N F T ™

Not For Tourists™ Guide to **ATLANTA**

2005-2006

Not For Tourists Inc New York

published and designed by
Not For Tourists Inc
NFT$_{TM}$—Not For Tourists$_{TM}$ Guide to ATLANTA 2005-2006
www.notfortourists.com

Publisher & Editor
Jane Pirone

Information Design
Jane Pirone
Rob Tallia
Scot Covey
Diana Pizzari

Managing Editors
Rob Tallia
Diana Pizzari

City Editors
Misti Hewatt
Joy Johnston

Writing and Editing
Cathleen Cueto
Misti Hewatt
Iya Perry
Joy Johnston
Diana Pizzari
Rob Tallia

Research
Ben Bray
Erin Kreindler

Editorial Interns
Amanda Fortier
Annie Karni
Tim O'Keefe

Research Interns
Bri Kapellas

Database Design
Scot Covey

**Graphic Design/
Production**
Scot Covey
Ran Lee
Christopher Salyers

Graphic Interns
Mike Ross
Juri Imamura

Contributors
Alli Hirschman
Annie Holt
Iya C. Perry

Proofreader
Jack Schieffer

Printed in China
ISBN# 0-9758664-3-5 $16.95
Copyright © 2005 by Not For Tourists, Inc.

Every effort has been made to ensure that the information in this book is as up-to-date as possible at press time. However, many details are liable to change—as we have learned. The publishers cannot accept responsibility for any consequences arising from use of this book.

Not For Tourists does not solicit individuals, organizations, or businesses for listings inclusion in our guides, nor do we accept payment for inclusion into the editorial portion of our book; the advertising sections, however, are exempt from this policy. We always welcome communications from anyone regarding ANYTHING having to do with our books; please visit us on our website at **www.notfortourists.com** for appropriate contact information.

Dear NFT User,

Welcome to the very first edition of the Not For Tourists Guide to Atlanta. Whether you live in Atlanta, work in Atlanta, or just find yourself in Atlanta, we trust that this book will help you get the most out of the city.

Compiling a locals' guide to Atlanta presented some unique challenges:

The majority of Atlantans are transplants (Yankees almost forget they are in the South if they stay within the city limits), making it tough to reflect a true "local" perspective. Move over mint juleps on verandas and say hello to martinis on swanky bar balconies. Atlanta has a day spa just for guys and more high-end designer boutiques than you can shake a stick at. The humidity is here to stay, however, so stop whining about it. The antiquated alcohol laws are not going anywhere either—just be sure to get drunk enough on Saturday to last you through Sunday.

Atlanta takes being "the city of the Phoenix" a bit too seriously. From road names to restaurants, the city is in a state of constant change. We are currently witnessing a construction renaissance not seen since, well, the Reconstruction Era. Due to Atlanta's reputation for tearing down landmarks at breakneck speed to erect ugly office parks or pseudo landmarks (think super-sized fish tank, a.k.a. the Georgia Aquarium), future NFT editions may require a section entitled, "What Used to Be There." The stinking sewers are supposed to go away, but we're not holding our breaths (unless we are near one of them). But there is much to be excited about—the new Atlanta Symphony Hall is going to feature movable rooftop wings!

With patience and persistence, we divided our sprawling city into digestible sections. Each neighborhood features a detailed map that pinpoints everything from the nearest post office to the hottest dance club—the necessities of life. If something doesn't jive, something pisses you off, or you want to sing our praises, go to **www.notfortourists.com** send us feedback.

hoping you find what you need.

i, Rob, Diana, and Jane

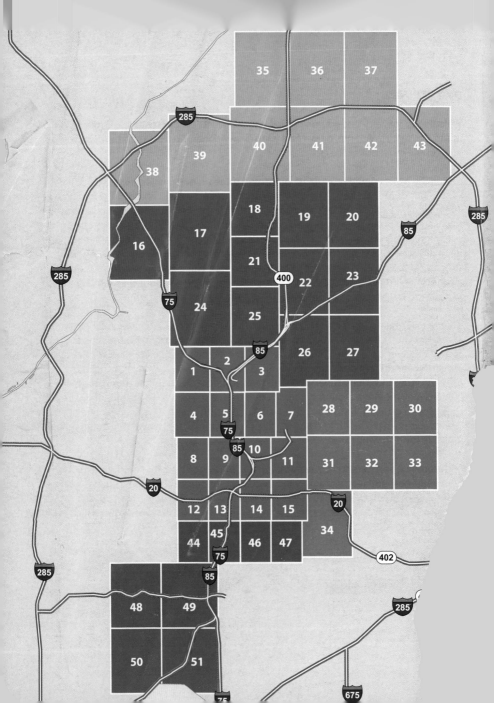

Map 1 • **Underwood Hills / Blandtown**

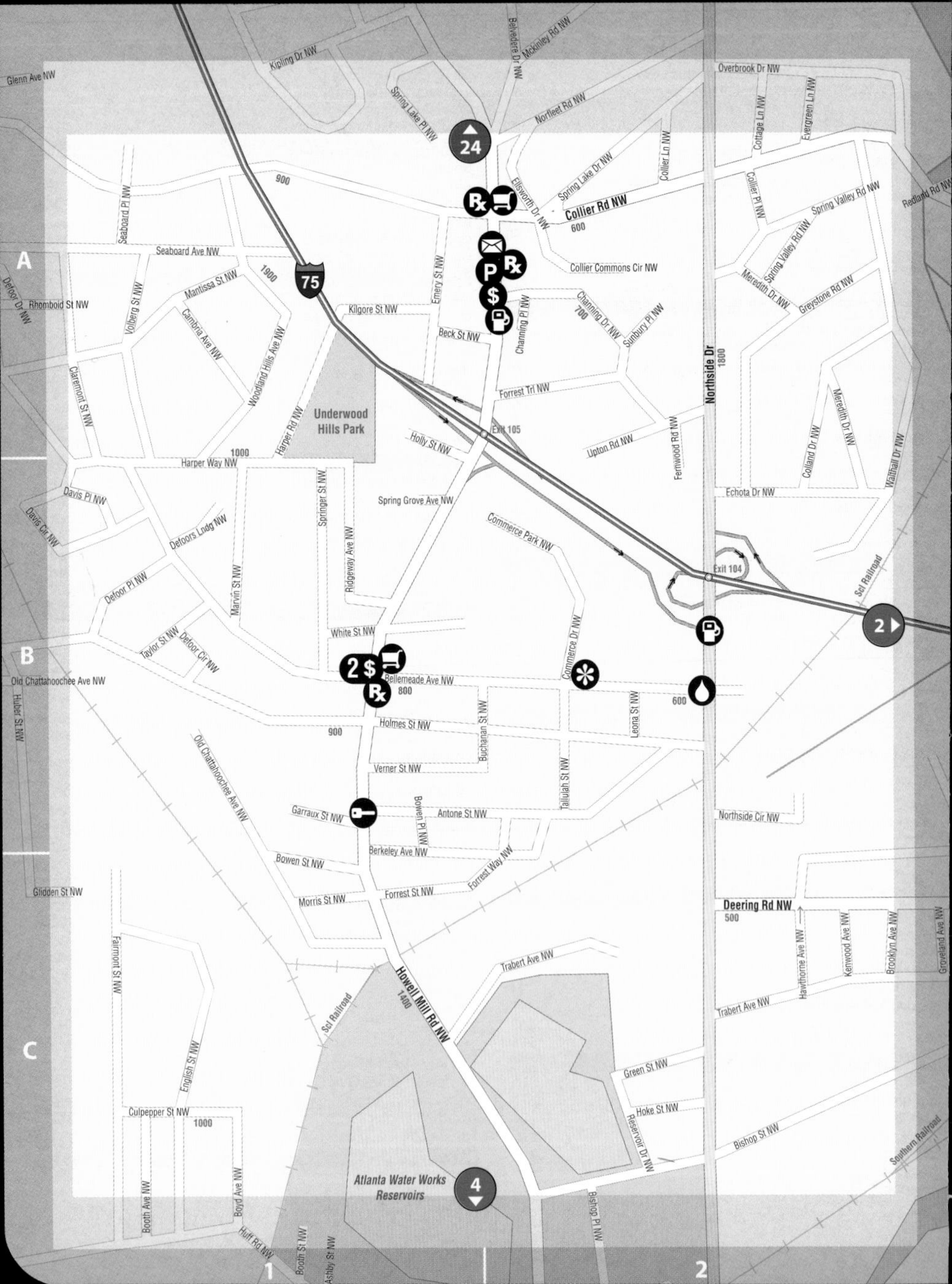

N

Glenn Ave NW

Kigling Dr NW

Berkeley Dr NW
McKinley Dr NW

Overbrook Dr NW

Spring Lake Pl NW

Norfleet Rd NW

Cottage Ln NW

Evergreen Ln NW

24

Collier Ln NW

Spring Lake Dr NW

Collier Pl NW

Spring Valley Rd NW

Redfield Rd NW

Seaboard Ave NW

900

Collier Rd NW
600

Meredith Dr NW

Spring Valley Rd NW

Greystone Rd NW

Meredith Dr NW

A

Rhomboid St NW

Defoor Dr NW

Volberg St NW

Mantissa St NW

Camfield Ave NW

Woodland Hills Ave NW

1900

Collier Commons Cir NW

Channing Dr NW
700

Sunbury Pl NW

Northside Dr
1800

Collard Dr NW

Walthall Dr NW

75

Kilgore St NW

Emery St NW

Beck St NW

Channing Pl NW

Claremont St NW

Harper Ave NW

Forrest Trl NW

Echota Dr NW

Underwood
Hills Park

Holly St NW

Exit 105

Upton Rd NW

Fernwood Rd NW

Davis Pl NW

Harper Way NW
1000

Springer St NW

Spring Grove Ave NW

Davis Cir NW

Defoors Long NW

Ridgeway Ave NW

Commerce Park NW

Sel Railroad

Defoor Pl NW

Marvin St NW

Commerce Dr NW

Exit 104

2

Taylor St NW

Defoor Cir NW

White St NW

B

Old Chattahoochee Ave NW

Haber St NW

2 $

Bellemeade Ave NW
800

Holmes St NW

Buchanan St NW

Talulah St NW

Leora St NW

600

900

Verner St NW

Old Chattahoochee Ave NW

Garraux St NW

Bowen Pl NW

Antone St NW

Northside Cir NW

Bowen St NW

Berkeley Ave NW

Forrest Way NW

Fairmont St NW

Morris St NW

Forrest St NW

Deering Rd NW
500

Glidden St NW

Trabert Ave NW

Hawthorne Ave NW

Kenwood Ave NW

Brooklyn Ave NW

Gresham Ave NW

C

English St NW

Trabert Ave NW

Culpepper St NW
1000

Howell Mill Rd NW

Sel Railroad

Green St NW

Booth Ave NW

Boyd Ave NW

Ashby St NW

Booth St NW

Atlanta Water Works
Reservoirs

4

Hoke St NW

Reservoir Dr NW

Bishop St NW

Bishop Pl NW

Southern Railroad

1

2

Essentials

	25			
1	2	3		26
4	5	6	7	28
8	9	10	11	31
12	13	14	15	
				34

Map 1

Once a railroad residential community, Underwood Hills lost steam when another form of transportation, namely Interstate 75, was constructed. It continues to be a modestly priced neighborhood with easy access to the interstate system and to intown Atlanta. Due to its industrial zoning, Blandtown is in danger of extinction, as development sweeps through.

Car Rental

- **Enterprise** · 1572 Howell Mill Rd

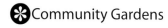 Community Gardens

Banks

- **Bank of America** · 1775 Howell Mill Rd
- **National Bank of Commerce** · 1715 Howell Mill Rd
- **Southtrust** · 1954 Howell Mill Rd

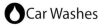 Car Washes

- **All American Pressure Washing** ·
  1650 Northside Dr NW

 Gas Stations

- **Shell** · 1695 Northside Dr
- **Shell** · 1892 Howell Mill Rd NW

 Parking

Rx Pharmacies

- **Eckerd** · 2020 Howell Mill Rd NW
- **Howell Mill Pharmacy** · 1970 Howell Mill Rd NW
- **Kroger** · 1715 Howell Mill Rd

✉ Post Offices

- **US Post Office** · 1984 Howell Mill Rd NW

🛒 Supermarkets

- **Kroger** · 1715 Howell Mill Rd
- **SaveRite** · 2020 Howell Mill Rd

Map 1 • **Underwood Hills / Blandtown**

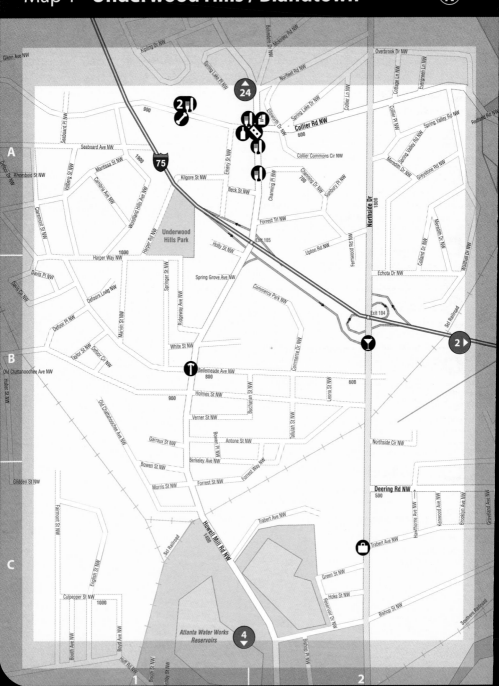

A retail renaissance continues on Howell Mill Road, and the once-industrial eyesore is becoming a haven for hip eats, such as Misto and The Real Chow Baby (Map 4). With three major commercial arteries (Howell Mill Road, Collier Road, and Northside Drive) and its proximity to Atlantic Station, this 'hood will become only more developed in the next few years.

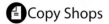Copy Shops
- **UPS Store** · 2020 Howell Mill Rd NW

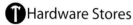Hardware Stores
- **Bates Ace Hardware** · 1709 Howell Mill Rd NW

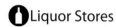Liquor Stores
- **Capital City Liquor Store** · 784 Collier Rd NW

Nightlife
- **Swinging Richards** · 1715 Northside Dr NW

Pet Shops
- **Pet Gallery** · 857 Collier Rd NW

Restaurants
- **Fellini's Pizza** · 1991 Howell Mill Rd
- **Malaya** · 857 Collier Rd NW
- **Melting Pot** · 857 Collier Rd NW
- **Misto** · 1950 Howell Mill Rd NW
- **Salsa** · 2020 Howell Mill Rd NW

Shopping
- **Sam Flax Art & Design Store** · 1460 Northside Dr

Video Rental
- **Blockbuster** · 2002 Howell Mill Rd

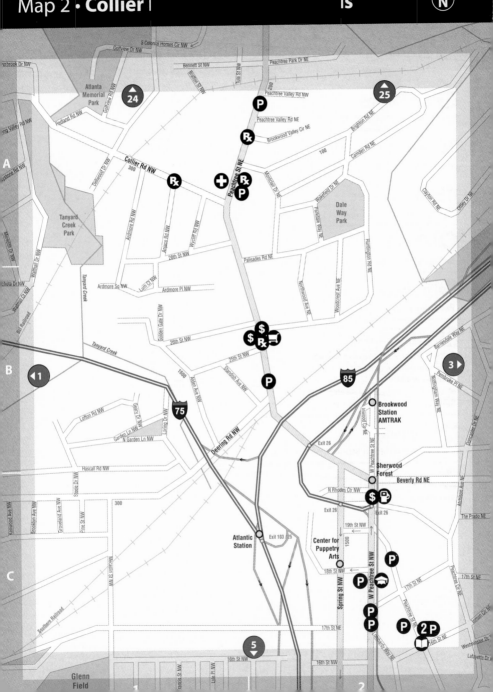

These primarily residential neighborhoods offer tranquil, tree-lined streets just minutes from the hustle and bustle of Buckhead and Midtown. Famed architect Neel Reid designed many of the original homes in Brookwood Hills. At the nexus of I-75 and I-85 lies Atlantic Station, a massive retail and residential development. Love it, hate it, you simply can't ignore it.

$ Banks
- **National Bank of Commerce** · 1745 Peachtree St
- **Regions** · 1745 Peachtree St NE
- **SunTrust** · 1503 Peachtree St

⛽ Gas Stations
- **Shell** · 1521 Peachtree St NE

➕ Hospitals
- **Piedmont** · 1968 Peachtree Rd NW

○ Landmarks
- **Atlantic Station** · Nexus of I75 & I85
- **Brookwood Station AMTRAK** · 1688 W Peachtree St NE
- **Center for Puppetry Arts** · 1404 Spring St NW
- **Sherwood Forest** · Beverly Rd & Peachtree St

📖 Libraries
- **Peachtree Branch** · 1315 Peachtree St NE

P Parking

℞ Pharmacies
- **CVS (24 hrs)** · 1943 Peachtree Rd
- **Kroger** · 1745 Peachtree St NE
- **Piedmont Hospital Apothecary** · 35 Collier Rd NW
- **Shepard Apothecary** · 2020 Peachtree Rd NW

🏫 Schools
- **John Marshall Law School** · 1422 W Peachtree St NW

🛒 Supermarkets
- **Kroger** · 1745 Peachtree St

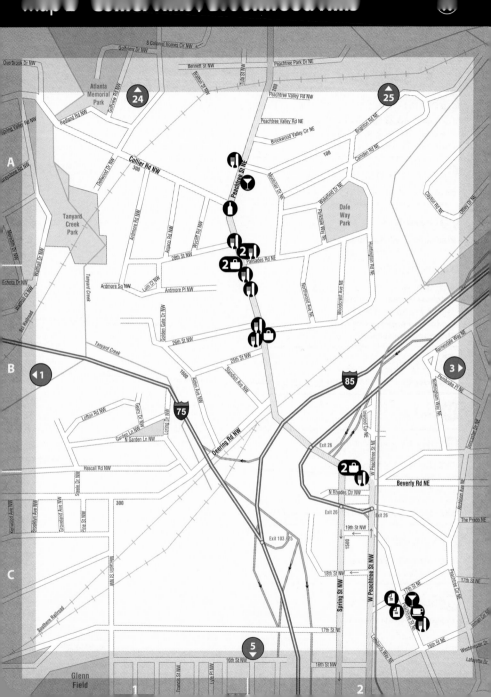

Map 2

Atlantic Station will offer high end shopping like IKEA and Dillard's, as well as a multiplex movie theater. Sip espresso and devour decadent desserts at Café Intermezzo. MidCity Cuisine draws a hip and rich crowd. Swoozies offers fun gift items and is located in the Brookwood Shopping Center, where you can grab gourmet lunch to go at Wolfgang Puck Express.

Copy Shops

- **FedEx Kinko's** · 1375 Peachtree St NE
- **Minuteman Press** · 1389 Peachtree St NE

Coffee

- **Starbucks** · 1375 W Peachtree St NW

Liquor Stores

- **Peachtree Road Liquor Store** ·
  1895 Peachtree Rd NE

Nightlife

- **Black Bear Tavern** · 1931 Peachtree Rd NE
- **The Loft** · 1374 W Peachtree St

Restaurants

- **Café Intermezzo** · 1845 Peachtree Rd
- **Huey's** · 1816 Peachtree Rd
- **Mamma Fu's** · 1935 Peachtree Rd
- **MidCity Cuisine** · 1545 Peachtree St
- **Nan** · 1350 Spring St NW
- **R Thomas Deluxe Grill** · 1812 Peachtree Rd NW
- **Satay Ria** · 1861 Peachtree Rd NE
- **Shipfeifer on Peachtree** · 1814 Peachtree St NE
- **Ted's Montana Grill** · 1874 Peachtree Rd
- **Wolfgang Puck Express** · 1745 Peachtree St NE

Shopping

- **Andrew: Men Women Home** · 1545 Peachtree St
- **Baby Cakes** · 1833 Peachtree Rd NE
- **Joq** · 1545 Peachtree St NE
- **Standard** · 1841 Peachtree Rd
- **Swoozies** · 1745 Peachtree St

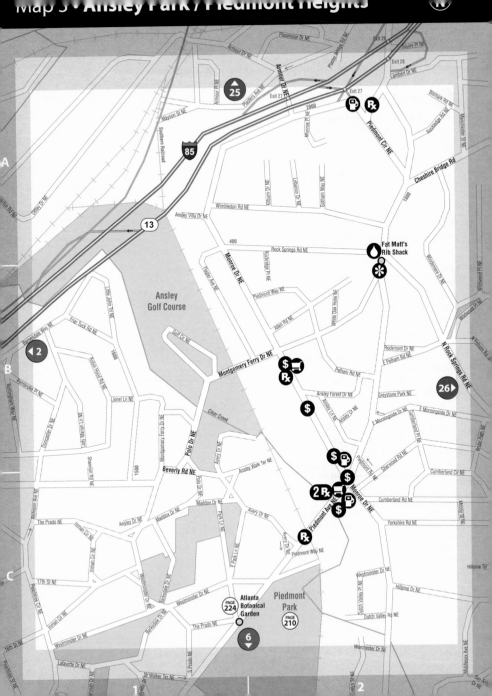

Map 5 • Ansley Park / Piedmont Heights

Essentials

1	2	3
4	5	6	7	28
8	9	10	11	31
12	13	14	15
				34

Map 3

Featuring gorgeous estates and winding roads that even locals get lost on, Ansley Park is one of Atlanta's most picturesque neighborhoods. This lush and tranquil neighborhood seems a million miles away from the city, yet really is in the center of it all. To feel further removed from the city grind, wander your way through the Atlanta Botanical Garden.

$ Banks

- **Bank of America** · 1674 Monroe Dr NE
- **Bank of America** · 1700 Monroe Dr NE
- **Regions** · 1544 Piedmont Ave NE
- **SunTrust** · 1544 Piedmont Ave NE
- **Wachovia** · 1605 Monroe Dr NE

Car Washes

- **Two-Minute Car Wash** · 1836 Piedmont Ave NE

Community Gardens

Gas Stations

- **Chevron** · 2195 Monroe Dr NE
- **Exxon** · 1570 Monroe Dr NE
- **Shell** · 1539 Piedmont Ave

o Landmarks

- **Atlanta Botanical Garden** ·
  1345 Piedmont Ave NE
- **Fat Matt's Rib Shack** · 1811 Piedmont Ave NE

Pharmacies

- **CVS** · 1544 Piedmont Ave NE
- **Eckerd** · 1512 Piedmont Ave NE
- **Kroger** · 1700 Monroe Dr
- **Publix** · 1544 Piedmont Ave NE
- **Stacy's Compounding Pharmacy** ·
  1953 Piedmont Cir NE

Supermarkets

- **Kroger** · 1700 Monroe Dr
- **Publix** · 1544 Piedmont Ave NE

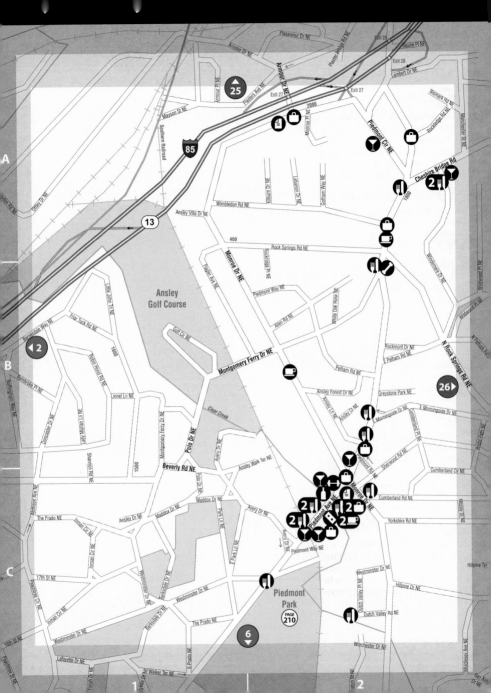

Throw down some ribs at Fat Matt's Rib Shack after a hard workout at LA Fitness in Ansley Square Mall. The gay version of Cheers can be found at Burkhart's Pub, while Smith's Olde Bar offers the best in live Rock music. For one of the best dining experiences in Atlanta, don't miss Woodfire Grill—try their Rocky the Free Range Chicken.

Coffee

- **Caribou Coffee** · 1551 Piedmont Ave NE
- **Einstein Bros** · 1870 Piedmont Ave NE
- **Einstein Bros** · 1676 Monroe Dr NE
- **Starbucks** · 1544 Piedmont Ave NE

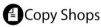 Copy Shops

- **Action Blueprint** · 2075 Monroe Dr NE
- **UPS Store** · 1579 Monroe Dr NE

Gyms

- **LA Fitness** · 1544 Piedmont Ave NE

 Liquor Stores

- **Ansley Wine Merchants** · 1544 Piedmont Ave NE

Nightlife

- **Burkhart's Pub** · 1492 Piedmont Ave NE
- **Deux Plex** · 1789 Cheshire Bridge Rd
- **New Order** · 1544 Piedmont Ave NE
- **Scandals** · 1510 Piedmont Ave NE
- **Smith's Olde Bar** · 1578 Piedmont Ave NE
- **Tripp's** · 1931 Piedmont Cir NE

Pet Shops

- **Pet Supplies Plus** · 1853 Piedmont Ave NE

Restaurants

- **Agnes and Muriel's** · 1514 Monroe Dr
- **Atmosphere** · 1620 Piedmont Ave NE
- **Bangkok Thai** · 1492 Piedmont Ave NE
- **Cowtippers** · 1600 Piedmont Ave NE
- **Fat Matt's Rib Shack** · 1811 Piedmont Ave NE
- **Green Sprout** · 1529 Piedmont Ave NE
- **King & I** · 1510 Piedmont Ave NE
- **Moe's Southwest Grill** · 1544 Piedmont Ave NE
- **Nakato** · 1776 Cheshire Bridge Rd NE
- **ONE.Midtown Kitchen** · 559 Dutch Valley Rd
- **Ru San's** · 1529 Piedmont Ave NE
- **Taco Cabana** · 1895 Piedmont Ave NE
- **Tierra** · 1425 Piedmont Ave NE
- **Woodfire Grill** · 1782 Cheshire Bridge Rd

 Shopping

- **Ansley Wine Merchants** · 1544 Piedmont Ave NE
- **Ansley Mall** · 1544 Piedmont Ave NE
- **Antique Collections** · 1579 Monroe Dr NE
- **Atlanta Costume** · 2089 Monroe Dr
- **Bookears** · 1579 Monroe Dr
- **The Boy Next Door** · 1447 Piedmont Ave NE
- **Classic Comics** · 1860 Piedmont Ave NE
- **Domus** · 1919 Piedmont Rd NE

Video Rental

- **Blockbuster** · 1544 Piedmont Ave NE

Map 4 • **West Midtown / Home Park**

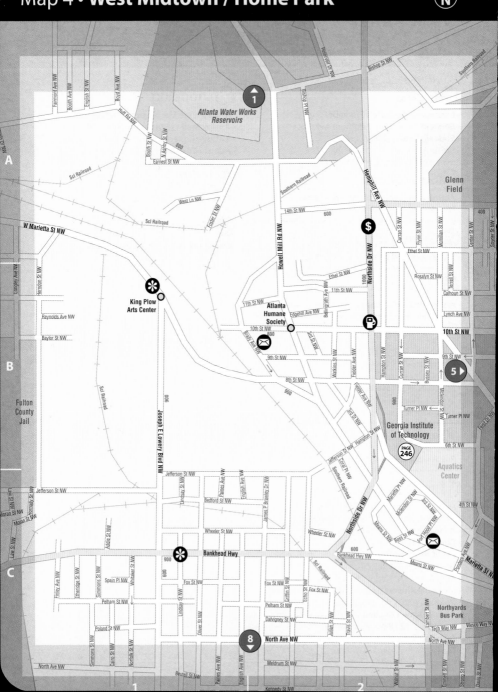

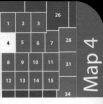

The 'hood of many names, including Midtown West and M West. Whatever you call it, most Atlantans will remember it as that warehouse and industrial district past the Georgia Tech campus. Now, thanks to hip, urban loft and condo projects, it's suddenly the place to be. Life necessities are still sorely lacking, but expect that to change soon.

Banks
- **Southtrust** · 1112 Northside Dr NW

Community Gardens

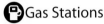Gas Stations
- **Marathon** · 1001 Northside Dr

o Landmarks
- **Atlanta Humane Society** · 981 Howell Mill Rd NW
- **King Plow Arts Center** · 887 W Marietta St NW

Post Offices
- **US Post Office** · 794 Marietta St NW
- **US Post Office** · 967 Brady Ave NW

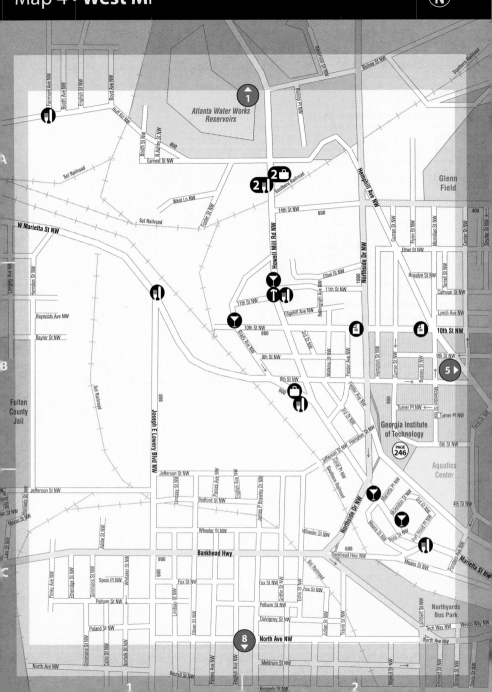

Map 4 • **West Mi**

N

Atlanta Water Works
Reservoirs

1

Glenn
Field

800

Booth St NW

Fairmont Ave NW
Booth Ave NW
English St NW
Boyd Ave NW

Huff Rd NW

N Lashby St NW

Earnest St NW

West Ln NW

Southern Railroad

Reservoir Dr NW

N Ira Brown Rd NW

Bishop St NW

Southern Railroad

2

2

14th St NW

600

Hemphill Ave NW

400

Curran St NW
Flynn St NW
McMillian St NW
Center St NW
Snyder St NW

W Marietta St NW

Scl Railroad

Estelle St NW

Scl Railroad

Herndon St NW

Reynolds Ave NW

Baylor St NW

Scl Railroad

11th St NW

Howell Mill Rd NW

Ethel St NW

11th St NW

Edgehill Ave NW

Bellingrath Ave NW

Northside Dr NW

1000

Ethel St NW

Rosalyn St NW

Calhoun St NW

Lynch Ave NW

Terrell St NW

10th St NW

800

Brady Ave NW

9th St NW

Watkins St NW

State St NW

Felder Ave NW

Hampton St NW

Curran St NW

Bissey St NW

9th St NW

5

10th St NW

Fulton
County
Jail

Joseph E Lowery Blvd NW

900

8th St NW

600

8th St NW

State St NW

Hamilton St NW

900

Turner Pl NW

Turner Pl NW

Fowler St NW

Georgia Institute
of Technology

PAGE
246

6th St NW

Aquatics
Center

Jefferson St NW

Herndon St NW

Jefferson St NW

Jefferson St NW

Lindsay St NW

Bedford St NW

Paines Ave NW

Angier Ave NW

James P Brawley Dr NW

Wheeler St NW

Wheeler St NW

EdgeH Pl NW

Southern Railroad

Northside Dr NW

Marietta Pl NW

McMendon Pl NW

Bissey St NW

3rd St NW

Fort Hood Pl NW

4th St NW

Marietta St NW

Bankhead Hwy

900

600

Fox St NW

Fox St NW

Echo St NW

Elm St NW

Griffin St NW

Pelham St NW

Dalvigney St NW

Scl Railroad

Jullian St NW

Travis St NW

600

Bankhead Hwy NW

Means St NW

Foundry St NW

Means St NW

Northyards
Bus Park

Lambert St NW

Tech Way NW

Wesco Way NW

Finley Ave NW
Etheridge St NW
Simmons St NW
Spain Pl NW
Whitaker St NW
Pelham St NW

Lindsay St NW

Oliver St NW

English St NW

8

North Ave NW

North Ave NW

Meldrum St NW

Walnut St NW

North Ave NW

Simmons St NW
Cairo St NW
Norfolk St NW

Poland St NW

Beutell St NW

Paines Ave NW

Kennedy St NW

Strong St NW

Emmett St NW

Fulton Ave NW
Haynes St NW
Law St NW

Jefferson St NW

Moran St NW

Mangum St NW
Adds St NW

A

B

C

1

2

Sundries / Entertainment

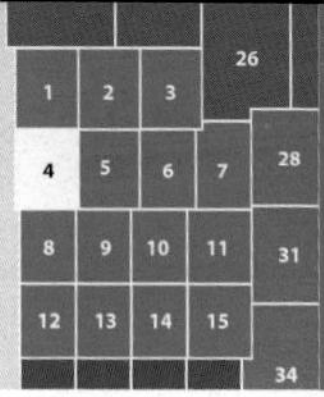

Bacchanalia's gamble on the area certainly paid off, as they are considered one of the best restaurants in the city. Compound is drawing clubbers with their multi-themed and multi-level nightclub. Octane is an ultra-hip, loft-style coffeehouse. The Food Studio is one of the city's most romantic restaurants, and is conveniently located next to Actor's Express, a cutting-edge theatre company.

Map 4

Copy Shops
• **Imaging Technologies Service** • 640 10th St NW
• **UPS Store** • 541 Tenth St NW

Hardware Stores
• **Atlanta Builders Supply** • 1034 Howell Mill Rd NW

Nightlife
• **Compound** • 1008 Brady Ave
• **The Library** • 800 Marietta St NW
• **Northside Tavern** • 1058 Howell Mill Rd NW

Restaurants
• **Bacchanalia** • 1198 Howell Mill Rd NW
• **Figo Pasta** • 1210 Howell Mill Rd NW
• **The Food Studio** • 887 W Marietta St NW
• **Octane** • 1009 Marietta St NW
• **Pangaea** • 1082 Huff Rd
• **The Real Chow Baby** • 1016 Howell Mill Rd NW
• **Taqueria Del Sol** • 1200 Howell Mill Rd NW
• **Thelma's Kitchen** • 768 Marietta St NW

Shopping
• **Bella Azul** • 1011-B Marietta St
• **Sprout** • 1198 Howell Mill Rd NW
• **Star Provisions** • 1198 Howell Mill Rd NW

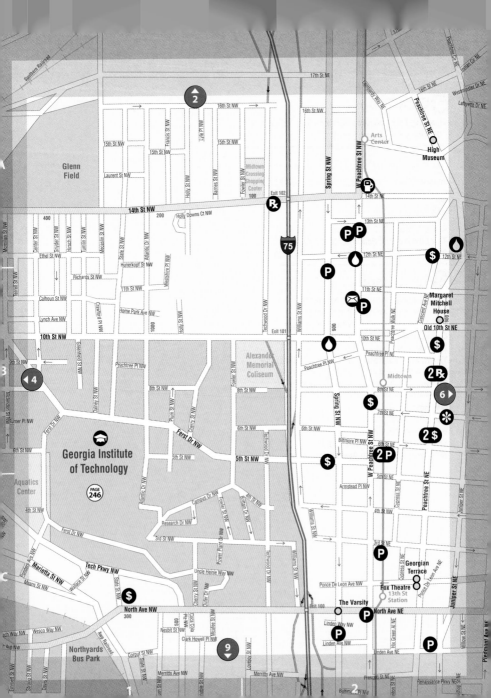

Essentials

	1	2	3		26	
4	**5**	6	7		28	
8	9	10	11		31	
12	13	14	15			
				34		

Map 5

The interstate used to separate Georgia Tech from the heart of Midtown, but Technology Square, a new pedestrian-friendly university and business district across from the Biltmore, has changed all of that. Many of Atlanta's jewels, including the Fox Theatre, the Margaret Mitchell House, and the High Museum, reside on this stretch of Peachtree Street from North Avenue to 16th St.

 Banks

• **Bank of America** • 600 Peachtree St NE
• **Bank of America** • 87 12th St NE
• **RBC Centura** • 75 5th St NW
• **SunTrust** • 760 W Peachtree St
• **Wachovia** • 615 Peachtree St NE
• **Wachovia** • 645 State St NW
• **Wachovia** • 999 Peachtree St

 Car Washes

• **Atlantic Center Car Wash** •
  1200 W Peachtree St NW
• **Chevron** • 970 Spring St NW

 Community Gardens

 **Gas Stations**

• **Chevron** • 970 Spring St NW
• **Shell** • 1184 Spring St NW

o **Landmarks**

• **Fox Theatre** • 660 Peachtree St NE
• **Georgian Terrace** • 659 Peachtree St NE
• **High Museum** • 1280 Peachtree St NE
• **Margaret Mitchell House** • 990 Peachtree St
• **The Varsity** • 61 North Ave NW

 Parking

Pharmacies

• **CVS** • 151 14th St NW
• **CVS** • 842 Peachtree St NE
• **Hawk's Drugs** • 849 Peachtree St NE

 Post Offices

• **US Post Office** • 1072 W Peachtree St NW

Schools

• **Georgia Tech** • Georgia Institute of Technology

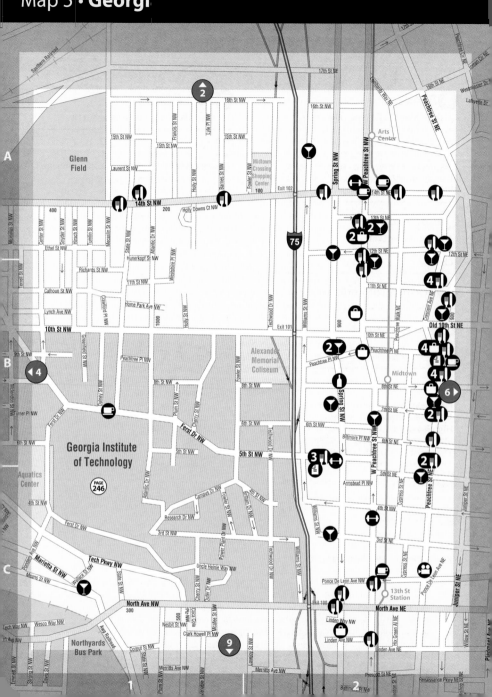

Map 5 · Georgia

On the Georgia Tech side, expect the college staples: chain fast food, pizza parlors, and coffeehouses. Go to Technology Square for cheap and tasty noodles at Tin Drum. Great eats (Eno, Park 75, Silk, South City Kitchen, Toast, Vinocity) can be found from near the Fox Theatre up to Arts Center. The clubbing action is hot in the Crescent Avenue district.

 ## Coffee
- **Atlantic Café** · 1180 W Peachtree St NW
- **Dunkin' Donuts** · 675 W Peachtree St NW
- **Starbucks** · 21 14th St NE
- **Starbucks** · 350 Ferst Dr NW
- **Starbucks** · 867 Peachtree St

 ## Copy Shops
- **Copy Club Parcel Plus** · 85 5th St NW
- **UPS Store** · 925B Peachtree St NE

Gyms
- **Atlantic Center Athletic Club** · 1180 W Peachtree St NW
- **Health Fitness** · 725 W Peachtree St NW
- **LA Fitness** · 75 5th St NW

Liquor Stores
- **Mac's Beer & Wine/Midtown Liquor** · 929 Spring St NW

Movie Theaters
- **Fox Theatre** · 660 Peachtree St NE

Nightlife
- **Apache Café** · 64 3rd St NW
- **Atlanta Brewery Company** · 1219 Williams St
- **Blu** · 960 Spring St NW
- **Bulldog's** · 893 Peachtree St NE
- **Charlie G's** · 1041 W Peachtree St NW
- **The Cheetah** · 887 Spring St NW
- **Churchill Grounds** · 660 Peachtree St
- **Cosmopolitan Lounge** · 45 13th St NE
- **Dragonfly** · 67 12th St NE
- **Fantasy Fare** · 700 Marietta St NW
- **Halo** · 817 W Peachtree St NW
- **Lava** · 57 13th St NE
- **Leopard Lounge** · 84 12th St NE
- **The Velvet Room** · 1021 Peachtree St
- **Wetbar** · 960 Spring St NW
- **Whiskey Peach** · 44 12th St NW

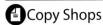 ## Restaurants
- **5th St Ribs n Blues** · 86 5th St NW
- **Baraonda** · 710 Peachtree St
- **Bobby & June's Country Kitchen** · 375 14th St NW
- **Bridgetown Grill** · 689 Peachtree St
- **Celebrity Café** · 903 Peachtree St NE
- **Cherry** · 1051 W Peachtree St NW
- **Eno** · 800 Peachtree St
- **Front Page News** · 1104 Crescent Ave NE
- **Fuego** · 1136 Crescent Ave
- **Gordon Biersch Brewery Restaurant** · 848 Peachtree St NE
- **JR Crickets** · 631 Spring St
- **Kool Korners Grocery** · 349 14th St NW
- **Little Azio** · 903 Peachtree St NE
- **Mick's** · 557 Peachtree St NE
- **Moe's Southwest Grill** · 85 5th St NW
- **Noodle** · 903 Peachtree St NE
- **Park 75** · 75 14th St NE
- **Pasta Da Pulcinella** · 1123 Peachtree Wk
- **The Savoy Bar and Grill** · 659 Peachtree St NE
- **Silk** · 919 Peachtree St
- **The Silver Skillet** · 200 14th St NW
- **South City Kitchen** · 1144 Crescent Ave NE
- **St Charles Deli** · 22 5th St NW
- **Tamarind** · 80 14th St NW
- **Tin Drum** · 88 5th St NW
- **Toast** · 817 W Peachtree St NE
- **Touch of India** · 1037 Peachtree St NE
- **Twisted Taco** · 66 12th St NE
- **The Varsity** · 61 North Ave NW
- **Veni Vidi Vici** · 41 14th St NE
- **Vickery's** · 1105 Crescent Ave NE
- **Vinocity** · 36 13th St NE
- **Vortex** · 878 Peachtree St

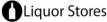 ## Shopping
- **The Barrel Man** · 800 Peachtree St
- **The Bath Experience** · 900 Peachtree St
- **Directions** · 915 Peachtree St
- **Earwax Records** · 565 Spring St NW
- **fab'rik** · 1114 W Peachtree St
- **French Kiss** · 900 Peachtree St
- **Inserection** · 1023 W Peachtree St
- **Lui-B** · 1116 W Peachtree St
- **Mac's Beer & Wine** · 21 Peachtree Pl NW
- **Universal Gear** · 935 Peachtree St

Map 6 · **Midtown**

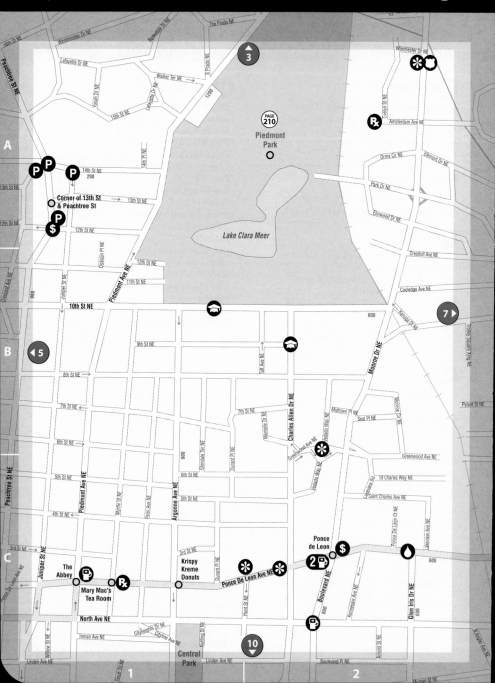

PAGE 210

Peachtree St NE
16th St NE
Westminster Dr NE
The Prado NE
Lafayette Dr NE
Barksdale Dr NE
S Prado NE
Worchester Dr NE
Walker Ter NE
Yonah St NE
15th St NE
Lafayette Dr NE
1200
Joslyn St NE
14th Pl NE
Amsterdam Ave NE
14th St NE
200
Piedmont Park
Orme Cir NE
Elkmont Dr NE
13th St NE
Corner of 13th St & Peachtree St
13th St NE
12th St NE
Dickson Pl NE
Park Dr NE
Lake Clara Meer
Elmwood Dr NE
Piedmont Ave NE
12th St NE
Juniper St NE
900
Crescent Ave NE
11th St NE
Cresthill Ave NE
10th St NE
Cooledge Ave NE
9th St NE
Taft Ave NE
600
Kanuga St NE
Trolley Square Way NE
8th St NE
7th St NE
7th St NE
Charles Allen Dr NE
Monroe Dr NE
Midtown Pl NE
Monroe Cir NE
Pylant St NE
Mentelle Dr NE
Seal Pl NE
6th St NE
Peachtree St NE
5th St NE
Piedmont Ave NE
Myrtle St NE
Penn Ave NE
Glendale Dr NE
800
Durant Pl NE
6th St NE
Velado Way NE
Greenwood Ave NE
Greenwood Ave NE
Charles Allen Dr NE
Velado Way NE
St Charles Way NE
4th St NE
Argonne Ave NE
5th St NE
Pasadena Ave NE
Saint Charles Ave NE
Ponce De Leon Ct NE
Lakeview Ave NE
3rd St NE
Juniper St NE
3rd St NE
Durant Pl NE
Ponce de Leon
600
The Abbey
Krispy Kreme Donuts
Ponce De Leon Ave NE
Boulevard NE
Glen Iris Dr NE
600
Mary Mac's Tea Room
North Ave NE
Hunt St NE
Kennesaw Ave NE
600
Ponce De Leon Pl NE
Inman Ave NE
Cityheights Dr NE
Glen Iris Dr NE
Ruffing St NE
Arnold St NE
Willow St NE
10
Linden Ave NE
Boulevard Pl NE
Finch Trl NE
Ponce De Leon Ave NE
Central Park
Linden Ave NE
Morgan St NE
N Angier Ave NE
Cypress St NE

A

B

C

1

2

3

5

7

10

Essentials

A true live-work-play community, Midtown boasts a dynamic gay population, a bustling business center, and a lively arts scene. Piedmont Park is a city treasure. Ponce de Leon Avenue retains its seedy charm, despite yuppie development. Shiny new parking meters mean street parking is no longer free, but hey, how else is the city going to pay for the new sewer system?

Banks

- **Bank of America** · 1088 Peachtree St NE
- **Southtrust** · 494 Ponce de Leon Ave NE

Car Washes

- **Automazing** · 1230 Peachtree St NE
- **Cactus Car Wash** · 575 Ponce de Leon Ave NE

Community Gardens

Gas Stations

- **BP** · 160 Ponce de Leon Ave NE
- **Chevron** · 180 Ponce de Leon Ave
- **Chevron** · 605 Boulevard NE
- **Exxon** · 486 Ponce de Leon Ave NE
- **Shell** · 689 Boulevard

Landmarks

- **The Abbey** · 163 Ponce de Leon Ave NE
- **Corner of 13th Street and Peachtree Street** · Peachtree St & 13th St
- **Krispy Kreme Doughnuts** · 295 Ponce de Leon Ave
- **Mary Mac's Tea Room** · 224 Ponce de Leon Ave NW
- **Piedmont Park** · 400 Park Dr NE
- **Ponce de Leon** · Ponce de Leon Ave & Monroe Dr

Parking

Pharmacies

- **CVS ProCare** · 560 Amsterdam Ave NE
- **The Medicine Shoppe** · 235 Ponce de Leon Ave NE

Police

- **APD Zone 5 Midtown Mini Precinct** · 1320 Monroe Dr NE

Schools

- **Atlanta College of Art** · 1280 Peachtree St NE
- **The Children's School** · 345 Tenth St NE
- **Grady High** · 929 Charles Allen Dr NE

Map 6

27

Map 6 · **Midtown**

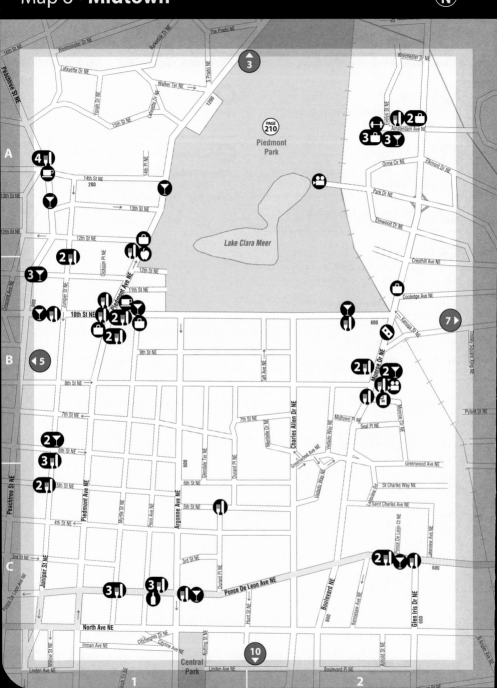

Map 6

Landmark Midtown Art Cinema shows indie flicks. Great restaurants (Apres Diem, Gilbert's, M.F. Sushibar, Nam) intermingle with mediocre ones (Salt, Nickiemoto), so choose wisely. Outwrite Bookstore is the gay meeting place. Satisfy your shoe fetish at Shoemaker's Warehouse. There's plenty of gay club action (Blake's, Hoedown's, Red Chair Lounge). Vision is a hip hop haven. Red Light Café is the place for live bluegrass.

Coffee
- **Caribou Coffee** · 1000 Piedmont Ave NE
- **Italia D'Oro** · 1197 Peachtree St NE

Copy Shops
- **UPS Store** · 931 Monroe Dr NE

Farmer's Markets
- **Green Market at Piedmont Park** · 1071 Piedmont Ave NE

Gyms
- **Fitness Factory** · 500 Amsterdam Ave NE

Liquor Stores
- **A&H Package Store** · 268 Ponce de Leon Ave NE

Movie Theaters
- **Landmark Midtown Art Cinema** · 931 Monroe Dr NE
- **Screen on the Green (outdoors)** · Piedmont Park, The Meadow, 10th St & Monroe Dr

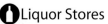

Nightlife
- **Armory** · 836 Juniper St NE
- **Atlanta Eagle** · 306 Ponce de Leon Ave
- **Blake's** · 227 10th St NE
- **Club 112** · 1055 Peachtree St NE
- **Eleven50** · 1150-B Peachtree St NE
- **The Highlander** · 931 Monroe Dr NE
- **Hoedown's** · 931 Monroe Dr NE
- **Jocks and Jills Midtown** · 112 10th St NE
- **Loca Luna** · 836 Juniper St NE
- **The Metro** · 1080 Peachtree St NE
- **Miss Q's** · 560 Amsterdam Ave NE
- **Park Tavern** · 500 10th St NE
- **Phoenix** · 567 Ponce de Leon Ave
- **Prince of Wales** · 1144 Piedmont Ave NE
- **Red Chair Lounge** · 550-C Amsterdam Ave
- **Red Light Café** · 553 Amsterdam Ave NE
- **Vision** · 1068 Peachtree St NE

Restaurants
- **Apres Diem** · 931 Monroe Dr NE
- **Babs** · 814 Juniper St NE
- **Bread Garden** · 549 Amsterdam Ave NE
- **Cha Gio/Wild Curry Thai Kitchen** · 132 10th St NE
- **Corner Bakery Café** · 1201 Peachtree St NE
- **DaVinci's** · 674 Myrtle St
- **Eats** · 600 Ponce de Leon Ave NE
- **Einstein's** · 1077 Juniper St NE
- **Fishmonger** · 980 Piedmont Ave NE
- **Flying Biscuit** · 1001 Piedmont Ave NE
- **Gilbert's Mediterranean Café** · 219 10th St NE
- **Jake's Ice Creams & Sorbets** · 970 Piedmont Ave NE
- **Joe's on Juniper** · 1049 Juniper St NE
- **Krispy Kreme** · 295 Ponce de Leon Ave
- **Las Palmeras** · 368 5th St NE
- **Mary Mac's Tea Room** · 224 Ponce de Leon Ave NE
- **Mellow Mushroom** · 931 Monroe Dr NE
- **MF Sushibar** · 265 Ponce de Leon Ave NE
- **Mitra** · 818 Juniper St NE
- **Moe's Southwest Grill** · 1197 Peachtree St NE
- **Mu Lan** · 824 Juniper St NE
- **Nam** · 931 Monroe Dr NE
- **Nancy's Pizza** · 265 Ponce de Leon Ave
- **Nickiemoto** · 990 Piedmont Ave NE
- **Papi's East Cuban Cuisine** · 216 Ponce de Leon Ave NE
- **Park Tavern** · 500 10th St NE
- **Salt** · 794 Juniper St NE
- **Shout** · 1197 Peachtree St NE
- **Silver Grill** · 900 Monroe Dr NE
- **Spice** · 793 Juniper St NE
- **Thai Chili** · 1197 Peachtree St NE
- **Thai Palate** · 265 Ponce de Leon Ave NE
- **Willy's Mexicana Grill** · 1071 Piedmont Ave NE
- **Zesto Drive-In** · 544 Ponce de Leon Ave NE
- **Zocalo** · 187 10th St NE

Shopping
- **Cook's Warehouse** · 549-I Amsterdam Ave NE
- **Gado Gado** · 549 Amsterdam Ave
- **Intown Bicycles** · 1035 Monroe Dr NE
- **Midtown Food Mart** · 225 10th St NE
- **Outwrite Bookstore and Coffeehouse** · 991 Piedmont Ave NE
- **Shoemaker's Warehouse** · 500 Amsterdam Ave NE
- **Skate Escape** · 1086 Piedmont Ave NE
- **Worthmore Jewelers** · 500 Amsterdam Ave NE

Video Rental
- **Blockbuster** · 985 Monroe Dr NE

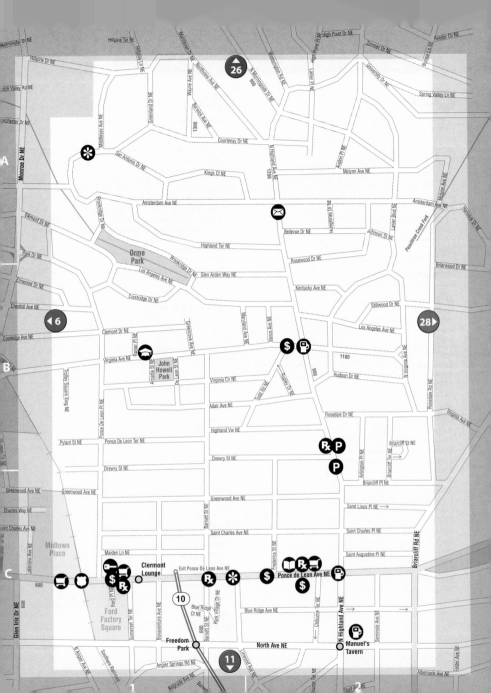

Virginia Highland is a friendly, artsy neighborhood that attracts city dwellers with kids. Public schools are above average, which isn't saying much. Housing is an eclectic mix of homes, apartments, and new condo and loft developments. Traffic and parking can be a real bitch on weekends, due to the area's concentrated nightlife district.

Banks
- **Bank of America** • 956 Ponce de Leon Ave
- **National Bank of Commerce** • 725 Ponce de Leon Ave NE
- **Southtrust** • 979 Virginia Ave NE
- **SunTrust** • 1001 Ponce de Leon Ave NE

Car Rental
- **Atlanta Rent-a-Car** • 718 Ponce de Leon Ave NE

 Community Gardens

Gas Stations
- **Chevron** • 1025 N Highland Ave NE
- **Citgo** • 1079 North Ave NE
- **Exxon** • 1161 Ponce de Leon Ave NE

o Landmarks
- **Clermont Lounge** • 789 Ponce de Leon Ave NE
- **Freedom Park** • North Ave & Freedom Pkwy
- **Manuel's Tavern** • 602 N Highland Ave NE

Libraries
- **Ponce de Leon Branch** • 980 Ponce de Leon Ave NE

Parking

Pharmacies
- **CVS** • 865 N Highland Ave NE
- **Eckerd** • 891 Ponce de Leon Ave NE
- **Kroger** • 725 Ponce de Leon Ave NE
- **Publix** • 1001 Ponce de Leon Ave NE

Police
- **APD Police Operations Bureau** • 675 Ponce de Leon Ave NE

Post Offices
- **US Post Office** • 1190 N Highland Ave NE

Schools
- **Inman Middle** • 774 Virginia Ave NE

Supermarkets
- **Kroger** • 725 Ponce de Leon Ave NE
- **Publix** • 1001 Ponce de Leon Ave NE
- **Whole Foods** • 650 Ponce de Leon Ave NE

26

6

28

3

10

11

Monroe Dr NE
Hillpine Dr NE
Hillpine Ter NE
Westminster Dr NE
Dutch Valley Rd NE
Worchester Dr NE
Greenland Dr NE
Northview Ave NE
Wayne Ave NE
Martindale Dr NE
N Morningside Dr NE
High Point Pl NE
High Point NE
Zimmer Dr NE
Raeder Cir NE
Bonnell Ln NE
University Dr NE
Spring Valley Ln NE
Courtenay Dr NE
N Highland Ave NE
Avalon Pl NE
Mclynn Ave NE
San Antonio Dr NE
Kings Ct NE
Amsterdam Ave NE
Amsterdam Ave NE
Lanier Blvd NE
Johnson St NE
Mayfair Pl NE
Harrold Ave NE
Peachtree Creek Park
Briarwood Dr NE
Highland Ter NE
Bellevue Dr NE
Humphries Dr NE
Rosewood Dr NE
Orme Park
Brookridge Dr NE
Glen Arden Way NE
Los Angeles Ave NE
Crestridge Dr NE
Kentucky Ave NE
Stillwood Dr NE
Elkmont Dr NE
Park Dr NE
Elmwood Dr NE
Cresthill Ave NE
Cooledge Ave NE
Clemont Dr NE
Barner Dr NE
Virginia Ave NE
Maryland Ave NE
Vance Ave NE
Los Angeles Ave NE
N Virginia Ave NE
Hudson Dr NE
Trolley Square Rd NE
Arcadia St NE
De Leon St NE
John Howell Park
Virginia Cir NE
Todd Rd NE
Rogers St NE
Adair Ave NE
Highland Vw NE
Rosedale Dr NE
Rosedale Rd NE
Virginia Ave NE
Arlington Pl NE
Briarcliff Ct NE
Briarcliff Ter NE
Briarcliff Pl NE
Briarcliff Rd NE
Ponce De Leon Pl NE
Pylant St NE
Ponce De Leon Ter NE
Drewry St NE
Barnett St NE
Greenwood Ave NE
Greenwood Ave NE
Saint Louis Pl NE
Charles Way NE
Saint Charles Ave NE
Saint Charles Pl NE
N Charles Ave NE
Frederica St NE
Saint Augustine Pl NE
Midtown Place
Maiden Ln NE
Ford Pl NE
Exit Ponce De Leon Ave NE
Ponce de Leon Ave NE
Somerset Ter NE
Bonaventure Ave NE
Blue Ridge Ave NE
Blue Ridge Ct NE
Park Village Dr NE
Cleburne Ave NE
N Highland Ave NE
Seminole Ave NE
Lakeview Ave NE
Glen Iris Dr NE
Ford Factory Square
North Ave NE
Angier Springs Rd NE
Belgrade Ave NE
Southern Railroad
Mourne Ter NE
Vaught Ave NE
Albemarle Ave NE
Eastern Ave NE

A
B
C

1

Virginia Highland offers a more relaxed nightlife scene. Don't miss the pizza and custom-made salads at Everybody's or the Sunday brunch at Murphy's. Atkins Park is the city's oldest bar, and Manuel's Tavern is a legendary watering hole. Surly servers and robust coffee can be found at Aurora Coffee. The cupcakes at Belly are awesome. Blues music is king at Blind Willie's.

Coffee
- **Aurora Coffee** · 992 N Highland Ave NE
- **Dunkin' Donuts** · 650 Ponce de Leon Ave NE
- **San Francisco Coffee Roasting** · 1192 N Highland Ave NE
- **San Francisco Coffee Roasting** · 664 N Highland Ave NE
- **Starbucks** · 800 N Highland Ave NE

Farmer's Markets
- **Morningside Farmers Market** · 1393 N Highland Ave

Gyms
- **Urban Body Fitness** · 742 Ponce de Leon Pl NE

Hardware Stores
- **Highland Hardware** · 1045 N Highland Ave NE
- **Home Depot** · 650 Ponce de Leon Ave NE
- **Intown Ace Hardware** · 854 N Highland Ave NE

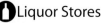Liquor Stores
- **Green's Beverage Store** · 737 Ponce de Leon Ave NE

Movie Theaters
- **Lefont Plaza Theatre** · 1049 Ponce de Leon Ave NE

Nightlife
- **10 High** · 816 N Highland Ave NE
- **Atkins Park** · 794 N Highland Ave NE
- **Blind Willie's** · 828 N Highland Ave NE
- **Dark Horse Tavern** · 816 N Highland Ave NE
- **Dugan's** · 777 Ponce de Leon Ave NE
- **Hand in Hand** · 752 N Highland Ave NE
- **Highland Tap** · 1026 N Highland Ave NE
- **Limerick Junction** · 822 N Highland Ave NE
- **The Local** · 758 Ponce de Leon Ave NE
- **Manuel's Tavern** · 602 N Highland Ave NE
- **Masquerade** · 695 North Ave NE
- **Midtown Saloon & Grill** · 736 Ponce de Leon Ave NE
- **MJQ Concourse** · 736 Ponce de Leon Ave NE
- **Model T's** · 699 Ponce de Leon Ave NE
- **Moe's and Joe's** · 1033 N Highland Ave NE
- **Neighbor's Pub** · 752 N Highland Ave NE
- **Rico's View** · 736 Ponce de Leon Ave NE
- **Righteous Room** · 1051 Ponce de Leon Ave NE

Pet Shops
- **Highland Pet Supply** · 1186 N Highland Ave NE
- **Petsmart** · 650 Ponce de Leon Ave NE

Restaurants
- **Alon's** · 1394 N Highland Ave NE
- **American Roadhouse** · 842 N Highland Ave NE
- **Babette's Café** · 573 N Highland Ave NE
- **Belly General Store** · 722 N Highland Ave NE
- **Cameli's Gourmet Pizza Joint** · 699 Ponce de Leon Ave NE
- **Caramba Café** · 1409 N Highland Ave NE
- **Chin Chin** · 699 Ponce de Leon Ave NE
- **Dish** · 870 N Highland Ave NE
- **Everybody's** · 1040 N Highland Ave NE
- **Fellini's Pizza** · 909 Ponce de Leon Ave NE
- **Fontaine's Oyster Bar** · 1026 1/2 N Highland Ave NE
- **Harry & Son's** · 820 N Highland Ave NE
- **Harvest** · 853 N Highland Ave NE
- **Horizon** · 1397 N Highland Ave NE
- **Java Jive** · 790 Ponce de Leon Ave NE
- **La Fonda Latina** · 923 Ponce de Leon Ave NE
- **La Tavola Trattoria** · 992 Virginia Ave NE
- **Majestic** · 1031 Ponce de Leon Ave NE
- **Mali** · 961 Amsterdam Ave
- **Mambo** · 1402 N Highland Ave NE
- **Moe's Southwest Grill** · 863 Ponce de Leon Ave NE
- **Murphy's** · 997 Virginia Ave NE
- **Noche** · 1000 Virginia Ave NE
- **Olive Bistro** · 650 Ponce de Leon Ave NE
- **Osteria 832** · 832 N Highland Ave NE
- **Pad Thai** · 1021 Virginia Ave NE
- **Paolo's Gelato Italiano** · 1025 Virginia Ave NE
- **Pura Vida** · 656 N Highland Ave NE
- **Qdoba** · 650 Ponce de Leon Ave NE
- **Sala** · 1186 N Highland Ave NE
- **Soul Vegetarian Restaurant** · 652 N Highland Ave NE
- **Surin of Thailand** · 810 N Highland Ave NE

Shopping
- **Belly General Store** · 772 N Highland Ave NE
- **Bill Hullman Boutique** · 792 N Highland Ave NE
- **Bill Hullman Shoes** · 776 N Highland Ave NE
- **Dakota J's** · 1030 N Highland Ave NE
- **Gazzelle's** · 842 N Highland Ave NE
- **Highland Hardware** · 1045 N Highland Ave NE
- **Home Concepts** · 729 Ponce de Leon Pl
- **Java Vino** · 579 N Highland Ave NE
- **Metropolitan Deluxe** · 1034 N Highland Ave NE
- **Movies Worth Seeing** · 1409 N Highland Ave NE
- **The Owl and the Pussycat** · 996 Virginia Ave
- **Paris on Ponce** · 716 Ponce de Leon Pl
- **Planetarian Ornaments** · 784 N Highland Ave NE
- **Ten Thousand Villages** · 1056 St Charles Ave

Video Rental
- **Blockbuster** · 882 Ponce de Leon Ave NE
- **Movies Worth Seeing** · 1409 N Highland Ave NE

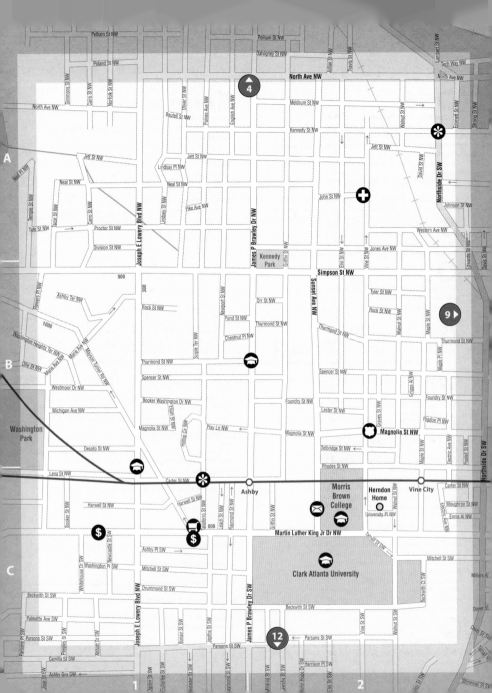

Vine City Surrounds Turner Field and often makes the local news for all of the wrong reasons, not just for crime, but for the broken sewer issues that cause destructive flooding in the area. Morris Brown College and Clark Atlanta University are historical African-American schools, that offer hope and revitalization to this once-thriving community.

 Banks
- **Citizens Trust Bank** ·
  965 Martin Luther King Jr Dr SW
- **SunTrust** · 825 Martin Luther King Jr Dr NW

 Community Gardens

 **Landmarks**
- **Herndon Home** · 587 University Pl NW

 **Police**
- **APD Zone 1 Magnolia Street Mini Precinct** ·
  612 Magnolia St NW

 Post Offices
- **US Post Office** · 50 Sunset Ave NW

Schools
- **Clark Atlanta University** · 223 James P Brawley Dr
- **KIPP WAYS Academy** · 80 Joseph E Lowery Blvd NW
- **Morris Brown College** ·
  643 Martin Luther King Jr Dr NW

Supermarkets
- **Publix** · 825 Martin Luther King Jr Dr NW

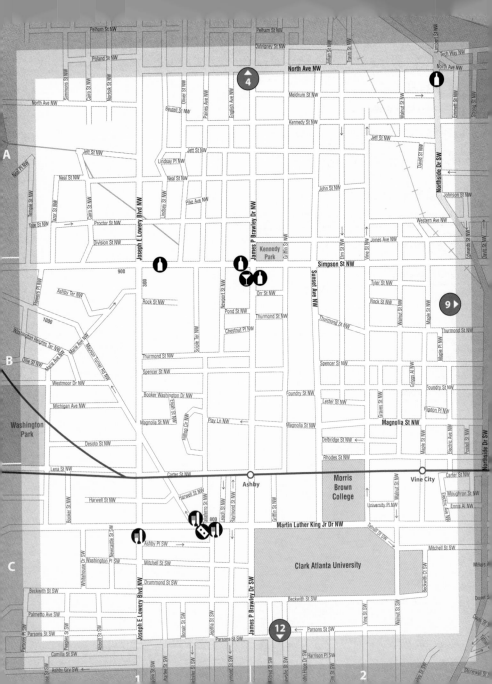

Busy Bee Café offers some of the best soul food in town. Enter 617 Club at your own risk. Package stores proliferate, so you'll never go thirsty. For more highbrow cultural entertainment, check out the events going on at Morris Brown and Clark Atlanta.

Liquor Stores

- **AJ Package** · 548 Northside Dr NW
- **C&H Package Store** · 900 Simpson St NW
- **D&J Beverage** · 307 Joseph E Lowery Blvd NW
- **HN Liquor Store** · 775 Simpson St NW

Nightlife

- **617 Club** · 310 Joseph E Lowery Blvd NW

Restaurants

- **Busy Bee Café** · 810 Martin Luther King Jr. SW
- **Eggroll Corner Chinese Restaurant** ·
  825 Martin Luther King Jr Dr NW
- **KFC** · 23 Joseph Lowery Blvd SW

Video Rental

- **Blockbuster** · 825 Martin Luther King Jr Dr

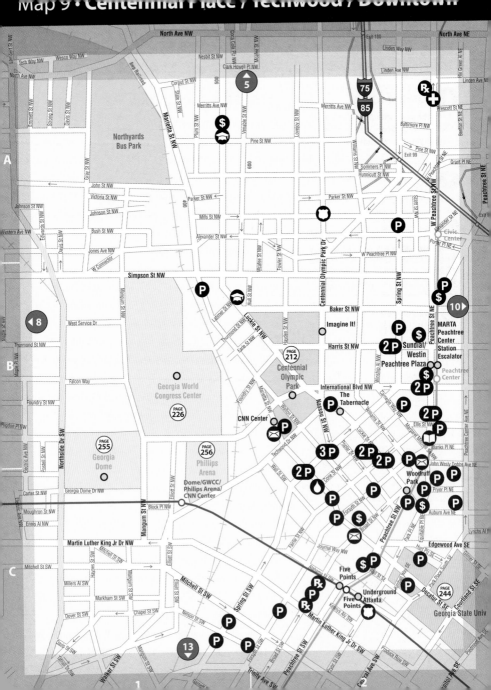

A new residential community has moved into the Downtown Atlanta area, formerly frequented by tourists and bums. An impressive mixed-income development replaced the Techwood projects. While a vigorous campaign has been launched to build up the residential community, basic services are still lacking. But who needs grocery stores when you've got Phillips Arena, Centennial Olympic Park, and the Georgia Dome at your doorstep?

Banks
- **Bank of America** · 231 Peachtree St NE
- **Bank of America** · 35 Broad St NW
- **Fidelity Bank** · 260 Peachtree St NE
- **SunTrust** · 225 Peachtree St NE
- **SunTrust** · 25 Park Pl
- **SunTrust** · 523 Luckie St NW
- **Wachovia** · 2 Peachtree St NW

Car Washes
- **Hoppy's Car Wash & Oil Change** ·
101 Marietta St NW

Hospitals
- **Emory Crawford Long** · 550 Peachtree St NW

o Landmarks
- **Centennial Olympic Park** · 265 Park Ave NW
- **CNN Center** · 1 CNN Ctr, 190 Marietta St NW
- **Five Points** · 30 Alabama St SW
- **Georgia Dome** · 1 Georgia Dome Dr
- **Georgia World Congress Center** · 285 Andrew Young International Blvd NW
- **Imagine It! The Children's Museum of Atlanta** · 275 Centennial Olympic Park Dr NW
- **MARTA Peachtree Center Station Escalator** · 216 Peachtree St NE
- **Sundial/Westin Peachtree Plaza** · 210 Peachtree St SW
- **The Tabernacle** · 152 Luckie St NW
- **Underground Atlanta** · 50 Upper Alabama St
- **Woodruff Park** · Auburn Ave & Peachtree St

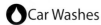
Libraries
- **Central (Main) Library** · 1 Margaret Mitchell Sq

Parking

Pharmacies
- **Concord Pharmacy** · 550 Peachtree St NW
- **CVS** · 12 Broad St SW
- **Millers Rexall Drugs** · 87 Broad St SW

Police
- **APD Zone 5 Station** ·
398 Centennial Olympic Park Dr NW
- **APD Zone 5 Underground Mini Precinct** ·
94 Pryor St SW

Post Offices
- **US Post Office** · 1 CNN Ctr, 190 Marietta St NW
- **US Post Office** · 133 Peachtree St NE
- **US Post Office** · 41 Marietta St NW

Schools
- **Atlanta New Century** · 300 Luckie St NW
- **Centennial Place Elementary** · 531 Luckie St NW

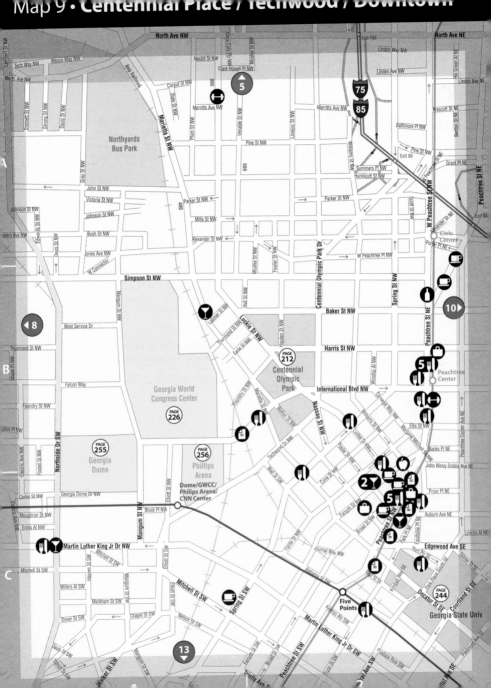

Map 9 • Centennial Place / Techwood / Downtown

High-end chains like Ted's Montana Grill and McCormick & Schmick's are good if you must entertain business associates or relatives. The Mark is where downtown clubbers head for some booty-shaking. City Grill is a fine way to introduce outsiders to Southern elegance. The new entertainment district at Underground Atlanta is supposed to invigorate the area, but we're not holding our breath.

Coffee

- **Caribou Coffee** · 303 Peachtree St NE
- **Dunkin' Donuts** · 303 Peachtree St NE
- **Dunkin' Donuts** · 98 Forsyth St NW
- **Frances Sweet Shoppe** · 75 Spring St SW
- **Starbucks** · 100 Peachtree St NE
- **Starbucks** · 240 Peachtree St NW

Copy Shops

- **Alphagraphics** · 34 Peachtree St NW
- **Bestway Copy Center** · 18 Decatur St SE
- **Document Resources** · 230 Peachtree St NW
- **Fedex Kinko's** · 100 Peachtree St NE
- **Fedex Kinko's** · 285 Andrew Young International Blvd NW

 Gyms

- **Gold's Gym** · 215 Peachtree St NE
- **YMCA** · 555 Luckie St NW

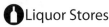 Liquor Stores

- **Peachtree Package Store** · 300 W Peachtree St NW

Nightlife

- **Club 720** · 904 Martin Luther King Jr Dr
- **Dailey's Downstairs** · 17 Andrew Young International Blvd
- **The Mark** · 79 Poplar St
- **Sidebar** · 79 Poplar St
- **Sun Dial Restaurant, Bar, and View** · 210 Peachtree St NW
- **Traxxx** · 339 Marietta St NW

Restaurants

- **Ali Baba** · 61 Broad St
- **Atlanta Bread Company** · 231 Peachtree St NE
- **Atlanta Grill** · 181 Peachtree St NE
- **Azio** · 229 Peachtree St NE
- **Benihana** · 229 Peachtree St NE
- **City Grill** · 50 Hurt Plz
- **Corner Bakery Café** · 270 Peachtree St NW
- **Ginseng Cafe** · 52 Broad St
- **Hard Rock Café** · 215 Peachtree NE
- **Landmark Diner** · 60 Luckie St NW
- **Lombardi's** · 94 Pryor St NE
- **Luxe** · 89 Park Pl
- **McCormick & Schmick's** · 190 Marietta St NW
- **Mick's** · 229 Peachtree St NE
- **Moe's Southwest Grill** · 1 CNN Ctr, 190 Marietta St NW
- **Moe's Southwest Grill** · 70 Peachtree St NE
- **Mr Everything Café** · 870 Martin Luther King Jr SW
- **Pittypat's Porch** · 25 International Blvd
- **Ray's in the City** · 240 Peachtree St NE
- **Sun Dial Restaurant, Bar, and View** · 210 Peachtree St NW
- **Ted's Montana Grill** · 133 Luckie St NW

Shopping

- **Americasmart Atlanta** · 240 Peachtree St NE
- **Estee's Children Shop** · 65 Peachtree St NE
- **The Executive Shop** · 56 Walton St

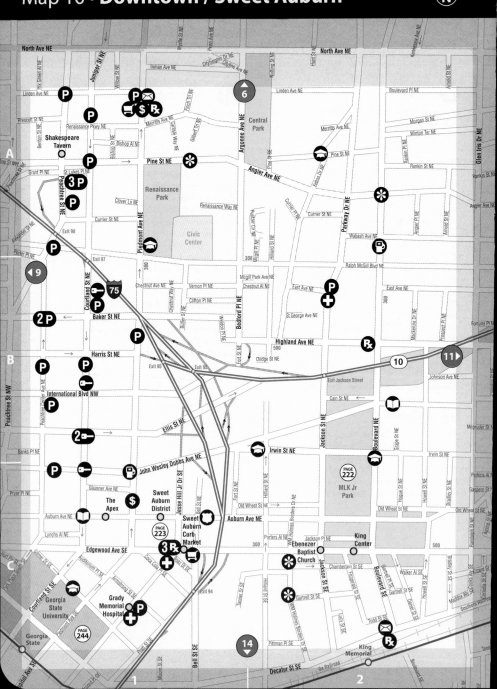

Map 10 · **Downtown / Sweet Auburn**

Build it, and they will come. Or will they? Downtown's revitalization efforts have been going on ever since the Olympics, and historical buildings keep being converted into high-priced condos, but where are the people? If there's not a major event happening, Downtown streets are still eerily quiet once the workday crowd heads back to the 'burbs.

Banks

- **Citizens Trust Bank** · 75 Piedmont Ave
- **Washington Mutual** · 595 Piedmont Ave NE

Car Rental

- **Avis** · 143 Courtland St NE
- **Budget** · 140 Courtland St NE
- **Enterprise** · 303 Courtland St NE
- **Hertz** · 202 Courtland St Ne
- **Thrifty** · 100 Courtland St NE

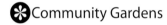Community Gardens

Gas Stations

- **Chevron** · 371 Boulevard NE
- **Shell** · 160 John Wesley Dobbs Ave NE

Hospitals

- **Atlanta Medical Center** · 303 Parkway Dr NE
- **Grady Memorial** · 80 Jesse Hill Jr Dr SE
- **Hughes Spalding Children's** · 35 Jesse Hill Jr Dr

o Landmarks

- **The Apex** · 135 Auburn Ave
- **Ebenezer Baptist Church** · 407 Auburn Ave NE
- **Grady Memorial Hospital** · 80 Jesse Hill Jr Dr SE
- **King Center** · 449 Auburn Ave NE
- **Shakespeare Tavern** · 499 Peachtree St NE
- **Sweet Auburn Curb Market** · 209 Edgewood Ave
- **Sweet Auburn District** · Auburn Ave b/w
  Courtland Ave & Jackson St

Libraries

- **Auburn Avenue Research Library** ·
  101 Auburn Ave NE
- **Martin Luther King Jr Branch** ·
  509 John Wesley Dobbs Ave

Parking

Pharmacies

- **Auburn Pharmacy** · 209 Edgewood Ave
- **CVS** · 439 Highland Ave NE
- **Express Drugs** · 9 Jesse Hill Jr Dr SE
- **HT Pharmacy & Medical Supplies** ·
  486 Decatur St SE
- **Market Pharmacy** · 209 Edgewood Ave SE
- **Walgreens (24 hrs)** · 595 Piedmont Ave NE

Police

- **APD Zone 5 Auburn Avenue Mini Precinct** ·
  247 Auburn Ave NE

Post Offices

- **US Post Office** · 486 Decatur St SE
- **US Post Office** · 570 Piedmont Ave NE

Schools

- **Georgia State University** · 33 Gilmer St SE
- **Hill Elementary** · 386 Pine St NE
- **Hope Elementary** · 112 Boulevard NE
- **Tech High** · 397 Piedmont Ave
- **Walden Middle** · 320 Irwin St NE

Supermarkets

- **Publix** · 595 Piedmont Ave NE
- **Sweet Auburn Curb Market** · 209 Edgewood Ave

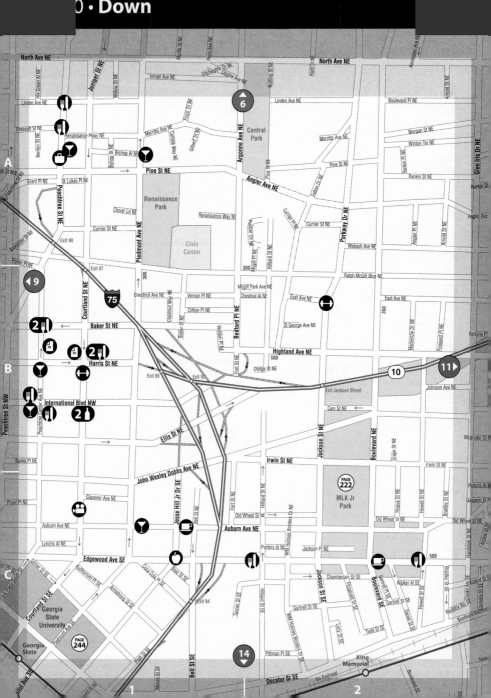

Sundries / Entertainment

The Sweet Auburn Curb Market offers everything from chitlins to chutney. Dinner at Nikolai's Roof may equal a mortgage payment, but it's worth it. Drive-thru barbecue is a hit at Rolling Bones. The Bard is never boring at Shakespeare Tavern (see Essentials).

Coffee
- **Javaology** · 466 Edgewood Ave
- **Sacred Grounds Bookstore Gallery Café** · 234 Auburn Ave NE

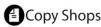Copy Shops
- **Fedex Kinko's** · 255 Courtland St NE
- **Fedex Kinko's** · 265 Peachtree Ctr Ave NE

Farmer's Markets
- **Sweet Auburn Curb Market** · 209 Edgewood Ave

Gyms
- **Highland Athletic Club** · 303 Parkway Dr NE
- **Peachtree Center Athletic Club** · 227 Courtland St NE

Liquor Stores
- **Peach Package** · 186 Courtland St NE
- **Sol's Liquor** · 186 Courtland St NE

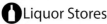Movie Theaters
- **Cinefest Film Theatre** · 66 Courtland St NE

Nightlife
- **Charlie and Barney's Bar & Grill** · 231 Peachtree Center Ave NE
- **O'Terrill's** · 510 Piedmont Ave
- **Royal Peacock** · 186 Auburn Ave NE
- **Shakespeare Tavern** · 499 Peachtree St NE

Restaurants
- **Dailey's** · 17 Andrew Young International Blvd
- **Gladys Knight Chicken and Waffles** · 529 Peachtree St
- **Hsu's Gourmet Chinese** · 192 Peachtree Center Ave NE
- **Morton's, The Steakhouse** · 303 Peachtree Center Ave NE
- **Nikolai's Roof** · 255 Courtland St NE
- **Pacific Rim Bistro** · 303 Peachtree Center Ave NE
- **Pleasant Peasant** · 555 Peachtree St NE
- **Rolling Bones Premium Pit BBQ** · 377 Edgewood Ave
- **Thumbs Up Diner** · 573 Edgewood Ave
- **Trader Vic's** · 255 Courtland St NE

Shopping
- **Bella Cucina Artful Food** · 493 Peachtree St

Map 10

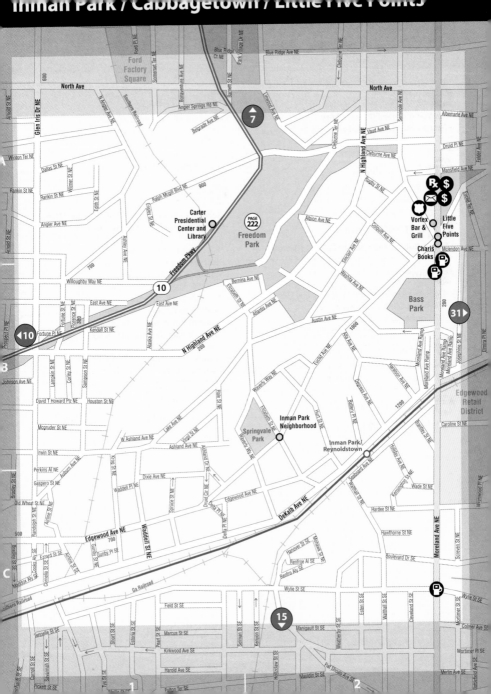

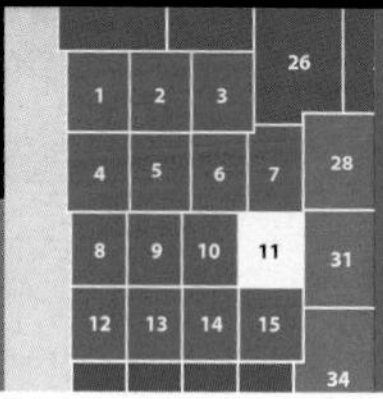

Map 11

Inman Park is known for its many beautifully restored Victorian homes, well-kept gardens, and a joyously bizarre annual neighborhood parade. Will an influx of big box chains threaten the bohemian Little Five Point's subversive spirit? Not likely. L5P is more than just a haven for hippies; it's one of Atlanta's most popular tourist destinations.

Banks

- **Bank of America (ATM)** · 437 Moreland Ave NE
- **BOND Federal Credit Union** · 433 Moreland Ave NE

Gas Stations

- **Chevron** · 372 Moreland Ave NE
- **Citgo** · 29 Moreland Ave SE
- **Shell** · 356 Moreland Ave

o Landmarks

- **Carter Presidential Center and Library** ·
  441 Freedom Pkwy
- **Charis Books** · 1189 Euclid Ave NE
- **Inman Park Neighborhood** · Euclid Ave &
  Elizabeth St
- **Little Five Points** · Moreland Ave NE & Euclid Ave NE
- **The Vortex Bar & Grill** · 438 Moreland Ave NE

Pharmacies

- **Little Five Points Pharmacy** · 484 Moreland Ave NE

Police

- **APD Zone 6 Little Five Points Mini Precinct** ·
  428 Seminole Ave NE

Post Offices

- **US Post Office** · 455 Moreland Ave NE

Ford Factory Square

North Ave   **North Ave**

PAGE 222

Freedom Park

Bass Park

Springvale Park

Inman Park / Reynoldstown

Edgewood Retail District

A

B

C

7

10

10

31

15

6

Glen Iris Dr NE · Winton Ter NE · Arnold St NE · Dallas St NE · Willmer St NE · Edith St NE · Rankin St NE · Angier Ave NE · Ralph McGill Blvd NE · Willoughby Way NE · East Ave NE · Fortune St SE · Florence St SE · Kendall St NE · Alaska Ave NE · N Highland Ave NE · Lampkin St NE · Corley St NE · Sampson St NE · Johnson Ave NE · David T Howard Plz NE · Houston St NE · Mcgruder St NE · W Ashland Ave NE · Ashland Ave NE · Irwin St NE · Perkins Al NE · Auburn Ave NE · Gaspero St NE · Bradley St NE · Old Wheat St NE · Randolph St NE · Edgewood Ave NE · Waddell St NE · Dixie Ave NE · DeKalb Ave NE · Seaboard Ave NE · Hardee St NE · Hawthorne St NE · Boulevard Dr NE · Moreland Ave NE · Ga Railroad · Southern Railroad · Field St SE · Marcus St SE · Kirkwood Ave SE · Harold Ave SE · Fulton Ter SE · Wylie St SE · Manigault St SE · Mollie St SE

Angier Springs Rd NE · Belgrade Ave NE · Blue Ridge Ave NE · Cleburne Ter NE · Albion Ave NE · Colquitt Ave NE · Seminole Ave NE · Euclid Ave NE · Austin Ave NE · Elizabeth St NE · Waverly Way NE · Moreland Ave Ramp · Josephine St NE · Brannon St NE · Caroline St NE

Cleburne Ave NE · Ruby St NE · Vaud Ave NE · Albemarle Ave NE · Druid Pl NE · Mansfield Ave NE · McLendon Ave NE

Bass Park · Hurt St NE · Battery Pl NE · Hansom Ave NE · Delta Pl NE · Delta Cir NE · Druid Cir NE · Sprite Lane NE

Hanover St NE · Renfroe Al NE · Renfro Aly NE · Wade St NE · Kensington Ave NE

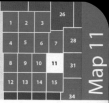
Sotto Sotto and its sister restaurant, the hip pizzeria Fritti, are standouts. Vegans drool over Lush, and hipsters inhale bubble tea at Teaspace. Terrific improv and clever silliness abound at Dad's Garage. Junkman's Daughter stocks everything your parents would hate. Counter-culture couture dominates the boutiques and shops of L5P (Wish, Lucky Devil).

Coffee
- **Starbucks** · 506 Moreland Ave

Gyms
- **Curves** · 701 Highland Ave NE

Liquor Stores
- **Little Five Point Liquor Store** ·
  448 Moreland Ave NE

Nightlife
- **97 Estoria** · 727 Wylie St SE
- **Brewhouse Café** · 401 Moreland Ave NE
- **Euclid Avenue Yacht Club** · 1136 Euclid Ave NE
- **Little 5 Points Corner Tavern** · 1174 Euclid Ave NE
- **Star Community Bar** · 437 Moreland Ave

Restaurants
- **Brewhouse Café** · 401 Moreland Ave NE
- **Fritti** · 311 N Highland Ave
- **Front Page News** · 351 Moreland Ave
- **Il Localino** · 467 N Highland Ave
- **Inman Park Patio** · 1029 Edgewood Ave
- **Lush** · 913 Bernina Ave
- **Miro's Garden** · 1150 Euclid Ave NE
- **Olive Bistro** · 1099 Euclid Ave NE
- **Rathbun's** · 112 Krog St
- **Roman Lily Café** · 668 Highland Ave
- **Savage Pizza** · 484 Moreland Ave NE
- **Son's Place** · 100 Hurt St NE
- **Sotto Sotto** · 313 N Highland Ave
- **Sweet Lime** · 1128 Euclid Ave NE
- **Teaspace** · 1133 Euclid Ave NE
- **Tijuana Garage** · 353 Moreland Ave NE
- **Two Urban Licks** · 820 Ralph McGill Blvd NE
- **The Vortex** · 438 Moreland Ave NE
- **Wisteria** · 471 N Highland Ave
- **Zesto** · 377 Moreland Ave

Shopping
- **A Cappella Books** · 1133 Euclid Ave
- **Abbadabbas** · 421 Moreland Ave
- **Cherry Bomb** · 1129-A Euclid Ave
- **The Clothing Warehouse** · 420 Moreland Ave
- **Criminal Records** · 466 Moreland Ave NE
- **Crystal Blue** · 1168 Euclid Ave NE
- **Envy** · 1143 Euclid Ave NE
- **Identified Flying Objects** · 1164 Euclid Ave NE
- **Junkman's Daughter** · 464 Moreland Ave NE
- **Lucky Devil** · 1158 Euclid Ave NE
- **Psycho Sisters Consignment Shop** ·
  428 Moreland Ave
- **Rene Rene** · 1142 Euclid Ave NE
- **Sevananda** · 467 Moreland Ave SE
- **Soul Kiss** · 1154 Euclid Ave NE
- **Stefan's Vintage Clothing** · 1160 Euclid Ave NE
- **Stratosphere Skateboards** · 1141 Euclid Ave NE
- **Tease** · 1166 Euclid Ave NE
- **Wax 'N' Facts** · 432 Moreland Ave NE
- **Wish** · 447 Moreland Ave

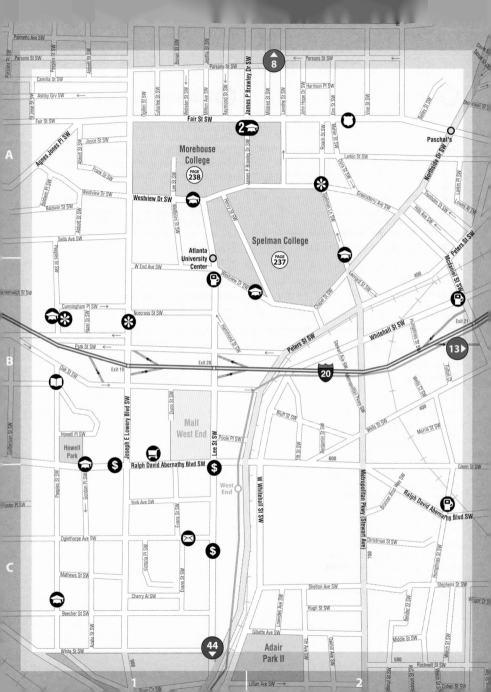

Named after the chic theatre district in London, and once considered to be the "ideal suburb of Atlanta," West End is now known for the Atlanta University Center, a bastion of African-American higher education and the home to six colleges. The surrounding area includes many longtime small businesses serving the black community.

Banks
- **Bank of America** · 711 Lee St SW
- **Wachovia** · 612 Lee St SW
- **Wachovia** · 921 Ralph David Abernathy Blvd SW

Community Gardens

Gas Stations
- **BP** · 535 Lee St SW
- **Chevron** · 490 Whitehall St SW
- **Exxon** · 507 Ralph David Abernathy Blvd SW

o Landmarks
- **Atlanta University Center** · 440 Westview Dr
- **Paschal's** · 180 Northside Dr SW

Libraries
- **West End Branch** · 525 Peeples St SW

Police
- **APD Zone 1 Fair Street Mini Precinct** · 676 Fair St SW

Post Offices
- **US Post Office** · 848 Oglethrope Ave SW

Schools
- **Brown Middle** · 765 Peeples St SW
- **Clark Atlanta University** · 223 James P Brawley Dr SW
- **Kennedy Middle** · 225 James P Brawley Dr NW
- **Morehouse College** · 830 Westview Dr SW
- **Morehouse School of Medicine** · 720 Westview Dr SW
- **Rusk Elementary** · 433 Peeples St SW
- **Spelman College** · 350 Spelman Ln SW
- **University Community Academy** · 953 Ralph David Abernathy Blvd SW

 Supermarkets
- **Everlasting Life Co-op** · 878 Ralph David Abernathy Blvd SW

Map 12 • West End

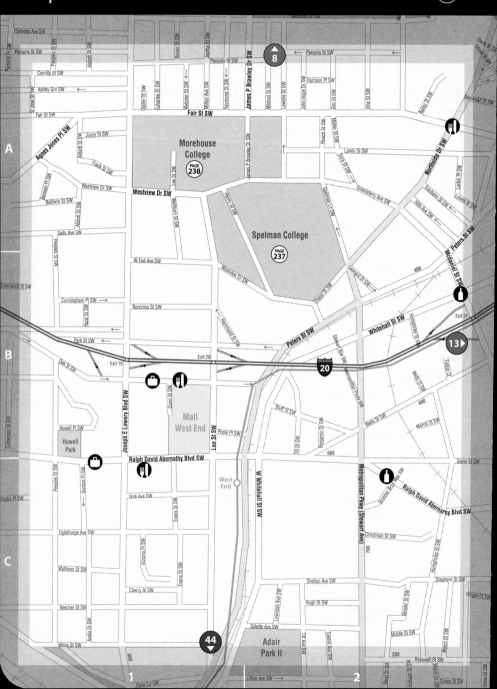

The Mall West End offers plenty of shopping. There's plenty of cheap meat and threes (Satterwhite's) to cater to the college crowd. Morehouse and Spelman offer cultural activities all year long.

Liquor Stores
- **D&M Liquor Store** ·
  595 Ralph David Abernathy Blvd SW
- **Whitehall Street Beer & Wine** ·
  495 Whitehall St SW

Restaurants
- **Pascal's Restaurant at Castleberry** ·
  180 Northside Dr SW
- **Satterwhite's** · 851 Oak St SW
- **Soul Vegetarian Restaurant** · 879 Ralph David
  Abernathy Blvd SW

Shopping
- **The Mall West End** · 850 Oak St SW
- **Shrine of the Black Madonna Cultural Center
  and Bookstore** · 946 Ralph David Abernathy Blvd

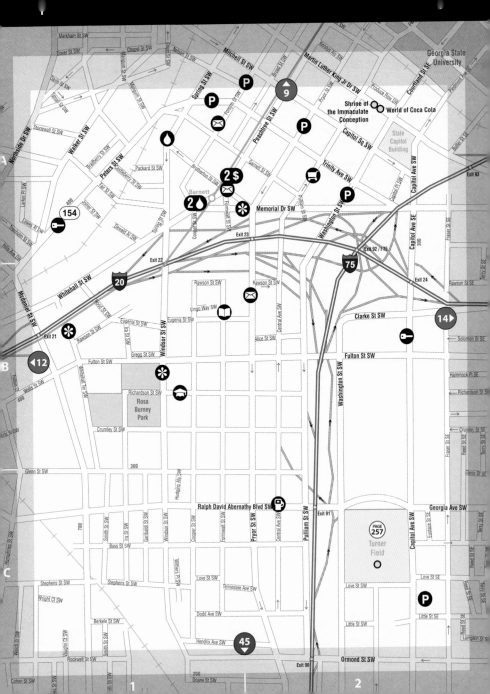

Both Mechanicsville and Summerhill were once home to thriving Jewish and African-American populations—until the Depression, and, later, housing projects and stadiums turned the area into a less vibrant community. On the outskirts of these blighted communities, back towards Downtown, lie some of Atlanta's most well-known landmarks (Turner Field, Westin Peachtree Plaza).

Banks

- **Southtrust** · 230 Peachtree St SW
- **Wachovia** · 240 Peachtree St SW

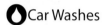 Car Rental

- **Enterprise** · 450 Capitol Ave
- **U-Haul** · 300 Peters St SW

 Car Washes

- **Atlanta Auto Spa** · 270 Peachtree St SW
- **Executive Clean Car** · 242 Peachtree St SW
- **Georgia Shine** · 216 Spring St SW

Community Gardens

Gas Stations

- **BP** · 180 Ralph David Abernathy Blvd SW

Landmarks

- **Shrine of the Immaculate Conception** · 48 Martin Luther King Jr Dr SW
- **Turner Field** · 755 Hank Aaron Dr SE
- **World of Coca Cola** · 55 Martin Luther King Jr Dr

Libraries

- **Mechanicsville Branch** · 400 Formwalt St SW

Parking

 Post Offices

- **US Post Office** · 183 Forsyth St SW
- **US Post Office** · 240 Peachtree St SW
- **US Post Office** · 400 Pryor St SW

Schools

- **Dunbar Elementary** · 403 Richardson St SW

Supermarkets

- **Kroger** · 235 Central Ave SW

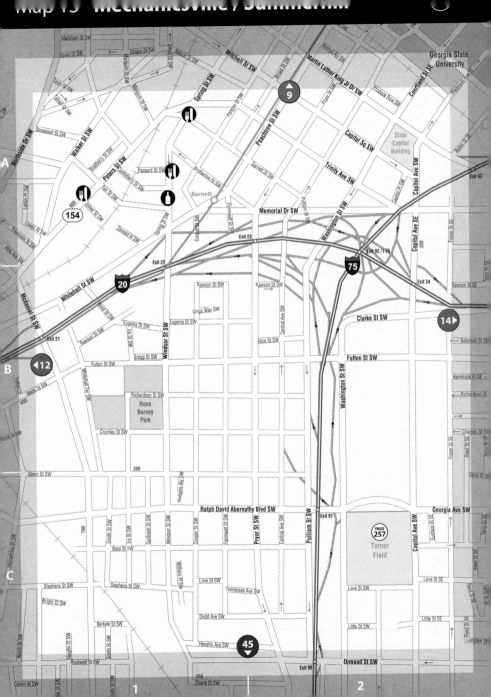

Do the tomahawk chop and cheer on the Braves at Turner Field. Cokeheads (the soda, not the powder) can sample international formulas at the World of Coca Cola. Check out the revolving Sun Dial Restaurant, Bar, and View for a sky-high perspective of the city. Slice is a hip pizza and martini joint. Formosa is such a cool bar it charges a cover.

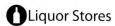

Liquor Stores

· **Atlanta Wholesale Wine** · 275 Spring St SW

Restaurants

· **Haveli Indian Cuisine** · 225 Spring St
· **Lunatique Café** · 160 Spring St
· **Slice** · 259 Peters St

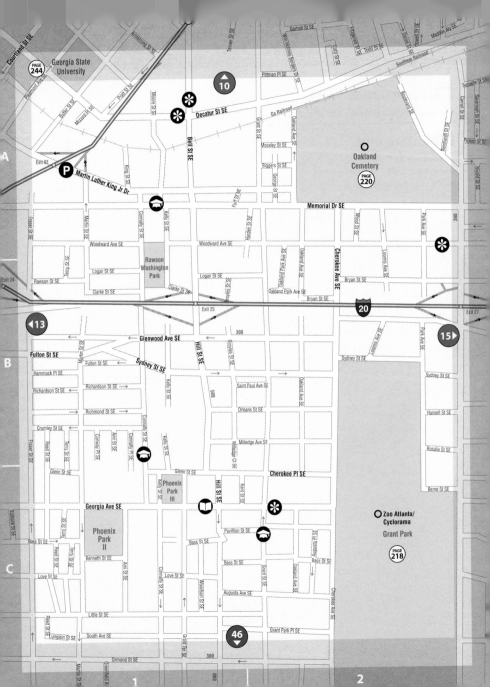

Essentials

Map 14

1	2	3		26
4	5	6	7	28
8	9	10	11	31
12	13	**14**	15	
				34

One of Atlanta's oldest neighborhoods has become one of the city's most successful revitalization efforts. The community is evenly split between middle- and lower-income white and black residents. Oakland Cemetery is an Atlanta landmark and a popular jogging trail. Grant Park is a nice piece of green space, and don't miss those bamboo noshing pandas at Zoo Atlanta.

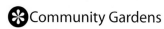 Community Gardens

o Landmarks
· **Cyclorama** · 800 Cherokee Ave SE
· **Oakland Cemetery** · 248 Oakland Ave SE
· **Zoo Atlanta** · 800 Cherokee Ave SE

 Libraries
· **Georgia-Hill Branch** · 250 Georgia Ave SE

 Parking

 Schools
· **Cook Elementary** · 211 Memorial Dr SE
· **MLK Jr Middle** · 582 Connally St SE
· **Neighborhood Charter** · 688 Grant St SE

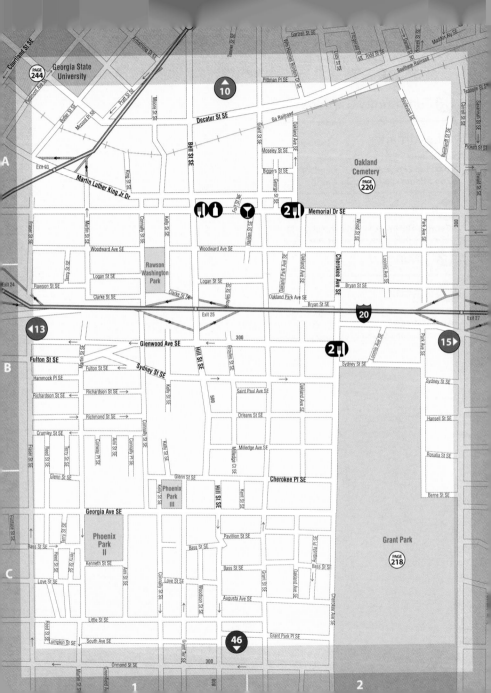

Daddy D'z has finger lickin' good barbecue. Six Feet Under is an aptly-named seafood shack overlooking Oakland Cemetery. Lenny's is as authentic a dive bar as one can find in Atlanta. Ria's Bluebird cooks up a mean breakfast.

Liquor Stores
· **Azar's Package Store** · 277 Memorial Dr SE

Nightlife
· **Lenny's** · 307 Memorial Dr SE

Restaurants
· **Daddy D'z** · 264 Memorial Dr SE
· **Dakota Blue** · 454 Cherokee Ave SE
· **Grand Central Pizza** · 451 Cherokee Ave SE
· **Ria's Bluebird** · 421 Memorial Dr
· **Six Feet Under** · 415 Memorial Dr SE

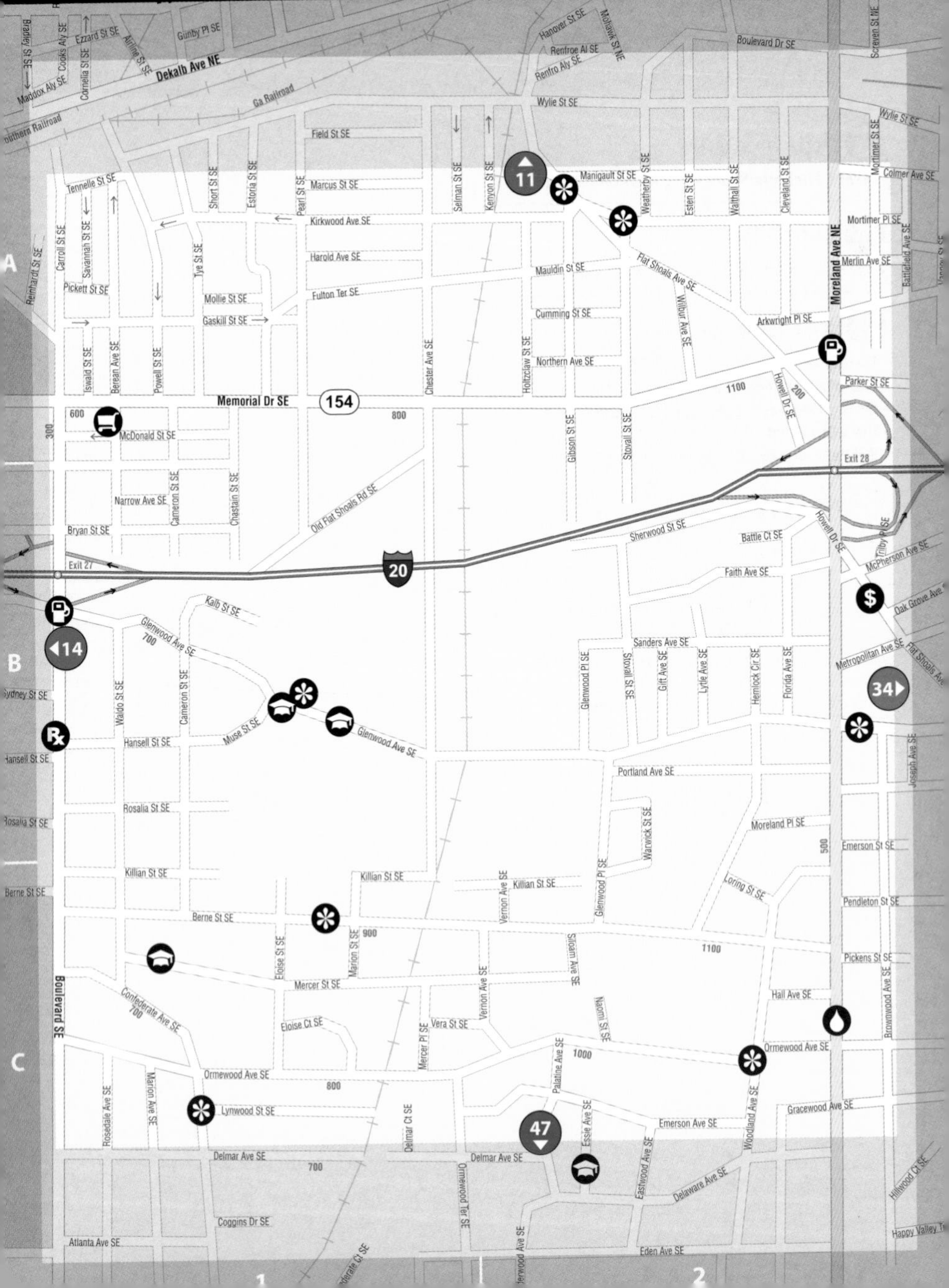

Map 15 • Ormewood Park North / Woodland Hills

Dekalb Ave NE

Ga Railroad

Holbreok Railroad

Maddox Aly SE
Cornelia St SE
Cooks Aly SE
Ezzard St SE
Airline St SE
Gunby St SE
Renfroe Al SE
Hanover St SE
Renfroe St SE
Mobbox St NE
Wylie St SE
Boulevard Dr SE
Screven St NE
Wylie St SE
Colmer Ave SE

Field St SE
Marcus St SE
Kirkwood Ave SE
Harold Ave SE
Fulton Ter SE

Tennelle St SE
Short St SE
Estoria St SE
Pearl St SE
Selman St SE
Kenyon St SE
Manigault St SE
Weatherly St SE
Esten St SE
Walthall St SE
Cleveland St SE
Mortimer PI SE
Merlin Ave SE

Carroll St SE
Savannah St SE
Pickett St SE
Tye St SE

Mollie St SE
Gaskill St SE

Iswald St SE
Berean Ave SE
Powell St SE

Mauldin St SE
Cumming St SE
Northern Ave SE

Flat Shoals Ave SE
Willard St SE

Moreland Ave NE
Arkwright PI SE
Parker St SE

Memorial Dr SE 154

Chester Ave SE

Gibson St SE
Stovall St SE

1100
200
Howell Dr SE

Exit 28

600
300
McDonald St SE

Narrow Ave SE
Cameron St SE
Chastain St SE

Bryan St SE

Old Flat Shoals Rd SE

Sherwood St SE
Battle Ct SE

Exit 27

I-20

Faith Ave SE

Howell Dr SE
Troy St SE
McPherson Ave SE

Kalb St SE
700

114

Glenwood Ave SE
Waldo St SE
Cameron St SE

Sydney St SE

Hansell St SE
Muse St SE
Glenwood Ave SE

Sanders Ave SE

Glenwood PI SE
Morris St SE
Gift Ave SE
Lytle Ave SE
Hemlock Cir SE
Florida Ave SE

Metropolitan Ave SE
Flat Shoals Ave SE
Josephine Ave SE

34

Rosalia St SE
Portland Ave SE

Moreland PI SE
Emerson St SE

Killian St SE

Berne St SE
Killian St SE
Warwick St SE
Loring St SE
Pendleton St SE

900
Eloise St SE
Marion St SE
Vernon Ave SE
Killian St SE
Vernon Ave SE
Glenwood PI SE
1100
Pickens St SE

Confederate Ave SE
700
Mercer St SE
Eloise Ct SE
Vernon Ave SE
Queen St SE
Hall Ave SE
Brownwood Ave SE

Ormewood Ave SE

Ormewood Ave SE
800
Lynwood St SE
Delmar Ave SE
Mercer PI SE
Vera St SE
Palatine Ave SE
1000
Emerson Ave SE
Woodland Ave SE
Gracewood Ave SE

Rosalia St SE
Berne St SE

Boulevard SE
Marion St SE
Rosedale St SE

Delmar Ave SE
700

47

Eisie Ave SE
Eastwood Ave SE
Delaware Ave SE
Hillcrest Ave SE
Happy Valley

Coggins Dr SE
Atlanta Ave SE

Eden Ave SE

Confederate Ct SE
Ormewood Ave SE
Sherwood Ave SE

1
2

Essentials

1	2	3		26
4	5	6	7	28
8	9	10	11	31
12	13	14	15	
				34

Map 15

These small residential neighborhoods are part of a community known as S.A.N.D. (South Atlantans for Neighborhood Development) bordered by the federal penitentiary and bisected by I-20. Despite this, new housing developments are slowly filtering in to the mix.

Banks
- **Bank of America** · 411 Flat Shoals Ave SE

Car Washes
- **Nolan's Car Wash** · 722 Moreland Ave SE

Community Gardens

Gas Stations
- **BP** · 448 Boulevard SE
- **Exxon** · 247 Moreland Ave SE

Pharmacies
- **CVS (24 hrs)** · 520 Boulevard SE

Schools
- **Atlanta Youth Academies** · 754 Glenwood Ave
- **McGill Elementary** · 820 Essie Ave SE
- **Parkside Elementary** · 685 Mercer St
- **Southside High** · 801 Glenwood Ave SE

Supermarket
- **Thunder Alley Grill & Grocery** ·
  632 McDonald St SE

Map 13 • Ormewood Park North / Woodland Hills

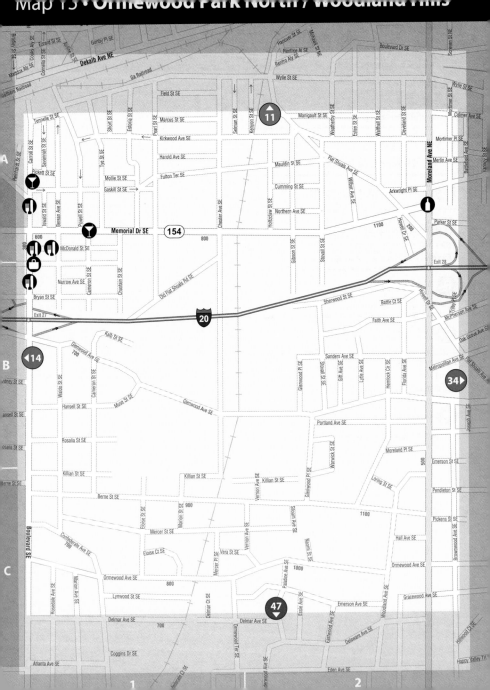

Agave offers sophisticated Southwestern cuisine. The Automatic is the city's coolest drive-thru. Carroll Street Café is a low-key neighborhood bar. Green thumbs delight in the Urban Gardener store. Da'Bomb Takeout Restaurant is, well, da bomb. And the giant skull entrance to the Vortex is pretty damn cool.

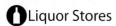Liquor Stores
· **Tower Beer and Wine Store** · 223 Moreland Ave SE

Nightlife
· **Carroll St Café** · 208 Carroll St SE
· **Crazy Horse Bar & Grill** · 687 Memorial Dr SE

Restaurants
· **Agave** · 242 Boulevard SE
· **The Automatic** · 313 Boulevard SE
· **Da'Bomb Take Out Restaurant** · 371 Boulevard SE
· **Thunder Alley Grill & Grocery** ·
  632 McDonald St SE

Shopping
· **Urban Gardner** · 347 Boulevard SE

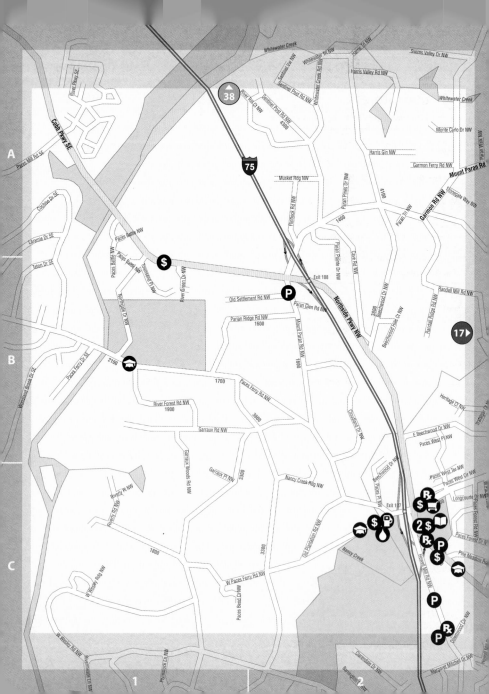

It's no doubt a lovely, wealthy community and a great place to raise kids, but any neighborhood that has "block captains" conjures up visions of *The Stepford Wives*. The neighborhood association challenged God (ok, a church), and limited its expansion in the neighborhood. You can bet the elite private schools in this area (such as Lovett) don't have no stinkin' evolution stickers on their science textbooks.

Banks

- **Bank of America** · 1280 W Paces Ferry Rd NW
- **Bank of America** · 3370 Northside Pkwy
- **Bank of North Georgia** · 4401 Northside Pkwy
- **Southtrust** · 1320 W Paces Ferry Rd
- **Wachovia** · 3290 Northside Pkwy NW
- **Wachovia** · 3393 Northside Pkwy NW

Car Washes

- **Shell** · 1313 W Paces Ferry Rd NW

Gas Stations

- **Exxon** · 1400 W Paces Ferry Rd NW
- **Shell** · 1313 W Paces Ferry Rd NW

Libraries

- **Northside Branch** · 3295 Northside Pkwy NW

Parking

Pharmacies

- **CVS** · 3401 Northside Pkwy NW
- **Pavillion Compounding Pharmacy** · 3193 Howell Mill Rd
- **Wender & Roberts Drugs** · 1262 W Paces Ferry Rd

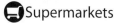Schools

- **Lovett** · 4075 Paces Ferry Rd
- **Trinity** · 3254 Northside Pkwy
- **Westminster** · 1424 W Paces Ferry Rd

Supermarkets

- **Publix** · 1250 W Paces Ferry Rd NW

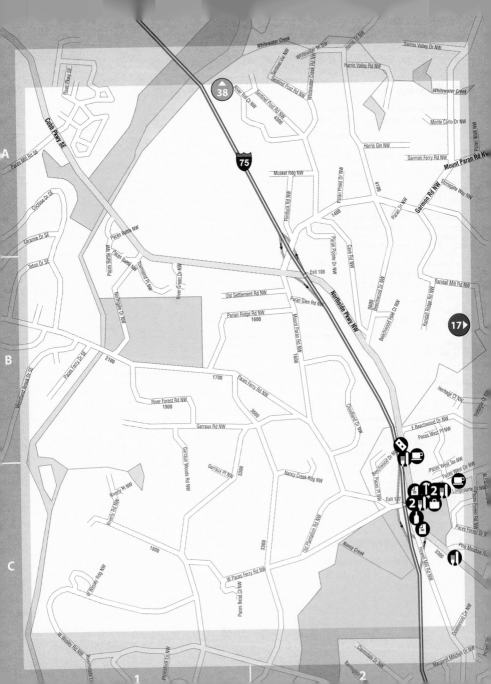

Northerner transplants flock to Goldberg's for the best bagels south of the Mason-Dixon line. Blue Ridge Grill offers sumptuous Southern cuisine. Joel is a chic, upscale dining destination with a happening singles bar scene. Dress your kids in designer threads at Gretchen's Children's Shop.

Coffee
- **Caribou Coffee** · 3487 Northside Pkwy
- **Starbucks** · 1200 W Paces Ferry Rd NW

Copy Shops
- **Fedex Kinko's** · 3401 Northside Pkwy NW
- **UPS Store** · 1266 W Paces Ferry Rd NW

Hardware Stores
- **West Paces Smith Ace Hardware** · 1248 W Paces Ferry Rd NW

Liquor Stores
- **Southern Wine & Spirits** · 3400 Northside Pkwy NW

Restaurants
- **Blue Ridge Grill** · 1261 W Paces Ferry Rd
- **Goldberg's Bagels and Deli** · 1272 W Paces Ferry Rd NW
- **Houston's** · 3539 Northside Pkwy
- **Joel** · 3290 Northside Pkwy NW
- **OK Café** · 1284 W Paces Ferry Rd NW
- **Pano's & Paul's** · 1232 W Paces Ferry Rd

Shopping
- **Gretchen's Children's Shop** · 1246 W Paces Ferry Rd

Video Rental
- **Blockbuster** · 3519 Northside Pkwy NW

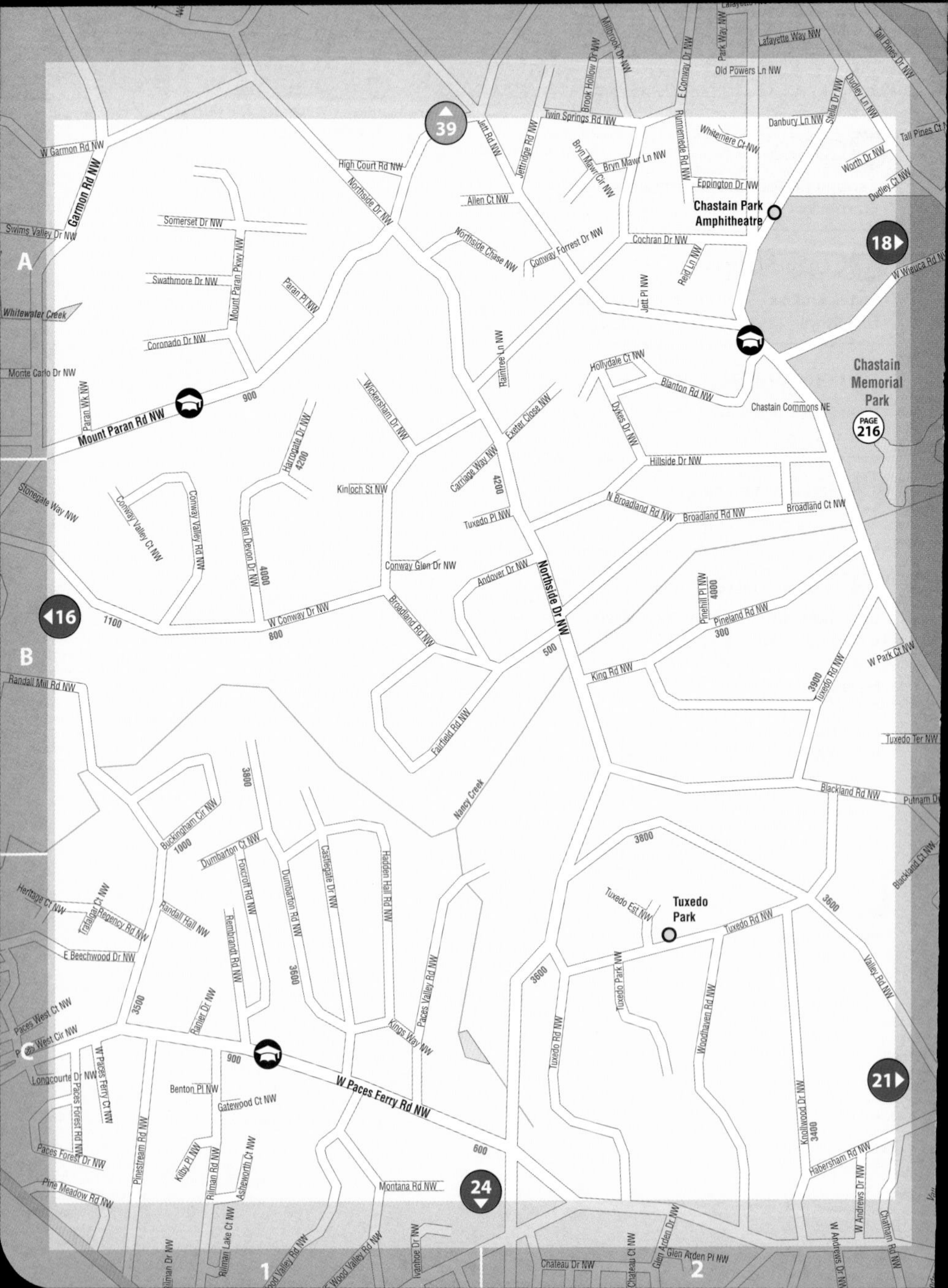

Map 17 · **Northwest Atlanta / Mt Paran** Ⓝ

W Garmon Rd NW

Garmon Rd NW

Swims Valley Dr NW

A

Whitewater Creek

Monte Carlo Dr NW

Paran Pkwy NW

Somerset Dr NW

Swathmore Dr NW

Coronado Dr NW

Mount Paran Pkwy NW

Paran Pl NW

High Court Rd NW

Northside Dr NW

Northside Chase NW

Allen Ct NW

39

Jett Rd NW

Ivanhoe Dr NW

Millbrook Dr NW

Park Way NW

Twin Springs Rd NW

Bryn Mawr Cir NW

Bryn Mawr Ln NW

Ridgewood Dr NW

E Conway Dr NW

Old Powers Ln NW

Lafayette Way NW

Whitemere Ct NW

Eppington Dr NW

Chastain Park Amphitheatre ○

Cochran Dr NW

Reid Ln NW

Conway Forrest Dr NW

Danbury Ln NW

Worth Dr NW

Dudley Ln NW

Tall Pines Ct NW

Dudley Ln NW

18▶

W Wieuca Rd NW

900

Mount Paran Rd NW 🚍

Stonegate Way NW

Conway Valley Rd NW

Harrogate Dr NW

4200

Glen Devon Dr NW

Wickersham Dr NW

Kinloch St NW

Raintree Ln NW

Conway Glen Dr NW

Exeter Close NW

4200

Tuxedo Pl NW

Andover Dr NW

Hollydale Ct NW

Blanton Rd NW

Dukes Dr NW

Hillside Dr NW

N Broadland Rd NW

Broadland Rd NW

Chastain Commons NE

Chastain Memorial Park

PAGE 216

Broadland Ct NW

🚍

4000

◀16

1100

W Conway Dr NW

800

Broadland Rd NW

Fairfield Pkwy NW

Northside Dr NW

500

King Rd NW

Pinehill Pl NW

4000

Pineland Rd NW

300

3800

Tuxedo Rd NW

W Park Ct NW

Tuxedo Ter NW

B

Randall Mill Rd NW

Buckingham Ct NW

1000

Dumbarton Ct NW

3800

Foxcroft Rd NW

Dumbarton Rd NW

Castlegate Dr NW

Hadden Hall Rd NW

Nancy Creek

Blackland Rd NW

Putnam Cir NW

Blackland Ct NW

Heritage Ct NW

Training Cir NW

Regency Rd NW

Randall Hall NW

Rembrandt Rd NW

E Beechwood Dr NW

3600

Pisces West Ct NW

West Cir NW

Longcourte Dr NW

3500

Ranier Ct NW

3800

3800

Paces Valley Rd NW

Kings Way NW

Tuxedo Est NW

3800

Tuxedo Park

○

Tuxedo Rd NW

Woodhaven Rd NW

Valley Rd NW

3600

3600

Blackland Rd NW

Knollwood Dr NW

21▶

🚍

900

Benton Pl NW

Pinestream Rd NW

W Paces Ferry Ct NW

W Paces Ferry Rd NW

Gatewood Ct NW

Paces Forest Rd NW

Paces Forest Dr NW

Kibby Ct NW

Rilman Rd NW

Gatewood Ct NW

Rilman Lake Cir NW

W Paces Ferry Rd NW

600

Montana Rd NW

24▼

Tuxedo Park NW

3400

Hakersham Rd NW

Glen Arden Pl NW

Glen Arden Dr NW

W Andrews Dr NW

Chatham Rd NW

Pine Meadow Rd NW

Heathcote Dr NW

Wood Valley Dr NW

1

Wood Valley Rd NW

Chateau Dr NW

Chateau Ct NW

Glen Arden Dr NW

2

With a community called Tuxedo Park in its midst, you know this neighborhood has to be loaded, and it is. Gorgeous, sprawling mansions attract tour buses on a regular basis. It should be no surprise that one of the city's best private schools (Pace Academy) is in this well-to-do neighborhood.

○ Landmarks

· **Chastain Park Amphitheatre** · 4469 Stella Dr NW
· **Tuxedo Park** · Vicinity of 3661 Tuxedo Rd NW

Schools

· **Jackson Elementary** · 1325 Mount Paran Rd NW
· **Pace Academy** · 966 W Paces Ferry Rd NW
· **Sutton Middle** · 4360 Powers Ferry Rd NW

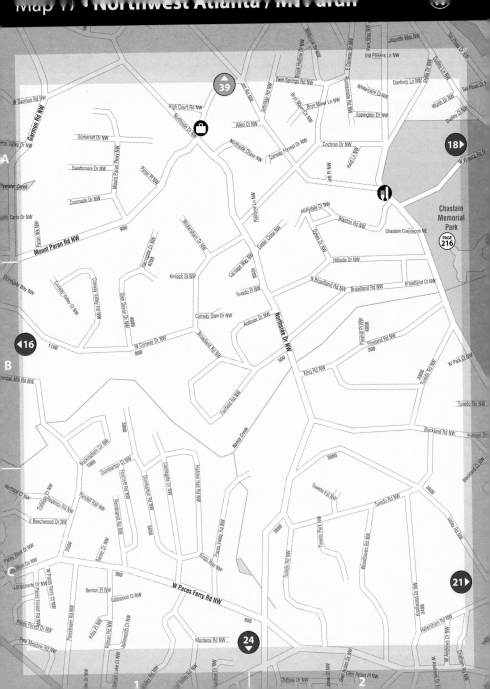

Chastain Park Amphitheatre is a great outdoor concert venue, unless you're stuck next to some cell-phone-chatting yuppie. Ride horses, play tennis, and engage in other rich folk hobbies at Chastain Memorial Park. Horseradish Grill is the city's oldest continuously operating restaurant, serving upscale Southern cuisine in a refined setting.

Restaurants

· **Horseradish Grill** · 4320 Powers Ferry Rd

Shopping

· **Mt Paran Country Store** · 4480 Northside Dr NW

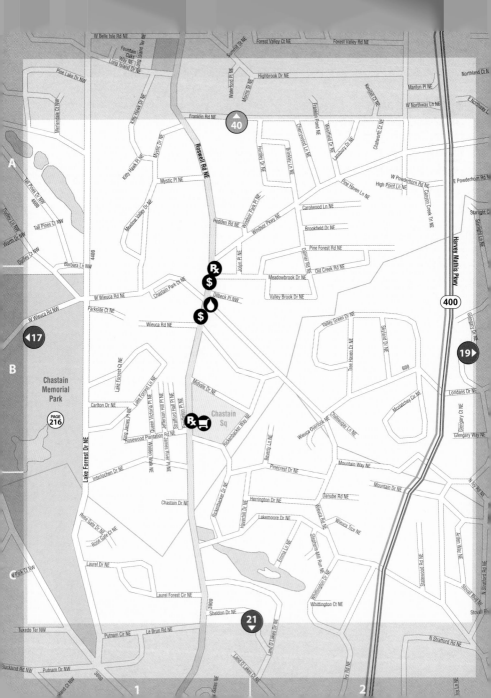

It's ironic that segregated almshouses for the poor once sat on the area now known for an entertainment center and a swim-tennis residential community. One of the city's prettiest neighborhoods, it boasts of a ton of recreational activities as well as convenient access to Buckhead, though you may have to fight formidable Roswell Road traffic.

$ Banks
- **Bank of America** · 4492 Roswell Rd NE
- **Wachovia** · 4454 Roswell Rd NE

Car Washes
- **Fast Lane Hand Car Wash** · 200 W Wieuca Rd NE

Pharmacies
- **Eckerd** · 4540 Roswell Rd NE
- **Publix** · 4279 Roswell Rd NE

Supermarkets
- **Publix** · 4279 Roswell Rd NE

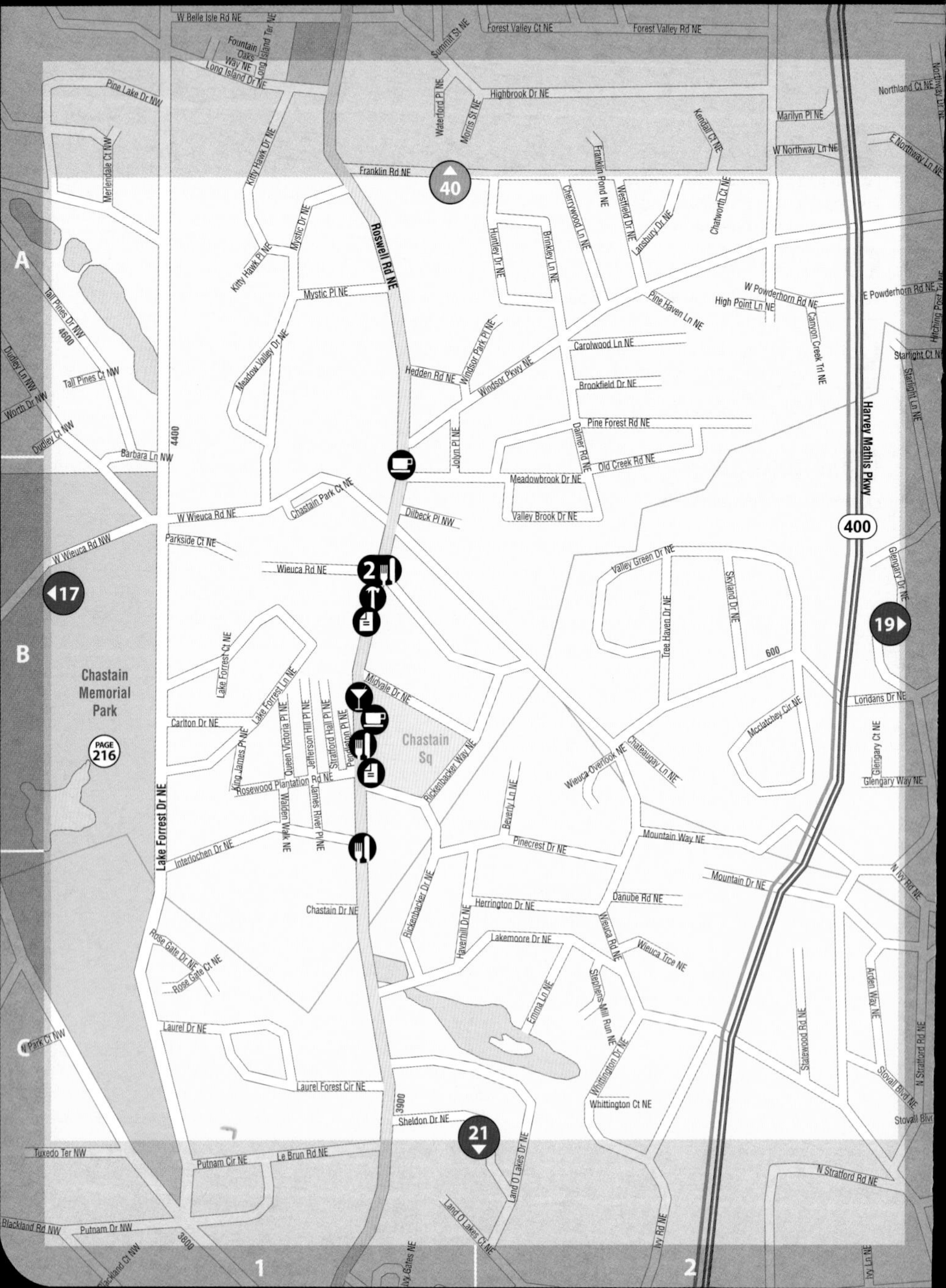

Map 18 · **Chastain Park**

N

A

B

C

W Belle Isle Rd NE
Pine Lake Dr NW
Fountain Dr NE
Long Island Dr NE
Long Island Ter NW
Summit St NE
Forest Valley Ct NE
Forest Valley Rd NE
Waterford Pl NE
Highbrook Dr NE
Mystic St NE
Northland Ct NE
Marilyn Pl NE
W Northway Ln NE
E Northway Ln NE
Kendall Ct NE
Meriendale Ct NW
Pine Lake Dr NW
Kitty Hawk Pl NE
Mystic Dr NE
Franklin Rd NE
40
Chatworth Ct NE
Landsburg Ct NE
Westfield Dr NE
Cherrywood Ln NE
Brinkley Ln NE
Huntley Dr NE
Franklin Pond Rd NE
W Powderhorn Rd NE
E Powderhorn Pl NE
High Point Ln NE
Tall Pines Dr NW
Tall Pines Ct NW
Worth Dr NW
Dudley Ct NW
Barbara Ln NW
Mystic Pl NE
Roswell Rd NE
Windsor Park Pl NE
Pine Haven Ln NE
Starlight Ct NE
Harvey Mathis Pkwy
Meadow Valley Dr NE
Hedden Rd NE
Windsor Pkwy NE
Carolwood Ln NE
Brookfield Dr NE
Pine Forest Rd NE
Joan Pl NE
Dalney Rd NE
Old Creek Rd NE
Chastain Park Ct NE
Dilbeck Pl NW
Meadowbrook Dr NE
Valley Brook Dr NE
400
Glengary Dr NE
W Wieuca Rd NE
Parkside Ct NE
Wieuca Rd NE
2
Valley Green Dr NE
Skyland Dr NE
19
Lake Forrest Ct NE
Lake Forest Dr NE
Carlton Dr NE
Lake Forest Pl NE
Queen Victoria Pl NE
Jefferson Hill Pl NE
Stratford Hill Pl NE
Kirby James Pl NE
Waddell Mill Pk NE
Rosewood Plantation Rd NE
James River Pl NE
Midvale Dr NE
Chastain Sq
Rickenbacker Way NE
Beverly Ln NE
Chattaway Ln NE
Wieuca Overlook NE
Tree Haven Dr NE
600
McClatchey Cir NE
Loridans Dr NE
Glengary Ct NE
Glengary Way NE
Chastain
Memorial
Park
PAGE
216
17
W Wieuca Rd NW
W Park Ct NW
Lake Forrest Dr NE
Interlochen Dr NE
Chastain Dr NE
Rickenbacker Dr NE
Haverhill Dr NE
Herrington Dr NE
Lakemoore Dr NE
Mountain Way NE
Pinecrest Dr NE
Danube Rd NE
Mountain Dr NE
Wieuca Rd NE
Wieuca Trce NE
N Ivy Rd NE
River Glen Dr NE
Rook Gate Ct NE
Laurel Dr NE
Laurel Forest Cir NE
3900
Sheldon Dr NE
Emma Ln NE
Shepherds Mill Run NE
Washington Dr NE
Whittington Ct NE
N Stratford Rd NE
Stovall Blvd NE
N Stratford Rd NE
Aiden Way NE
Stovall Blvd NE
Asden Rd NE
Asden Pl NE
21
Tuxedo Ter NW
Putnam Cir NE
Le Brun Rd NE
Land O Lakes Dr NE
Land O Lakes Ct NE
Blackland Rd NW
Putnam Dr NW
3900
N Ivy Rd NE
Ivy Rd NE

1   2

Well, duh, the Chastain Park Amphitheatre, not just for concerts, but also for horseback riding, tennis, golf, and an arts center. 10 Degrees South offers an upscale take on South African cuisine. Brandy House and Tavern offers such a diverse set of live music acts, you never know what to expect.

Coffee

- **Caribou Coffee** · 4520 Roswell Rd NE
- **Starbucks** · 4285 Roswell Rd NE

Copy Shops

- **Diazo Specialty Blueprint** · 4385 Roswell Rd NE
- **UPS Store** · 4279 Roswell Rd NE

Hardware Stores

- **Workbench Ace Hardware** · 4405 Roswell Rd NE

Nightlife

- **Brandy House and Tavern** · 4365 Roswell Rd NE

Restaurants

- **10 Degrees South** · 4183 Roswell Rd NE
- **Chopstix** · 4279 Roswell Rd NE
- **Fellini's Pizza** · 4429 Roswell Rd NE
- **La Fonda Latina** · 4427 Roswell Rd NE

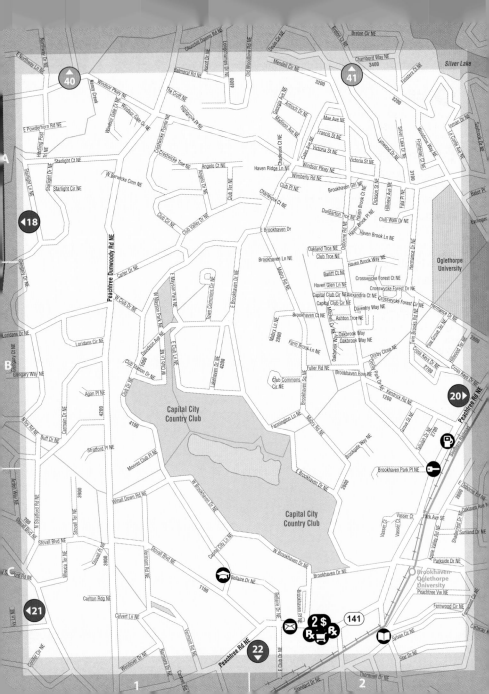

Essentials

Map 19

Fittingly, Brookhaven was Atlanta's first ritzy "country club" community. Nothing much has changed over the years. Well-maintained homes on winding streets, good public and private schools, and an active neighborhood community makes this area perfect for affluent families that don't want to deal with the hellish suburban commute.

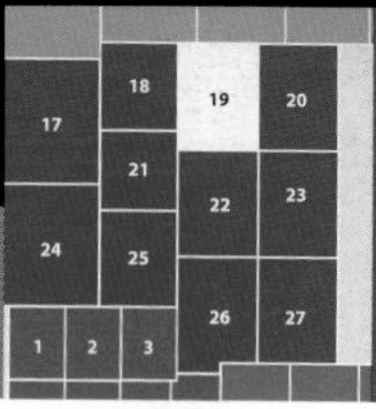

$ Banks

• **IronStone Bank** • 3871 Peachtree Rd NE
• **Wachovia** • 3890 Peachtree Rd NE

Car Rental

• **Accent Auto & Truck Rental** • 4208 Peachtree Rd NE

Gas Stations

• **Chevron** • 4234 Peachtree Rd NE

Libraries

• **Brookhaven Library** • 1242 N Druid Hills Rd

Pharmacies

• **Eckerd** • 3964 Peachtree Rd NE
• **Kroger** • 3871 Peachtree Rd NE

 Post Offices

• **US Post Office** • 3851 Peachtree Rd NE

Schools

• **Sophia Academy** • 1199 Bellaire Dr NE

Supermarkets

• **Kroger** • 3871 Peachtree Rd NE

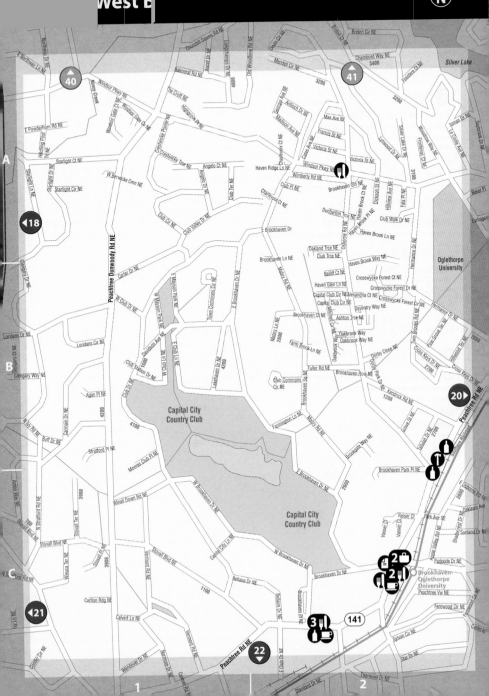

If you're a Capital City Country Club member (and if you live in the neighborhood you probably are), then you can golf and play tennis to your heart's delight. Sherlock's Wine Merchants offers an excellent international wine selection. For some down-to-earth BBQ, Pig-N-Chik is the place to go. Chin Chin offers dependable, upscale Chinese that is perfect for this non-adventurous neighborhood crowd.

Coffee
- **Dunkin' Donuts** · 4040 Peachtree Rd NE
- **Starbucks** · 3901 Peachtree Rd NE

Copy Shops
- **UPS Store** · 4060 Peachtree Rd NE

Hardware Stores
- **General Hardware** · 4218 Peachtree Rd NE

Liquor Stores
- **Alex Package** · 4200 Peachtree Rd NE
- **Olympic Package Store** · 4244 Peachtree Rd NE
- **Peachtree Wine** · 3891 Peachtree Rd NE

Restaurants
- **Au Rendez-Vous** · 1328 Windsor Pkwy
- **Bajaritos** · 3877 Peachtree Rd NE
- **Chin Chin** · 3887 Peachtree Rd NE
- **Jack's & Jill's Sports Grill** · 4046 Peachtree Rd NE
- **Meehan's Ale House** · 4058 Peachtree Rd NE
- **Mellow Mushroom** · 4058 Peachtree Rd NE
- **Pig-N-Chik** · 3929 Peachtree Rd NE

Shopping
- **Cook's Warehouse** · 4062 Peachtree Rd NE
- **Sherlock's Wine Merchants** · 4062 Peachtree Rd NE

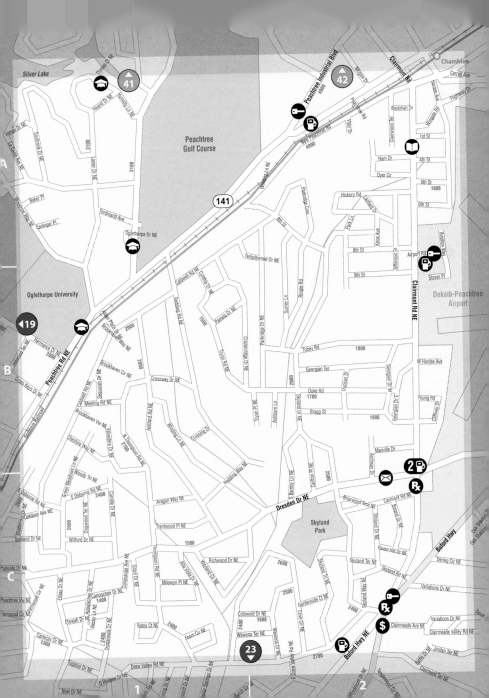

This section of Brookhaven is an interesting mix of an affluent golf club and a university community, along with a growing international community as one ventures east towards Buford Highway. The private DeKalb-Peachtree Airport was once a military installation.

Banks

• **Colonial Bank** • 3361 Clairmont Rd NE

Car Rental

• **Auto Save** • 4945 Peachtree Industrial Blvd
• **Budget** • 3892 Buford Hwy NE
• **Hertz** • 1954 Airport Rd

Gas Stations

• **Chevron** • 3630 Clairmont Rd
• **Citgo** • 3637 Clairmont Rd
• **Marathon** • 4930 Peachtree Rd
• **Philips 66** • 1950 Airport Rd
• **Shell** • 3799 Buford Hwy NE

Libraries

• **Chamblee Library** • 4115 Clairmont Rd

Pharmacies

• **CVS** • 3615 Clairmont Rd
• **Kroger** • 3855 Buford Hwy

Post Offices

• **US Post Office** • 1920 Dresden Dr NE

Schools

• **Oglethorpe University** • Peachtree Rd NE
• **Our Lady of The Assumption** • 1320 Hearst Dr NE
• **St Martin's Episcopal** • 3110 Ashford Dunwoody

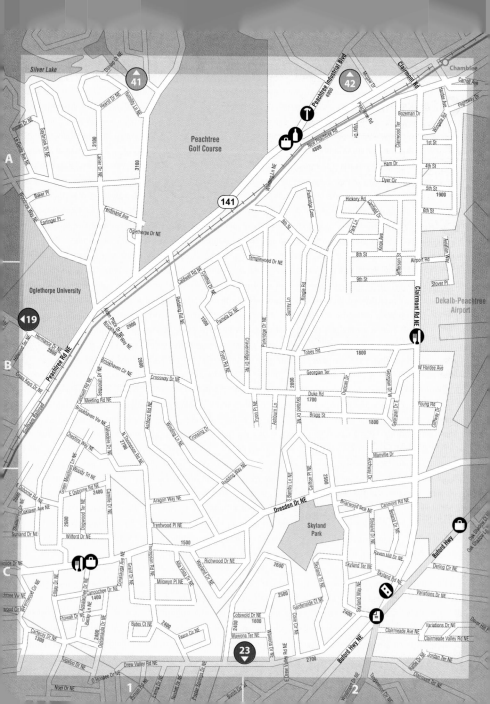

Sundries / Entertainment

Map 20

17	18	19	20
21	22	23
24	25	26	27
1	2	3

Haven is a hip dining spot. If you're an ice cream fanatic who's trying to find that unique flavor you had at an Atlanta restaurant, then head to the Greenwood Ice Cream Company Outlet Store. The 57th Fighter Group is an aviation-themed dining landmark that has some tasty beer-cheese soup that will wreck any diet.

Copy Shops
- **Action Printing Center** · 3400 Clairmont Rd NE

Hardware Stores
- **Lowes** · 4950 Peachtree Industrial Blvd

Liquor Stores
- **S&S Bottle Shop** · 4865 Peachtree Rd

Restaurants
- **57th Fighter Group** · 3829 Clairmont Rd
- **Haven** · 1411 Dresden Dr

Shopping
- **Burlington Coat Factory** · 4166 Buford Hwy NE
- **Fiddle-dee-dee** · 1441 Dresden Dr
- **Greenwood Ice Cream Co Outlet Store** ·
  4829 Peachtree Rd

Video Rental
- **Trade A Video** · 3432 Clairmont Rd NE

Map 21 · **Central Buckhead**

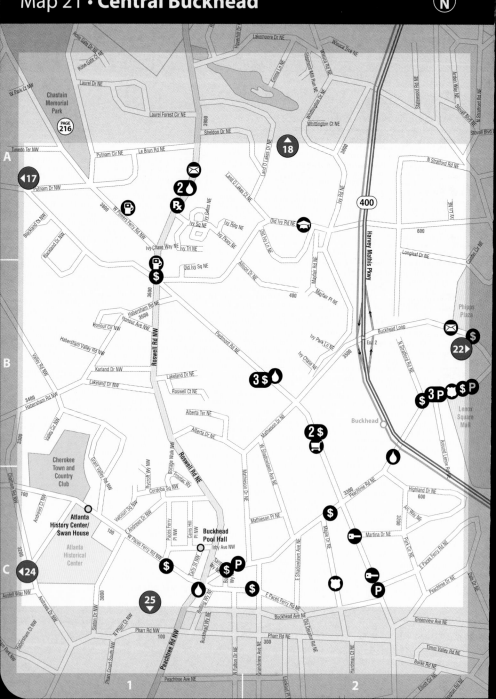

There really are two Buckheads, the first belonging to the city's silver-haired matriarchs and patriarchs, and the other belonging to the hell-bent partygoers of the area's notorious club scene. Expect the best (and most expensive) amenities and services, and expect the worst traffic, especially on weekends, when surface streets resemble a parking lot.

Banks

- **Bank of America** · 3116 Peachtree Rd NE
- **Bank of America** · 3414 Peachtree Rd NE
- **The Buckhead Community Bank** ·
  415 E Paces Ferry Rd NE
- **Colonial Bank** · 3379 Peachtree Rd NE
- **Fidelity Bank** · 3490 Piedmont Rd NE
- **Flag Bank** · 3475 Piedmont Rd NE
- **National Bank of Commerce** · 3330 Piedmont Rd
- **RBC Centura** · 3475 Piedmont Rd NE
- **Regions** · 3655 Roswell Rd
- **Riverside Bank** · 334 E Paces Ferry Rd NE
- **Wachovia** · 3235 Peachtree Rd NE
- **Wachovia** · 3465 Buckhead Loop NE
- **Washington Mutual** · 3330 Piedmont Rd

 Car Rental

- **Atlanta Rent-a-Car** · 3129 Piedmont Rd
- **Enterprise** · 3088 Piedmont Rd NE

Car Washes

- **Buckhead Autobath** · 3060 Peachtree Rd NE
- **Buckhead Car Wash and Detail** ·
  3340 Peachtree Rd NE
- **Buckhead's Finest Car Wash** · 3827 Roswell Rd NE
- **Carbuffs Car Wash and Detail Salon** ·
  3721 Roswell Rd NE
- **JP Express Detail** · 3475 Piedmont Rd NE

Gas Stations

- **Shell** · 3669 Powers Ferry Rd NW
- **Texaco** · 3658 Roswell Rd NE

o Landmarks

- **Atlanta History Center** · 130 W Paces Ferry Rd NW
- **Buckhead Pool Hall** · 30 Irby Ave NW
- **Swan House** · 130 W Paces Ferry Rd NW

Parking

Pharmacies

- **CVS** · 3788 Roswell Rd

Police

- **APD Zone 2 Lenox Mall Mini Precinct** ·
  3393 Peachtree Rd NE
- **APD Zone 2 Station** · 3120 Maple Dr NE

 Post Offices

- **US Post Office** · 3495 Buckhead Loop NE
- **US Post Office** · 3840 Roswell Rd NE

Schools

- **Smith Elementary** · 370 Old Ivy Rd NE

Supermarkets

- **Kroger** · 3330 Piedmont Rd NE

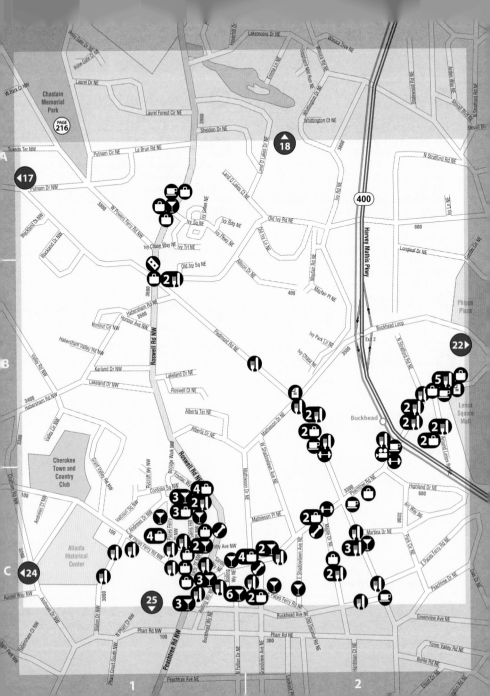

If hanging with drunken frat boys and gold-toothed rappers is your idea of a good time, head to Buckhead Village for the meat-market club scene. Get your steak on at Bone's, savor the finest sushi in the Southeast at Soto, and, if you're really lucky, see Whitney Houston and Bobby Brown get tipsy at The Palm. Distant Replays offers cool vintage sports jerseys.

Coffee
- **Buckhead Bread Company** · 3070 Piedmont Rd
- **Caribou Coffee** · 3261 Peachtree Rd NE
- **Dunkin' Donuts** · 3802 E Roswell Rd
- **Starbucks** · 3330 Piedmont Rd
- **Starbucks** · 3343 Peachtree Rd
- **Starbucks** · 3393 Peachtree Rd

Copy Shops
- **Ameripress** · 3400 Peachtree Rd NE
- **Photo Factory Imaging & Copy Center** · 3420 Piedmont Rd NE

Gyms
- **Crunch** · 3340 Peachtree Rd NE
- **Crunch** · 3365 Piedmont Rd NE
- **LA Fitness** · 3232 Peachtree Rd NE

Movie Theaters
- **AMC Buckhead Backlot 6** · 3340 Peachtree Rd NE

Nightlife
- **Andrew's Upstairs** · 56 E Andrews Dr NW
- **Beluga Martini Bar** · 3115 Piedmont Rd
- **Buckhead Amusement Center** · 30 Irby Ave NW
- **Buckhead Saloon** · 3107 Peachtree Rd NE
- **Che** · 268 E Paces Ferry Rd NE
- **Churchill Arms** · 3223 Cains Hill Pl NW
- **Coyote Ugly** · 287 E Paces Ferry Rd NE
- **East Andrews Bar** · 56 E Andrews Dr NW
- **Electra** · 3081 E Shadowlawn Ave NE
- **Fado** · 3035 Peachtree Rd NE
- **Five Paces Inn** · 41 Irby Ave NW
- **Fluid** · 3067 Peachtree Rd NE
- **Hole in the Wall** · 3177 Peachtree Rd NE
- **Jellyroll's Dueling Pianos** · 295 E Paces Ferry Rd NE
- **Johnny's Hideaway** · 3771 Roswell Rd NE
- **The Living Room** · 3069 Peachtree Rd NE
- **Lulu's Bait Shack** · 3057 Peachtree Rd NE
- **Mako** · 3065 Peachtree Rd NE
- **McDuff's Irish Pub** · 56 E Andrews Dr NW
- **Mike 'n Angelo's** · 312 E Paces Ferry Rd

- **Moondogs** · 3179 Peachtree Rd NE
- **Park Bench** · 256 E Paces Ferry Rd NE
- **Rose and Crown** · 288 E Paces Ferry Rd NE
- **Sambuca Jazz Café** · 3102 Piedmont Rd NE
- **Sanctuary** · 3209 Paces Ferry Pl
- **Tongue and Groove** · 3055 Peachtree Rd
- **Uranus** · 3049 Peachtree Rd NE
- **World Bar** · 3071 Peachtree Rd NE

Pet Shops
- **Atlantis Aquarium** · 3125 Roswell Rd NE
- **The Fish Store & More** · 3145 Peachtree Rd NE
- **Petsmart** · 3221 Peachtree Rd NE

Restaurants
- **Aiko** · 128 E Andrews Dr NW
- **Anthony's** · 3109 Piedmont Rd NE
- **Antica Posta** · 519 E Paces Ferry Rd NE
- **Atlanta Bread Company** · 3365 Piedmont Rd NE
- **Au Pied de Cochon** · 3315 Peachtree Rd NE
- **Bone's** · 3130 Piedmont Rd NE
- **Brasserie Le Coze** · 3393 Peachtree Rd NE
- **Buckhead Diner** · 3073 Piedmont Rd NE
- **Café at East Andrews** · 56 E Andrews Dr NW
- **The Capital Grille** · 255 E Paces Ferry Rd NE
- **Chipotle** · 3424 Piedmont Rd NE
- **Chops** · 70 W Paces Ferry Rd NW
- **Clubhouse** · 3393 Peachtree Rd NE
- **Copeland's** · 3365 Piedmont Rd NE
- **Corner Bakery Café** · 3368 Peachtree Rd NE
- **Corner Bakery Café** · 3393 Peachtree Rd NE
- **Dantanna's** · 3400 Around Lenox Dr
- **Dante's Down the Hatch** · 3380 Peachtree Rd NE
- **Fogo de Chao** · 3101 Piedmont Rd NE
- **Hal's on Old Ivy** · 30 Old Ivy Rd NE
- **Hashiguchi** · 3400 Around Lenox Dr
- **Henri's Bakery** · 61 Irby Ave NW
- **Kyma** · 3085 Piedmont Rd NE
- **Landmark Diner** · 3652 Roswell Rd
- **Maggiano's** · 3368 Peachtree Rd NE
- **McKinnon's Louisiane** · 3209 Maple Dr NE
- **Milan** · 3377 Peachtree Rd NE
- **Moe's Southwest Grill** · 3722 Roswell Rd NE
- **Morton's - The Steakhouse** · 3379 Peachtree Rd NE
- **Nava** · 3060 Peachtree Rd NE
- **The Palm** · 3391 Peachtree Rd NE
- **Portofino** · 3199 Paces Ferry Pl NW

- **Prime** · 3393 Peachtree Rd NE
- **Roy's** · 3475 Piedmont Rd NE
- **Seeger's** · 111 W Paces Ferry Rd NW
- **Soleil** · 3081 Maple Dr NE
- **Soto** · 3330 Piedmont Rd NE
- **Souper Jenny** · 56 E Andrews Dr NW
- **Surin of Thailand** · 318 E Paces Ferry Rd NE
- **Swan Coach House** · 3130 Slaton Dr NW
- **White House** · 3172 Peachtree Rd NE

Shopping
- **Almanac** · 22 E Andrews Dr NW
- **Apple Store** · 3393 Peachtree Rd NE
- **Atlanta Beach** · 3145 Peachtree Rd NE
- **BD Jeffries** · 3736 Roswell Rd NE
- **Binders** · 3330 Piedmont Rd NE
- **Blue Genes** · 3400 Around Lenox Dr
- **Buckhead's Upscale Resale** · 3655 Roswell Rd NE
- **Buckles** · 3145 Peachtree Rd NE
- **C'est Moi** · 3198 Paces Ferry Pl NW
- **Distant Replays** · 324 E Paces Ferry Rd NE
- **DR Mercantile** · 324 E Paces Ferry Rd NE
- **Eatzi's** · 3221 Peachtree Rd NE
- **Fitigues** · 26 E Andrews Dr
- **Henri's** · 61 Irby Ave
- **Interior Dimensions** · 3185 Maple Dr NE
- **Joe Muggs Newstand** · 3275 Peachtree Rd NE
- **K-la** · 3400 Around Lenox Dr
- **Merci Woman** · 3209 Paces Ferry Pl NW
- **Now & Again** · 56 E Andrews Dr
- **Oh! Fine Lingerie** · 3209 Paces Ferry Pl
- **The Owl and the Pussycat** · 3145 Peachtree Rd NE
- **Patagonia** · 34 E Andrews Dr
- **Pearl Paints** · 3756 Roswell Rd NE
- **Pearson's Wine of Atlanta** · 3072 Early St NW
- **Pink Lemonade** · 3802 E Roswell Rd NE
- **Pollen** · 22 E Andrews Dr
- **Razzle Dazzle** · 49 Irby Ave NW
- **Sage Clothing** · 37 W Paces Ferry Rd NE
- **Susan Lee** · 56 E Andrews Dr
- **Topaz Gallery** · 3145 Peachtree Rd NE
- **Tower Records** · 3232 Peachtree Rd NE
- **Urban Frontier** · 3210 Paces Ferry Pl NW
- **Urban Outfitters** · 3393 Peachtree Rd NE
- **White Dove** · 18 E Andrews Dr NW
- **World Market** · 3330 Piedmont Rd NE

Video Rental
- **Blockbuster** · 3655 Roswell Rd NE

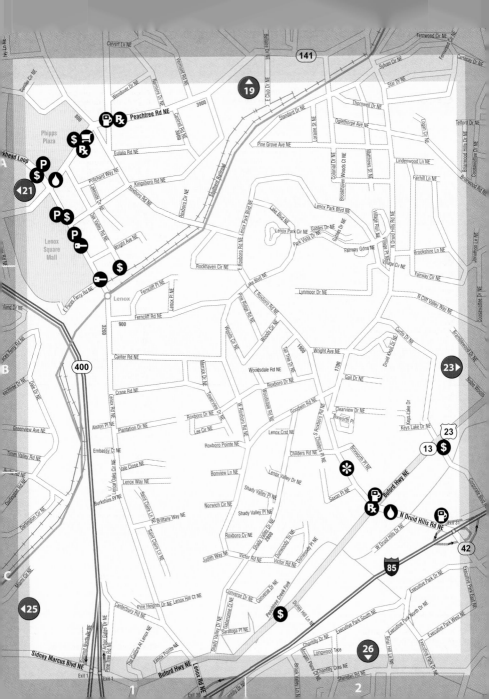

For upscale living around upscale malls, the Lenox area can't be beat. You could go shopping on foot, but why would you bother when you can drive your Mercedes or BMW? Upscale condo and town home communities dot the area, including some senior living communities, because even the rich eventually get old.

$ Banks

- **Bank of America** · 3535 Peachtree Rd NE
- **BB&T** · 950 E Paces Ferry Rd NE
- **Main Street Bank** · 3500 Lenox Rd
- **Southtrust** · 3424 Peachtree Rd NE
- **Wachovia** · 2750 Buford Hwy
- **Wachovia** · 3019 Buford Hwy NE

Car Rental

- **Avis** · 3405 Lenox Rd NE
- **Hertz** · 3300 Lenox Rd NE

Car Washes

- **Hi-Speed Car Wash** · 2024 N Druid Hills Rd NE
- **Pinnacle Detailing** · 3445 Peachtree Rd NE

Community Gardens

Gas Stations

- **BP** · 2080 N Druid Hills Rd NE
- **BP** · 3639 Peachtree Rd NE
- **Chevron** · 2024 N Druid Hills Rd NE
- **Chevron** · 2911 Buford Hwy NE

Parking

Pharmacies

- **CVS** · 2910 Buford Hwy
- **CVS** · 3637 Peachtree Rd NE
- **Publix** · 3535 Peachtree Rd NE

Supermarkets

- **Publix** · 3535 Peachtree Rd NE

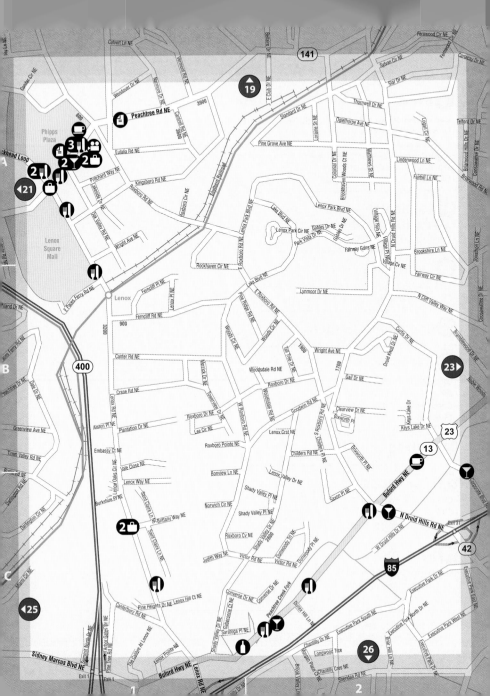

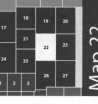
Shopping sprees at Lenox Square and Phipps Plaza are a must. Bluepointe is a dramatic, Asian-inspired restaurant. Twist and The Tavern at Phipps draw a rich, single, and attractive crowd. The Dining Room at the Ritz Carlton offers some of the finest formal dining in the city. Filene's Basement is good for bargain hunters with upscale tastes.

Coffee
- **Dunkin' Donuts** · 3007 Buford Hwy NE
- **Starbucks** · 3500 Peachtree Rd NE

Copy Shops
- **Fedex Kinko's** · 3637 Peachtree Rd NE
- **UPS Store** · 3535 Peachtree Rd NE

Liquor Stores
- **Green's Beverage Store** · 2614 Buford Hwy NE

Movie Theaters
- **AMC Phipps Plaza 14** · 3500 Peachtree Rd NE

Nightlife
- **Chapparel** · 2715 Buford Hwy NE
- **Fuzzy's Place** · 2015 N Druid Hills Rd NE
- **Pink Pony** · 1837 Corporate Blvd NE
- **The Tavern at Phipps** · 3500 Peachtree Rd NE
- **Twist** · 3500 Peachtree Rd NE

Restaurants
- **Ali Oli** · 3535 Peachtree Rd NE
- **Bluepointe** · 3455 Peachtree Rd NE
- **The Cabin Room** · 2678 Buford Hwy
- **The Dining Room at the Ritz Carlton** ·
  3434 Peachtree Rd NE
- **Emeril's** · 3500 Lenox Rd
- **Havana Sandwich Shop** · 2905 Buford Hwy NE
- **Houston's** · 3321 Lenox Rd
- **Johnny Rockets** · 3500 Peachtree Rd NE
- **New York Prime** · 3424 Peachtree Rd NE
- **Phuket Thai Restaurant** · 2839 Buford Hwy NE
- **Roaster's** · 2770 Lenox Rd NE
- **Twist** · 3500 Peachtree Rd NE

Shopping
- **Dick's Sporting Goods** · 3535 Peachtree Rd
- **Fem Deluxe** · 2770 Lenox Rd NE
- **Filene's Basement** · 3535 Peachtree Rd NE
- **Metropolitan Deluxe-Phipps Plaza** ·
  3500 Peachtree Rd NE
- **Signature Boutique** · 2770 Lenox Rd NE

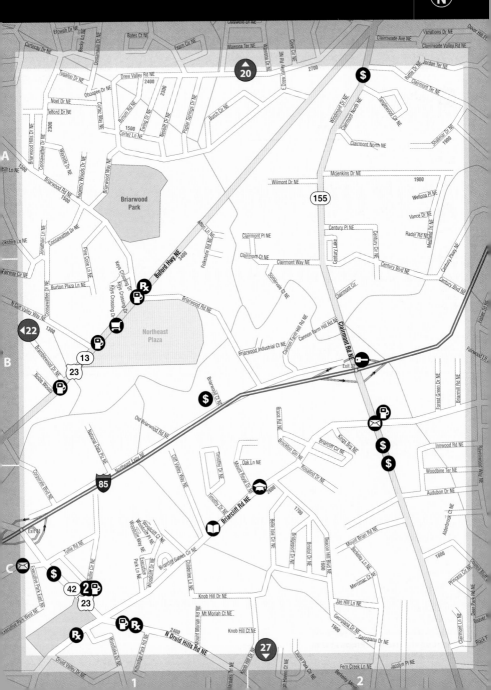

A pine tree-lined residential community clashes with high-density commercial and industrial development and a rapidly growing international community in this evolving area.

$ Banks

- **Bank of America** · 2223 N Druid Hills Rd
- **CDC Federal Credit Union** · 1947 Briarwood Ct NE
- **Southtrust** · 2700 Clairmont Rd
- **Wachovia** · 2725 Clairmont Rd NE
- **Washington Mutual** · 3300 Clairmont Rd NE

Car Rental

- **National** · 1716 NE Expy

Gas Stations

- **Chevron** · 2289 N Druid Hills Rd NE
- **Chevron** · 2755 Clairmont Rd NE
- **Citgo** · 2320 N Druid Hills Rd
- **Citgo** · 3390 Buford Hwy NE
- **Philips 66** · 3107 Buford Hwy NE
- **Quicktrip** · 2375 N Druid Hills Rd NE
- **Quicktrip** · 3292 Buford Hwy NE

Libraries

- **Briarcliff Library** · 2775 Briarcliff Rd

Pharmacies

- **Eckerd** · 2480 Briarcliff Rd NE
- **Eckerd** · 3397 Buford Hwy
- **Target** · 2400 N Druid Hills NE

Post Offices

- **US Post Office** · 4 Executive Park Dr NE
- **US Post Office** · Briarcliff & Clairmont

Schools

- **Immaculate Heart of Mary** · 2855 Briarcliff Rd NE

Supermarkets

- **Publix** · 3317 Buford Hwy NE

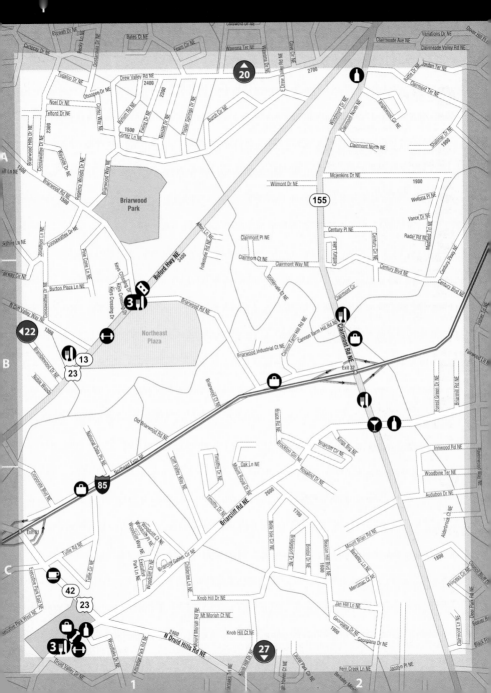

A little bit of everything when it comes to dining, from French (Violette) to Bangladeshi (Panahar), to South American (Machu Picchu). Sidelines is a decent neighborhood sports bar. Spoil your furry friend at The Pet Set.

Coffee

- **Einstein Bros** · 2240 North Druid Hills Rd NE

Gyms

- **LA Fitness** · 2480 Briarcliff Rd NE
- **Planet Fitness** · 3293 Buford Hwy NE

Liquor Stores

- **Cheers Beer & Wine** · 2490 Briarcliff Rd NE
- **DeKalb Bottle House** · 3111 Briarcliff Rd NE
- **Skyland Beverage & Party Center** · 3342 Clairmont Rd NE

Nightlife

- **Sidelines** · 2775 Clairmont Rd NE

Pet Shops

- **The Pet Set** · 2480 Briarcliff Rd NE

Restaurants

- **El Porto Mexican Restaurant** · 3396 Buford Hwy NE
- **El Rey de Todos Mexican Restaurant** · 3249 Buford Hwy NE
- **El Torero Mexican Restaurant** · 2484 Briarcliff Rd NE
- **Fortune Cookie** · 2480 Briarcliff Rd NE
- **Machu Picchu** · 3375 Buford Hwy NE
- **Moe's Southwest Grill** · 2484 Briarcliff Rd
- **Panahar** · 3375 Buford Hwy
- **Violette** · 2948 Clairmont Rd NE
- **Waffle House** · 2886 Clairmont Rd NE

Shopping

- **Guitar Center** · 1485 Northeast Expy NE
- **The Pet Set** · 2480 Briarcliff Rd
- **REI** · 1800 Northeast Expy NE
- **Sam's Club** · 2901 Clairmont Rd NE

Video Rental

- **Hollywood Video** · 3395 Buford Hwy NE

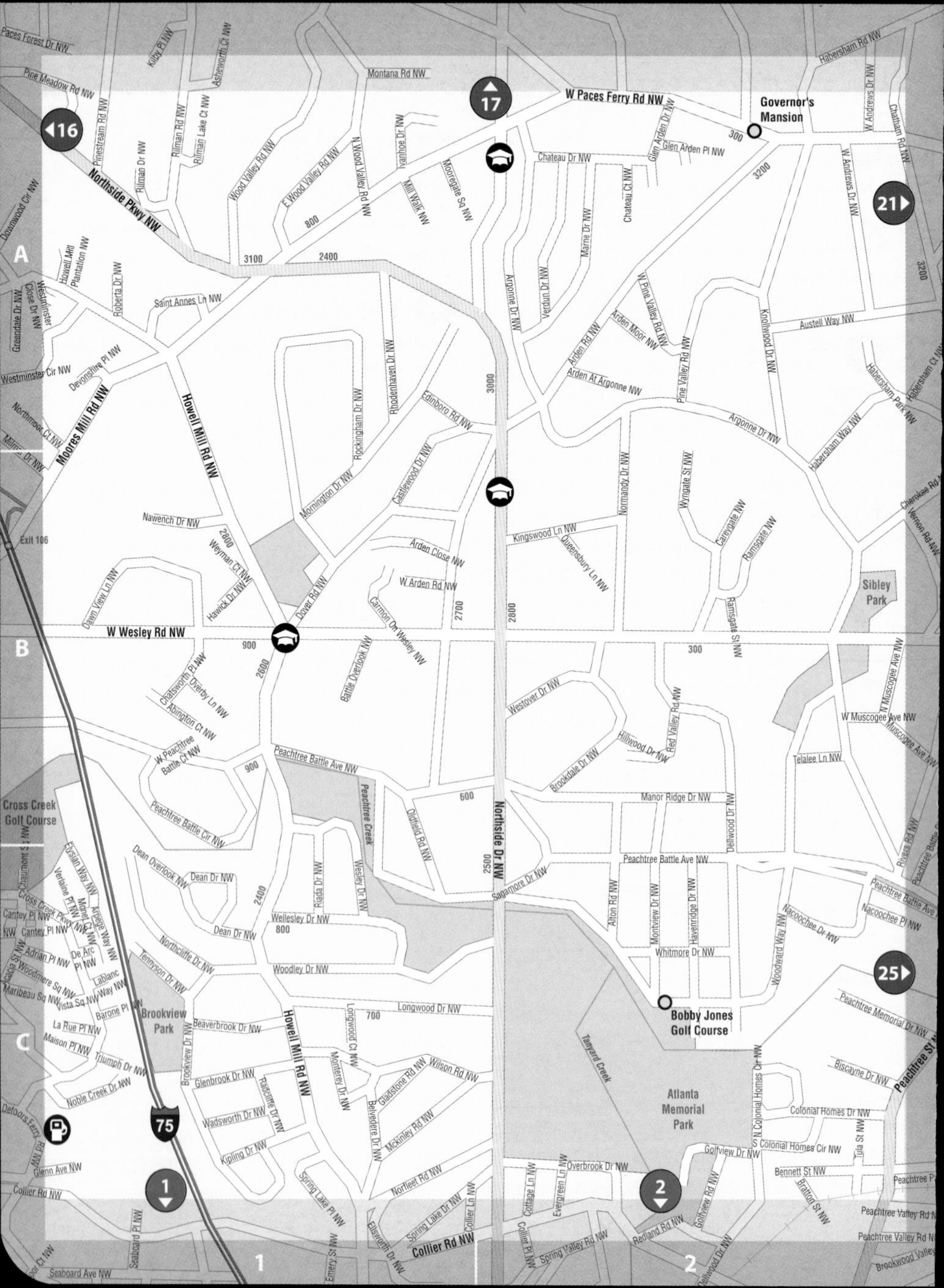

Map 24 · **Peachtree Battle / Woodfield**

N

Paces Forest Dr NW

Pine Meadow Ln NW

Montana Rd NW

W Paces Ferry Rd NW

Governor's Mansion

◄16

Northside Pkwy NW

17

Chateau Dr NW

21►

Howell Mill Rd NW

Moores Mill Rd NW

Saint Annes Ln NW

3100   2400

3000

Austell Way NW

Arden Rd NW

Arden At Argonne NW

Argonne Dr NW

Habersham Park NW

Nawench Dr NW

Exit 106

Arden Close NW

Kingswood Ln NW

W Arden Rd NW

Sibley Park

2700   2600

B

W Wesley Rd NW

900

300

Peachtree Battle Ave NW

W Muscogee Ave NW

Telalee Ln NW

Peachtree Creek

Cross Creek Golf Course

Manor Ridge Dr NW

2500

500

Peachtree Battle Ave NW

25►

Dean Overlook NW

Dean Dr NW

Wellesley Dr NW   800

Peachtree Memorial Dr NW

Woodley Dr NW

Brookview Park

Beaverbrook Dr NW

Bobby Jones Golf Course

Howell Mill Rd NW

Longwood Dr NW   700

Whitmore Dr NW

Biscayne Dr NW

Peachtree St NW

Glenbrook Dr NW

Wadsworth Dr NW

Colonial Homes Dr NW

Atlanta Memorial Park

Noble Creek Dr NW

75

Kipling Dr NW

Northfleet Dr NW

Wilson Rd NW

Bennett St NW

Collier Rd NW

Seaboard Ave NW

1   **2**

Collier Rd NW

Spring Valley Rd NW

Peachtree Valley Rd NW

1   **2**

Essentials

The Bobby Jones Golf Course and Governor's Mansion anchor this residential neighborhood, which is conveniently located near all of the shopping and dining options that Buckhead has to offer. Giant oak and magnolia trees line the streets of these Buckhead neighborhoods, with a mix of modest-to-upscale homes.

 Gas Stations

• **Shell** • 2118 Defoors Ferry Rd NW

o Landmarks

• **Bobby Jones Golf Course** • 384 Woodward Way NW
• **Governor's Mansion** • 391 W Paces Ferry Rd NW

 Schools

• **Brandon Elementary** • 2741 Howell Mill Rd NW
• **Heiskell** • 3260 Northside Dr NW
• **North Atlanta High** • 2875 Northside Dr NW

Map 24

99

Map 24 · **Peachtree Battle / Woodfield**

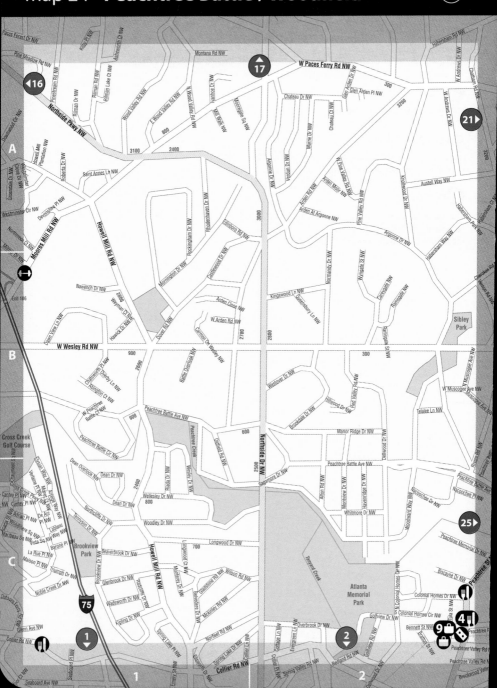

Justin's is P Diddy's dining digs. There's plenty of boutique and antique shopping (City Art Works, Nottingham Antiques). Libby's Cabaret is practically a legend. Café Sunflower cooks up some tasty vegetarian cuisine. Sherlock's Wine Merchants offers a vast vino selection.

Gyms
• **YMCA** • 1160 Moores Mill Rd NW

Nightlife
• **Libby's, A Cabaret** • 3401 Northside Pkwy

Restaurants
• **Benihana** • 2143 Peachtree Rd NE
• **Café Sunflower** • 2140 Peachtree Rd
• **Figo Pasta** • 1170 Collier Rd NW
• **Fratelli di Napoli** • 2101 Tula St NW
• **Houston's** • 2166 Peachtree Rd NW
• **Justin's** • 2200 Peachtree Rd

Shopping
• **Bittersweet Ltd** • 45 Bennett St NW
• **City Art Works** • 2140 Peachtree Rd NW
• **Interiors Market** • 55 Bennett St NW
• **Jules Burt Gallery** • 75 Bennett St
• **Monkee's** • 2140 Peachtree Rd
• **Nottingham Antiques** • 45 Bennett St NW
• **Pickles and Ice Cream** • 2140 Peachtree Rd
• **Precious Soles** • 2140 Peachtree Rd
• **Sherlock's Wine Merchants** •
  3401 Northside Pkwy
• **The Stalls** • 116 Bennett St NW

Video Rental
• **Blockbuster** • 2099 Peachtree Rd NE

Garden Hills / Peachtree Heights / Peachtree Hills

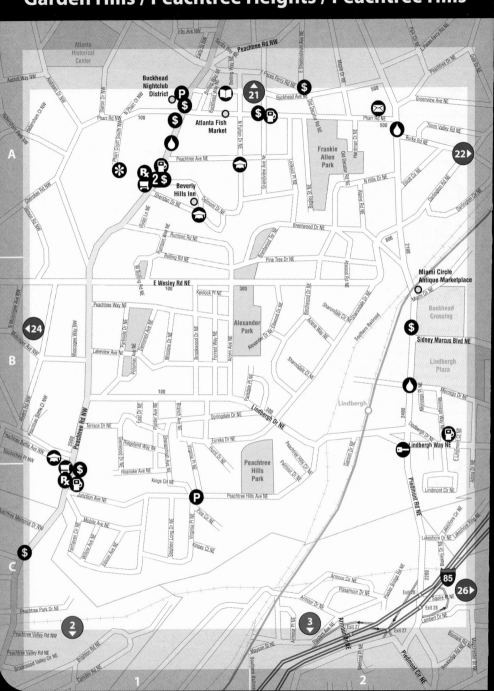

From the lush greenery of Garden Hills to the duck pond in Peachtree Heights, to the eclectic multicolored houses of Peachtree Hills, these picturesque Buckhead residential neighborhoods are nestled within lush landscaping and winding roads. Superior public schools and easy access to all of Buckhead's business and entertainment destinations make these in-town neighborhoods attractive.

Banks

- **Bank of America** · 2367 Peachtree Rd NE
- **Bank of America** · 2625 Piedmont Rd NE
- **Bank of America** · 340 Pharr Rd
- **National Bank of Commerce** · 2900 Peachtree Rd NW
- **Southtrust** · 79 W Paces Ferry Rd NW
- **SunTrust** · 2900 Peachtree Rd NE
- **SunTrust** · 3020 Peachtree Rd NW
- **Wachovia** · 2204 Peachtree St NW
- **Wachovia** · 31 Pharr Rd NW

Car Rental

- **Budget** · 2399 Piedmont Rd

 Car Washes

- **Cactus Car Wash** · 2980 Piedmont Rd NE
- **California Autobuff** · 2955 Peachtree Rd NE
- **Chevron** · 639 Morosgo Dr NE

 Community Gardens

Gas Stations

- **Chevron** · 2331 Peachtree Rd NE
- **Chevron** · 639 Morosgo Dr NE
- **Exxon** · 2901 Peachtree Rd NE
- **Exxon** · 635 Lindbergh Dr NE
- **Texaco** · 345 Pharr Rd NE

o Landmarks

- **Atlanta Fish Market** · 265 Pharr Rd NE
- **Beverly Hills Inn** · 65 Sheridan Dr
- **Buckhead Nightclub District** · Peachtree Rd, Pharr Rd, and Paces Ferry Rd
- **Miami Circle Antique Marketplace** · 700 Miami Cir NE

Libraries

- **Buckhead Branch** · 269 Buckhead Ave NE

Parking

 Pharmacies

- **Kings Peachtree Battle Drugs** · 2345 Peachtree Rd NE
- **Publix** · 2900 Peachtree Rd NW

Post Offices

- **US Post Office** · 575 Pharr Rd NE

Schools

- **Atlanta International** · 2890 N Fulton Dr NE
- **E Rivers Elementary** · 8 Peachtree Battle Ave NW
- **Garden Hills Elementary** · 285 Sheridan Dr NE

Supermarkets

- **Publix** · 2365 Peachtree Rd NE
- **Publix** · 2900 Peachtree Rd NW

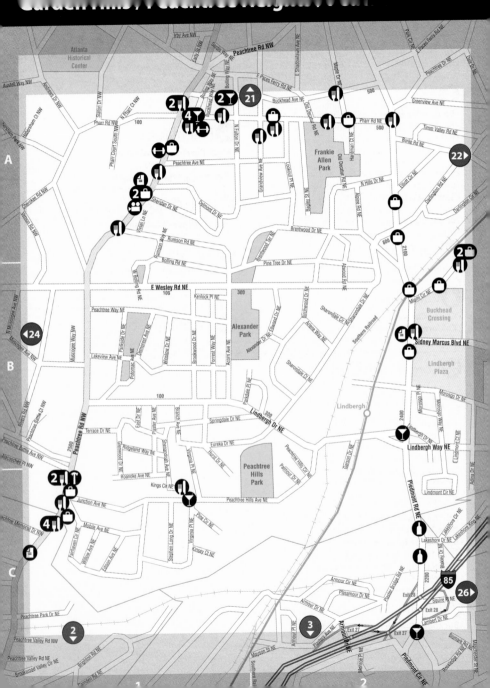

Map 25

You can't miss the giant fish outside of the Atlanta Fish Market. Miami Circle is an antique lover's dream. Buckhead's nightlife district features veteran dance clubs like Tongue and Groove (Map 21), along with the smoky salsa beats at the Havana Club. Imperial Fez features authentic Moroccan cuisine and belly dancing. Lefont Garden Hills Cinema is a good place to catch an indie or foreign flick.

 Coffee

• **Starbucks** • 2333 Peachtree Rd
• **Starbucks** • Barnes & Noble, 2900 Peachtree Rd NE

Copy Shops

• **UPS Store** • 2221 Peachtree Rd NE
• **UPS Store** • 2625 Piedmont Rd NE
• **UPS Store** • 2870 Peachtree Rd NE

 Gyms

• **Best Fitness** • 211 Pharr Rd NE
• **Curves** • 2900 Peachtree Rd NE

 Hardware Stores

• **Workbench Ace Hardware** •
  2365 Peachtree Rd NE

Liquor Stores

• **New World Wines** • 2175 Piedmont Rd NE
• **Tower Beer and Wine & Spirits** •
  2161 Piedmont Rd NE

 Movie Theaters

• **Lefont Garden Hills Cinema** •
  2835 Peachtree Rd NE

Nightlife

• **Bell Bottoms** • 225 Pharr Rd
• **CJ's Landing** • 270 Buckhead Ave NE
• **Frequency** • 220 Pharr Rd
• **Havana Club** • 247 Buckhead Ave
• **Jack Rabbit Lounge** • 3055 Bolling Wy NE
• **Tattletale Lounge** • 2075 Piedmont Rd NE
• **Three Dollar Café** • 3002 Peachtree Rd
• **Treehouse Restaurant and Pub** • 7 Kings Cir NE
• **Woofs on Piedmont** • 2425 Piedmont Rd NE

Restaurants

• **Anis Café & Bistro** • 2974 Grandview Ave NE
• **Aria** • 490 E Paces Ferry Rd NE
• **Atlanta Fish Market** • 265 Pharr Rd
• **Bite** • 10 Kings Cir NE
• **Café Tu Tu Tango** • 220 Pharr Rd NE
• **The Cheesecake Factory** • 3024 Peachtree Rd NE
• **Coco Loco** • 2625 Piedmont Rd NE
• **Eclipse Di Luna** • 764 Miami Cir NE
• **Fellini's Pizza** • 2809 Peachtree Rd NE
• **Georgia Grille** • 2290 Peachtree Rd NE
• **Imperial Fez** • 2285 Peachtree Rd
• **Jalisco** • 2337 Peachtree Rd NE
• **Jim White's Half Shell Restaurant** •
  2349 Peachtree Rd NE
• **Moe's Southwest Grill** • 2915 Peachtree Rd
• **Pasta Vino** • 2391 Peachtree Rd NE
• **Pricci** • 500 Pharr Rd
• **Ray's New York Pizza** • 3021 Peachtree Rd NE
• **Restaurant Eugene** • 2277 Peachtree Rd
• **Taka Sushi Café** • 375 Pharr Rd NE
• **Toulouse** • 2293 Peachtree Rd NE
• **Waffle House** • 3016 Piedmont Rd NE

Shopping

• **Animals** • 375 Pharr Rd
• **Architectural Accents** • 2711 Piedmont Rd NE
• **Bennie's Shoes** • 2581 Piedmont Rd
• **Beverly Hall Furniture Gallery** •
  2789 Piedmont Rd NE
• **Books & Cases & Prints Etc** • 800 Miami Cir NE
• **Fantasyland Records** • 2839 Peachtree Rd NE
• **Highlighters** • 690 Miami Cir NE
• **Just the Thing!** • 529 Pharr Rd NE
• **Luxe** • 764 Miami Cir NE
• **Oxford Comics and Books** • 2855 Piedmont Rd NE
• **Pet Pearls** • 2819 Peachtree Rd
• **Richards Variety Store** • 2347 Peachtree Rd NE
• **Spin Street Music** • 2327 Peachtree Rd NE
• **Unity Natural Foods** • 2955 Peachtree Rd NE

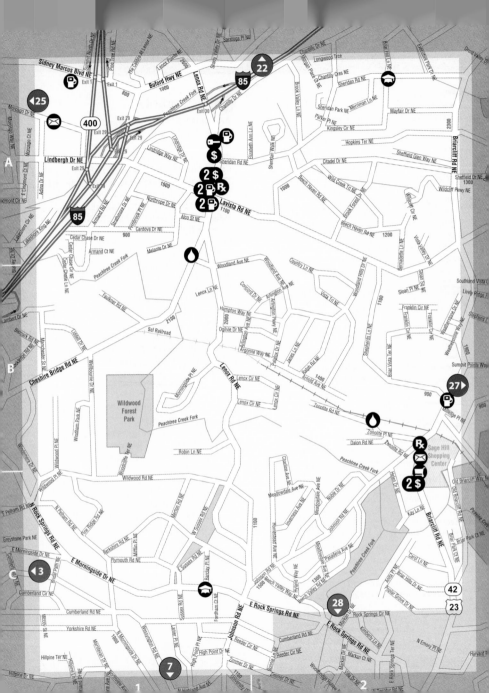

Being a Morningside mom isn't just a title; it's a lifestyle. It's a gorgeous neighborhood, if you can dodge the botox-injected breeders in their Lexus SUV's, as they drive precious little Madison and Tyler to school. At the other end of the spectrum, the industrial Cheshire Bridge Road area is home to seedy strip clubs and adult video stores.

 Banks

- **National Bank of Commerce** ·
  1799 Briarcliff Rd NE
- **Southtrust** · 2349 Cheshire Bridge Rd NE
- **SunTrust** · 1799 Briarcliff Rd NE
- **Wachovia** · 2419 Cheshire Bridge Rd NE
- **Washington Mutual** · 2350 Cheshire Bridge Rd NE

 **Car Rental**

- **Enterprise** · 2441 Cheshire Bridge Rd NE

Car Washes

- **Clubhouse Services on Zonolite** ·
  1155 Zonolite Rd NE
- **Leo's Auto Detailing and Hand Car Wash** ·
  2195 Cheshire Bridge Rd NE

 Gas Stations

- **BP** · 2320 Cheshire Bridge Rd NE
- **Citgo** · 2239 Cheshire Bridge Rd NE
- **Conoco** · 2353 Cheshire Bridge Rd NE
- **Philips 66** · 2319 Cheshire Bridge Rd NE
- **Quiktrip** · 761 Sidney Marcus Blvd NE
- **Quiktrip** · 1836 Briarcliff Rd
- **Shell** · 2448 Cheshire Bridge Rd

Pharmacies

- **CVS (24 hrs)** · 2350 Cheshire Bridge Rd NE
- **Eckerd** · 1799 Briarcliff Rd NE

Post Offices

- **US Post Office** · 1799 Briarcliff Rd NE
- **US Post Office** · 780 Morosgo Dr NE

 Schools

- **Heritage Preparatory** · 1438 Sheridan Rd NE
- **Morningside Elementary** ·
  1053 Rock Springs Rd NE

 **Supermarkets**

- **Kroger** · 1799 Briarcliff Rd NE

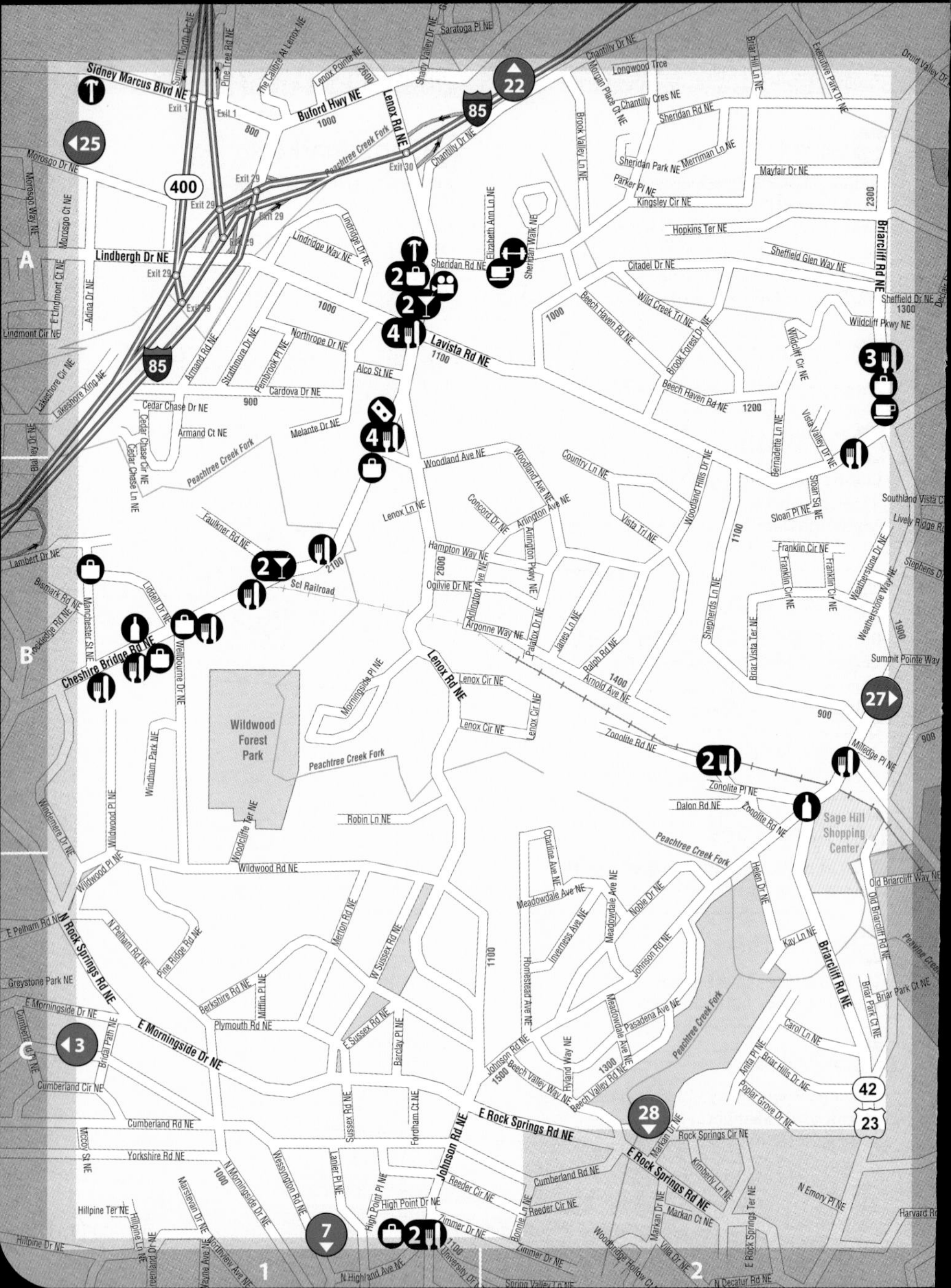

Map 26 • **Morningside / Lenox Hills**

Sidney Marcus Blvd NE

25

400

Lindbergh Dr NE

85

Buford Hwy NE

Lenox Rd NE

85

22

Lavista Rd NE

3

Cheshire Bridge Rd NE

2

27

Wildwood Forest Park

2

Sage Hill Shopping Center

13

28

42

23

7

2

E Rock Springs Rd NE

E Morningside Dr NE

Briarcliff Rd NE

Most of the Morningside eats are family-friendly and cheap (Doc Chey's Noodle House, Olde Towne Pizza). Cheshire Bridge Road offers an eclectic ethnic restaurant selection (Alfredo's, Jitlada, Meskerem, Taverna Plaka), along with a health food store (Return to Eden) and a dining institution, The Colonnade.

Coffee
- **Café Central** · 1515 Sheridan Rd NE
- **Starbucks** · 2135 Briarcliff Rd NE

Gyms
- **Athletic Club Northeast** · 1515 Sheridan Rd NE

Hardware Stores
- **Home Depot** · 815 Sidney Marcus Blvd
- **La Vista Ace Hardware** ·
  2301 Cheshire Bridge Rd NE

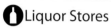Liquor Stores
- **Pitch & Putt Liquor Store** · 1890 Johnson Rd NE
- **Terrific Package Store** · 1899 Cheshire Bridge Rd NE

Movie Theaters
- **United Artists Tara Cinemas-Atlanta** ·
  2345 Cheshire Bridge Rd NE

Nightlife
- **24K Club** · 2284 Cheshire Bridge Rd NE
- **Buddies** · 2345 Cheshire Bridge NE
- **Doll House** · 2050 Cheshire Bridge NE
- **Heretic** · 2069 Cheshire Bridge Rd

Restaurants
- **Alfredo's** · 1989 Cheshire Bridge Rd NE
- **The Colonnade** · 1879 Cheshire Bridge Rd NE
- **Broadway Café** · 2168 Briarcliff Rd NE
- **Doc Chey's** · 1424 N Highland Ave NE
- **Dusty's Barbecue** · 1815 Briarcliff Rd NE
- **Floataway Café** · 1123 Zonolite Rd
- **Hong Kong Harbour** · 2184 Cheshire Bridge Rd NE
- **Jitlada** · 2329 Cheshire Bridge Rd NE
- **Las Margaritas** · 1842 Cheshire Bridge Rd NE
- **Little Bangkok** · 2225 Cheshire Bridge Rd
- **Mambo** · 1402 N Highland Ave NE
- **Meskerem** · 2329 Cheshire Bridge Rd NE
- **Nicola's** · 1602 LaVista Rd NE
- **Nino's** · 1931 Cheshire Bridge Rd NE
- **Olde Town Pizza** · 1394 N Highland Ave
- **Red Snapper** · 2100 Cheshire Bridge Rd NE
- **Rustic Gourmet** · 1145 Zonolite Rd NE
- **South of France** · 2345 Cheshire Bridge Rd NE
- **Sundown Café** · 2165 Cheshire Bridge Rd NE
- **Taverna Plaka** · 2196 Cheshire Bridge Rd NE
- **Thai Chili** · 2169 Briarcliff Rd
- **The Varsity Jr.** · 1085 Lindbergh Dr NE

Shopping
- **A Flea Antique II** · 1853 Cheshire Bridge Rd NE
- **Canine Showcase & Wild Bird** · 2036 Manchester St
- **Cherub's Attic** · 2179 Cheshire Bridge Rd NE
- **Fickle Manor** · 1402-4 N Highland Ave
- **Happy Herman's** · 2299 Cheshire Bridge Rd NE
- **Milou's Market** · 1927 Cheshire Bridge Rd NE
- **Quality Kosher Emporium** · 2153 Briarcliff Rd
- **Return to Eden** · 2335 Cheshire Bridge Rd NE

Video Rental
- **Southern Nights Video** ·
  2205 Cheshire Bridge Rd NE

Toco Hills is the home to much of Atlanta's affluent Jewish community and is a serene, picturesque neighborhood. The Emory University campus was designed to blend in with its surrounding woodsy neighborhood, and it succeeds. But hey, the CDC's work with plagues and viruses should keep residents on their toes.

Banks

- **Bank of America** · 2205 Lavista Rd
- **Fidelity Bank** · 2936 N Druid Hills Rd
- **National Bank of Commerce** · 2851 N Druid Hills Rd
- **Southtrust** · 2920 N Druid Hills Rd
- **Wachovia** · 2942 N Druid Hills Rd NE
- **Wachovia** · 725 Houston Mill Rd NE
- **Washington Mutual** · 2105 Lavista Rd

Community Gardens

Gas Stations

- **Shell** · 2374 Briarcliff Rd NE

Hospitals

- **Children's Healthcare of Atlanta at Egelston** · 1405 Clifton Rd NE

o Landmarks

- **Center for Disease Control and Prevention** · 1600 Clifton Rd NE

Pharmacies

- **CVS (24 hrs)** · 2830 N Druid Hill Rd
- **Kroger** · 2205 Lavista Rd
- **Publix** · 2969 N Druid Hills Rd NE

Schools

- **Benjamin Franklin Academy** · 1585 Clifton Rd NE
- **Emory University** · Houston Mill Rd NE & Clifton Rd NE
- **Intown Community School** · 2059 LaVista Rd
- **Temima High School for Girls** · 1839 LaVista Rd

Supermarkets

- **Kroger** · 2205 Lavista Rd
- **Publix** · 2969 N Druid Hills Rd NE
- **Whole Foods** · 2111 Briarcliff Rd NE

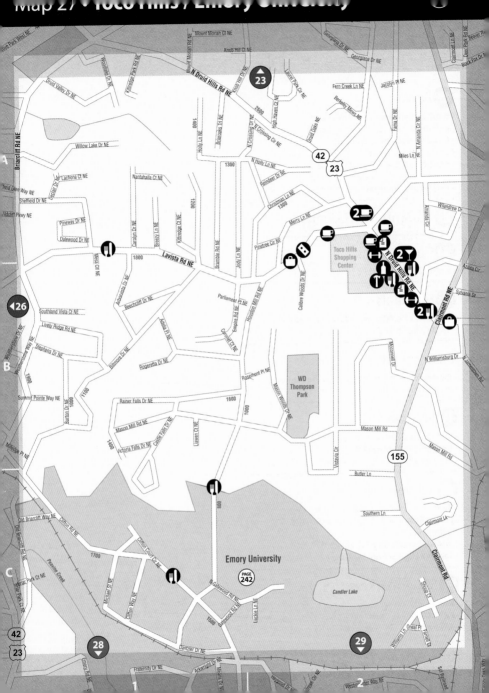

Sundries / Entertainment

Map 27

Cheap, ethnic eats (Top Spice, Touch of India) abound for the nearby college population. Petite Auberge, located in the Toco Hills Shopping Center, offers homestyle French and German cuisine. Atlanta Coffee Roasters brews some good, strong java.

Coffee

- **Atlanta Coffee Roasters** • 2205 Lavista Rd NE
- **Caribou Coffee** • 2870 North Druid Hills Rd NE
- **Dunkin' Donuts** • 2827 N Druid Hills Rd NE
- **Einstein Bros** • 2870 North Druid Hills Rd NE
- **Starbucks** • 2830 N Druid Hills Rd

Copy Shops

- **Toco Instant Printing** • 2960 N Druid Hills Rd NE
- **UPS Store** • 2897 N Druid Hills Rd NE

Gyms

- **Curves** • 2987 N Druid Hills Rd NE
- **LA Fitness** • 2880 N Druid Hills Rd NE

Hardware Stores

- **The Workbench Ace Hardware** • 2943 N Druid Hills Rd NE

Liquor Stores

- **Toco Giant** • 2941 N Druid Hills Rd NE

Nightlife

- **Famous Pub & Sports Palace** • 2947 N Druid Hills Rd NE
- **Maggie's** • 2937 N Druid Hills Rd NE

Restaurants

- **Edo** • 2945 N Druid Hills Rd NE
- **Houston Mill House** • 849 Houston Mill Rd
- **Le Giverny** • 1641 Clifton Rd NE
- **Mellow Mushroom** • 1679 LaVista Rd NE
- **Petite Auberge** • 2935 N Druid Hills Rd NE
- **Top Spice** • 3007 N Druid Hills Rd
- **Touch of India** • 3017 N Druid Hills Rd

Shopping

- **Book Nook** • 3037 N Druid Hills Rd NE
- **Pike's Nursery** • 2101 LaVista Rd NE

Video Rental

- **Blockbuster** • 2161 LaVista Rd NE

113

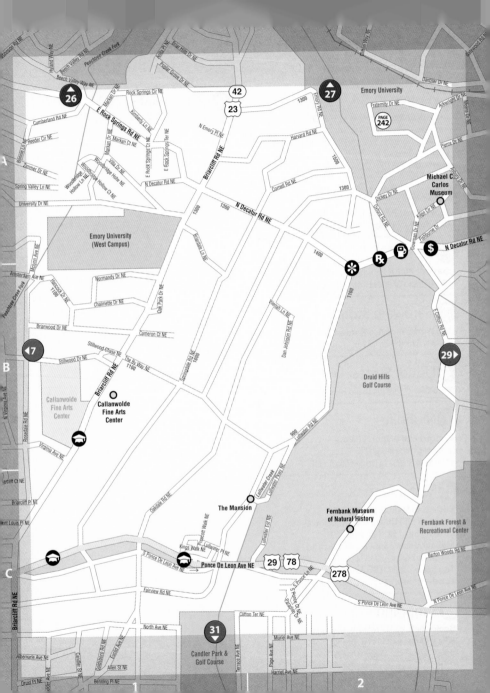

Adjacent to Emory University, Druid Hills was designed by landscape architect Frederick Law Olmstead, and it features some of the finest residential architecture in Georgia. This neighborhood also features some of the city's best fine arts and cultural institutions (Callanwolde, Fernbank). The Druid Hills Golf Club is taking heat for not providing equal benefits to gay couples. Several homes in the area were featured in the movie *Driving Miss Daisy*.

Banks
• **Bank of America** • 1615 N Decatur Rd NE

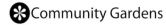 Community Gardens

Gas Stations
• **Chevron** • 1574 N Decatur Rd NE

o Landmarks
• **Callanwolde Fine Arts Center** •
980 Briarcliff Rd NE
• **Fernbank Museum of Natural History** •
767 Clifton Rd NE
• **The Mansion** • 822 Lullwater Rd NE
• **Michael C Carlos Museum** • 571 S Kilgo Cir NE

 Pharmacies
• **CVS (24 hrs)** • 1554 N Decatur Rd NE

Schools
• **Charter BHC at Laurel Heights** •
934 Briarcliff Rd NE
• **Howard** • 1246 Ponce de Leon NE
• **Paideia** • 1509 Ponce de Leon Ave

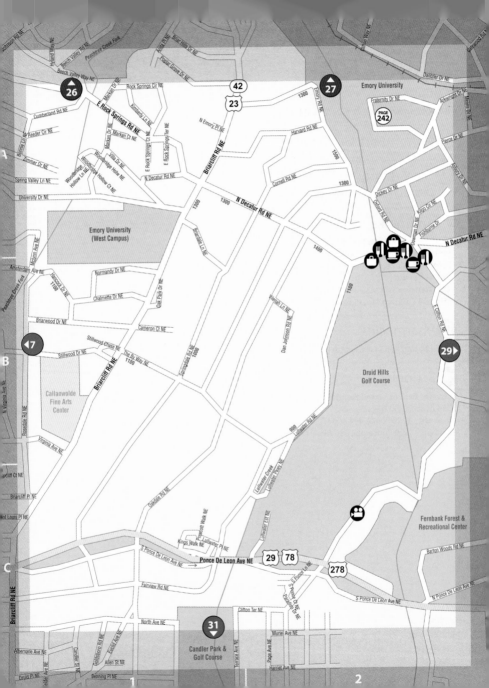

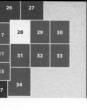

Map 28

The IMAX-and-martini night at Fernbank is way cool. Everybody's offers killer pizzas and salads. Ego is the place to find designer jeans. Golf fans claim that the Druid Hills Golf Course has extremely fast greens and one of the best holes in the state (#8). Callanwolde offers everything from poetry readings to string quartets to tango dancing.

Coffee

· **Caribou Coffee** · 1593 N Decatur Rd NE
· **Starbucks** · 1569 N Decatur Rd NE

Movie Theaters

· **Fernbank Museum's IMAX Theatre** ·
  767 Clifton Rd NE

Restaurants

· **Burrito Art** · 1451 Oxford Rd NE
· **Doc Chey's Noodle House** · 1556 N Decatur Rd NE
· **Everybody's** · 1593 N Decatur Rd NE

⬛Shopping

· **Ego** · 1581 N Decatur Rd NE
· **Shield's Market** · 1554 N Decatur Rd NE

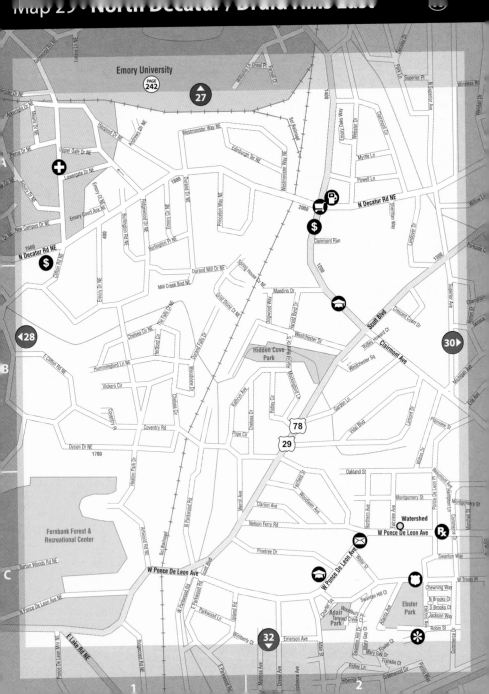

Naturally curving roads and a lush, almost woodsy environment envelop this area, where beautiful estates often sell for a million dollars. One of the city's best hospitals, Emory University Hospital, is in the area.

 Banks
• **BB&T** • 1221 Clairmont Rd
• **SunTrust** • 1685 N Decatur Rd NE

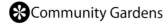 Community Gardens

 **Gas Stations**
• **Shell** • 1265 Clairmont Rd

Hospitals
• **Emory University** • 1364 Clifton Rd NE

Landmarks
• **Watershed** • 406 W Ponce de Leon Ave

Pharmacies
• **CVS** • 225 W Ponce de Leon Ave

Police
• **Decatur Police Department** • 420 W Trinity Pl

Post Offices
• **US Post Office** • 520 W Ponce de Leon Ave

Schools
• **Cliff Valley** • 1004 Clairmont Ave
• **St Thomas More** • 630 W Ponce de Leon

Supermarkets
• **Publix** • N Decatur Rd & Clairmont Ave

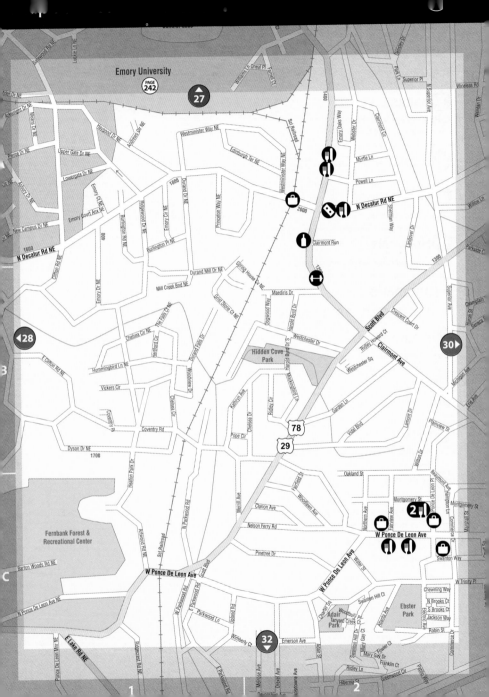

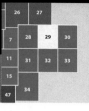
The shops and restaurants of Emory Village are nearby. Don't miss Chef Scott Peacock's heavenly fried chicken at Watershed (partially owned by Emily Saliers of the Indigo Girls). The Supper Club is your best bet for an intimate meal that will get you out of the dog house with your mate. Northern Indian cuisine is the star at Bhojanic.

Gyms
• **YMCA** • 1100 Clairemont Ave

Liquor Stores
• **Decatur Package Store** • 1220 Clairmont Rd

Restaurants
• **Athens Pizza** • 1341 Clairmont Rd NE
• **Bhojanic** • 1363 Clairmont Rd
• **Café Lily** • 308 W Ponce de Leon Ave
• **Mexico City Gourmet** • 2134 N Decatur Rd
• **The Supper Club** • 308 W Ponce de Leon Ave
• **Taqueria Del Sol** • 359 W Ponce de Leon Ave
• **Watershed** • 406 W Ponce de Leon Ave

Shopping
• **Boogaloos** • 246 W Ponce de Leon Ave
• **The 17 Steps** • 235 Ponce de Leon Pl
• **Sole** • 415 W Ponce de Leon Ave
• **Wuxtry Records** • 2096 N Decatur Rd NE

Video Rental
• **Blockbuster** • 2115 N Decatur Rd

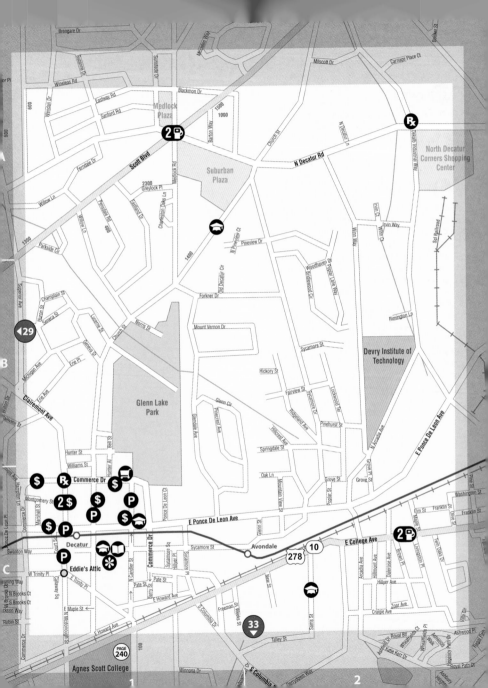

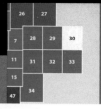
Like the suburbs, but way cooler. Decatur has a thriving town square, a well-developed arts community, and almost-affordable housing. The residential community around the town square is best for ex-city slickers. The population is quite diverse, with young families, lesbians, and African-Americans all calling Decatur home.

 Banks
- **Bank of America** · 163 Clairmont Ave
- **Decatur First Bank** · 1120 Commerce Dr
- **Decatur First Bank** · 720 Commerce Dr
- **Fidelity Bank** · 160 Clairmont Ave
- **Southtrust** · 101 W Ponce de Leon Ave
- **SunTrust** · 198 W Ponce de Leon Ave
- **Wachovia** · 250 E Ponce de Leon Ave

Community Gardens

 Gas Stations
- **Chevron** · 1486 Scott Blvd
- **Citgo** · 2767 East College Ave
- **Marathon** · 1489 Scott Blvd
- **Shell** · 2781 E College Ave

○ Landmarks
- **Eddie's Attic** · 515 N McDonough St

Libraries
- **Decatur Library** · 215 Sycamore St

Parking

Pharmacies
- **The Medicine Shoppe** · 215 Clairmont Ave
- **Walgreens (24 hrs)** · 585 Dekalb Industrial Wy

 Schools
- **Decatur First Methodist Kindergarten** ·
  300 E Ponce de Leon Ave
- **Decatur Montessori** · 1429 Church St
- **Decatur Presbyterian Kindergarten** ·
  205 Sycamore St
- **Friend's School** · 121 Sams St

 Supermarkets
- **Kroger** · 720 Commerce Dr

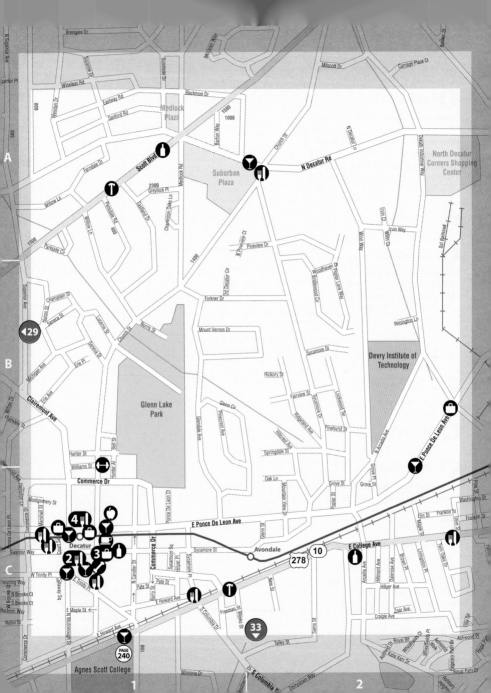

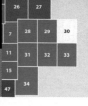
The old courthouse square offers a great collection of coffeeshops (East of Java), restaurants (Sage, Zocalo), and shopping (Square Roots). My Sister's Room is where Atlanta-area sapphos congregate. Eddie's Attic is an amazing live acoustic music venue, and helped John Mayer get his start in the music biz.

Coffee

· **East of Java** · 425 Church St

Farmer's Markets

· **Downtown Decatur Market** ·
Downtown Decatur on the square, behind the old court house

Gyms

· **Sonz** · 701 Church St

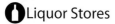Hardware Stores

· **Decatur Smith Ace Hardware** · 601 E College Ave
· **Intown Ace Hardware** · 1404 Scott Blvd

Liquor Stores

· **ABC Liquor Store** · 2765 E College Ave
· **College Inn Package Store** · 2683 E College Ave
· **Fiesta Package Store** · 1445 Scott Blvd

Nightlife

· **Azul Tequila and Wine Bar** · 141 Sycamore St
· **Brick Store Pub** · 125 E Ct Square
· **Eddie's Attic** · 515 N McDonough St
· **Java Monkey** · 205 E Ponce de Leon Ave
· **My Sister's Room** · 222 E Howard Ave
· **Pin-ups** · 2788 E Ponce de Leon Ave
· **Suburban Lanes Bowling** · 2619 N Decatur Rd

Pet Shops

· **The Posh Pup** · 419 Church St

Restaurants

· **Atlanta Bread Company** · 205 E Ponce de Leon
· **Café Alsace** · 121 E Ponce de Leon Ave
· **Carpe Diem** · 105 Sycamore Pl
· **Crescent Moon** · 174 W Ponce de Leon Ave
· **Eurasia Bistro** · 129 E Ponce de Leon Ave
· **Johnny's New York Pizza** · 340 Church St
· **Moe's Southwest Grill** · 1524 Church St
· **Noodle** · 205 E Ponce de Leon Ave
· **Our Way Café** · 2831 E College Ave
· **Raging Burrito** · 141 Sycamore St
· **Sage on Sycamore** · 121 Sycamore Sq
· **Zocalo** · 123 E Court Sq

Shopping

· **Domestic Instincts** · 416 Church St
· **Kudzu Antiques** · 2874 E Ponce de Leon Ave
· **The Posh Pup** · 419 Church St
· **Rue de Leon** · 131 E Ponce de Leon Ave
· **Square Roots** · 117 E Court Square
· **Squash Blossom** · 427 Church St

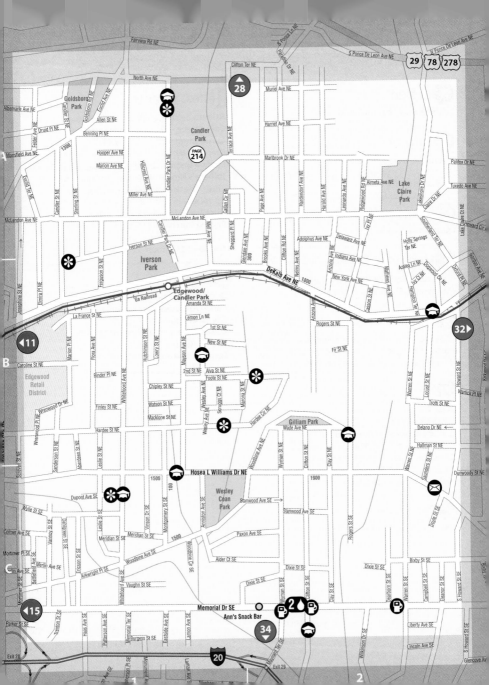

Overshadowed by Inman Park, but actually older, this colorful and diverse community is well on its way to revitalization. Fancifully painted houses of all styles dot the landscape, as do quirky businesses. The public Candler Park Golf Course is family-friendly.

Car Washes

- **Exxon** · 1675 Memorial Dr
- **Hand Clean Car Wash** · 1674 Memorial Dr SE

Community Gardens

Gas Stations

- **Citgo** · 1860 Memorial Dr
- **Citgo** · 225 Clifton St SE
- **Exxon** · 1675 Memorial Dr

○ Landmarks

- **Ann's Snack Bar** · 1615 Memorial Dr SE

Post Offices

- **US Post Office** · 1926 Hosea L Williams Dr NE

Schools

- **Coan Middle** · 1550 Hosea L Williams Dr SE
- **Crim High** · 256 Clifton St SE
- **Horizons** · 1900 DeKalb Ave NE
- **Lin Elementary** · 586 Candler Park Dr NE
- **Ragsdale Elementary** · 187 Wesley Ave NE
- **Toomer Elementary** · 65 Rogers St NE
- **Whitefoord Elementary** · 35 Whitefoord Ave SE

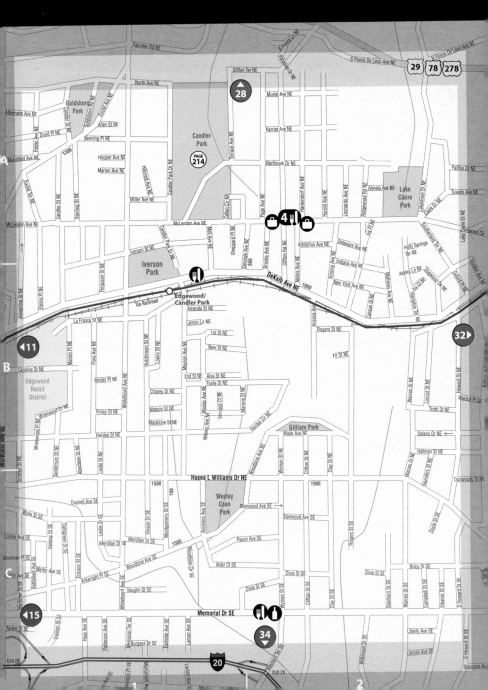

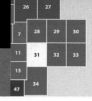
Radial Cafe offers terrific brunches, as does the original Flying Biscuit Cafe. Gato Bizco is a true neighborhood hangout. Frock of Ages is a cool vintage clothing store. The ghetto burger is the bomb at Ann's Snack Bar- just make sure you don't piss Ann off.

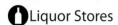
Liquor Stores
• **Zee Package Store** • 1621 Memorial Dr SE

Restaurants
• **Ann's Snack Bar** • 1615 Memorial Dr SE
• **Cold Cream** • 1645 McLendon Ave NE
• **Fellini's Pizza** • 1634 McLendon Ave NE
• **Flying Biscuit Café** • 1655 McLendon Ave
• **Gato Bizzo Café** • 1660 McLendon Ave
• **Radial Café** • 1530 DeKalb Ave NE

Shopping
• **Frock of Ages** • 1653 McLendon Ave
• **Kelly's Closet** • 1649 McLendon Ave NE

Map 32 · **Kirkwood**

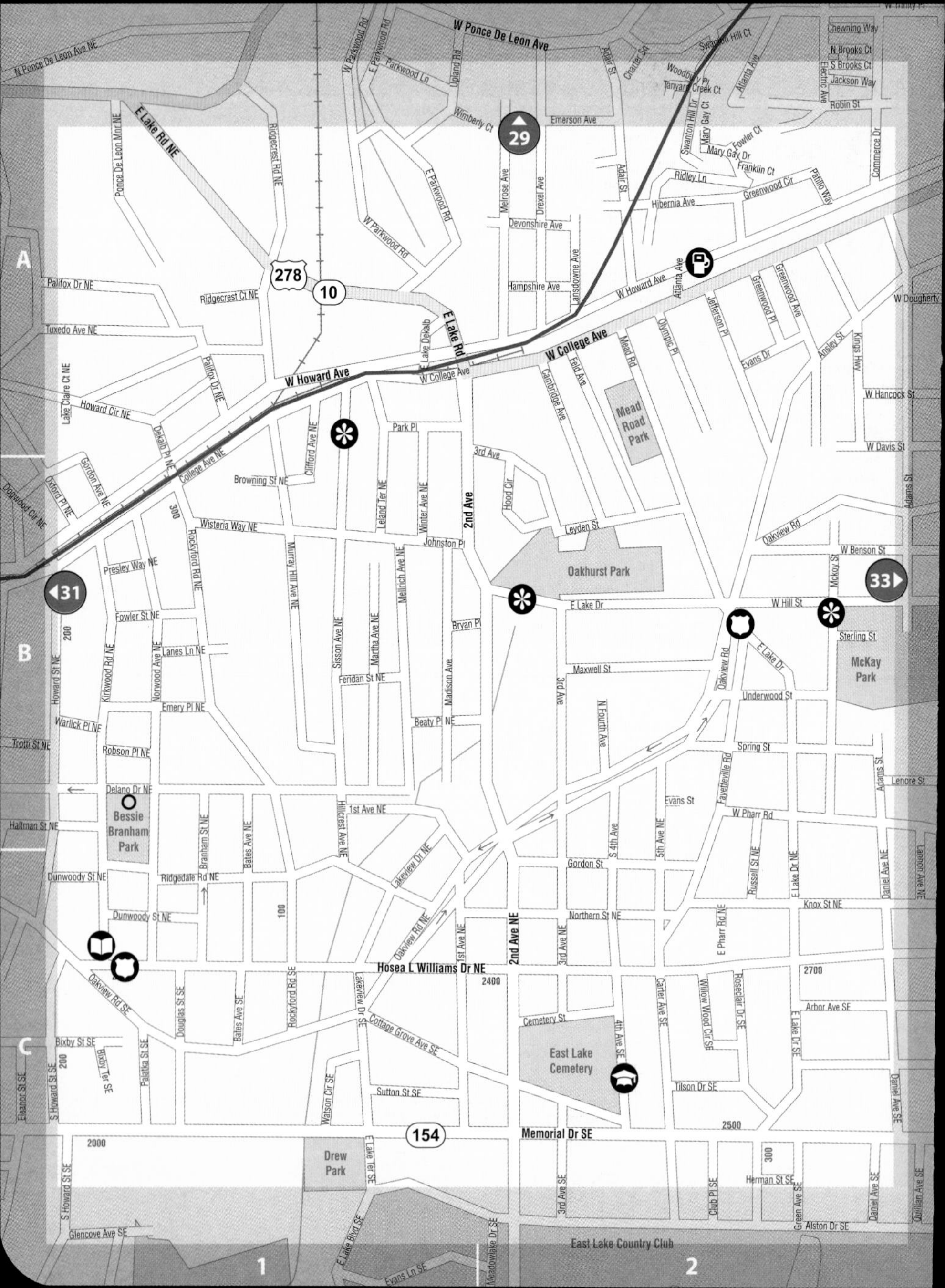

N

W Bexley Ct

N Brooks Ct
S Brooks Ct
Jackson Way
Electric Ave
Atlanta Ave
Robin St

W Ponce De Leon Ave

N Ponce De Leon Ave NE

W Parkwood Rd
E Parkwood Rd
Parkwood Rd

Wimberly Ct

Emerson Ave

Stephen Hill Ct
Woodfin Pl Dr
Stanton Hill Dr
Tanyard Creek Ct
Stephen Hill Dr
Mary Gay Dr
Mary Gay Ct
Fowler Ct
Franklin Ct

Chester Ave

E Lake Rd Mtn NE

Ponce De Leon Ave NE

Ridgecrest Rd NE

Melrose Ave
Drexel Ave

Devonshire Ave

Ridley Ln
Hibernia Ave

Greenwood Cir
Pharr Way

W Parkwood Rd

E Lake Ave

Atlanta Ave

Commerce Dr

A

Palifox Dr NE

278

10

Ridgecrest Ct NE

E Lake Delsab

W Howard Ave

Hampshire Ave

Jefferson Pl
Olympic Pl
Mead Rd

W Howard Ave
Jefferson Pl
Greenwood Pl

W Dougherty

W Hancock St

W Davis St

Tuxedo Ave NE

Lake Claire Ct NE

Howard Cir NE

Palifox Dr NE

W Howard Ave

W College Ave

W College Ave

Cambridge Ave

Evans Dr

Greenwood Pl
Airline St
Rocky Hwy

Park Pl

3rd Ave

Hood Dr

Mead
Road
Park

Ridgecrest Rd NE

College Ave NE

Browning St NE

Clifford Ave NE

Leland Dr NE

Winter Ave NE

2nd Ave

Leyden St

Oakview Rd

W Benson St

300

Gordon Pl NE
Garden Ave NE

Wisteria Way NE

Johnston Pl

Oakhurst Park

E Lake Dr

W Hill St

31

Presley Way NE

Rockford Rd NE

Murray Hill Ave NE

Mellrich Ave NE

Bryan Pl

E Lake Dr

Sterling St

McKay
Park

Oakview Rd

200

Howard St NE

Fowler St NE

Lanes Ln NE

Sisson Ave NE

Martha Ave NE

Feridan St NE

Maxwell St

N Clariendon Ave
N Druid Ave

E Lake Dr

B

Kirkwood Rd NE

Norwood Ave NE

Emery Pl NE

Beaty Pl NE

Underwood St

Adams St

Lenore St

Trotti St NE

Warlick Pl NE

Robson Pl NE

Madison Ave

Spring St

Fayetteville Rd

Evans St

Delano Dr NE

1st Ave NE

Hillcrest Ave NE

Branham St NE

Bates Ave NE

W Pharr Rd

Russell St NE

E Lake Dr NE

Knox St NE

Halfman St NE

Bessie
Branham
Park

Ridgedale Rd NE

100

Oakview Rd NE

2nd Ave NE

3rd Ave NE

5th Ave NE

E Pharr Rd NE

Daniel Ave NE

Dunwoody St NE

Dunwoody St NE

Northern St NE

2700

Arbor Ave SE

Daniel Ave SE

Douglas St SE

Bates St SE

Rockford Rd SE

Cottage Grove Ave SE

Hosea L Williams Dr NE

2400

2nd Ave NE

3rd Ave SE

4th Ave SE

Carter Ave SE

Willow Wood Cir SE
Rossevelt Dr SE

Carter Ave SE

Cub Pl SE

Green Ave SE

C

Bixby St SE

Palaka St SE

Cemetery St

East Lake
Cemetery

Tilson Dr SE

300

Elsanor St SE

S Howard St SE

Bixby St SE

Bixby Ter SE

Watson Cir SE

Sutton St SE

2500

Herman St SE

2000

Drew
Park

154

E Lake Blvd SE

Memorial Dr SE

3rd Ave SE

Clifton Pl SE

Alston Dr SE

Green Ave SE

Glencove Ave SE

Evans Ln SE

Meadowdale Dr SE

East Lake Country Club

1

2

29

33

Gentrification is grinding its way through Kirkwood, though you will still find more package stores and pawn shops than you will find hip shops. The urban pioneers moving into this blighted area are trying to bring modern services to the area, which is being met with a mixed reaction by the long-term residents, many of whom feel they are being priced out of the neighborhood.

Community Gardens

Gas Stations

- **Citgo** • 600 W Howard St

Landmarks

- **Bessie Branham Park** • 2051 Delano Dr NE

Libraries

- **Kirkwood Branch** • 11 Kirkwood Rd NE

Police

- **APD Zone 6 Station** • 2025 Hosea L Williams Dr NE
- **Decatur Police Department-Oakhurst Office** • 707 E Lake Dr

Schools

- **East Lake Elementary** • 145 Fourth Ave SE

Map 32 · **Kirkwood**

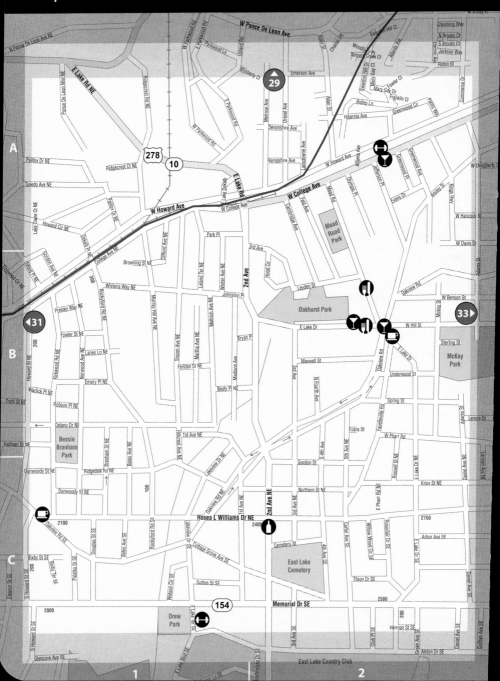

There's a state-of-the-art YMCA as well as Bessie Branham Park for all of your recreational needs. Sweet Java Brown will satisfy your sugar and caffeine cravings. Sweet Devil Moon offers wicked tapas, Universal Joint is an easygoing watering hole, Billy Goat's Cantina offers fun and fajitas, and Jupiter Coffee is out of this world.

Coffee

- **Jupiter Coffee** · 707B E Lake Dr
- **Sweet Java Brown** · 1994 Hosea L Williams Dr NE

Gyms

- **Core Body Decatur** · 533 W Howard Ave
- **YMCA** · 275 E Lake Blvd SE

Liquor Stores

- **Town & Country Liquor** · 15 2nd Ave SE

Nightlife

- **Mulligan's** · 630 E Lake Dr
- **Thinking Man Tavern** · 537 W Howard Ave
- **Universal Joint** · 906 Oakview Rd

Restaurants

- **Billy Goat's Cantina** · 653 E Lake Dr
- **Sweet Devil Moon** · 350 Mead Rd

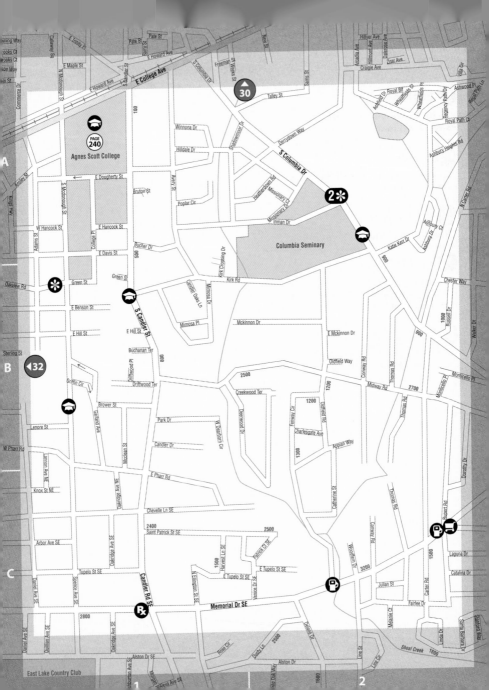

Agnes Scott College is a premier women's studies institution. East Lake is the home to Atlanta's first country club, and while the area sank into slumhood, it is on an upswing. Golf is still a focal point, with a private and a public course. Low-income projects have been transformed into mixed-income residential developments.

✳ Community Gardens

⛽ Gas Stations
• **Citgo** • 3335 Memorial Dr
• **Shell** • 3152 Memorial Dr

℞ Pharmacies
• **Eckerd** • 2886 Memorial Dr SE

🎓 Schools
• **Agnes Scott College** • 141 E College Ave
• **College Heights Elementary School** •
  917 S McDonough St
• **Lullwater** • 705 S Candler St
• **Waldorf School of Atlanta** • 711 S Columbia Dr

🚚 Supermarkets
• **Big T Supermarket** • 3354 Memorial Dr

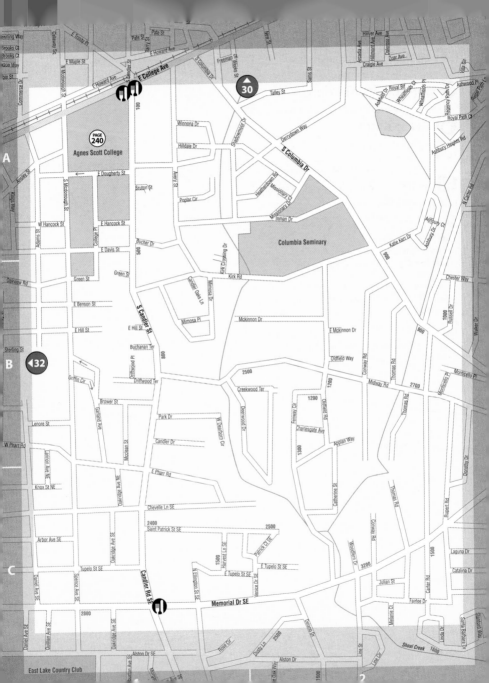

Sundries / Entertainment

26	27		
7	28	29	30
11	31	32	33
15			
47	34		

Map 33

Oz Pizza is considered to have some of the best pies in the Atlanta area. The Wing Factory is a popular hangout for the college crowd. Golf is the main recreational activity, though Agnes Scott offers many cultural activities that are open to the public.

Restaurants

- **Oz Pizza** · 309 E College Ave
- **Subway** · 2889 Memorial Dr SE
- **Wing Factory** · 307 E College Ave

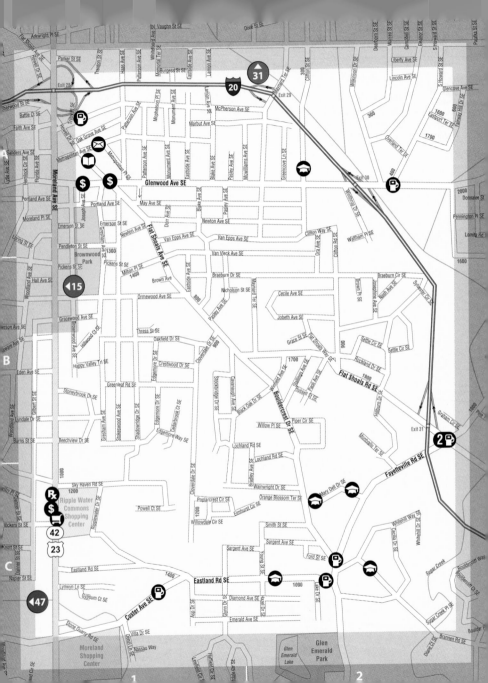

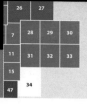
The events of 9/11 and the tanking economy wrecked the renaissance of this urban hipster outpost, but residents don't seem to mind. East Atlanta Village still maintains its funky, edgy vibe and continues to draw healthy crowds. The residential renaissance has been a bit slower in coming, but new developments are cropping up, so gentrification may soon become a reality.

$ Banks
- **National Bank of Commerce** ·
  1160 Moreland Ave SE
- **Southtrust** · 1246 Glenwood Ave SE
- **SunTrust** · 514 Flat Shoals Ave SE

Gas Stations
- **Chevron** · 1865 Glenwood Ave SE
- **Exxon** · 1981 Flat Shoals Rd SE
- **Philips 66** · 1181 McPherson Ave SE
- **Philips 66** · 1988 Flat Shoals Rd SE
- **Shell** · 1420 Custer Ave SE
- **Shell** · 2000 Flat Shoals Rd SE
- **Texaco** · 1668 Eastland Rd SE

Libraries
- **East Atlanta Branch** · 457 Flat Shoals Ave SE

Pharmacies
- **Kroger** · 1160 Moreland Ave SE

Post Offices
- **US Post Office** · 1273 Metropolitan Ave SE

Schools
- **Burgess Elementary** · 480 Clifton St SE
- **Carver High** · 1820 Mary Dell Dr
- **First Steps Christian Academy** ·
  1863 Brannen Rd SE
- **New Generation Learning Center** ·
  1572 Eastland Rd SE
- **Peterson Elementary** · 1757 Mary Dell Dr SE

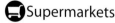 Supermarkets
- **Kroger** · 1160 Moreland Ave SE

Map 34 • **East Atlanta**

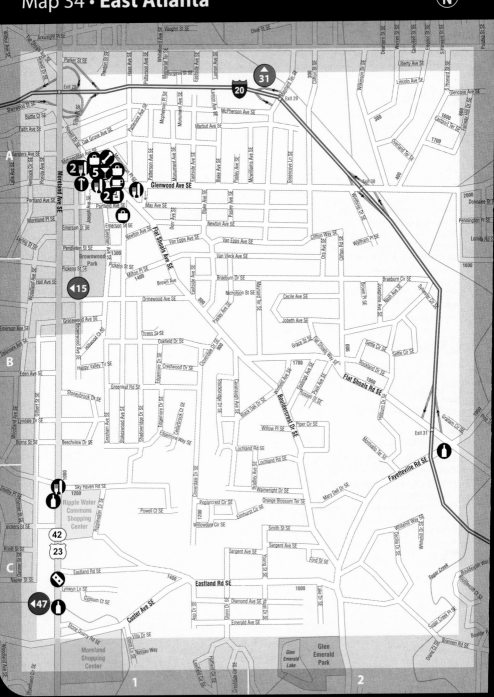

Iris offers upscale cuisine in a former gas station. Heaping Bowl and Brew serves cheap and creative meals in a bowl. The Flatiron and Gravity Pub are good neighborhood joints to guzzle down a PBR. Mary's is a friendly gay bar that offers a fun karaoke night. The Earl is all about indie rock. Traders and Earthshaking Music are cool shops at which to drop some cash.

☕ Coffee
- **East Atlanta Coffee Shop** · 510 Flat Shoals Ave SE

🖨 Copy Shops
- **Digital Images** · 1287 Glenwood Ave SE
- **East Atlanta Copy Center** · 1287 Glenwood Ave SE

🔧 Hardware Stores
- **East Atlanta Ace Hardware** · 1231 Glenwood Ave SE

🍾 Liquor Stores
- **F&S Package Store** · 1391 Moreland Ave SE
- **Ike & Ann's Package Store** · 1046 Fayetteville Rd SE
- **Southeast Package Store** · 1139 Moreland Ave SE

🍸 Nightlife
- **The Earl** · 488 Flat Shoals Ave SE
- **The Flatiron** · 520 Flat Shoals Ave SE
- **Fountainhead Lounge** · 485 Flat Shoals Ave SE
- **Gravity Pub** · 1257 Glenwood Ave SE
- **Mary's** · 1287 Glenwood Ave SE

🐾 Pet Shops
- **Park Pet Supply** · 491 Flat Shoals Ave SE

🍴 Restaurants
- **East Atlanta Thai & Sushi** · 467 Flat Shoals Ave SE
- **Heaping Bowl and Brew** · 469 Flat Shoals Ave SE
- **Iris** · 1314 Glenwood Ave SE
- **Pastificio Cameli** · 1263 Glenwood Ave SE
- **Zesto** · 1181 E Confederate Ave SE

🛍 Shopping
- **The Dressing Room** · 504 Flat Shoals Ave SE
- **Earthshaking Music** · 543 Stokewood Ave SE
- **Traders** · 485 Flat Shoals Ave SE

📀 Video Rental
- **Alan's Video** · 1241 Moreland Ave SE

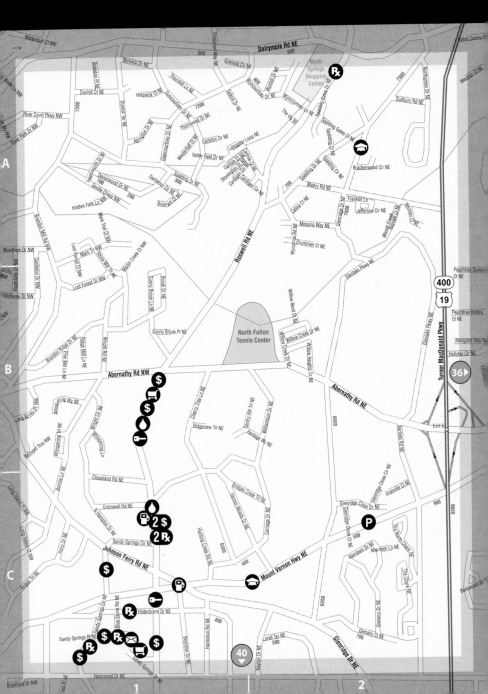

This diverse community located mainly within the Perimeter is a collection of 18 separate neighborhoods. The oldest homes date back to the 1950's, and there are many newly constructed homes as well. Residents include affluent singles, young families, and married couples.

$ Banks

- **Bank of America** · 227 Sandy Springs Pl NE
- **Bank of America** · 6075 Roswell Rd NE
- **Buckhead Community Bank** ·
  6000 Sandy Springs Cir NE
- **Fidelity Bank** · 225 Sandy Springs Cir NE
- **National Bank of Commerce** · 6344 Roswell Rd NE
- **Regions** · 6637 Roswell Rd NE
- **Wachovia** · 6300 Roswell Rd NE
- **Washington Mutual** · 6601 Roswell Rd NE

Car Rental

- **Budget** · 6509 Roswell Rd NE
- **Enterprise** · 6189 Roswell Rd NE

Car Washes

- **Mikael's Auto Detailing & Hand Washing** ·
  6380 Roswell Rd NE
- **Sandy Springs Car Wash** · 6585 Roswell Rd NE

Gas Stations

- **Chevron** · 295 Mount Vernon Hwy NE
- **Chevron** · 6385 Roswell Rd NE

Pharmacies

- **CVS** · 6330 Roswell Rd
- **Eckerd** · 6014 Sandy Springs Cir NE
- **EZ Med Pharmacy** · 199 Hilderbrand Dr NE
- **Kroger** · 227 Sandy Springs Pl NE
- **Sandy Springs Pharmacy** · 6329 Roswell Rd NE
- **Wender & Roberts Drugs** · 7306 Roswell Rd NE

Parking

Post Offices

- **US Post Office** · 227 Sandy Springs Pl NE

Schools

- **Mount Vernon Presbyterian** ·
  471 Mount Vernon Hwy NE
- **St Jude the Apostle** · 7171 Glenridge Dr NE

Supermarkets

- **Kroger** · 227 Sandy Springs Pl NE
- **Publix** · 6615 Roswell Rd NE

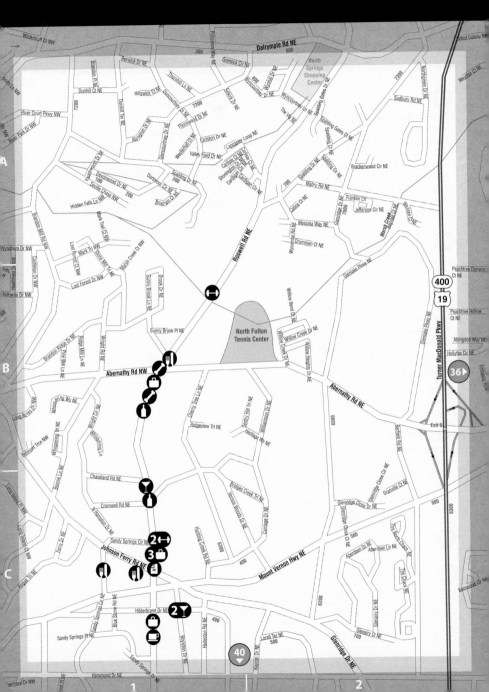

Plenty of suburban chains, because this is practically the 'burbs. Minado is a supersized and high-quality sushi and Japanese food buffet. The Punchline comedy club provides plenty of ha-ha's. Flashers is a strip club that will probably be shut down if the good people of Sandy Springs get their way.

Coffee
· **Dunkin' Donuts** · 6060 Roswell Rd NE

Copy Shops
· **Fedex Kinko's** · 6280 Roswell Rd NE

Gyms
· **Bally Total Fitness** · 6780 Roswell Rd NE
· **Curves** · 6303 Roswell Rd NE
· **Gold's Gym** · 6335 Roswell Rd NE

Liquor Stores
· **Parman's Wine & Spirits** · 6623 Roswell Rd NE
· **Roswell Road Package Store** · 6401 Roswell Rd NE

Nightlife
· **Café 290** · 290 Hilderbrand Dr NE
· **Flashers** · 6420 Roswell Rd NE
· **The Punchline** · 280 Hilderbrand Dr NE

Pet Shops
· **Pet Supermarket** · 6690 Roswell Rd NE
· **Red Bandanna Pet Food** · 6649 Roswell Rd NE

Restaurants
· **Atlanta Bread Company** ·
  220 Sandy Springs Cir NE
· **Minado** · 6690 Roswell Rd NE
· **Savories Bistro** · 206 Johnson Ferry Rd NE

Shopping
· **Bell Carpet Galleries** · 6223 Roswell Rd NE
· **Chocolate Soup** · 6681 Roswell Rd NE
· **the petite place** · 6309 Roswell Rd NE
· **The Scarlet Tassel** · 6235 Roswell Rd NE
· **Smoke 911** · 6124 Roswell Rd NE

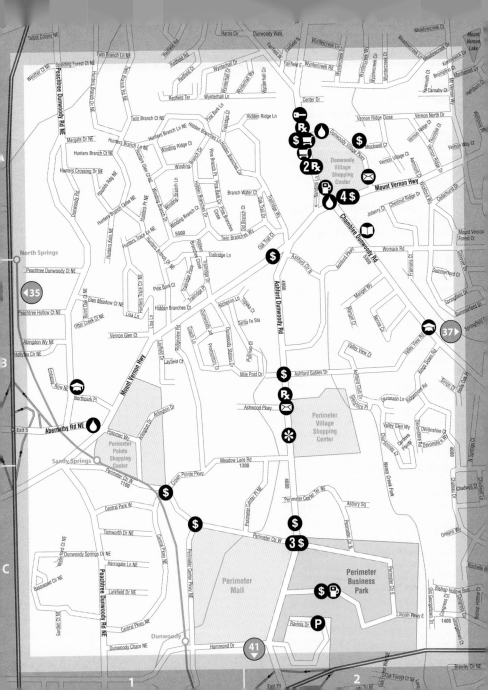

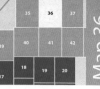
Anchored by Perimeter Mall, Dunwoody is a proud swim/tennis community at the top-end perimeter. Generally a quiet, safe, and affluent community; even P. Diddy has a home here. If you are in the tech industry, you may find yourself working in the area.

$ Banks

- **Bank of America** · 1 Perimeter Ctr E
- **Buckhead Community Bank** · 6000 Sandy Springs Cir NE
- **Colonial Bank** · 4800 Ashford Dunwoody Rd
- **Fidelity Bank** · 135 Perimeter Ctr W
- **Fidelity Bank** · 1425 Dunwoody Village Pkwy
- **Fidelity Bank** · 2 Perimeter Ctr E
- **Flag Bank** · 1614 Mount Vernon Rd
- **Main Street Bank** · 1636 Mount Vernon Rd
- **National Bank of Commerce** · 84 Perimeter Ctr E
- **Regions** · 1457 Mount Vernon Rd
- **Southtrust** · 1660 Mount Vernon Rd
- **Southtrust** · 4540 Ashford-Dunwoody Rd NE
- **SunTrust** · 121 Perimeter Ctr W
- **Wachovia** · 1630 Mount Vernon Rd
- **Wachovia** · 4570 Ashford Dunwoody Rd
- **Washington Mutual** · 5550 Chamblee Dunwoody Rd

Car Rental

- **Avis** · 5578 Chamblee-Dunwoody Rd

Car Washes

- **Coast & Valley Northpark** · 1100 Abernathy Rd NE
- **Shell** · 5546 Chamblee Dunwoody Rd
- **Sunshine Car Wash of Dunwoody** · 1244 Dunwoody Village Pkwy

Community Gardens

Gas Stations

- **Chevron** · 5456 Chamblee Dunwoody Rd
- **Exxon** · 77 Perimeter Ctr E
- **Shell** · 5546 Chamblee Dunwoody Rd

Libraries

- **Dunwoody Library** · 5339 Chamblee-Dunwoody Rd

P Parking

Rx Pharmacies

- **Carlton's Pharmacy** · 5484 Chamblee Dunwoody Rd
- **Eckerd** · 5556 Chamblee Dunwoody Rd
- **Wal-Mart** · 4725 Ashford Dunwoody Rd
- **Walgreens** · 5511 Chamblee Dunwoody Rd

Post Offices

- **US Post Office** · 1551 Dunwoody Village Pkwy
- **US Post Office** · 4707 Ashford Dunwoody Rd

Schools

- **American Intercontinental University** · 6600 Peachtree-Dunwoody Rd 500 Embassy Row
- **Atlanta North School of SDA** · 5123 Chamblee-Dunwoody Rd

Supermarkets

- **Fresh Market** · 5511 Chamblee Dunwoody Rd
- **Publix** · 5550 Chamblee Dunwoody Rd

Map 36 · **West Dunwoody**

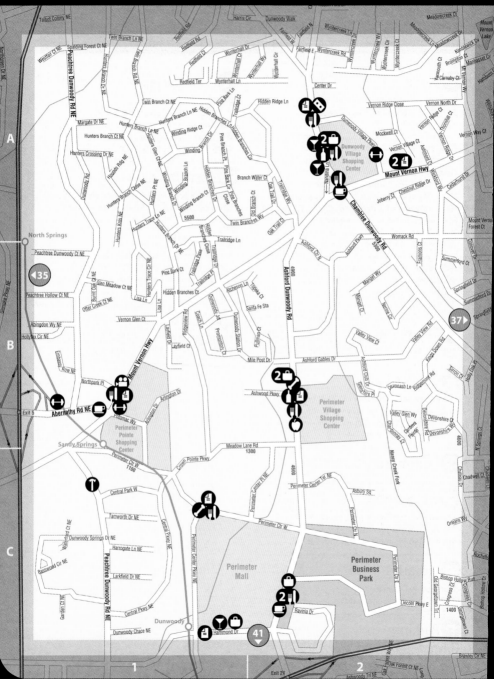

Perimeter Mall offers all of your standard mall necessities. The area surrounding the mall generally favors slightly upscale chains like Houston's and The Cheesecake Factory. Eatzie's is for gourmet on the go. The Farmhouse Tea Shoppe is a great way to recover from a trip to the mall. D'Vine Wine Bar and Shop offers a good selection of vino.

Coffee
- **Bistro New York** · 4400 Ashford Dunwoody Rd
- **Dunkin' Donuts** · 1594 Mount Vernon Rd
- **Italia D'Oro** · 1100 Abernathy Rd NE

Copy Shops
- **Advanced Imaging** · 1140 Hammond Dr NE
- **Alphagraphics** · 4729 Ashford Dunwoody Rd
- **Dunwoody Atlanta Printing** · 1720 Mount Vernon Rd
- **Fedex Kinko's** · 126 Perimeter Ctr W
- **Mount Vernon Printing and Copying** · 1713 Mount Vernon Rd
- **Office Depot** · 1155 Mount Vernon Hwy
- **Postnet** · 5588 Chamblee Dunwoody Rd

Farmer's Markets
- **Farmers Market at Spruill Gallery** · 4681 Ashford Dunwoody Rd

Gyms
- **Curves** · 1424 Dunwoody Village Pkwy
- **LA Fitness** · 1155 Mt Vernon Hwy
- **Northpark 400 Health Club** · 1000 Abernathy Rd NE

Hardware Stores
- **Home Depot** · 6400 Peachtree Dunwoody Rd

Liquor Stores
- **Dunwoody Bottle Shop** · 5479 Chamblee Dunwoody Rd
- **Perimeter Bottle Shop** · 4719 Ashford Dunwoody Rd

Movie Theaters
- **Regal Perimeter Pointe 10** · 1155 Mount Vernon Hwy

Nightlife
- **CB South** · 5500 Chamblee Dunwoody Rd
- **Derby Food & Spirits** · 1155 Hammond Dr NE
- **Dunwoody Tavern** · 5488 Chamblee Dunwoody Rd

Pet Shops
- **Petland** · 4733 Ashford Dunwoody Rd
- **Petsmart** · 128 Perimeter Ctr W

Restaurants
- **Atlanta Bread Company** · 1155 Mount Vernon Hwy
- **CB South** · 5500 Chamblee Dunwoody Rd
- **The Cheesecake Factory** · 4400 Ashford Dunwoody Rd
- **Corner Bakery Café** · 4400 Ashford Dunwoody Rd
- **Eatzie's** · 4504 Ashford Dunwoody Rd NE
- **Farmhouse Tea Shoppe** · 5455 Chamblee Dunwoody Rd
- **Fire of Brazil** · 118 Perimeter Ctr W
- **Houston's** · 4701 Ashford Dunwoody Rd
- **Moe's Southwest Grill** · 5562 Chamblee-Dunwoody Rd

Shopping
- **Best Buy** · 1201 Hammond Dr NE
- **Chickenlips** · 5484 Chamblee Dunwoody Rd
- **D'Vine Wine Bar and Shop** · 5486 Chamblee Dunwoody Rd
- **Eatzie's** · 4504 Ashford Dunwoody Rd NE
- **REI** · 1800 NE Expressway NE

Video Rental
- **Dunwoody Versatile Video** · 5575 Chamblee Dunwoody Rd

Map 37 • **East Dunwoody**

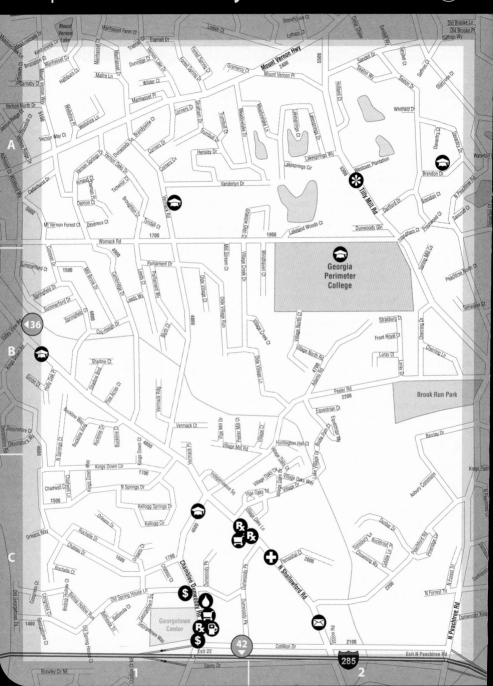

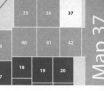

Just outside of the Perimeter (I-285), but still close to all the city has to offer, this is an attractive neighborhood for singles and families, and a bit more affordable than other communities north of the perimeter.

$ Banks
· **Bank of America** · 4545 Chamblee Dunwoody Rd
· **National Bank of Commerce** · 4498 Chamblee Dunwoody Rd

Car Washes
· **Cartique** · 4530 Chamblee Dunwoody Rd
· **Chevron** · 4479 Chamblee-Dunwoody Rd

Community Gardens

Gas Stations
· **Amoco** · 5500 Northside Dr NW
· **BP** · 3340 Cobb Pkwy
· **Chevron** · 4479 Chamblee-Dunwoody Rd
· **Chevron** · 5545 New Northside Dr
· **Shell** · 5640 Northside Dr NW

Hospitals
· **Emory-Dunwoody Medical Center** ·
4575 N Shallowford Rd

Pharmacies
· **Eckerd** · 4621 N Shallowford Rd
· **Kroger** · 4498 Chamblee Dunwoody Rd
· **The Medicine Shoppe** · 4675 N Shallowford Rd

Post Offices
· **US Post Office** · 4444 N Shallowford Rd

Schools
· **Chamblee Middle** · 4680 Chamblee-Dunwoody Rd
· **Deo Preparatory** · 5067 Chamblee-Dunwoody Rd
· **Dunwoody High** · 5035 Vermack Rd
· **Georgia Perimeter College** · 2101 Womack Rd
· **Kingsley Elementary** · 2051 Brendon Dr

Supermarkets
· **Dunwoody Food Mart** · 4639 N Shallowford Rd
· **Kroger** · 4498 Chamblee-Dunwoody Rd

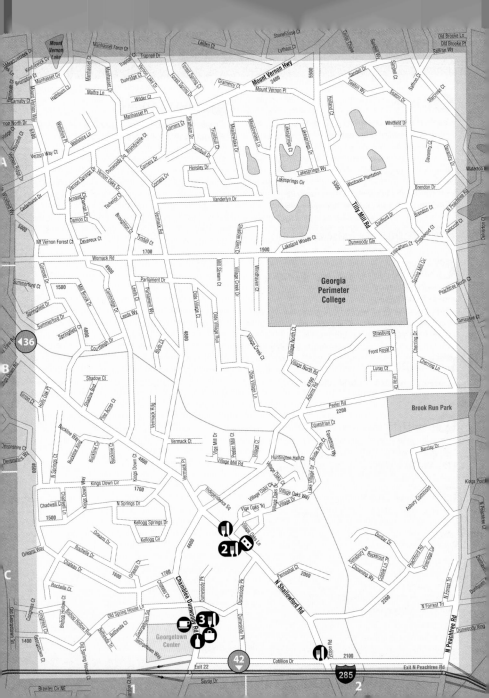

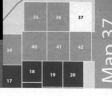

Goldberg's is the closest you'll get to a New York City bagel in the South. Ethnic restaurants are popular, including the always dependable Chopsticks and Garcia's Mexican Restaurant.

Coffee
· **Starbucks** · 4520 Chamblee Dunwoody Rd

Liquor Stores
· **Georgetown Package Store** ·
4516 Chamblee Dunwoody Rd

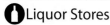Restaurants
· **Chopsticks** · 4639 N Shallowford Rd
· **Garcia's Mexican Restaurant** ·
4515 Chamblee Dunwoody Rd
· **Goldberg's Bagel Company** ·
4520 Chamblee Dunwoody Rd
· **Hot Dogs Etc** · 4639 N Shallowford Rd
· **Milano Pizza & Subs** ·
4498 Chamblee Dunwoody Rd
· **Moe's Southwest Grill** · 4401 N Shallowford Rd
· **Santi Thai Restaurant** · 4639 N Shallowford Rd

Shopping
· **Pet Supermarket** · 4498 Chamblee Dunwoody Rd

Video Rental
· **Video Connections** · 4639 N Shallowford Rd

Surprisingly trendy considering it's the gateway to Cobb County, Vinings is where conservative and wealthy singles live until they find one another, marry, and start a family in the 'burbs. The fact that the Chattahoochee River runs through the area may sound like an attractive selling point, but with the Hooch as polluted as it is, a riverside location is not nearly as enticing.

 ## Banks

· **Flag Bank** · 5340 New Northside Dr
· **Georgia Bank** · 6190 Powers Ferry Rd NW
· **Wachovia** · 6370 Powers Ferry Rd

 ## Car Washes

· **Shell** · 5640 New Northside Dr

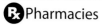 ## Gas Stations

· **Amoco** · 5500 Northside Dr NW
· **BP** · 3340 Cobb Pkwy
· **Chevron** · 5545 New Northside Dr
· **Shell** · 5640 New Northside Dr

 ## Pharmacies

· **CVS** · 6300 Powers Ferry Rd

 ## Supermarkets

· **Kroger** · 3300 Cobb Pkwy
· **Publix** · 6300 Powers Ferry Rd NW

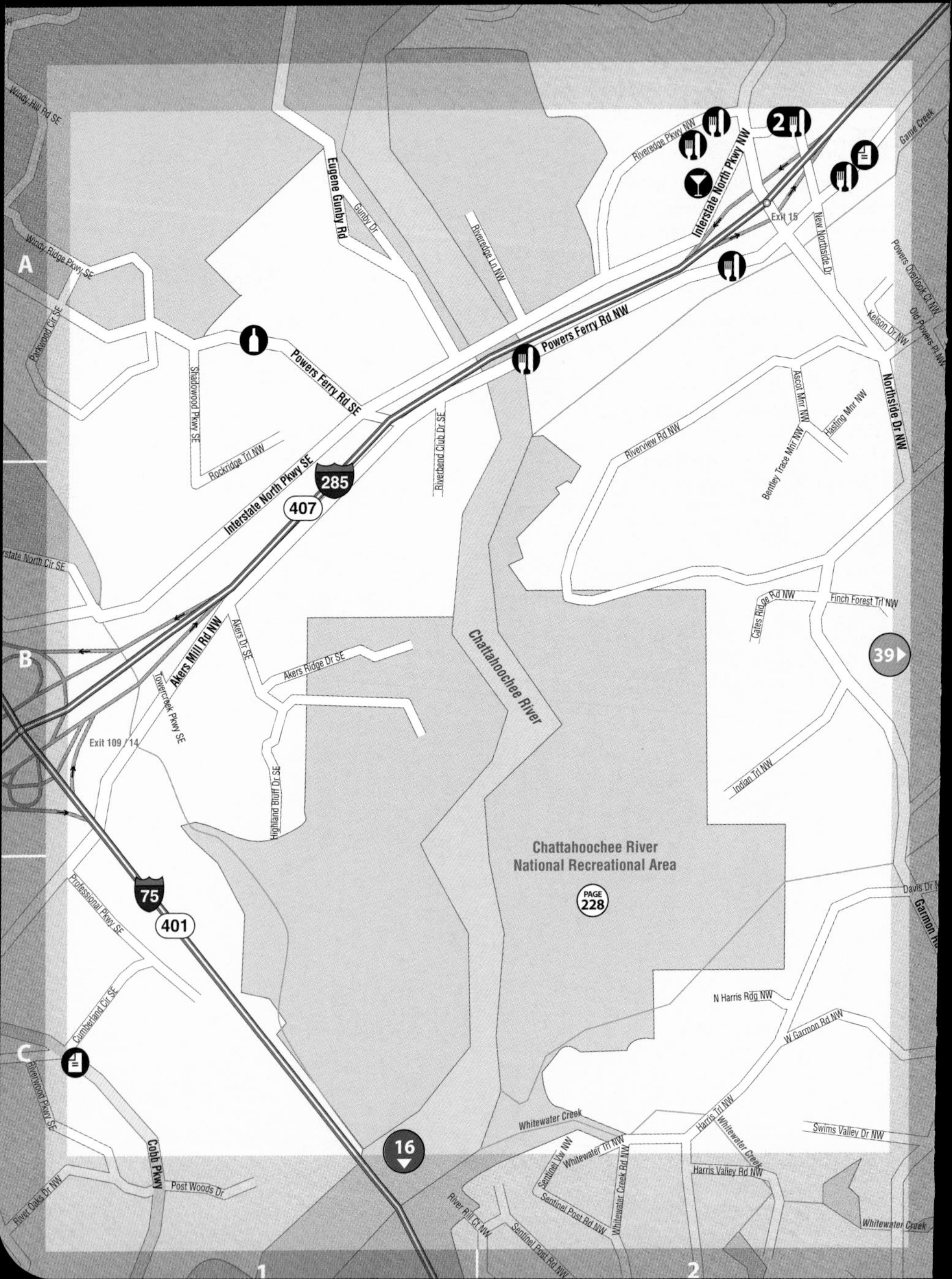

Map 38 · **Vinings**

N

A

B

C

Windy Hill Rd SE

Windy Ridge Pkwy SE

Briarwood Cir SE

Interstate North Cir SE

Briarwood Pkwy SE

Cumberland Cir SE

Professional Pkwy SE

Cobb Pkwy

River Oaks Dr NW

Post Woods Dr

Eugene Gunby Rd

Gunby Dr

SE Pkwy Shipsbrough

Rockridge Trl NW

Powers Ferry Rd SE

Interstate North Pkwy SE

285

407

Akers Mill Rd NW

Travertine Pkwy SE

Akers Rd SE

Akers Ridge Dr SE

SE Dr Bluff Highland

Exit 109 / 14

75

401

Exit 110

Riveredge Dr NW

Powers Ferry Rd NW

Riverband Club Dr SE

Riverview Rd NW

Chattahoochee River

Riveredge Pkwy NW

Interstate North Pkwy NW

2

Exit 16

New Northside Dr

Game Creek

Powers Overlook Ct NW

Kelson Dr NW

Old Powers Pl NW

Northside Dr NW

Bentley Trace Mnr NW

Ascot Mnr NW

Hasting Mnr NW

Cates Ridge Rd NW

Finch Forest Trl NW

39▶

Indian Trl NW

Chattahoochee River
National Recreational Area

PAGE
228

Davis Dr N

N Harris Rdg NW

W Garmon Rd NW

Garmon Rd NW

**16
▼**

Whitewater Creek

Sentinel Vw NW

Sentinel Whitewater Trl NW

River Rdl Ct NW

Sentinel Post Rd NW

Whitewater Creek Rd NW

Harris Trl NW

Whitewater Creek

Harris Valley Rd NW

Swims Valley Dr NW

Whitewater Creek

1

2

Sundries / Entertainment

Dining on the Chattahoochee is still considered romantic and quite popular, as Ray's on the River and Olives Waterside indicate. Sushi-Huku is popular with sushi fanatics.

Copy Shops
· **UPS Store** · 3232 Cobb Pkwy
· **UPS Store** · 6300 Powers Ferry Rd NW

Liquor Stores
· **Hillside Liquor** · 2150 Powers Ferry Rd SE

Nightlife
· **Sidelines Bar & Grille** · 5525 Interstate North Pkwy

Restaurants
· **Café the Pointe** · 5660 New Northside Dr NW
· **Chevy's** · 5565 New Northside Dr NW
· **Get Away Café** · 1600 Riveredge Pkwy NW
· **Olives Waterside** · 6450 Powers Ferry Rd NW
· **Ray's on the River** · 6700 Powers Ferry Rd NW
· **Riveredge Café** · 1500 Riveredge Pkwy NW
· **Sushi-Huku** · 6300 Powers Ferry Rd NW

Map 38

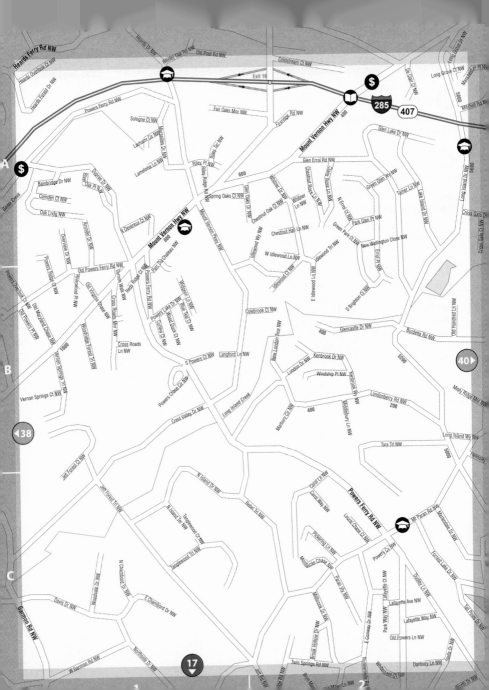

This Sandy Springs neighborhood just south of the Perimeter offers high-quality schools, a low crime rate, and large, well maintained homes. The neighborhood association is quite active in maintaining the community's high standard of living. A thriving gardening community is the pride of the neighborhood.

 Banks

- **Georgia Banking Company** ·
  6190 Powers Ferry Rd NW
- **IronStone Bank** · 325 Mount Vernon Hwy NW

 Libraries

- **Sandy Springs Regional** · 395 Mt Vernon Hwy

 Schools

- **First Montessori of Atlanta** ·
  5750 Long Island Dr NW
- **Holy Innocents' Episcopal** ·
  805 Mount Vernon Hwy
- **Riverwood High** · 5900 Heards Dr NW
- **Schenck** · 282 Mt Paran Rd

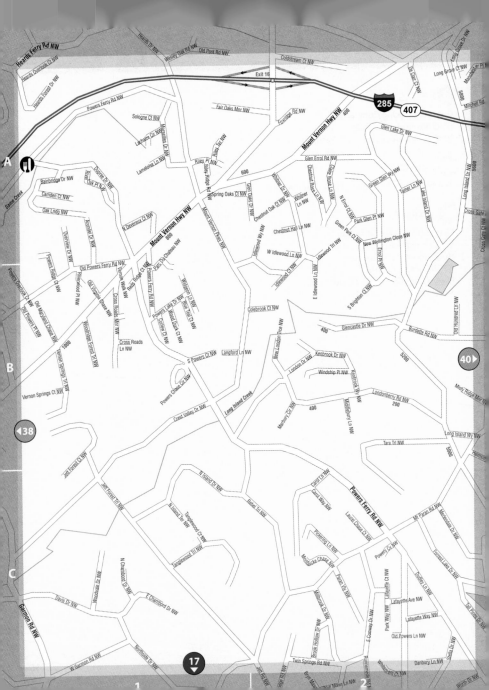

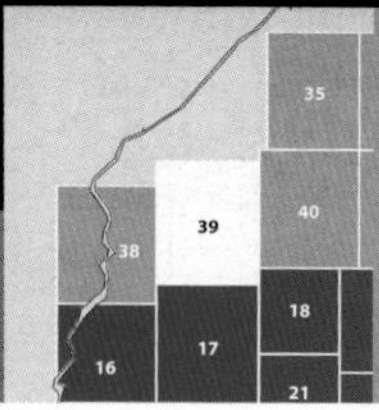

Sundries / Entertainment

Map 39

Since the community is almost entirely residential, you won't find much in way of dining or entertainment in the area. However, the people that live in this community no doubt have at least one car, if not more, so driving to nearby Buckhead or Sandy Springs is not a problem.

 Restaurants

· Powers Ferry East Café ·
6151 Powers Ferry Rd NW

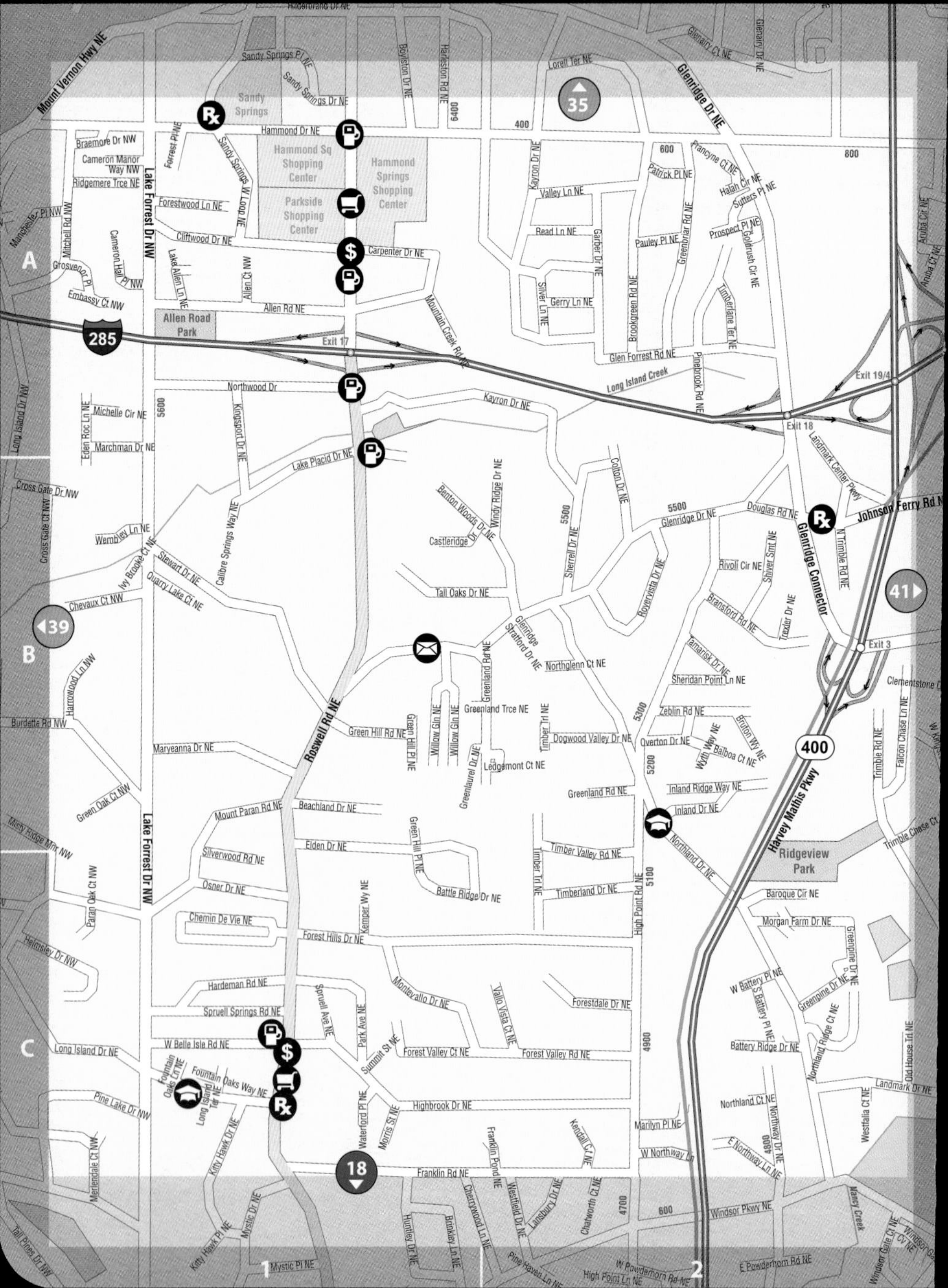

Map 40 · **Sandy Springs (South)**

N

Sandy Springs

Hammond Sq Shopping Center

Hammond Springs Shopping Center

Parkside Shopping Center

Allen Road Park

285

Castleridge

Ridgeview Park

35

139

41

400

18

Mount Vernon Hwy NE
Braemore Dr NW
Cameron Manor Way NW
Ridgemere Trce NE
Forrest Dr NE
Sandy Springs Pl NE
Sandy Springs Dr NE
Brighton Dr NE
Helmsdon Pl NE
Loreli Ter NE
6400
400
Glenlei Ct NE
Glenridge Dr NE
Gresham Ct NE
Mitchell Rd NE
Forestwood Ln NE
Sandy Springs Cir NE
Hammond Dr NE
600
Francyne Ct NE
Patrick Pl NE
Suttars Ct NE
800
Grosvenor St NE
Cameron Trail
Embassy Ct NW
Cliffwood Dr NE
Allen Ct NW
Allen Rd NE
Valley Ln NE
Gifford Dr NE
Read Ln NE
Brookgreen Rd NE
Pauley Ln NE
Prospect Pl NE
Goldmann Cir NE
Exit 17
Glen Forrest Rd NE
Gerry Ln NE
Marchman Creek Rd NE
Long Island Creek
Pinebrook Rd NE
Exit 19/4
Northwood Dr
Kingston Dr NE
Kayron Dr NE
Exit 18
Lake Placid Dr NE
Michelle Cir NE
Eden Roc Ln NE
Marchman Dr NE
Cross Gate Dr NW
Benton Woods Dr NE
Windy Ridge Dr NE
Colquitt Rd NE
5500
Glenridge Dr NE
Douglas Rd NE
Lacomte Center Pkwy
Wembley Ln NE
Calibre Springs Way NE
Ivy Brook Ct NE
Quarry Lake Ct NE
Stewart Dr NE
Tall Oaks Dr NE
Sherrell Dr NE
Rivoli Cir NE
Skinner Sprt NE
N Trimble Rd NE
Chevaux Ct NW
Burdette Rd NW
Hammond Ln NW
Maryeanna Dr NE
Green Hill Rd NE
Green Hill Pl NE
Willow Glen NE
Greenland Trce NE
Northglenn Ct NE
Sheridan Point Ln NE
Clementstone
Green Oak Ct NW
Paran Oak Ct NW
Heimlin Dr NW
Roswell Rd NE
Lake Forrest Dr NW
Mount Paran Rd NE
Beachland Dr NE
Green Hill Ln NE
Greenland Dr NE
Ledgemont Ct NE
Dogwood Valley Dr NE
Timber Trl NE
5300
Zeblin Rd NE
Overton Dr NE
Worth Way NE
Balboa Ln NE
Greenland Rd NE
Inland Ridge Way NE
Inland Dr NE
Harvey Mathis Pkwy
Baroque Cir NE
Silverwood Rd NE
Elden Dr NE
Battle Ridge Dr NE
Timberland Dr NE
Timber Valley Rd NE
5100
Northland Dr NE
Morgan Farm Dr NE
Osner Dr NE
Chemin De Vie NE
Forest Hills Dr NE
W Battery Pl NE
S Battery Pl NE
Greenpine Dr NE
Greenland Ridge Ct NE
Hardeman Rd NE
Spruell Springs Rd NE
Monticello Dr NE
Forestdale Dr NE
4900
Battery Ridge Dr NE
Northland Ridge Ct NE
Oak House Ln NE
Landmark Dr NE
Long Island Dr NE
W Belle Isle Rd NE
Fountain Oaks Way NE
Park Ave NE
Summit St NE
Forest Valley Ct NE
Forest Valley Rd NE
Marilyn Pl NE
Northland Ct NE
Northway Dr NE
Westfalia Ct NE
Long Island Ct NE
Pine Lake Dr NW
Fountain Oaks Ct NE
Highbrook Dr NE
Franklin Pond Rd NE
Kendall Dr NE
E Northway Ln NE
Mystic Ms NE
Waterford Pl NE
Franklin Rd NE
Coventry Rd NE
W Northway Dr
4700
600
Terr Park Ct NE
Kelly Hope Pl NE
Kirk Hope Ct NE
Mystic Pl NE
Mystic Pl NE
W Powderhorn Rd NE
High Point Ln NE
E Powderhorn Rd NE
Windsor Pkwy NE

Now that the Republicans are in charge of the state, Sandy Springs is strutting its stuff, ready to shed the albatross around its neck—better known as the city of Atlanta. The only problem with this WASP wet dream is that pesky ethnic community that's cropped up along Roswell Road, with their run-down shops and non-English signs. It's like reverse gentrification!

Banks
· **Bank of America** · 4920 Roswell Rd NE
· **SunTrust** · 5895 Roswell Rd NE

Gas Stations
· **Citgo** · 4968 Roswell Rd NE
· **Citgo** · 5645 Roswell Rd NE
· **Philips 66** · 6024 Roswell Rd NE
· **Shell** · 5700 Roswell Rd NE
· **Shell** · 5866 Roswell Rd NE

Pharmacies
· **Eckerd** · 6014 Sandy Springs Cir NE
· **Health for Life Pharmacy** ·
  860 Johnson Ferry Rd NE
· **Kroger** · 4920 Roswell Rd NE

Post Offices
· **US Post Office** · 5400 Glenridge Dr NE

Schools
· **Donnellan** · 4820 Long Island Dr NE
· **Greenfield Hebrew Academy** ·
  5200 Northland Dr NE

Supermarkets
· **Kroger** · 4920 Roswell Rd NE
· **Whole Foods** · 5930 Roswell Rd

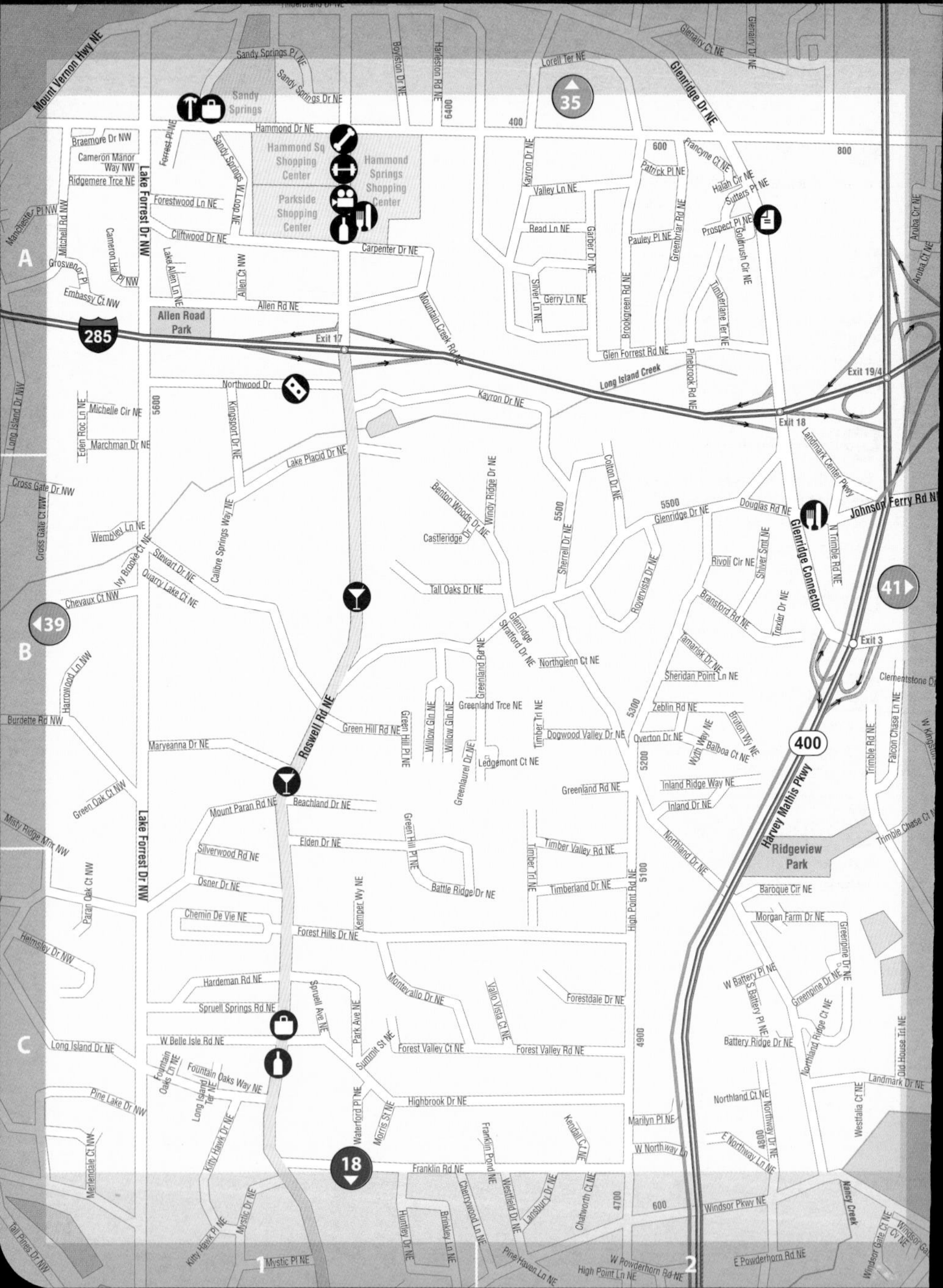

Map 40 · Sandy Springs (South)

N

35

39

41

18

Mount Vernon Hwy NE
Sandy Springs Pl NE
Sandy Springs Dr NE
Sandy Springs
Corell Ter NE
Glenridge Dr NE
Glenriry Ct NE

Hammond Dr NE
6400
400
800
600
Francyne Ct NE
Patrick Pl NE

Hammond Sq
Shopping
Center
Hammond
Springs
Shopping
Center
Kayron Dr NE
Valley Ln NE
Halah Cir NE
Suttary Pl NE

Parkside
Shopping
Center
Read Ln NE
Prospect Pl NE
Golltush Cir NE

Braemore Dr NW
Cameron Manor Way NW
Ridgemere Trce NE
Forestwood Ln NE
Carpenter Dr NE
Pauley Ln NE
Greenridge Rd NE
Timberline Ter NE

Cliffwood Dr NE
Gerry Ln NE

Mitchell Rd NE
Lake Allen Ln NE
Allen Ct NE
Allen Rd NE
Mountain Creek Rd NE
Glen Forrest Rd NE

Grosvenor Pl NW
Embassy Ct NW

285

Allen Road Park
Exit 17
Long Island Creek
Exit 19/4

Northwood Dr NE
5600
Kayron Dr NE
Exit 18
Landmark Center Pkwy

Michelle Cir NE
Marchman Dr NE
Lake Placid Dr NE
Glenridge Dr NE
Douglas Rd NE
N Trimble Rd NE
Johnson Ferry Rd NW

Eden Roc Ln NE
Kingussoll Dr NE
Benton Woods Dr NE
Windy Ridge Dr NE
5500
Rivoli Cir NE
Silver Oint Dr NE
Glenridge Connector

Wernield Ln NE
Ivy Brooke Ct NE
Stewart Dr NE
Castleridge
Sherrell Dr NE
Rosemonte Dr NE
Bransford Rd NE
Trasler Dr NE

Chevaux Ct NW
Quarry Lake Ct NE
Caldere Springs Way NE
Tall Oaks Dr NE
Exit 3

Burdette Rd NW
Roswell Rd NE
Green Hill Rd NE
Green Hill Dr NE
Glenridge Stratford Dr NE
Northglenn Ct NE
Sheridan Point Ln NE
Clementstone Ct

Maryeanna Dr NE
Willow Gln NE
Greenland Trce NE
Timber Trl NE
Zeblin Rd NE
Overton Dr NE
Brilon Wy NE
Falcon Chase Ln NE

Green Oak Ct NW
Greenland Ct NE
Dogwood Valley Dr NE
5200
125th Way NE
Balboa Ct NE
400

Mount Paran Ct NE
Beachland Dr NE
Ledgemont Ct NE
Greenland Rd NE
Inland Ridge Way NE
Harvey Mathis Pkwy

Silverwood Rd NE
Elden Dr NE
Green Trl NE
Inland Dr NE
Ridgeview Park

Osner Dr NE
Battle Ridge Dr NE
Timber Valley Rd NE
Northland Dr NE
Baroque Cir NE

Chemio De Vie NE
Kempel Wy NE
Timberland Dr NE
5100
Morgan Farm Dr NE

Pazan Oak Ct NW
Forest Hills Dr NE
High Point Rd NE
W Battery Pl NE
Greenpine Ct NE

Helmsby Dr NW
Hardeman Rd NE
Montevallo Dr NE
S Battery Pl NE
Greenpine Dr NE

Spruell Springs Rd NE
Spruell Ave NE
Forest Valley Ct NE
Forestdale Dr NE
Battery Ridge Dr NE
Northland Ridge Trl NE

W Belle Isle Rd NE
Park Ave NE
Summit St NE
Forest Valley Rd NE
4900
Oak House Trl NE
Westfalia Ct NE
Landmark Dr NE

Long Island Ln NE
Fountain Oaks Way NE
Highbrook Dr NE
Northland Ct NE
E Northway Dr NE

Pine Lake Dr NW
Waterford Pl NE
Morris St NE
Marilyn Pl NE
W Northway Dr NE
Windsor Pkwy NE

Meridian Ct NW
Franklin Rd NE
Kendall Ct NE
600
Nancy Creek

Kiry Park Ct NW
Kiry Hawk Dr NE
Huntley Rd NE
Brinkley Ln NE
Charmwood Dr NE
Lancaster Dr NE
Chatworth Ct NE
Pine Haven Ln NE
W Powderhorn Rd NE
E Powderhorn Rd NE

Mystic Pl NE
Franklin Rd NE
High Point Ln NE

1
2

Ricesticks offers exquisite upscale Vietnamese cuisine in an unlikely strip mall locale. Maxim Cabaret is a classy and upscale adult entertainment venue. American Pie is a popular partying destination. Petco offers discount pet supplies.

Copy Shops
- **Ameripress** · 5881 Glenridge Dr NE

Gyms
- **Sandy Springs Fitness** · 5920 Roswell Rd NE

Hardware Stores
- **Sandy Springs Smith Ace Hardware** ·
  6010 Sandy Springs Cir NE

Liquor Stores
- **Bailey's Bottle Shop** · 4920 Roswell Rd NE
- **Jax Fine Wines & Spirits** · 5901 Roswell Rd NE

Movie Theaters
- **Lefont Sandy Springs** · 5920 Roswell Rd NE

Nightlife
- **American Pie** · 5480 Roswell Rd NE
- **Maxim Cabaret** · 5275 Roswell Rd NE

Pet Shops
- **Petco** · 5938 Roswell Rd NE

Restaurants
- **Moe's Southwest Grill** · 860 Johnson Ferry Rd
- **Ricesticks** · 5920 Roswell Rd NE

Shopping
- **Fragile** · 6010 Sandy Springs Cir NE
- **Sunlighting Lamp and Shade Center** ·
  4990 Roswell Rd NE

Video Rental
- **La Fiesta (Spanish)** · 215 Northwood Dr NE

Map 41 · **North Atlanta West**

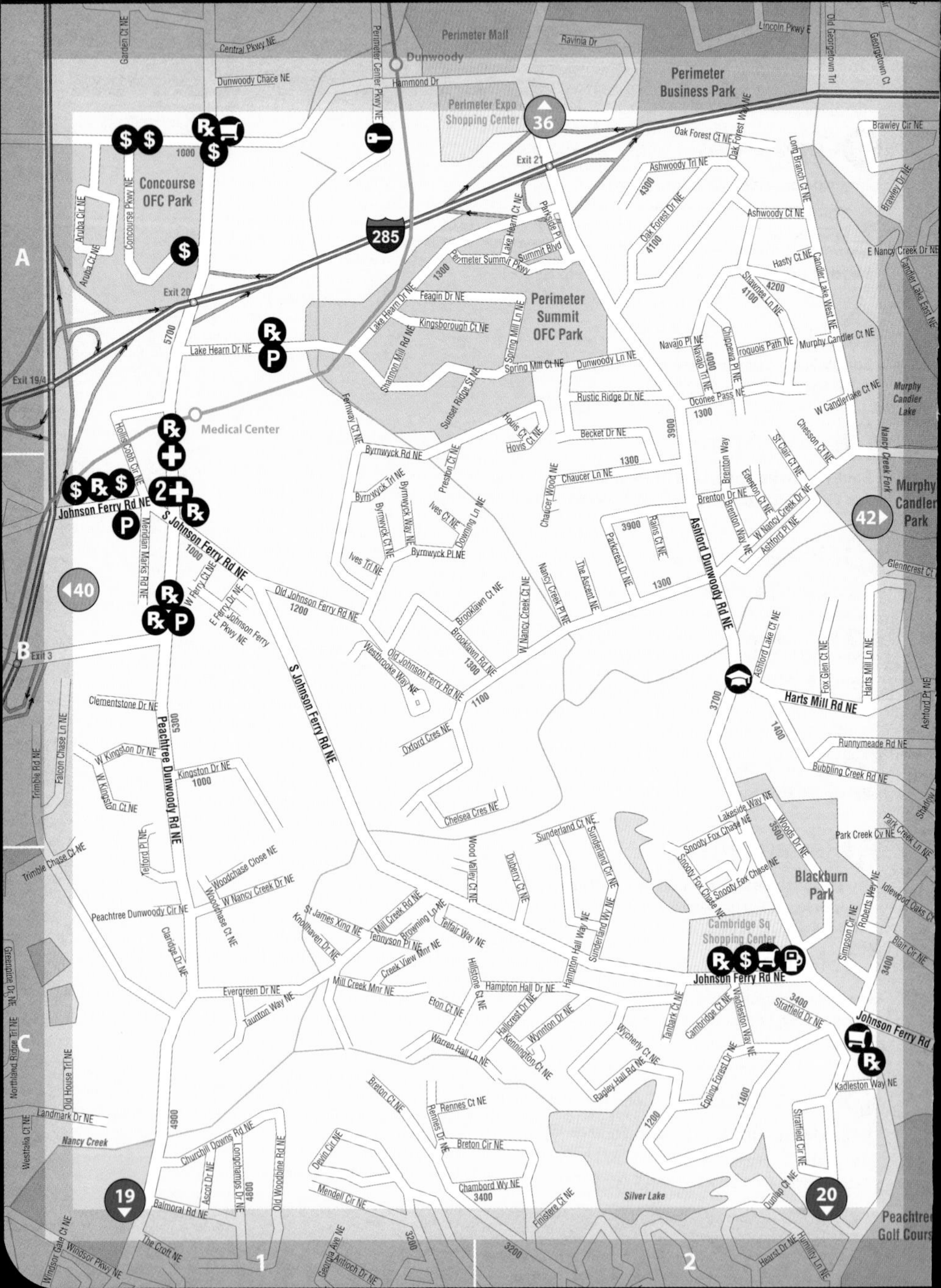

N

Perimeter Mall
Ravinia Dr
Lincoln Pkwy E
Old Georgetown Trl
Garden Ct NE
Central Pkwy NE
Dunwoody
Dunwoody Chace NE
Hammond Dr
Perimeter Business Park
Brawley Cir NE
Aruba Ct NE
Perimeter Ctr Pkwy NE
1000
Perimeter Expo Shopping Center
36
Oak Forest Ct NE
Oak Forest Way NE
Brawley Cir NE

$ $
Rx
$
Concourse OFC Park
Concourse Pkwy NE
Exit 21
Ashwoody Trl NE
Long Branch Dr NE
4300
Ashwoody Dr NE
Hasty Ct NE
E Nancy Creek Dr NE
Candler Lake West Ct NE

A
$
Exit 20
5700
Lake Hearn Dr NE
Lake Hearn Dr NE
285
Summit Blvd
Perimeter Summit Pkwy
1000
Perimeter Summit Pkwy
4100
Savoia Ct NE
Stavola Ct NE
8200
4100

Exit 19/4
Feagin Dr NE
Kingsborough Ct NE
Perimeter Summit OFC Park
Navajo Pl NE
Chippewa Pl NE
4000
Navajo Trl NE
Iroquois Path NE
Murphy Candler Ct NE

Rx
P
Sutton Mill Rd NE
Sunset Ridge Ct NE
Spring Mill Ln NE
Dunwoody Ln NE
Rustic Ridge Dr NE
Ocofee Pass NE
W Candlerlake Ct NE
1300
Murphy Candler Lake

Medical Center
Rx
+
Byrnwyck Rd NE
Hovis Ct NE
Hovis Ln NE
Becket Dr NE
3900
Chauncer Ln NE
1300
Chesson Ct NE
St Clair Ct NE
Murphy Candler Park
42

$ Rx $
P
Johnson Ferry Rd NE
2 +
Rx
Meridian Marsh NE
S Johnson Ferry Rd NE
1000
Byrnwyck Trl NE
Byrnwyck Way NE
Byrnwyck Ct NE
Ives Ct NE
Byrnwyck Pl NE
Ives Trl NE
Preston Ln NE
Distelling Ln NE
Chauncer Wood Ave NE
Chauncer Ln NE
3900
Brenton Ln NE
Baxes Ct NE
Brenton Way
Cromer Ct NE
W Nancy Creek Dr NE
Ashford Dr NE
Ashford Dunwoody Rd NE
St Clair Ct NE

40
Rx
Rx P
E Perry Ct NE
E Perry Ct NE
Johnson Ferry Pkwy NE
Old Johnson Ferry Rd NE
1200
Brooklawn Ct NE
Brooklawn Rd NE
W Nancy Creek Dr NE
Parkaires Ct NE
The Ascent NE
1300
Ashford Lake Ct NE
Fox Glen Ct NE
Harts Mill Ln NE

B
Exit 3
Clementstone Dr NE
Peachtree Dunwoody Rd NE
5300
Westbrooke Way NE
Old Johnson Ferry Rd NE
1000
1100
Oxford Cres NE
3700
Harts Mill Rd NE
Runnymeade Rd NE
Bubbling Creek Rd NE

Trimble Rd NE
W Kingston Dr NE
Kingston Dr NE
1000
Telford Pl NE
Kingston Ct NE
S Johnson Ferry Rd NE
Chelsea Cres NE
Lakeside Way NE
Snooty Fox Chase NE
Woods Ct NE
Park Creek Cv NE
Park Creek Dr NE

C
Trimble Chase Ct NE
Falcon Chase Ln NE
Peachtree Dunwoody Cir NE
Clairidge Ct NE
Woodchase Close NE
W Nancy Creek Dr NE
Woodchase Ct NE
Clarkdell Ct NE
St James Xing NE
Mill Creek Rd NE
Tennyson Dr NE
Browning Ln NE
Telfair Way NE
Sunderland Ct NE
Dunbarton Ct NE
Sutherland Ct NE
Sutherland Dr NE
Snooty Fox Chase NE
Hampton Hall Way NE
Cambridge Sq Shopping Center
Rx $
Johnson Ferry Rd NE
Simpson Ct NE
Roberts Way NE
Ketteredge Cours Ct NE
Blair Ct NE
Blackburn Park
3400
3400

Greenway Dr NE
Northland River Rd NE
Westside Ct NE
Landmark Dr NE
Nancy Creek
Churchill Downs Rd NE
Old Woodbine Rd NE
Peachtree Dunwoody Rd NE
Evergreen Dr NE
Taunton Way NE
Mill Creek Mnr NE
Hampton Hall Dr NE
Creek View Mnr NE
Hillcrest Dr NE
Eton Ct NE
Halfcreek Ct NE
Warren Hall Ln NE
Wynnton Ct NE
Kennington Ct NE
Wychern Ct NE
Cambridge Dr NE
Widdlesten Way NE
Gapora Escaed Dr NE
Strattield Dr NE
Johnson Ferry Rd
Rx
Kadleston Way NE

19
Old House Dr NE
Ardale Ct NE
Winston Gate Ct NE
Windsor Pkwy NE
Balmoral Rd NE
The Croft Dr NE
Shadowcliff Ct NE
Mendell Cir NE
Dover Hts NE
Breton Ct NE
Rennes Ct NE
Breton Cir NE
Chambord Wy NE
3400
4800
4900
5200
Timbers Ct NE
Silver Lake
1200
Dunsley Ct NE
Peachtree Golf Course
20

1 2

Home to Atlanta's medical center, with 3 major hospitals in the area (Scottish Rite, Northside, and St. Joseph's). Marist School is a well-respected private Catholic school. Blackburn Park is home to the Atlanta Silverbacks, which are part of the United Soccer League.

Banks

- **Bank of America** · 2 Concourse Pkwy
- **National Bank of Commerce** · 2036 Johnson Ferry Rd
- **National Bank of Commerce** · 990 Hammond Dr NE
- **SunTrust** · 1100 Hammond Dr
- **SunTrust** · 993 Johnson Ferry Rd NE
- **Wachovia** · 1034 Hammond Dr NE
- **Wachovia** · 960 Johnson Ferry Rd NE

Car Rental

- **Hertz** · 246 Perimeter Ctr Pkwy NE

Gas Stations

- **Chevron** · 3500 Ashford Dunwoody Rd

Hospitals

- **Children's Healthcare of Atlanta at Scottish Rite** · 1001 Johnson Ferry Rd NE
- **Northside** · 1000 Johnson Ferry Rd NE
- **St Joseph's of Atlanta** · 5665 Peachtree Dunwoody Rd NE

Parking

Pharmacies

- **Concord Drugs** · 5505 Peachtree Dunwood Rd NE
- **Concord Drugs** · 5555 Peachtree Dunwoody Rd NE
- **Concord Pharmacy** · 1150 Lake Hearn Dr NE
- **Concord Pharmacy** · 960 Johnson Ferry Rd NE
- **Concord Pharmacy** · 993 Johnson Ferry Rd NE
- **CVS** · 3439 Ashford Dunwoody Rd
- **Eckerd** · 1100 Hammond Dr NE
- **Kroger** · 2036 Johnson Ferry Rd NE
- **St Joseph's Apothecary** · 5671 Peachtree Dunwoody Rd NE

Schools

- **Marist** · 3790 Ashford-Dunwoody Rd

Supermarkets

- **Kroger** · 2036 Johnson Ferry Rd NE
- **Publix** · 1100 Hammond Dr NE
- **Publix** · 3435 Ashford Dunwoody Rd NE

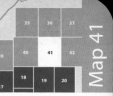

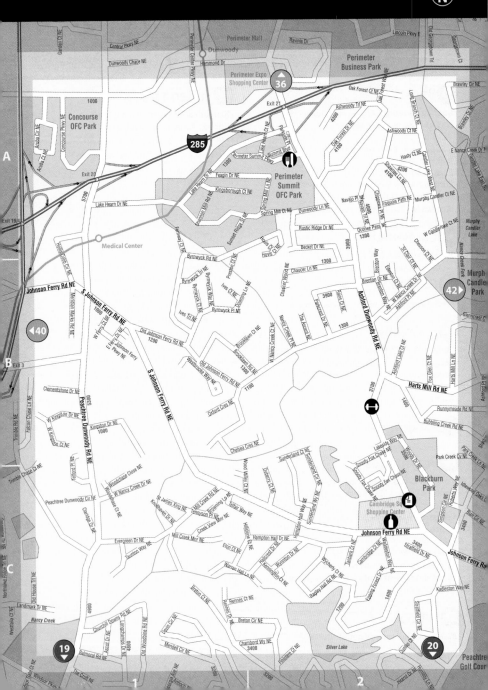

Villa Christina, a replica of an Italian villa, offers a fine dining restaurant, special events facilities, and Caffe Christina, for exquisite takeout food.

Copy Shops

· **UPS Store** · 3530 Ashford Dunwoody Rd NE

Gyms

· **YMCA** · 3692 Ashford Dunwoody Rd

Liquor Stores

· **Cambridge Package Store** ·
2036 Johnson Ferry Rd NE

Restaurants

· **Caffe Christina** · 4000 Summit Blvd

Map 42 · **North Atlanta East / Silver Lake**

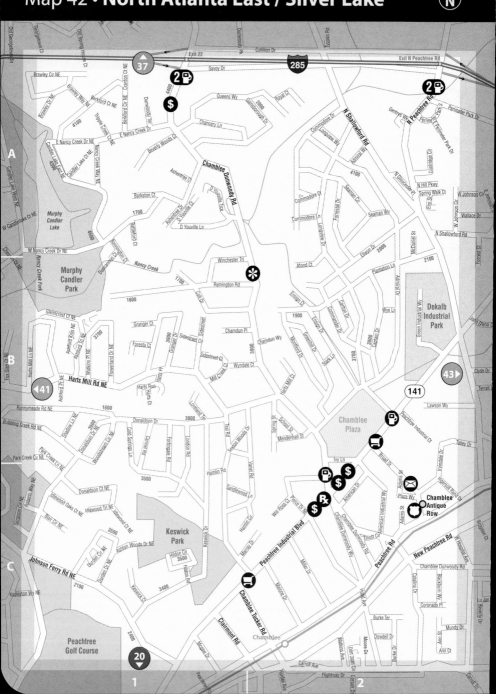

Essentials

The influx of immigrants of all races to the neighboring Chamblee/Doraville area is spilling over into this section of North Atlanta. The International Farmers Market attracts not only Atlanta's minority communities, but people of all races who are searching for authentic, high-quality ingredients to make ethnic dishes at home.

$ Banks

- **Bank of America** · 5442 Peachtree Industrial Blvd
- **Summit National** · 4360 Chamblee Dunwoody Rd
- **SunTrust** · 5370 Peachtree Industrial Blvd
- **Wachovia** · 5425 Peachtree Industrial Blvd

Car Washes

- **Exxon** · 4401 Chamblee Dunwoody Rd
- **Shell** · 4301 N Peachtree Rd

Community Gardens

Gas Stations

- **Chevron** · 3640 Chamblee Dunwoody Rd
- **Citgo** · 5560 Peachtree Industrial Blvd
- **Exxon** · 4401 Chamblee Dunwoody Rd
- **Philips 66** · 4291 N Peachtree Rd
- **Philips 66** · 4400 Chamblee Dunwoody Rd
- **Shell** · 4301 N Peachtree Rd

o Landmarks

- **Chamblee Antique Row** · 3519 Broad St

Pharmacies

- **Walgreens (24 hrs)** · 5373 Peachtree Industrial Blvd

Police

- **Chamblee Police Department** · 3518 Broad St

Post Offices

- **US Post Office** · 3545 Broad St

Supermarkets

- **International Farmers Market** · 5193 Peachtree Industrial Blvd
- **SaveRite** · 5528 Peachtree Industrial Blvd

Map 42

Map 42 • **North Atlanta East / Silver Lake**

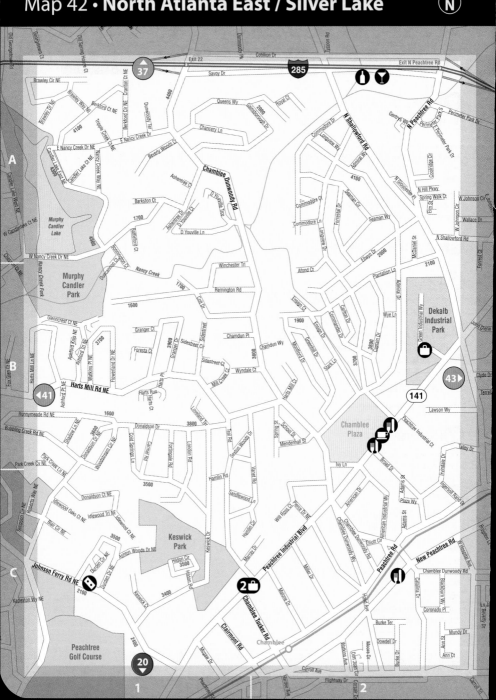

If you're short on space, head to Wallbedzzz for the best selection of hide-a-beds. Oriental Pearl in Chinatown Plaza specializes in seafood prepared Asian-style. Salsa con Sabor cooks up an eclectic blend of Peruvian and Puerto Rican dishes.

Coffee
· **Dunkin' Donuts** · 5558 Peachtree Industrial Blvd

Liquor Stores
· **Winery the NO II** · 2101 Savory Dr

Nightlife
· **Bleachers Sports Bar & Billiards** · 2175 Savoy Dr

Restaurants
· **Athens Pizza House** ·
  5550 Peachtree Industrial Blvd
· **Oriental Pearl** · 5399 New Peachtree Rd
· **Salsa con Sabor** · 5567 Peachtree Industrial Blvd

Shopping
· **Great Estates Antiques and Auctions** ·
  5180 Peachtree Industrial Blvd
· **International Farmers Market** ·
  5193 Peachtree Industrial Blvd
· **Wallbedzzz** · 3838 Green Industrial Wy

Video Rental
· **Hollywood Video** · 2221 Johnson Ferry Rd NE

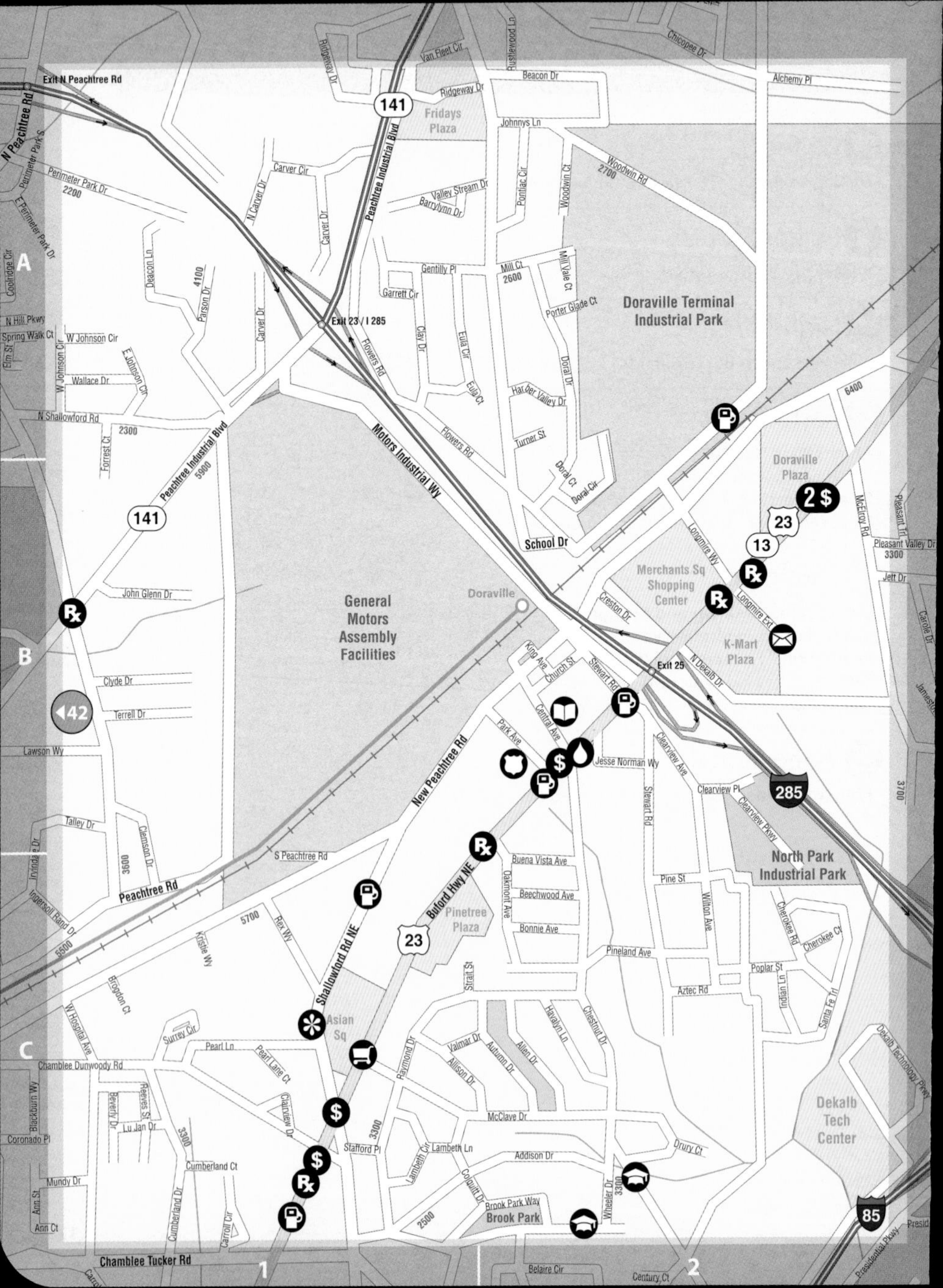

Map 43 · **Chamblee / Doraville**
N

Exit N Peachtree Rd

141

Fridays Plaza

Ridgeway Dr
Beacon Dr
Alchemy Pl
Van Fleet Ct.
Rushwood Ln
Chisopea Dr

N Peachtree Rd
Perimeter Park S
Dunwoody Park S
E Perimeter Park Dr
Perimeter Park Dr. 2200

Carver Cir
N Carver Dr
Carver Cir
Carver Dr

Johnnys Ln
Valley Stream Dr
Barrylynn Dr
Pontiac Dr
Woodwin Ct
Woodwin Dr 2700
Woodwin Rd 2700

Goolhege Dr
N. Hill Pkwy
Spring Walk Ct
W Johnson Cir
W Johnson Dr
E Johnson Dr
Wallace Dr
N Shallowford Rd
Forrest Dr 2300

Deacon Ln
Faison Dr 4100
Carver Dr
Peachtree Industrial Blvd

Gentilly Pl
Garrett Cir
Clay Dr
Euid Dr
Euid Ct
Mill Ct. 2600
Mill Walk Ct
Porter Glade Ct
Doral Dr

A

Exit 23 / I 285

Flowers Rd
Flowers Rd

Turner St
Doral Ct
Doral Cir

Doraville Terminal Industrial Park

6400

McElroy Rd
Pleasant Hill Rd
Pleasant Valley Rd 3300
Jeff Dr
Carnie Dr
Janestown Dr

Motors Industrial Wy

School Dr

Doraville Plaza
2 $
13 23

141

John Glenn Dr

General Motors Assembly Facilities

Doraville

Merchants Sq Shopping Center

Rx

K-Mart Plaza

Rx

B

Rx

42

Clyde Dr
Terrell Dr
Lawson Wy

Talley Dr
Ironwood Dr
Lynburn Dr 3000

S Peachtree Rd
Peachtree Rd

New Peachtree Rd

King Ct
Church St
Church St
Park Ave
Camille Ave

Stewart Rd
Creston Dr
Longmire Ext
Longmire Dr
Exit 25
N Dekalb Dr
Clearway Ave

Jesse Norman Wy
Stewart Rd
Clearview Pl
Clearview Pkwy

285

3700

North Park Industrial Park

Rx
Buena Vista Ave
Oakmont Ave
Beechwood Ave
Bonnie Ave
Pineland Ave
Pine St
Wilton Ave
Aztec Rd
Poplar St
Chamblee Rd
Cherokee Ct
Santa Fe Trl

Ingersoll Rand Dr
W Hospital Ave
Brogdon Ct
Rex Wy
5700
Shallowford Rd NE

Buford Hwy NE
Pinetree Plaza
23

C

Chamblee Dunwoody Rd
Blackburn Wy
Coronado Pl
Beverly Dr
Lu Jan Dr
Reeves St
Chanticleer Dr
Cumberland Dr
Mundy Dr
Ann St
Ann Ct

Krista Wy

Pearl Ln
Surrey Cir
Pearl Lane Ct
Chevron Wy
Cumberland Ct
Carroll Dr

Asian Sq
$
Raymond Dr
Stratt St
Harwell Dr
Hartz Dr
$
Stafford Pl
Rx
Lambert Dr
Lambeth Ln
2300

Valmar Dr
Allison Dr
Autumn Dr
Alan Dr
McClave Dr
Addison Dr
Brook Park Way
Brook Park

Valmar Dr
Chestnut Dr
Harvard Ln
Chamell Rd
Drury Ct
Wheeler Dr

Dekalb Tech Center

Dekalb Technology Pkwy

85

Chamblee Tucker Rd
Century Ct
Belaire Cir

1   2

An international village, Chamblee is home to a wide array of immigrant populations. Here the signs will often be in a language other than English. The area is crowded with pawn shops, nail salons, and ethnic grocery stores. Real estate is still relatively cheap for being so close to the city and major interstates.

Banks
- **Bank of America** · 5001 Buford Hwy NE
- **RBC Centura** · 5424 Buford Hwy NE
- **Southtrust** · 5770 Buford Hwy NE
- **Summit National** · 3490 Shallowford Rd
- **Wachovia** · 5772 Buford Hwy NE

Car Washes
- **Carnett's Auto Appearance Centers** · 5432 Buford Hwy NE

Community Gardens

Gas Stations
- **Chevron** · 4026 Winters Chapel Rd
- **Citgo** · 3666 Shallowford Rd NE
- **Exxon** · 4926 Buford Hwy NE
- **Philips 66** · 5425 Buford Hwy NE
- **Shell** · 5500 Buford Hwy NE

Libraries
- **Doraville Library** · 3748 Central Ave

Pharmacies
- **Collier's Pharmacy** · 5705 Buford Hwy NE
- **CVS (24 hrs)** · 5764 Peachtree Industrial Blvd
- **Family Pharmacy** · 4897 Buford Hwy
- **K-Mart** · 5597 Buford Hwy NE
- **Kim's Pharmacy** · 5280 Buford Hwy NE

Police
- **Doraville Police Department** · 3760 Park Ave

Post Offices
- **US Post Office** · 4700 Longmire Ext

Schools
- **Northwoods Montessori** · 3340 Chestnut Dr
- **Yeshiva Atlanta High** · 3130 Raymond Dr

Supermarkets
- **Ranch 99** · 5150 Buford Hwy NE

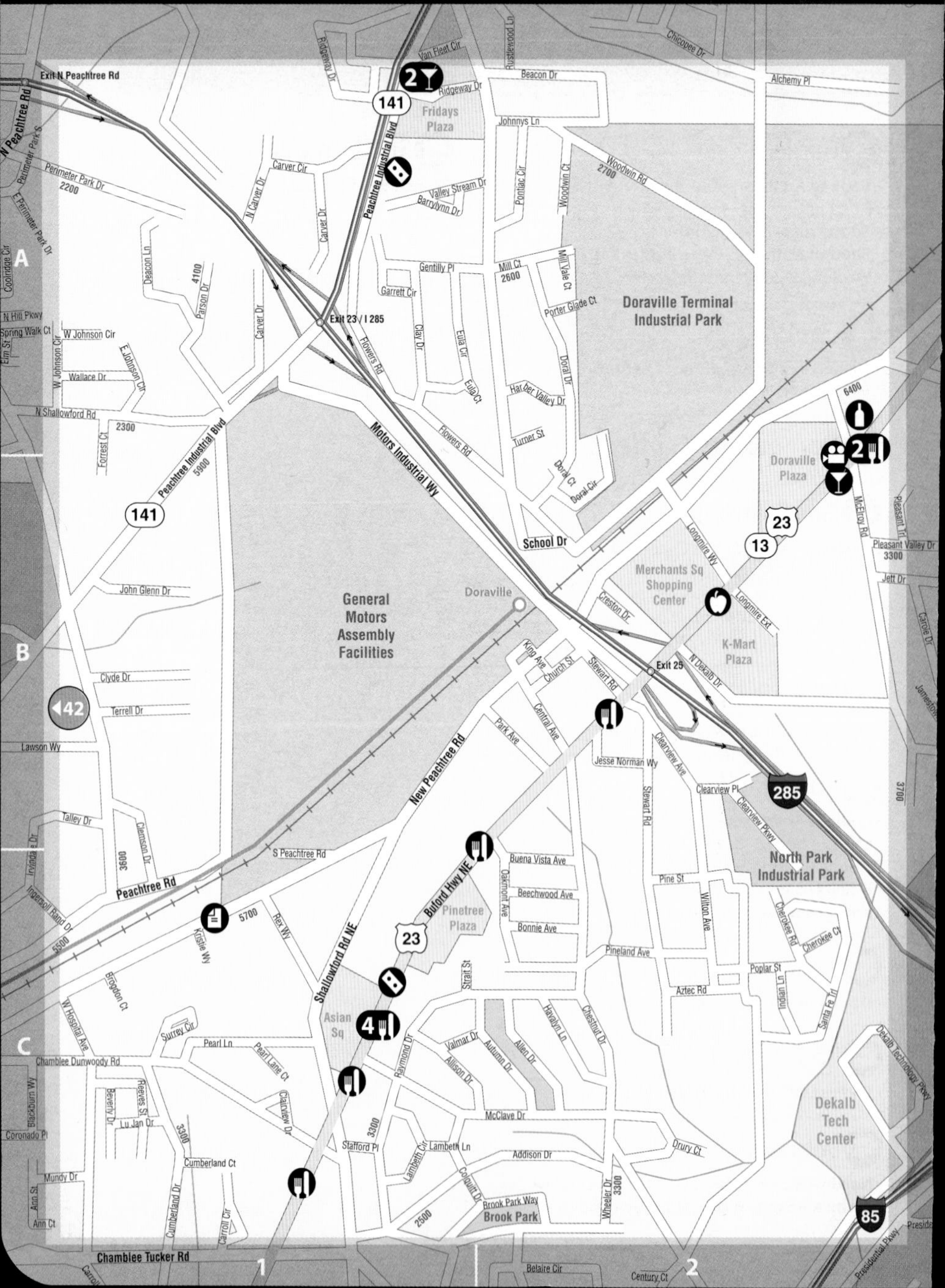

Map 43 · **Chamblee / Doraville**

N

Exit N Peachtree Rd

N Peachtree Rd
Perimeter Park S
E Perimeter Park Dr
Perimeter Park Dr 2200
Coolidge Dr

141
Fridays Plaza
Ridgeway Dr
Van Fleet Cir
Beacon Dr
Alchemy Pl
Chicopee Dr
Birchwood Ln

Carver Cir
N Carver Dr
Carver Dr
Carver Dr
Deason Ln
4100
Parson Dr

Johnnys Ln
Woodrun Rd 2700
Woodrun Dr
Pontiac Dr

Valley Stream Dr
Barrydorm Dr

Gentilly Pl
Garrett Cir
Mill Ct 2600
Mill Vale Ct
Porter Glade Dr

Doraville Terminal Industrial Park

A

N Hill Pkwy
Spring Walk Ct
W Johnson Cir
E Johnson Ct
Wallace Dr
N Shallowford Rd
2300
Forrest Ct

Exit 23 / I 285
Clay Dr
Estia Ct
Eda Ct
Hat Der Valley Dr
Turner St

Flowers Rd

Dena Ct
Bona Cir

6400

Doraville Plaza

2

23
13

McStroy Rd
Pleasant Valley Dr 3300
Pleasant Trl
Jeff Dr

141
Peachtree Industrial Blvd 5900

Motors Industrial Wy

School Dr

John Glenn Dr

General Motors Assembly Facilities

Doraville

Longmire Wy
Longmire Ext
Creston Dr
Merchants Sq Shopping Center

K-Mart Plaza

Exit 25

B

42

Clyde Dr
Terrell Dr
Lawson Wy
Talley Dr

New Peachtree Rd

Kings Ave
Church St
Stewart Rd

Park Ave
Central Ave

Jesse Norman Wy

Clearview Ave
Clearview Pl
Clearview Pkwy

285

North Park Industrial Park

3700

Ingersoll Island Ct
Clemson Dr
9500

S Peachtree Rd

Peachtree Rd
5700
Kristie Wy
Red Wy

Shallowford Rd NE
Buford Hwy NE

Pinetree Plaza
23

Buena Vista Ave
Dahlonega Wy
Beechwood Ave
Bonnie Ave

Pine St
Pineland Ave
Wilson Ave

Poplar St
St Limngo
Aztec Rd

Chamblee Rd
Cherokee Cy

Okaba Technology Pkwy

Surrey Cir
W Hospital Ave
Pearl Ln
Pearl Lane Ct

Asian Sq
4

Raimond Dr
3300
Strait St
Valmar Dr
Allison Dr
Allison Dr

Harold St
Chestnut Dr

Pineland Ave

Dekalb Tech Center

C

Chamblee Dunwoody Rd
Beverly Dr
Reeves St
Lu Jan Ct
3300
Blossom Wy
Coronado Pl

Stafford Pl
Lambeth Ln
Lambeth Ln
2500

McClave Dr
Addison Dr
Conrad Dr
Wheeler Dr 3300
Drury Ct

Mundy Dr
Ann Ct

Cumberland Ct
Cumberland Dr
Carrol Ct

Chamblee Tucker Rd

Brook Park Wy
Brook Park

Betaire Cir

Century Ct

85

1
2

An ethnic food lover's dream come true. Nosh at Toyo Ta Ya's sushi bar for lunch, do dim-sum for dinner at the Oriental Pearl, and satisfy midnight snack attacks at the 24-hour 88 Tofu House. Spicy describes more than the cuisine—a thriving sex industry can be found in those "Asian massage parlors." Good antique shopping is worth the drive.

Copy Shops
· **AAA Digital Imaging** · 5706 New Peachtree Rd

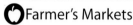Farmer's Markets
· **Buford Highway Farmers Market** ·
5600 Buford Hwy NE

Liquor Stores
· **Tower Beer, Wine, & Spirits** · 5877 Buford Hwy NE

Movie Theaters
· **Buford Highway Twin Theaters** ·
5805 Buford Hwy

Nightlife
· **Barnacles** · 6365 Peachtree Industrial Blvd
· **Oasis Goodtime Emporium** · 6363 Peachtree
Industrial Blvd
· **Rooster's Barnyard** · 5805 Buford Hwy

Restaurants
· **88 Tofu House** · 5490 Buford Hwy NE
· **Bien Thuy** · 5095 Buford Hwy NE
· **El Azteca** · 5800 Buford Hwy NE
· **El Taco Veloz** · 5000 Buford Hwy
· **First China** · 5295 Buford Hwy
· **Hae Woon Dae** · 5805 Buford Hwy NE
· **Little Szechuan** · 5091 Buford Hwy NE
· **Pho Hoa** · 5150 Buford Hwy NE
· **Phung Mie** · 5145 Buford Hwy NE
· **Toyo Ta Ya** · 5082 Buford Hwy NE

Video Rental
· **L&T Vietnamese Videos (Vietnamese)** ·
5150 Buford Hwy NE
· **Rainbow Video (Japanese)** · 6255 Peachtree
Industrial Blvd

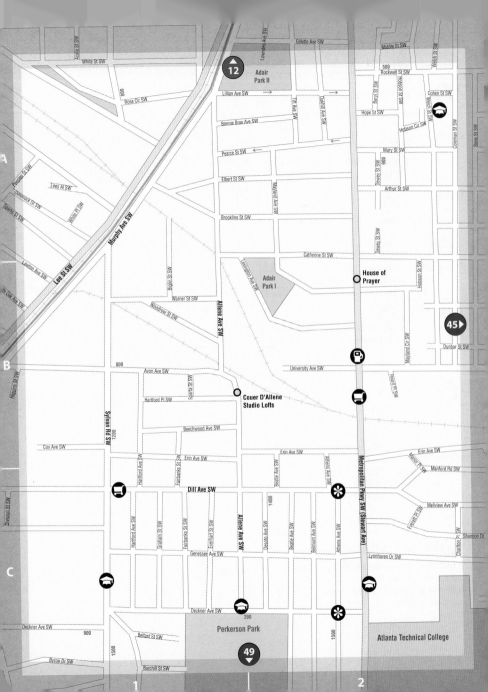

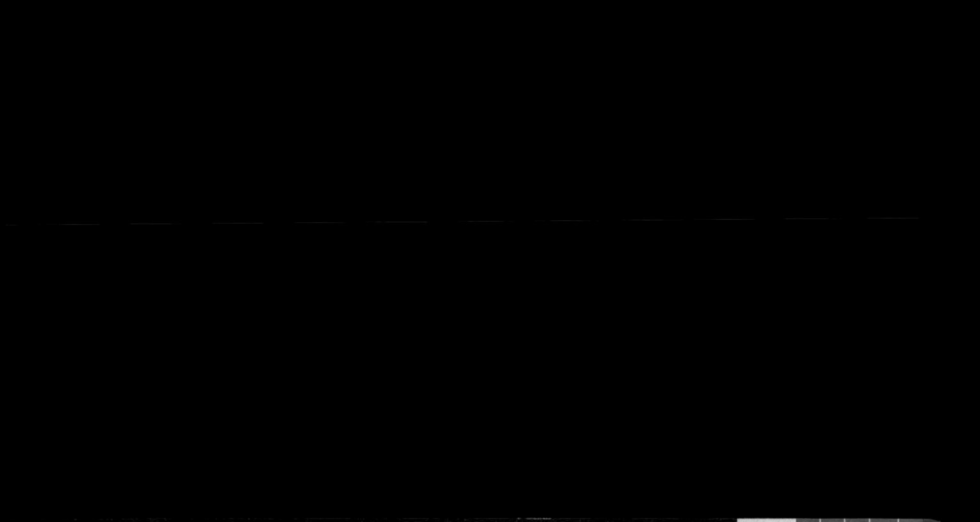

Essentials

Map 44

This struggling neighborhood, which encompasses Capitol View, has plenty of graffiti and package stores, but early signs of revitalization do exist. Case in point—the area's first loft community, Couer D'Allene Studios, has sold out phase one. The notorious House of Prayer, whose pastor went to prison after telling his flock that the Bible instructed them to whip their kids, is a neighborhood fixture.

✪ Community Gardens

🅿 Gas Stations

- **Amoco** · 1163 Metropolitan Pkwy SW

⊙ Landmarks

- **Couer D'Allene Studio Lofts** · 1213 Allene Ave SW
- **House of Prayer** · 1136 Metropolitan Pkwy SW

🏫 Schools

- **Capitol View Elementary** · 1442 Metropolitan Pkwy SW
- **Gideons Elementary** · 897 Welch St SW
- **Lena Jean Campbell Elementary** · 770 Deckner Ave SW
- **Sylvan Hills Middle** · 1461 Sylvan Rd SW

🛒 Supermarkets

- **Chico's Food Mart** · 902 Dill Ave SW
- **Han's Big H Food Store** · 1217 Metropolitan Pkwy SW

Map 44 · **Adair Park**

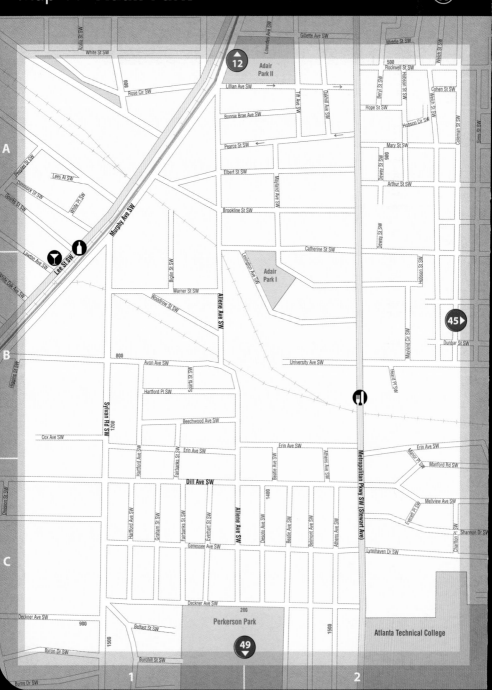

Adair Park II

Adair Park I

Perkerson Park

Atlanta Technical College

Battered and deep-fried dominates this neighborhood's eating establishments. Yag's Soul Food offers some real home cookin'. Little King Lounge is where the homeboys hang out. Perkerson Park Recreation Center offers neighborhood kids a safe haven from the mean streets.

Liquor Stores
· **Li Package Store** · 1061 Lee St SW

Nightlife
· **Little King Lounge** · 1081 Lee St SW

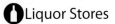Restaurants
· **Yag's Soul Food** · 1219 Metropolitan Pkwy SW

Map 45 · **Pittsburgh**

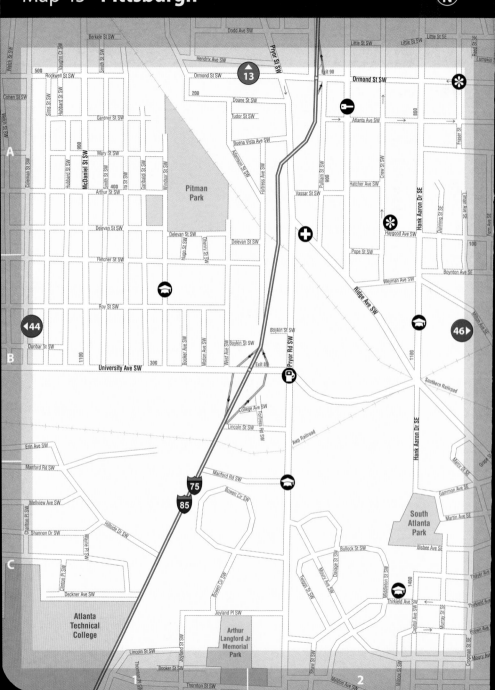

Another struggling South Atlanta community, Pittsburgh has high child poverty and unemployment rates. But thanks to a UPS-affiliated charity, the Annie E. Casey Foundation, this community is seeing the construction of Habitat for Humanity homes, which will hopefully lay the groundwork for a middle-class community to blossom. For urban pioneers, the home prices here are among the lowest in the city.

 Car Rental
· **Ryder** · 875 Washington St NW

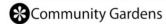 Community Gardens

 Gas Stations
· **Exxon** · 180 University Ave SW

 Hospitals
· **Southside Medical Center** · 21 Thirkield Ave SW

 Schools
· **Lena Jean Campbell Elementary** ·
  21 Thirkield Ave SW
· **Nur Academy** · 1127 Hank Aaron Dr SE
· **Parks Middle** · 1090 Windsor St SW
· **Slater Elementary** · 1320 Pryor Rd

Map 45 · **Pittsburgh**

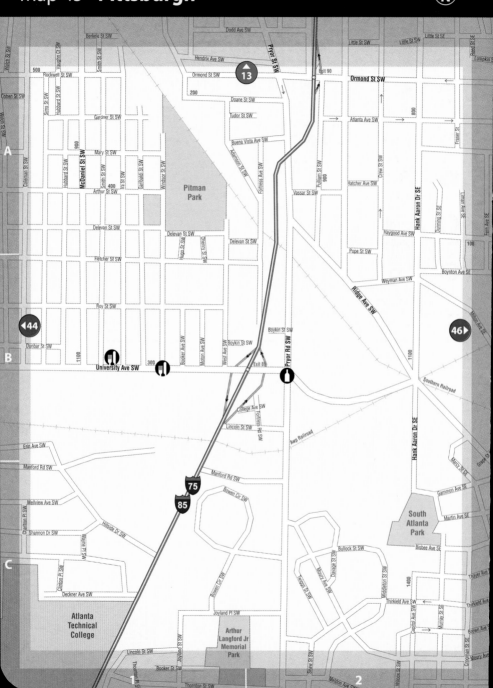

Sundries / Entertainment

12	13	14	15
44	45	46	47	34

48	49
50	51

Map 45

Modest neighborhood restaurants like Brook's Family Restaurant and Oceanfront are located on the neighborhood's main thoroughfare, University Avenue.

 Liquor Stores
- **All American Package Store** · 1238 Pryor Rd SW

 Restaurants
- **Brook's Family Restaurant** ·
  309 University Ave SW
- **Oceanfront** · 355 University Ave SW

Map 46 · **Peoplestown**

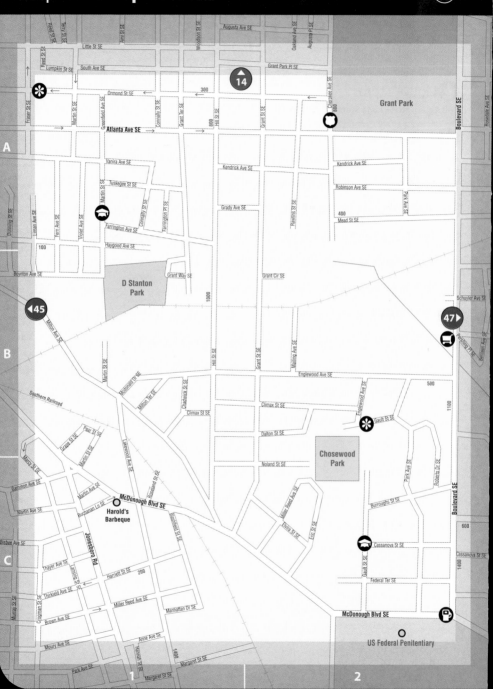

Reed St SE
Reed St Terr SE
Little St SE
Lumpkin St SE
South Ave SE
Augusta Ave SE
Grant Park Pl SE
Oakland Ave SE
Augusta Pl SE
Woodson St SE
SE

14

300

Ormond St SE
Fraser St SE
Martin St SE
Greenfield Ave SE
Connally St SE
Grant Ter SE
Hill St SE
Grant St SE
Chelsea Ave SE
800

Grant Park

Boulevard SE
Rosalind Ave SE

Atlanta Ave SE

A

Vanira Ave SE
Kendrick Ave SE
Kendrick Ave SE
Robinson Ave SE

Dunning St SE
Liman Ave SE
Fern Ave SE
Martin St SE
Tuskegee St SE
Connally St SE
Farrington Pl SE
Grady Ave SE
Rawlins St SE
Park Ave SE

Farrington Ave SE
400
Mead St SE

Voigt Ave SE
Haygood Ave SE

100

Boynton Ave SE
Grant Way SE
Grant Cir SE

**D Stanton
Park**

1000

◄45
Miller Ave SE

47►

Schuyler Ave SE
Pershing Ter SE
Bertram Ave SE

B

Martin St SE
McDonald Dr SE
Milton Ter SE
Chadwick St SE
Hill St SE
Grant St SE
Maling Ave SE
Englewood Ave SE
500
1100

Southern Railroad
Climax St SE
Climax St SE
Climax St SE
Gault St SE

Pear St SE
Grace St SE
Martin St SE
Lakewood Ave SE
Dalton St SE
Englewood Ave SE
Park Ave SE
Roberts Dr SE

Marcy St SE
Noland St SE

Sammon Ave SE
**Chosewood
Park**

Martin Ave SE
Martin St SE
Buchanan Ln SE
Boulevard SE
Bradfield St SE

Bisbee Ave SE
McDonough Blvd SE

**Harold's
Barbeque**
Burroughs St SE
600

C
Jonesboro Rd
Miller Reed Ave SE
Elvira St SE
Eric St SE
Gault St SE
Cassanova St SE
Cassanova St SE
1400

Thayer Ave SE
Harriett St SE
200

Thirkield Ave SE
Coleman St SE
Brown Ave SE
Manhattan Dr SE
Federal Ter SE

Moury Ave SE
SE

Murray St SE
Anne Ave SE
McDonough Blvd SE

P

US Federal Penitentiary

Park Ave SE
Margaret St SE
1400
Margaret St SE

1   **2**

It's never a good sign when the prison is the major landmark in your neighborhood. The US Federal Penitentiary borders the neighborhood, yet there are new residential developments cropping up, though it would take a marketing czar to spin the prison locale as an amenity.

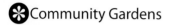 Community Gardens

 Gas Stations
· **Chevron** · 580 McDonough Blvd SE

o Landmarks
· **Harold's Barbeque** · 171 McDonough Blvd SE
· **US Federal Penitentiary** ·
  601 McDonough Blvd SE

Police
· **APD Zone 3 Station** · 880 Cherokee Ave SW

Schools
· **Benteen Elementary** · 200 Casanova St SE
· **DH Stanton Elementary** · 970 Martin St SE

Supermarkets
· **Kaira Food Mart** · 1181 Boulevard SE

Map 46 · **Peoplestown**

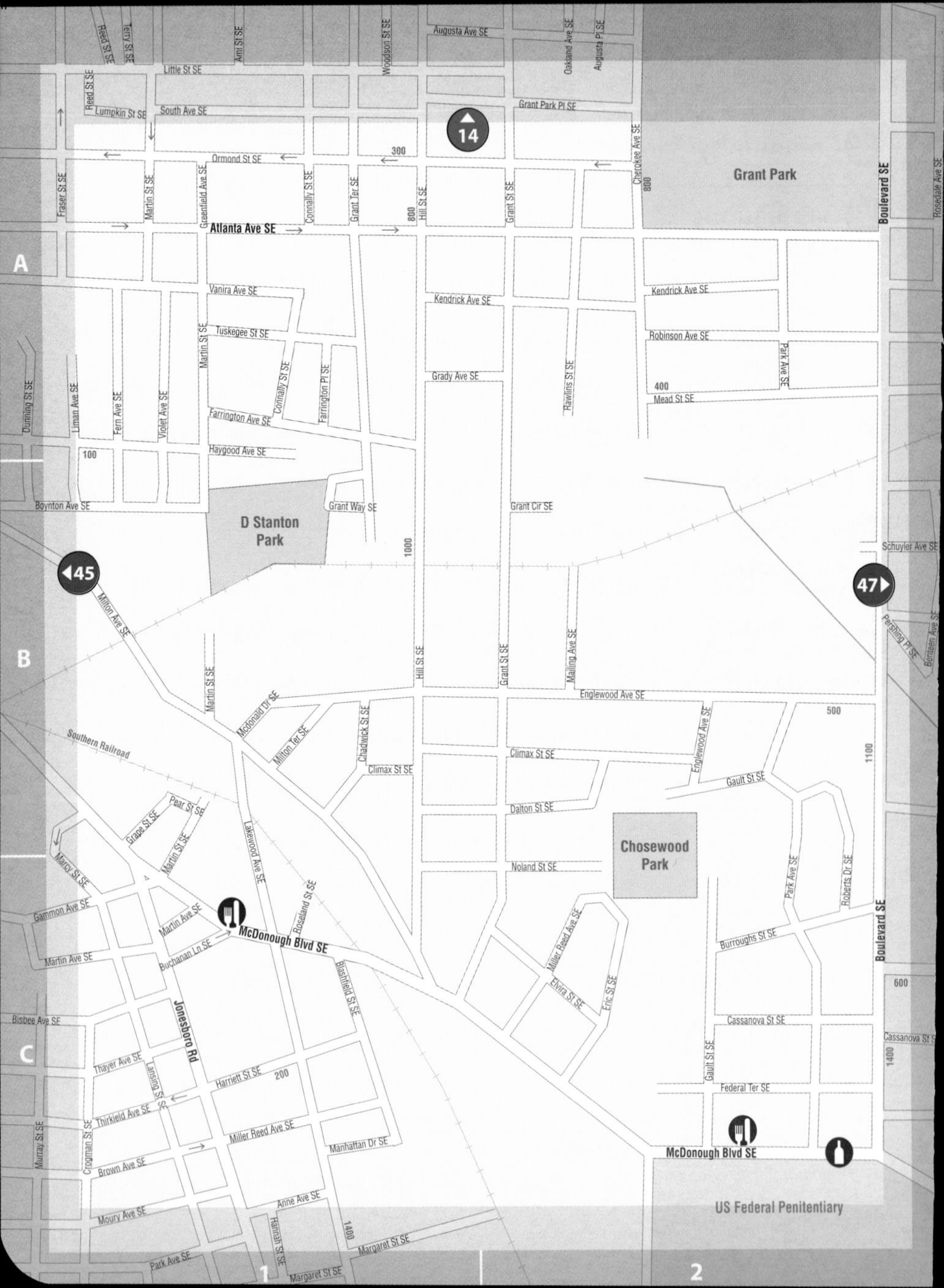

N

Reed St SE
SE IS IS
Terry St SE
Ann St SE
Woodson St SE
Augusta Ave SE
Oakland Ave SE
Augusta Pl SE

Little St SE
Lumpkin St SE
South Ave SE
Grant Park Pl SE

14

300
Ormond St SE
Connally St SE
Grant Ter SE
Hill St SE
Grant St SE
Cherokee Ave SE
800

Grant Park

Fraser St SE
Martin St SE
Greenfield Ave SE
800

Atlanta Ave SE

Boulevard SE
Brookdale Ave SE

A

Vanira Ave SE
Kendrick Ave SE
Kendrick Ave SE

Robinson Ave SE
Park Ave SE

Dunning St SE
Liman Ave SE
Fern Ave SE
Violet Ave SE
Martin St SE
Tuskegee St SE
Connally St SE
Farrington Pl SE

Grady Ave SE
Rawlins St SE

400
Mead St SE

Farrington Ave SE

Haygood Ave SE

100

Grant Way SE
Grant Cir SE

Boynton Ave SE

**D Stanton
Park**

1000

Schuyler Ave SE

◀**45**

Milton Ave SE

47▶

Pershing Pl SE
Benteen Ave SE

B

Martin St SE
McDonald Dr SE
Milton Ter SE
Chadwick St SE
Hill St SE
Grant St SE
Mailing Ave SE

Englewood Ave SE

500

Southern Railroad
Climax St SE
Climax St SE

Climax St SE

Gault St SE

1100

Pear St SE
Grape St SE
Dalton St SE

Englewood Ave SE

Martin St
Martin St SE
Lakewood Ave SE

Noland St SE

**Chosewood
Park**

Park Ave SE
Roberts Dr SE

Marco St SE

Gammon Ave SE

Martin Ave SE
Roseland St SE

Miller Reed Ave SE
Eloir St SE
Eric St SE

Burroughs St SE

Martin Ave SE
Buchanan Ln SE
🍴 **McDonough Blvd SE**

Bisbee Ave SE
Bushfield St SE

Cassanova St SE

Cassanova St SE
1400

C

Thayer Ave SE
Harnett St SE
200
Gault St SE
Federal Ter SE

Croghan St SE
Thirkield Ave SE
Brown Ave SE
Miller Reed Ave SE
Manhattan Dr SE

Murray St SE
Moury Ave SE

🍴 **McDonough Blvd SE** 🚹

Anne Ave SE

SE IS IS

Boulevard SE
600

Park Ave SE
Margaret St SE
Margaret St SE
1400

US Federal Penitentiary

1 | **2**

Sundries / Entertainment

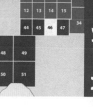

Map 46

Opening a package store just across from the prison (556 Package Store) was a stroke of genius, because when does one need a drink more than when entering or leaving the slammer? Harold's Barbecue is an Atlanta landmark, offering tasty smoked meats and kick-ass Brunswick stew for over 50 years.

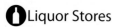 Liquor Stores
• **556 Package Store** • 556 McDonough Blvd SE

 Restaurants
• **El Potosino Restaurant** • 500 McDonough Blvd SE
• **Harold's Barbeque** • 171 McDonough Blvd SE

Map 47 · **Ormewood Park**

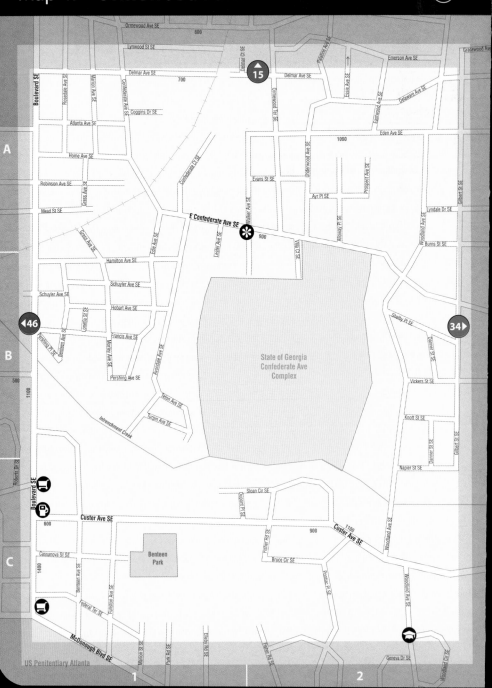

Ormewood Ave SE

800

Lynwood St SE

Gracewood Ave

Emerson Ave SE

Delmar Ave SE

700

Delmar Ave SE

15

Boulevard SE

Rosedale Ave SE

Marion St SE

Confederate Ave SE

Coggins Dr SE

Atlanta Ave SE

Ormewood Ter SE

Pracine Ave SE

Essie Ave SE

Eastwood Ave SE

Delaware Ave SE

Eden Ave SE

1000

Home Ave SE

Underwood Ave SE

Prospect Ave SE

Gilbert St SE

A

Robinson Ave SE

Gress Ave SE

Evans St SE

Mead St SE

Ayr Pl SE

Alleyway Pl SE

Woodland Ave SE

Lyndale Dr SE

Gress Ave SE

Eagle Ave SE

E Confederate Ave SE

Lester Ave SE

Walker Ave SE

900

BMA St SE

Burns St SE

Hamilton Ave SE

Schuyler Ave SE

Schuyler Ave SE

Hobart Ave SE

Shelby Pl SE

Dalmer St SE

46

34

Lonetta St SE

Pershing Pl SE

Benteen Ave SE

Francis Ave SE

Avondale Ave SE

Willow Ave SE

Vickers St SE

B

500

1100

Pershing Ave SE

State of Georgia
Confederate Ave
Complex

Knott St SE

Teton Ave SE

Dalner St SE

Gilbert St SE

Turpin Ave SE

Intrenchment Creek

Napier St SE

Roberts Dr St

Boulevard SE

Sloan Cir SE

Dupont Pl SE

Custer Ave SE

600

Custer Ave SE

Fuller Rd SE

900

1100

Woodland Ave SE

Cassanova St SE

Bruce Cir SE

Pontiac Pl SE

Benteen Ave SE

Funston St SE

Benteen
Park

C

1400

Woodland Ave SE

Federal Ter SE

Marion St SE

Park Rd SE

Foley Rd SE

Fisher Rd SE

Geneva Dr SE

McDonough Blvd SE

US Penitentiary Atlanta

1

2

One of the largest South Atlanta neighborhoods, Ormewood Park is a residential community that features a mixture of Craftsman homes, along with shotgun-style houses and brick bungalows. S.A.N.D. (South Atlantans for Neighborhood Development) is working hard to improve the availability of basic necessities in the area.

Community Gardens

Gas Stations
· **Citgo** · 1362 Boulevard SE

Schools
· **Guice Elementary** · 1485 Woodland Ave SE

Supermarkets
· **Discount Grocery** · 1334 Boulevard SE
· **Franklin Supermarket** · 1460Boulevard SE

Map 47 · **Ormewood Park**

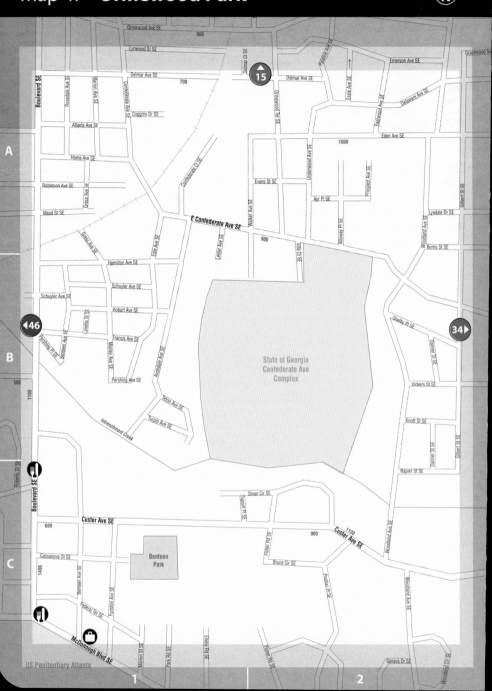

Ormewood Ave SE
800
Lynwood St SE
Delmar Ct SE
Piedmont Ave SE
Gracewood Av
Emerson Ave SE
Delmar Ave SE
700
Delmar Ave SE
Ormewood Ter SE
Eastwood Ave SE
Delaware Ave SE
15
Boulevard SE
Rosedale Ave SE
Marion Ave SE
Confederate Ave SE
Coggins Dr SE
Eden Ave SE
Atlanta Ave SE
A
1000
Underwood Ave SE
Prospect Ave SE
Gilbert St SE
Home Ave SE
Confederate Ct SE
Evans St SE
Walker Ave SE
Robinson Ave SE
Grass Ave SE
Ayr Pl SE
Lyndale Dr SE
Mead St SE
Alloway Pl SE
Woodland Ave SE
Cross Ave SE
E Confederate Ave SE
Mill St SE
Burns St SE
Lester Ave SE
900
Edie Ave SE
Hamilton Ave SE
Schuyler Ave SE
Schuyler Ave SE
Shelby Pl SE
Hobart Ave SE
Tanner St SE
◄46
Lynette Ave SE
Benteen Ave SE
Francis Ave SE
Morley Ave SE
34►
Pershing Ter SE
Avondale Ave SE
Vickers St SE
B
500
1100
Pershing Ave SE
State of Georgia
Confederate Ave
Complex
Knott St SE
Teflin Ave SE
Tanner St SE
Turpin Ave SE
Gilbert St SE
Intrenchment Creek
Napier St SE
Roberts Dr SE
Sloan Cir SE
Lullwater Pl SE
Boulevard SE
Custer Ave SE
600
Woodland Dr SE
1100
Custer Ave SE
Cassanova St SE
Fisher Rd SE
900
Pontiac Pl SE
1400
Benteen Ave SE
Bruce Cir SE
Union Ave SE
C
Benteen
Park
Woodland Ave SE
Woodland Cir SE
Federal Ter SE
Henry Ford Ave SE
Park St SE
Fisher Rd SE
Geneva Dr SE
McDonough Blvd SE
US Penitentiary Atlanta
1
2

Charlie's Trading Post, right near the prison, is where adventurous hipsters head for denim threads and industrial work boots.

Restaurants

· **Cinco de Mayo** · 1332 Boulevard SE
· **Mrs Winner's Chicken & Biscuits** ·
  590 McDonough Blvd SE

Shopping

· **Charlie's Trading Post** · 648 McDonough Blvd SE

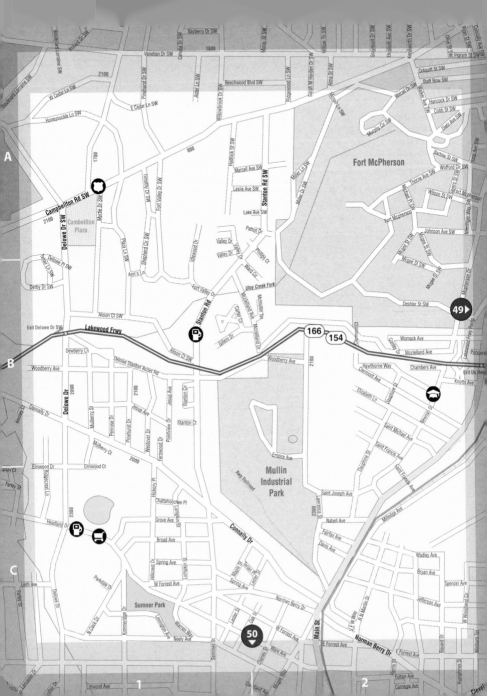

A mile from the airport and a city in itself, East Point is undergoing an urban renewal. Fort McPherson has always been a fixture of the community, providing jobs and industry to the area.

Gas Stations

- **Chevron** · 2091 Headland Dr
- **Citgo** · 2048 Stanton Rd

Police

- **APD Zone 4 Campbellton Road Mini Precinct** · 2000 Campbellton Rd SW

Schools

- **Romar Academy** · 2148 Newnan St

Supermarkets

- **SaveRite** · 2020 Headland Dr

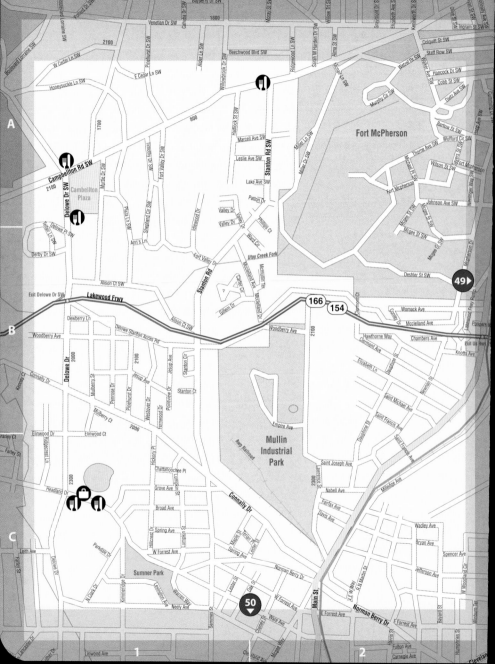

Map 48 · **East Point**

Sundries / Entertainment

Looking for some shag carpeting? Then head to the Carpet Mill Outlet. Restaurants tend to be on the greasy and fried side (Chester Fried Chicken, Philly & Wings). Check out Ida's Country Kitchen and Keur Khadim African Restaurant for a change from the area's primarily fast food options.

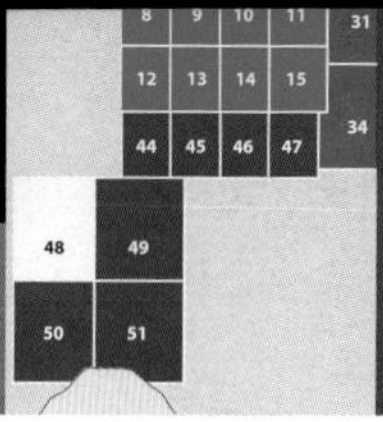

Restaurants

- **Chester Fried Chicken** · 2091 Headland Dr
- **Family Griddle** · 1722 Campbellton Rd SW
- **Ida's Country Kitchen** · 1821 Delowe Dr SW
- **Keur Khadim African Restaurant** ·
  2105 Campbellton Rd SW
- **Philly & Wings** · 2062 Headland Dr

Shopping

- **Carpet Mill Outlet** · 2084 Headland Dr

Map 48

Map 49 • **Sylvan Hills**

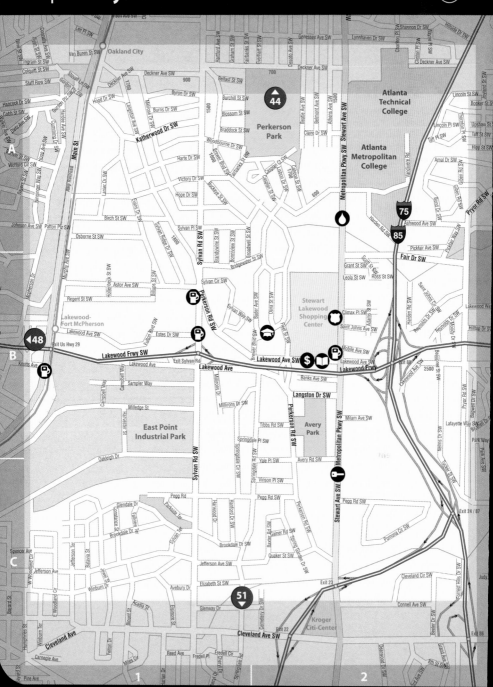

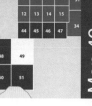
The residential community of this area has to combat lots of low-end commercial businesses, pawn shops, check-cashing places, and package stores, along with the sex industry along Metropolitan Parkway. On the flip side, there's easy access to the city's major interstates and reasonable home prices for bungalow homes with spacious porches. The area is considered one of the last low-priced 'hoods inside the Perimeter.

 Banks
• **Wachovia** • 2891 Lakewood Ave SW

 Car Rental
• **Acceptance Car Rentals** • 2263 Metropolitan Pkwy SW

 Car Washes
• **Inside Out** • 1731 Metropolitan Pkwy SW

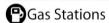 **Gas Stations**
• **Amoco** • 2095 Metropolitan Pkwy SW
• **Chevron** • 2050 Sylvan Rd SW
• **Citgo** • 2139 Main St
• **Philips 66** • 1974 Sylvan Rd SW

 Libraries
• **Stewart-Lakewood Branch** • 2893 Lakewood Ave

 Police
• **APD Zone 3 Metropolitan Parkway Mini Precinct** • 2027 Metropolitan Pkwy SW

 Schools
• **Perkerson Elementary** • 2040 Brewer Blvd SW

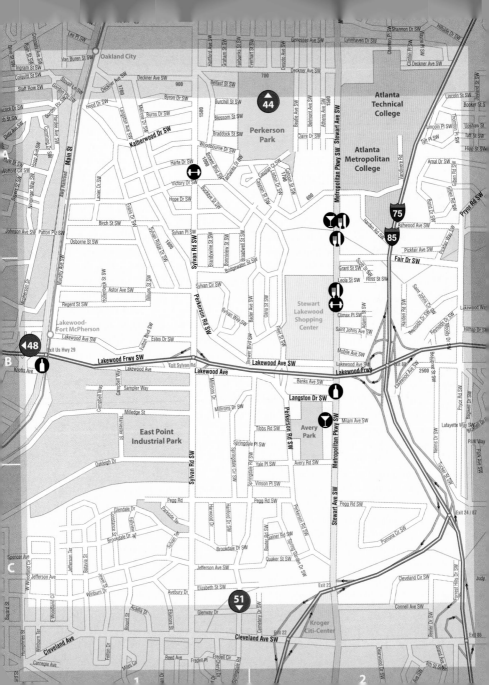

Where you go to be bad, whether it's to find a "date" with one of the ladies of the night or pay a visit to your dealer of "alternative medicine." Club Nikki is a rough strip club. Seedy Metropolitan Parkway and Cleveland Avenue are good places to run into a police sting operation.

Gyms
- **Curves** · 1683 Sylvan Rd SW
- **Run 'n Shoot Athletic Center** · 1959 Metropolitan Pkwy SW

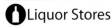Liquor Stores
- **Banks Liquor Store** · 2151 Metropolitan Pkwy SW
- **Track One Package Store** · 2099 Main St

Nightlife
- **Club Nikki** · 1785 Stewart Ave SW
- **FJ's Tavern** · 2202 Metropolitan Pkwy SW

Restaurants
- **Afro Dish** · 1919 Metropolitan Pkwy SW
- **Caribbean Experience Restaurant** · 1747 Metropolitan Pkwy SW
- **Hot Spicy Fast Food** · 1780 Metropolitan Pkwy SW

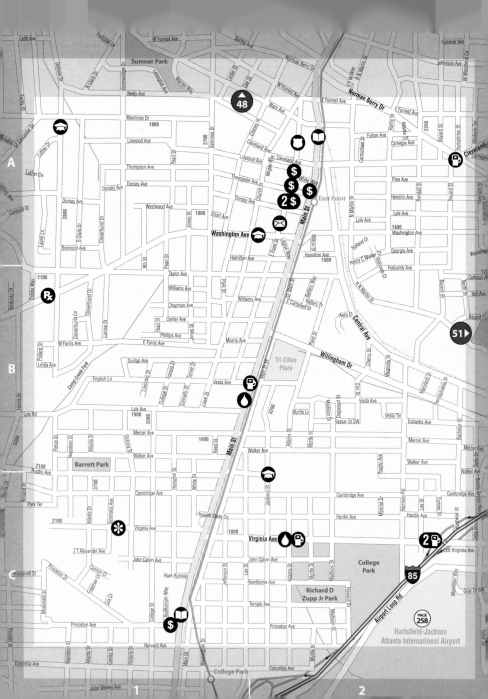

Another neighborhood close to the airport, College Park has long been an industrial center and African-American residential community, but signs of diversification are rising, especially on sleepy Main Street, where new ventures mix in with dusty relics of the past.

$ Banks

- **Bank of America** · 1876 Princeton Ave
- **Bank of America** · 2818 East Point St
- **Citizens Trust Bank** · 2840 East Point St
- **Regions** · 2833 Main St
- **Southtrust** · 2860 East Point St
- **Wachovia** · 2791 East Point St SW

Car Washes

- **K&B Carwash** · 1633 Virginia Ave
- **Minit Car Wash** · 3207 Main St

Community Gardens

Gas Stations

- **Chevron** · 1337 Virginia Ave
- **Citgo** · 1270 Cleveland Ave
- **Shell** · 1338 Virginia Ave
- **Shell** · 1633 Virginia Ave
- **Shell** · 3257 Main St

Libraries

- **College Park Branch** · 3647 Main St
- **East Point Branch** · 2757 Main St

Pharmacies

- **Eckerd** · 3055 Washington Rd

Police

- **East Point Law Enforcement Center** ·
  2727 East Point St

Post Offices

- **US Post Office** · 2905 East Point St

Schools

- **Christ Lutheran** · 2719 Delowe Dr
- **Pathway Christian** · 1706 Washington Ave
- **Woodward Academy** · 1662 Rugby Ave

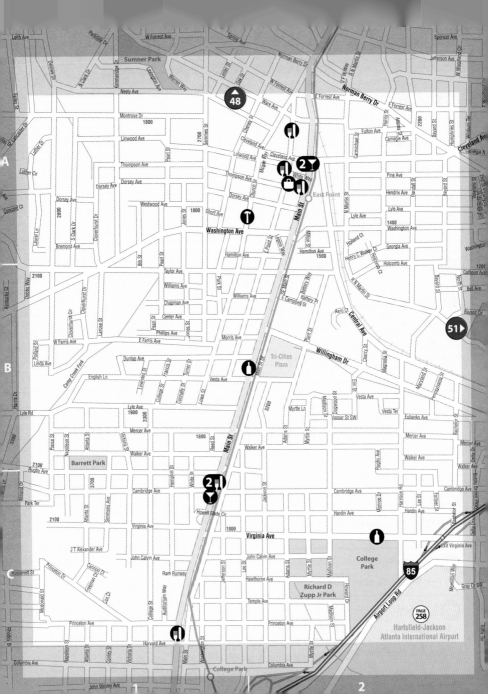

Head to Main Street, across from the old railroad depot and the MARTA station. The Brake Pad features casual eats, and the sophisticated ambience of Oscar's lights up an otherwise sleepy thoroughfare. Patio Daddy-O offers barbecue tofu for a healthy alternative. East Point Antiques is a must for treasure hunters.

Hardware Stores
- **East Point Hardware** · 2891 Church St

Liquor Stores
- **Beverage City Liquor Store** · 1451 Virginia Ave
- **Main Street Package Store** · 3215 Main St

Nightlife
- **The Brake Pad** · 3403 Main St
- **East Point Corner Tavern** · 2783 Main St
- **Main Street Bar & Grill** · 2787 Main St

Restaurants
- **The Brake Pad** · 3403 Main St
- **Kosmos** · 3383 Main St
- **Liz and Lee's Live** · 1613 White Way St
- **Matilda Bean** · 1603 White Way
- **Oscar's** · 3725 Main St
- **Patio Daddy-O** · 2714 East Point St

Shopping
- **East Point Antiques** · 1595 White Way

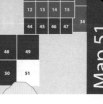
The airport outpost of Atlanta has long been a forgotten community. However, due to its proximity to Hartsfield, there are plenty of Delta and Airtran employees that call this place home (when they're not flying). Hence a bit of sophistication around the rough edges of this primarily industrial area, along with plenty of car mechanics and storage facilities.

Banks

- **Bank of America** · 2685 Metropolitan Pkwy SW
- **Regions** · 600 S Central Ave
- **Wachovia** · 590 S Central Ave

Car Rental

- **Enterprise** · 3080 Sylvan Rd

Gas Stations

- **BP** · 610 Spring St
- **Citgo** · 501 N Central Ave
- **Citgo** · 655 Cleveland Ave SW
- **Citgo** · 971 Virginia Ave
- **Marathon** · 2685 Beeler Dr SW
- **Philips 66** · 2711 Metropolitan Pkwy
- **Philips 66** · 816 S Central Ave
- **Shell** · 751 N Central Ave

Hospitals

- **South Fulton Medical Center** · 1170 Cleveland Ave

Libraries

- **Hapeville Branch** · 525 King Arnold St

Parking

Pharmacies

- **Chapman Drug** · 615 N Central Ave
- **CVS** · 1043 Cleveland Ave
- **CVS** · 2720 Metropolitan Pkwy SW
- **Eckerd** · 437 N Central Ave
- **Kroger** · 2685 Metropolitan Ave SW

Police

- **Hapeville Police Department** · 700 Doug Davis Dr

Post Offices

- **US Post Office** · 650 S Central Ave

Schools

- **Hutchinson Elementary** · 650 Cleveland Ave SW

Supermarkets

- **Kroger** · 2685 Metropolitan Pkwy SW

Map 51 • **Hapeville**

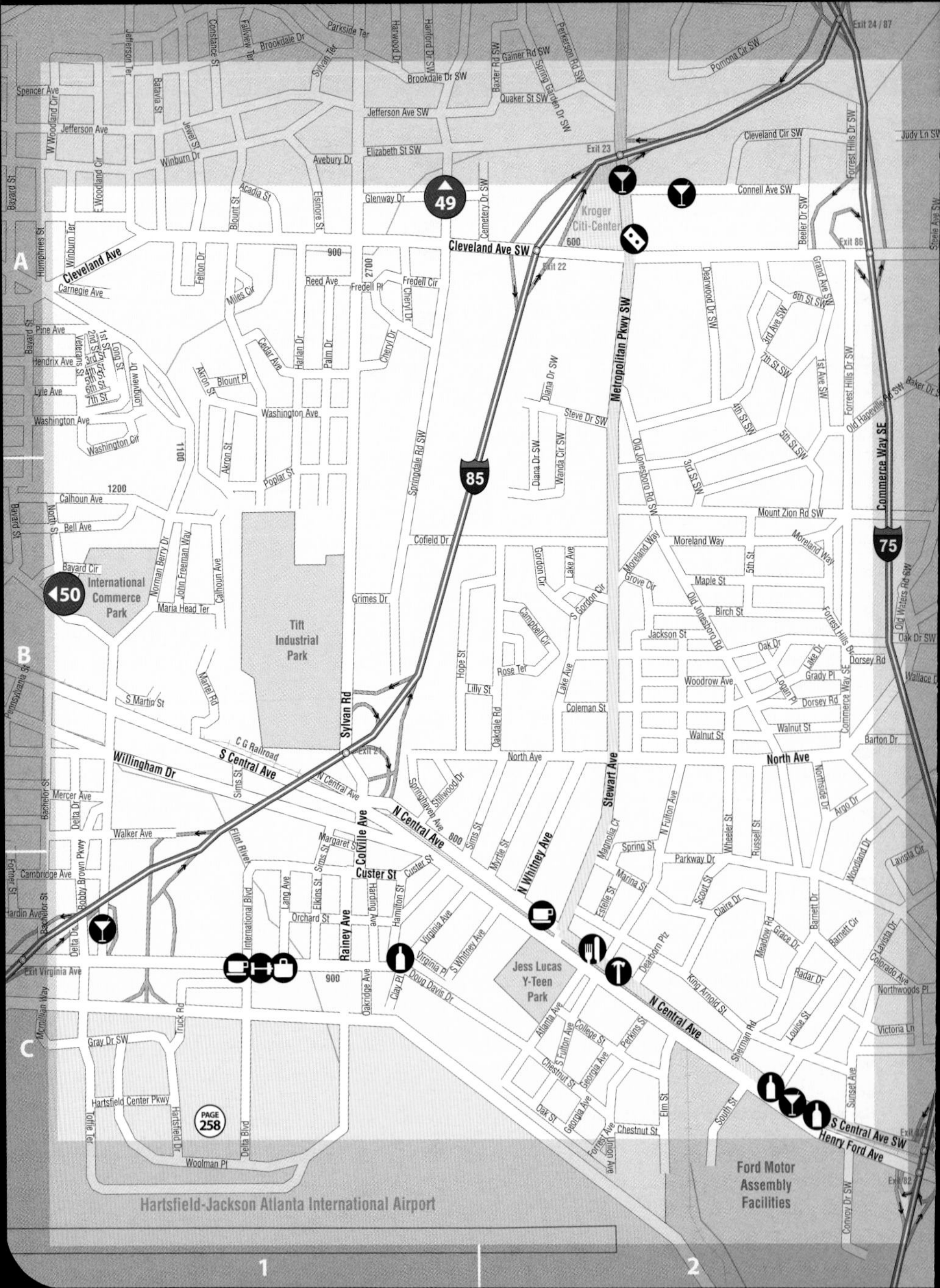

N

Parkside Ter
Spencer Ave
Jefferson Ave
W Woodland Ave
W Woodland Dr
Brookdale Dr
Brookdale Dr SW
Jefferson Ave SW
Quaker St SW
Baxter Rd SW
Gainer Rd SW
Spring Dr SW
Peachtree Rd SW
Pomona Cir SW
Exit 24 / 87

Winburn Dr
Avebury Dr
Elizabeth St SW
Cleveland Cir SW
Judy Ln SW
Bayard St
Winburn Ter
Humphries St
Acadia St
Glenway Dr
Cemetery Dr SW
Exit 23
Connell Ave SW
Beeler Dr SW
Forrest Hills Dr SW

49

Kroger
Citi-Center

Exit 86

A

Cleveland Ave
Carnegie Ave
Felton St
Miles Cir
Reed Ave
2700
Fredell Rd
Fredell Cir
Cherry St
Palm Dr
Cleveland Ave SW
Exit 22
500
600
Metropolitan Pkwy SW
Old Dixie Way SW
6th St SW
Deerwood Dr SW
Stone St SW

Pine Ave
Hendrix Ave
Lyle Ave
Washington Ave
Washington Cir
1st Ave
Longview Dr
Cedar Ave
Harlan Dr
Washington Ave
Poplar St
Afton St
Blount Pl
1100
Springdale Rd SW
Diana Dr SW
Wenda Cir SW
Steve Dr SW
Old Jonesboro Rd SW
5th St SW
3rd St SW
6th St SW
Sun Valley Dr SW
5th St SW
Sun Valley Dr
Way SW

Calhoun Ave
Bell Ave
1200
S Bayard St
Cofield Dr
Gordon Dr
Lake Ave
Mount Zion Rd SW
Moreland Way
5th St
Moreland Way
Commerce Way SE
75

◄150
Bayard Cir
International
Commerce
Park
Norman Berry Dr
John Freeman Way
Maria Head Ter
Calhoun Dr
Grimes Dr
Campbell Dr
S Gordon Cir
Grove Cir
Maple St
Birch St
Old Jonesboro Rd SW
Forrest Hills Rd SW
Oak Dr SW

B
Tift
Industrial
Park
S Martin St
Maret Rd
Hope St
Lilly St
Rose Ter
Jackson St
Oak Ave
Woodrow Ave
Lake Cir
Grady Pl
Dorsey Rd
Dorsey Rd
Barton Dr

C G Railroad
Willingham Dr
S Central Ave
Exit 2
Sylvan Rd
Oakdale Rd
North Ave
Coleman St
Walnut St
Stewart Ave
Walnut St
North Ave
Northside Dr

Sims St
N Central Ave
Springdale Dr
Sedalwood Dr
Murray St
Sims St
800
N Fulton Ave
Magnolia Ct
Spring St
Marina St
Parkway Dr
Scout St
Clara Pl
Barnett Dr
Laurel Cir

Mercer Ave
Bachelor Ave
Delta Dr
Walker Ave
Flint River St
Margaret St
Custer St
Hamilton St
N Central Ave
Colville Ave
N Whitney Ave
Estelle Dr
Clarmon Plz
Meadow Rd
King Arnold St
Grace Dr
Radar Rd
Colorado Ave
Northwoods Dr

Cambridge Ave
Hardin Ave
Delta Dr
Exit Virginia Ave
International Blvd
Orchard St
Rainey Ave
Oakridge Ave
900
Virginia Ave
N Whitney Ave
Clara Pl
Virginia Ave
Doug Davis Dr
Jess Lucas
Y-Teen
Park
N Central Ave
Sherman Rd
Louise St
Victoria Ln

C
McMillan Way
Gray Dr SW
Truck Rd
Delta Blvd
Hartsfield Center Pkwy
PAGE 258
Atlanta Ave
S Station Ave
College St
Chestnut St
George Ave
Perkins St
Oak St
Forrest Ave
Georgia Ave
Chestnut St
Elm St
South St
S Central Ave SW
Henry Ford Ave
Sunset Ave
Conroy Dr SW
Exit

Woolman Pl
Hartsfield-Jackson Atlanta International Airport
Ford Motor
Assembly
Facilities

85
I-75

1   **2**

Map

48 49
50 51

For the most sophisticated spot you will find in Hapeville, head to 623, the upscale restaurant on the main square that offers New American cuisine. B-52's offers a lively karaoke scene. Crystal Palace and Goldrush Show Bar, somewhat seedy Southside strip clubs, are one way to make time fly when your flight gets delayed.

Coffee
- **Perk Place** · 673 N Central Ave
- **Wing Walkers Coffee Shop** · 1003 Virginia Ave

Gyms
- **Olympus Gym** · 1001 Virginia Ave

Hardware Stores
- **Tri-City True Value** · 597 N Central Ave

Liquor Stores
- **Ace Package** · 409 N Central Ave
- **Crest Liquors** · 371 N Central Ave
- **Virginia Curve Liquor Store** · 856 Virginia Ave

Nightlife
- **B-52's** · 3420 Norman Berry Dr
- **Central Station** · 387 N Central Ave
- **Crystal Palace** · 502 Connell Ave SW
- **Goldrush Show Bar** · 2608 Metropolitan Pkwy SW

Restaurants
- **623** · 623 N Central Ave

Shopping
- **M3** · 996 Virginia Ave

Video Rental
- **Blockbuster** · 2685 Metropolitan Pkwy SW

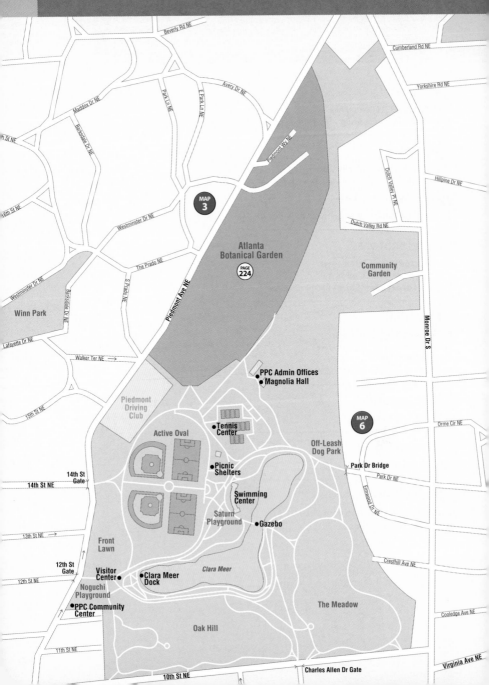

General Information

NFT Maps: 3 & 6
Address: Piedmont Park Conservatory
            400 Park Dr NE
            Atlanta, GA 30306
Website: www.piedmontpark.org
Phone: 404-875-7275
Hours: 6 am-11 pm daily

Overview

If the SAT analogy was: New York: Central Park, Atlanta: _____, the only possible answer would be Piedmont Park. It is by far the most beloved, popular, and well-kept park in the city. Whether you are looking to bake, bike, skip, skate, play tennis, or simply play, Piedmont Park will make you happy.

Georgia's first ever football game, featuring the University of Georgia vs. Auburn, was played in the park in 1892. Hunker down hairy dawgs! In 1895, the Cotton States and International Exposition, a "Southern" World's Fair, visited the park and so did President Grover Cleveland. The park was also home to the Atlanta Crackers baseball team from 1902 until 1904 (the Crackers won 17 pennants). In 1969, love came to town when some hippies decided to host a giant love-in complete with a free Allman Brothers concert.

In addition to good historical company, you will also find yourself in the company of the many homeless people who linger in the park. While harmless for the most part, Atlanta's homeless can be rather assertive, so don't be surprised if you are approached.

Activities & Events

One hundred years after its foundation, the triangular-shaped park is home to standard park fare: playgrounds (including a great playground designed by Japanese artist Isamu Noguchi), community gardens, tennis courts, a historic stone bathhouse, a swimming center, covered picnic areas, and an off-leash dog park. There are ball fields available for baseball and soccer. For the able angler, Lake Clara Meer is routinely stocked with large mouth bass, crappie, bream, and catfish, although we don't advise eating fish from the lake. "Catch and release" is our motto!

Planned additions to the park include more ball fields, sandy volleyball courts, and a running track; until then, joggers can choose between a 2.75-mile grassy trail around the perimeter of the park and a 1.2-mile paved circle around Lake Clara Meer.

The park is also used for organized events including the Dogwood Festival (April 8-10; www.dogwood.org) and Gay Pride celebrations (June 24-26; www.atlantapride.org), as well as musical performances. Turner Classic Movies hosts Screen on the Green—free movies on The Meadow during the summer. And just in case you doubt that Atlanta is the "New York of the South," check out Shake at the Lake during May, the ATL's version of Shakespeare in the Park.

Piedmont Park Conservancy Community Center

1071 Piedmont Ave, 404-876-4024
The Piedmont Park Conservancy Community Center, located next to the 12th Street Gate on Piedmont Avenue, serves as the headquarters for all community programs in Piedmont Park. From yoga to acting to photography, the center offers classes and activities for the youngest to the oldest Atlanta residents. Classes usually cost between $5 and $15, with discounts for PPC members. Check the website for a current schedule of activities and program fees.

How to Get There—Driving

Parking is not allowed in the park, which makes driving there a rather frustrating situation.

From GA 400 S, merge onto I-85 S. Exit at 10th-14th Streets. Go straight through the traffic light at the end of the ramp, crossing 14th Street. Stay to the left when the road splits and at the next traffic light, turn left at 10th Street.

From I-75/I-85 N, exit at 10th-14th Streets. Turn right on 10th Street. Follow 10th Street to Monroe Drive. Turn left onto Elmwood Drive NE, then left onto Park Drive NE.

If you're taking surface roads, head south on Piedmont Avenue towards Midtown and turn left onto Monroe Drive. Take Monroe to 10th Street and turn right. The park will be on your right.

How to Get There—Mass Transit

The Midtown MARTA stop is a ten-minute walk from the park. Walk east (right) on 10th Street toward the park.

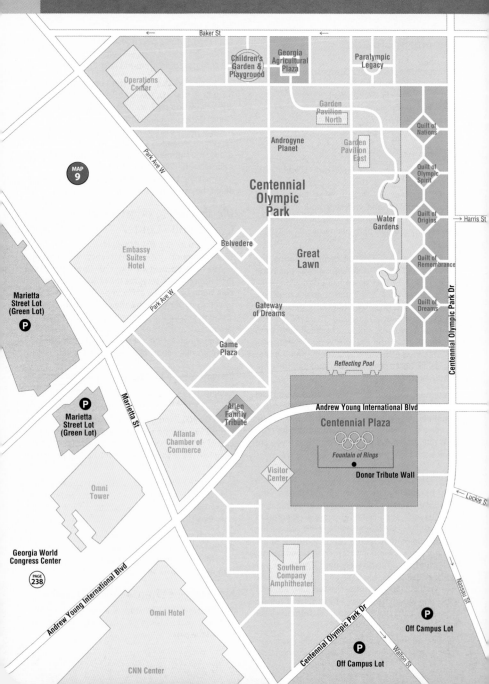

General Information

NFT Map:	9
Address:	265 Park Ave West NW
	Atlanta, GA 30313
Phone:	404-222-7275
Website:	www.centennialpark.com
Hours:	7 am-11 pm daily
Admission:	Free

Overview

The 1996 Olympics were the biggest thing to happen to Atlanta since it was burned to the ground by Sherman in 1864; Muhammad Ali came to town, Bill Clinton was around, and Michael Johnson wore those smashing gold shoes. A nail bomb killed one person and injured 110 but, according the official Olympic website, "the Atlanta Games are best remembered for their sporting achievements." Right.

Regardless, Atlanta did deliver an impressive games and a $2.5 million, 21-acre park—Centennial Olympic Park. Following the games, the grass and granite plaza was temporarily closed, redesigned for public use, and re-opened in 1998 as the largest US city park to be created in the past twenty years.

One of the park's major attractions is bricks—many Atlantans purchased and dedicated bricks to help offset the cost of construction. But the biggest attraction, by far, is the Fountain of Rings. In the summer months you'll see hoards of kids triggering the jets and generally getting soaked by the world's largest interactive fountain. If you don't feel like getting wet, you can sit and watch the Fountain Show, where the water is synchronized to music and lighting (12:30 pm, 3:30 pm, 6:30 pm, and 9 pm daily).

The PR pundits would have you believe that the park is "one of Atlanta's biggest tourist attractions and a popular destination for families and first dates." During the day, there's not a whole lot to do in the park besides basking in the fading aura of athletic greatness, playing in the fountain, or searching for the names of people you know on the bricks. From time to time, however, there are some interesting events held in the park.

Ice Skating Rink

The only outdoor skating rink in Atlanta is in Centennial Olympic Park. The rink is located at the north end of the park and features a canopy for protection from the elements, theatrical lighting on the ice, and decorative lighting in the surrounding trees. The rink is open only for the holidays from late November to early January. Check the website for up-to-date opening hours and admission fees.

Events in the Park

There are many events held in the park throughout the year. Some regular features include:

- **Music at Noon**: Tuesday and Thursday; 12 pm-1 pm during the spring season. Musical groups perform jazz, blues, and R&B in the amphitheater free of charge.
- **NuSoul Concert Series**: First Tuesday of the month; 5:30 pm-8 pm. Free poetry readings, hip hop, funk, and R&B performances.
- **On the Bricks**: Friday nights, May-August. Headlining bands (like Creed, Live, and Train) perform outdoors for a nominal fee (usually $5). www.onthebricks.com
- **Fourth of July Celebration**: Fireworks sensation.
- **Holiday in Lights**: Who needs snow when you have a park full of marvelous lights and shiny decorations.

How to Get There—Driving

From I-75/85 N, get off at Andrew Young International Boulevard (Exit 248C). Turn left onto Andrew Young International Boulevard, then turn right on Marietta Street. The Green Lot will be on the left, across the street from Embassy Suites.

From I-75/85 S, take the Williams Street exit (249C). Turn right onto Alexander Street, left on Marietta Street.

If you take I-20 E, get off at Spring Street (Exit 56B). Turn left onto Spring Street, then left onto Marietta Street. From I-20 W, take the Spring Street exit (56B). Turn right onto Spring Street, then left onto Marietta Street.

Parking

The closest lot is the Green Lot, which costs $6 per day. Parking is also available in other lots around the perimeter of the park.

How to Get There—Mass Transit

Take the MARTA West Line to the Phillips Arena/Dome/GWCC Station (W-1), or take the North Line to Peachtree Center (N-1), and follow signs to the park.

Euclid Ave NE

Clifton Ter NE

North Ave NE

Muriel Ave NE

Oakdale Rd NE

Candler Park
Golf Course

Terrace Ave NE

Page Ave NE

Benning Pl NE

Candler Park Dr NE

MAP
31

Marlbrook Dr NE

Golf
Center

Tennis
Courts

Soccer Field

Miller Ave NE

Callan Cir NE

Pool

Candler Park

McLendon Ave NE

Mell Ave NE

Sheppard Pl NE

Glendale Ave NE

Brooks Ave NE

Iverson St NE

Iverson St NE

Iverson Park

General Information

NFT Map:	31
Address:	585 Candler Park Dr NE
	Atlanta, GA 30307
Phone Numbers:	404-817-6757 (Reservations)
Website:	www.candlerpark.org
Park Hours:	6 am-11 pm daily

Overview

There's more dirt than grass, and more potholes than cement at Candler Park. The "au natural terrain" is either unkempt or charming, depending on your view. Biking and rollerblading can be challenging. Walking and running are manageable, and many of the trails in Candler Park meet up with the nearby Freedom Park paths. At 55 acres, Candler is quite large, but there's a special neighborhood quality that makes the park feel more intimate than Piedmont.

The Candler Park neighborhood is filled with small, privately-owned businesses, restaurants, and bars. We recommend chowing down on biscuits and apple butter at the Flying Biscuit, which will later require heading to the park for a couple of laps. Other park fun can be found on the tennis courts, playgrounds, picnicking pavilions, outdoor basketball courts, or in the swimming pool. Plenty of undeveloped woods are also available for public use. Oh, and don't forget the golf course—9 cheap holes of urban extreme golf: great for beginners, terrible for golf snobs.

Reservations

If you're planning on using one of the two pavilions with grills, you'll need to make a reservation with Atlanta's Bureau of Parks on 404-817-6757. If you're planning on playing an organized game of soccer or football, you'll also need to call the Bureau to make a reservation. The lovely tennis courts, however, are available on a first-come, first-served basis.

Swimming Pool

1500 McLendon Ave NE, 404-373-4849
The outdoor swimming pool is managed and operated by the Candler Park Pool Association (CPPA). In order to extricate control from the city, the CPPA had to invite pool subscribers to offset some of its operational costs. In return, subscribers are afforded exclusive swimming times throughout the week. At all other times, the pool is open to the general public. The privatization of pool management has seen some vast improvements in maintenance, cleanliness, and refreshment stocks.

Swim times are as follows:

Mon – Fri:	9 am-10 am	Subscribers swim
Mon – Fri:	10 am-1 pm	Free swim
Mon – Fri:	1 am-5 pm	Pay swim
Sat:	10 am-5 pm	Pay swim
Sun:	12 pm-5 pm	Pay swim
Every Day:	5 pm-8:30 pm	Subscriber swim

In 2004, the cost for "pay swim" times was $1 for children and $3 for everyone over 16. Costs for subscription were $75 for seniors, $125 for adults, $175 for two adults living at the same address, $225 for two adults and one child, and $250 for two adults and two or more children. For 2005 season rates and to subscribe, call 404-373-4849.

Candler Park Golf Course

585 Candler Park Dr NE, 404-371-1260
The park's nine-hole golf-course is open to the public and costs $7-$10 per game. Atlanta residents play for less. (Note: The golf course is fun and easy, but not particularly well-maintained. In other words, you get what you pay for.)

How to Get There—Driving

From the north, take I-85 to the North Avenue exit. Turn left and drive through the light at Moreland Avenue. Freedom Park will be on your right. Drive through two stop signed intersections and turn right (it's a dead end so you won't have a choice). On your left will be the world famous Candler Park Master's Links Country Club (a.k.a. our own little nine-hole public course) and Candler Park.

From the south, east, or west, take I-20 to the Moreland Avenue exit and head north. (If you're coming from the east, there is only one Moreland Avenue exit. If you're coming from the west, there are two, and you'll want the second one.) Drive through five stop lighted intersections. Keep going through the tunnel under the railroad tracks to the next stoplight. Turn right onto McLendon Avenue and you'll be in Candler Park.

Parking

Your best bet is to make use of the large, free parking lot across the street from McLendon Avenue. Street parking is often available as well.

How to Get There—Mass Transit

Take MARTA to the Candler Park/Edgewood Station, located on DeKalb Avenue. Walk north (to the right) up Oakdale Road.

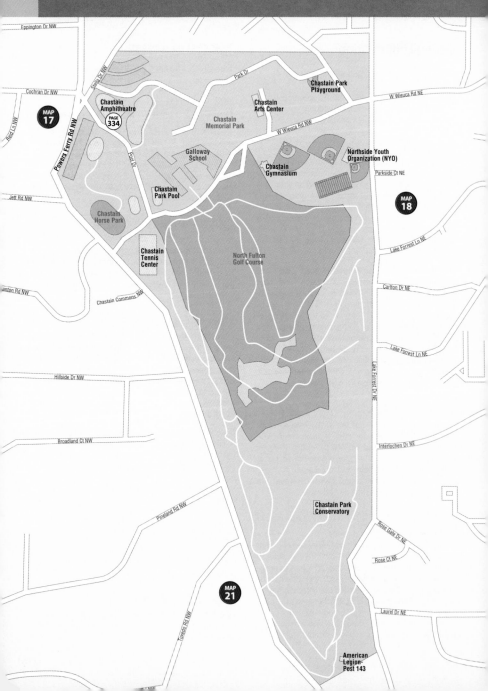

Eppington Dr NW

Cochran Dr NW

Park Dr

Chastain Park
Playground

W Wieuca Rd NE

MAP
17

Scott Dr NW

Powers Ferry Rd NW

Reid Ln NW

Chastain
Amphitheatre

PAGE
334

Chastain
Arts Center

Chastain
Memorial Park

W Wieuca Rd NW

Pool Dr

Galloway
School

Chastain
Gymnasium

Northside Youth
Organization (NYO)

Parkside Ct NE

Jeff Rd NW

Chastain
Park Pool

MAP
18

Chastain
Horse Park

Lake Forrest Ln NE

Chastain
Tennis
Center

North Fulton
Golf Course

Carlton Dr NE

anton Rd NW

Chastain Commons NW

Lake Forrest Ln NE

Hillside Dr NW

Lake Forrest Dr NE

Broadland Ct NW

Interlochen Dr NE

Chastain Park
Conservatory

Pineland Rd NW

Rose Gate Dr NE

Rose Ct NE

MAP
21

Laurel Dr NE

American
Legion-
Post 143

General Information

NFT Map: 17 & 18
Address: 135 W Wieuca Rd NW
             Atlanta, GA 30327
Website: www.chastainparkconservancy.com

Overview

Atlanta is teeming with urban parks, each one with a unique neighborhood feel; lots of yuppy people live near Chastain Park, so lots of yuppy people can be found there.

If you are looking for outdoor privacy, the Troy G. Chastain Memorial Park gets the job done—at 262 acres, Chastain is Atlanta's largest park, with many undeveloped areas. If you don't live nearby and use the park on a regular basis, you might find yourself visiting the main attraction at Chastain: a 6,000-seat outdoor amphitheater. This is where the locals go to sip champagne and listen to the symphony, but every now and then the six-pack crowd shows up for ZZ Top.

The park contains one of the few children's playgrounds in the area, and is home to other creatures including foxes, great horned owls, deer, and coyotes. If you're after some physical activity, the park houses a golf course, tennis center, basketball courts, baseball fields, a swimming pool, and numerous walking and running paths.

North Fulton Golf Course

216 W Wieuca Rd NE, 404-255-0723
One of Chastain Memorial Park's biggest attractions is the beautifully kept 18-hole North Fulton Golf Course. Formerly home to a pre-Masters PGA tournament, the course is now open to the public for $34 per person during the week and $41 per person on the weekends. Don't be intimidated if you're not a pro—golfers of all levels swing their clubs here. The signature hole is #18, a 446-yard par 4. The course is open year-round, but remember that no tank tops or cut-offs are allowed, even in the summer.

Chastain Arts Center & Gallery

135 W Wieuca Rd, 404-252-2927 (art center); 404-257-1804 (art gallery)
The art gallery, open Tuesday-Saturday from 1 pm-5 pm, puts on a host of edgy exhibitions, which are always free and open to the public. The art center also runs year-round art classes for amateur artists, including pottery, ceramics, jewelry making, glasswork, drawing, and painting courses, and a summer art camp for kids.

Outdoor Amphitheater

4469 Stella Dr, 404-233-2227
The outdoor amphitheater, home of the Atlanta Symphony Orchestra Summer Concert Series, also brings in aging rockers to entertain baby-boomers wielding picnic baskets filled with cheese spreads. The cozy venue snuggled in the woods of Chastain Park might be more conducive to picnicking, drinking, and socializing than it is to music-appreciation, but hey, how often do you get to see Heart perform live?

Chastain Horse Park

4371 Powers Ferry Rd, 404-252-4244;
www.chastainhorsepark.org
Chastain Horse Park provides a Therapeutic Riding Program for riders with cognitive, physical, or emotional disabilities. It also caters to inner-city and at-risk children through its Outreach Program. The horse park holds many events throughout the year including fundraisers that help maintain the programs. Check the website for details.

Chastain Park Conservancy

4001 Powers Ferry Rd NW, 404-237-2177;
www.chastainparkconservancy.com
The aim of the Chastain Park Conservancy is to "restore, enhance, maintain and preserve Chastain Park." If you're interested in volunteering for a project or becoming a member, visit the conservancy website.

How to Get There—Driving

From I-285 take the Roswell Road exit (Exit 25) and head south. Turn right on W Wieuca Rd NW, which leads you into the park. From the 400, take Exit 2 and go west on Ivy Road NE. Turn right onto Piedmont Road NE and at the fork in the road, veer left onto Powers Ferry Road NW for points west or Roswell Road NE for points east.

How to Get There—Mass Transit

Take MARTA's North Line to Lindbergh Station (N6) or ride MARTA bus 38, which also stops at N6.

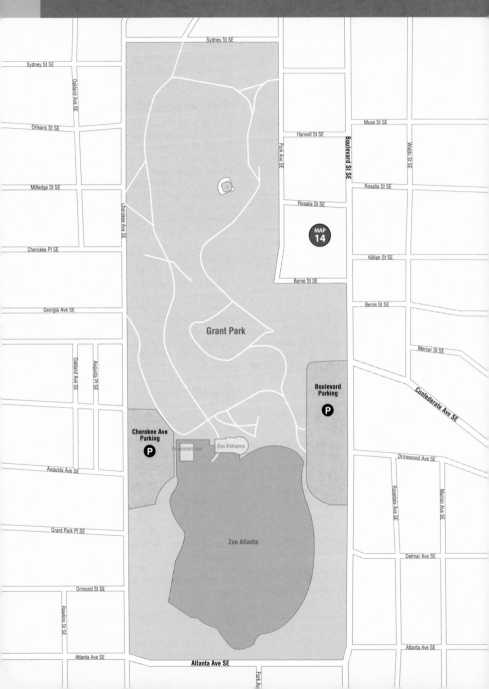

Sydney St SE

Sydney St SE

Oakland Ave SE

Orleans St SE

Muse St SE

Hansell St SE

Waldo St SE

Milledge St SE

Park Ave SE

Boulevard St SE

Rosalia St SE

Cherokee Ave SE

Rosalia St SE

Cherokee Pl SE

MAP
14

Killian St SE

Georgia Ave SE

Berne St SE

Berne St SE

Grant Park

Mercer St SE

Oakland Ave SE

Augusta Pl SE

Confederate Ave SE

Boulevard
Parking

P

Cherokee Ave
Parking

P

Ormewood Ave SE

Administration

Zoo Entrance

Augusta Ave SE

Rosedale Ave SE

Marion Ave SE

Grant Park Pl SE

Zoo Atlanta

Delmar Ave SE

Ormond St SE

Rawlins St SE

Atlanta Ave SE

Atlanta Ave SE

Atlanta Ave SE

Park Ave

General Information

NFT Map: 14
Address: 840 Cherokee Ave SE
              Atlanta, GA 30319
Phone: 404-624-0697
Website: www.grantpark.org

Overview

With Zoo Atlanta and the gigantic Cyclorama panoramic painting as major attractions, Grant Park is the destination of countless school fieldtrips. Although most Atlantans without children don't have the time or the desire to chill with Lun-Lun and Yang-Yang (the famous giant panda pair), the top-notch Zoo Atlanta features natural environments for over 150 species of animals, and it's worth a one-time $17 splurge if you've never visited.

Another of the park's major attractions is the Victorian houses surrounding the park; the Grant Park neighborhood is a nationally recognized historical district. (A tour of homes is held in late September.) The Oakland Cemetery where Margaret Mitchell and Bobby Jones are buried is also nearby (see Page 220).

Smaller and quieter than Piedmont Park, Grant Park is Atlanta's historic green pasture. The 132 acres, which are free and open to the public, are dotted with picnic tables, playgrounds, basketball and tennis courts, and soccer and baseball fields. Like other Atlanta parks, though, it's no Piedmont when it comes to upkeep.

Picnic Facilities

There are two pavilions and one gazebo (all with grills) that can be reserved for private functions. With your booking, you'll also get a key to the outdoor bathrooms. Bookings can be made through the Bureau of Parks by calling 404-817-6757. There are other smaller picnic shelters (for fewer than 30 people and without grills) that do not require a reservation.

Recreation Center

537 Park Ave SE, 404-624-0697
Tennis courts, basketball courts and outdoor ball fields are operated by the Recreation Center. The center offers kids' programs in t-ball, softball, baseball, soccer, and track and field. For the adults, there's yoga and step-aerobics.

Zoo Atlanta

800 Cherokee Ave SE, 404-624-5600; www.zooatlanta.org
Rated in the 1980s as one of the top ten least-humane zoos in the country (animals were kept in tiny cages that allowed no room for physical activity), Zoo Atlanta underwent major revamping to become a nationally-recognized wildlife habitat. Today, animals roam more freely than the zoo's visitors. Lun Lun and Yang Yang are the zoo's most famous inhabitants—one of only three Chinese giant panda pairs in the world. The rebirth of the zoo initiated the renaissance of the entire surrounding neighborhood, which was ripped apart when the six-lane I-20 cut the neighborhood in half in the 1960s. Tickets cost $17 for adults, $12 for children (aged 3-11), and $13 for seniors (55+). The zoo is open daily 9:30 am-4:30 pm, except on Thanksgiving, Christmas, and New Year's Day.

Cyclorama

800 Cherokee Ave SE, 404-624-1071
The Cyclorama was the 19th-century's version of the IMAX film. The painting, which depicts the Battle of Atlanta in 1864, stands 42-feet high and wraps 358-feet around a circular room. It is one of the few remaining examples of this bizarre art form that became popular in America toward the end of the 19th-century and fizzled out just twenty years later, when motion pictures became far more exciting to watch than motionless murals. The attraction claims to be the largest painting in the world (and everyone knows that good art is about quantity, not quality). Tickets cost $7 for adults, $5 for children (aged 6-12) and $6 for seniors (60+). The cyclorama is open daily, 9:30 am-4:30 pm.

How to Get There—Driving

Heading north on I-75/85, take Exit 246 (Fulton Street). Follow signs to Fulton Street, turn right, and drive three blocks to a fork in the road. Take the right fork, Sydney Street, and go three blocks to Broyles Street.

Parking

Parking for Grant Park is free. There are two lots next to the zoo entrance that are almost always empty. Street parking is also pretty easy to find around the park.

How to Get There—Mass Transit

From the Five Points MARTA station, take the 97 bus to Grant Park.

Carroll St SE

Shelton St SE

Reinhardt St SE

N

Boulevard SE

Potters Field

Park Ave SE

Carrie Steele Logan

Jacob Elsas
Mausoleum

Bishop Wesley
John Gaines

Morris and Emmanuel Rich

African-
American
Section

Joseph Jacobs
Mausoleum

MAP
14

Jewish
Section

Loomis Ave SE

Martin Luther King Jr Dr SE

Memorial Dr

Oakland Cemetery

The Confederate
Obelisk

Confederate
Section

Robert Tyre
"Bobby" Jones

Wood St SE

Cherokee Ave SE

Decatur St SE

Margaret
Mitchell Marsh

Watch House

Joel Hurt

Oakland Ave SE

Oakland Ave SE

Entrance

General Information

NFT Map: 14
Main Entrance: 248 Oakland Ave SE
                         Atlanta, Georgia 30312
Phone: 404-688-2107
Website: www.oaklandcemetery.com

Overview

"Tranquil public park" and "old cemetery" are generally not used to describe the same place, but some wacky Atlantans think that since Oakland Cemetery is the third-largest green space in downtown Atlanta, they should use it as a park. Creepy.

If you're looking for a tranquil park, stick with Piedmont. But if you're looking for an old cemetery with semi-famous dead people you don't know, Oakland Cemetery is your destination. Established in 1850, the 88-acre cemetery is as much a museum as it is a macabre cemetery. As you stroll the grounds, you will traverse a 150-year history of Atlanta. Monuments in the cemetery represent a variety of styles and eras—from Victorian and Greek-Revival to Neo-classical, Gothic, Egyptian, and Exotic-Revival. The socially-constructed layout that mirrors the segregation that dominated the late 1800s is significant. The grounds are divided into several distinct sections: the Original Six Acres, the African-American Section, the Confederate Section, the Jewish Section, and Potter's Field.

Walking Tours

Oakland Cemetery offers many unique walking tours including: "Pioneers of Atlanta—The First 20 Years" (1st Saturday of every month), "Dying in 19th-Century Atlanta" (2nd Saturday of every month), "Oakland Cemetery & the Civil War" (3rd Saturday of every month), and "Victorian Symbolism at Oakland" (4th Saturday of every month). Many other tours are offered throughout the year. Check the website for details.

Walking tour prices are $10 for adults, $5 for children 6 and older, and $3 for seniors (65+). Family and group rates are available.

Famous Graves

You probably haven't heard of half these people, but it is your civic duty as an Atlantan to pretend that you have:

- **Margaret Mitchell**—Author of *Gone With the Wind*.
- **Carrie Steele Logan**—Ex-slave who established the first African-American orphanage (The Carrie Steele-Pitts Home) in Atlanta.
- **Bishop Wesley John Gaines**—Second pastor of Big Bethel African Methodist Episcopal Church and founder of Morris Brown College.
- **Joseph Jacobs**—Pharmacist who introduced Coca-Cola as a beverage in 1896.
- **Jacob Elsas**—Owned the Fulton Bag & Cotton Mill.
- **Morris and Emmanuel Rich**—Founders of one of the largest retail chains in the South (Rich's).
- **Joel Hurt**—Neighborhood developer and founder of the first electric trolley system in Atlanta.
- **Bobby Jones**—Renowned golfer.
- **Maynard Jackson**—Atlanta's first African-American mayor.

How to Get There—Driving

From I-75/85, take Exit 247 to I-20 E. Take Exit 59A to Boulevard. Turn left (north) and drive two intersections to Memorial Drive and turn left. At the third traffic signal turn right onto Grant Street, then right onto Martin Luther King Drive. The gates of Oakland should be straight ahead.

Parking

Oakland was created before the motor vehicle, and it shows. There are no parking lots and the paved roads within the park are rather narrow. When you park your car on the paved roads, make sure you leave enough room for other cars to pass. There's no parking permitted on any of the brick roads.

How to Get There—Mass Transit

Take MARTA East Line to King Memorial Station. Exit the station and walk south on Grant Street. Turn left at the stop sign onto MLK Drive and you will be facing Oakland's front gates.

221

General Information

NFT Maps: 10 & 11
Address: North Ave & Freedom Pkwy
              Atlanta, GA 30307
Phone: 404-875-7284

Overview

Located on the city's edge, Freedom Park gives visitors an awesome view of downtown Atlanta. The best vantage point is the corner of Boulevard and Freedom Parkway. The 45-acre Freedom Park is not a prime picnicking destination; its main attraction is six miles of paved trails, which are part of the PATH trail system. If you're heading there, it should be to exercise or visit one of the historic attractions.

Freedom Park commemorates the lives of two of Georgia's most influential peacemakers: Martin Luther King, Jr. and Jimmy Carter. An outdoor tribute to the two Nobel Peace Prize Laureates runs along a 1.5 mile stretch of the Freedom Park trail. The permanent exhibition combines photographs with memorable quotes and historical facts.

Carter Center

452 Freedom Pkwy NE 404-865-7100; www.cartercenter.org
Founded in 1982 by former President Jimmy Carter and his wife, Rosalynn, the non-profit Carter Center addresses national and international issues of human rights and participates in conflict mediation around the world. The center consists of six circular, UFO-like buildings but only the Presidential Library and Museum are open to the public. Admission to the museum costs $7 for adults, $5 for seniors or students, and is free for children under 16. The museum is open Monday-Saturday, 9 am–4:45 pm and Sunday, 12 pm-4:45 pm. The library is open weekdays, 9 am–4:45 pm.

How to Get There—Driving

Take I-85 to the North Avenue exit. Turn left off of the exit and go through the light at Moreland Avenue. Freedom Park will be on your right.

How to Get There—Mass Transit

To get to the Carter Center, take MARTA bus 16 to Five Points Station. To get to the King Center, take the 3 Auburn bus to either Five Points Station or E2 Station.

General Information

NFT Map: 10
Guided Tour Phone: 404-876-2041
                        (Atlanta Preservation Center)
Websites: www.sweetauburn.com
                        www.thekingcenter.org

Overview

Largely due to the Jim Crow laws that kept races segregated, many African-Americans established businesses, congregations, and social organizations in the Sweet Auburn District during the 1930s. It was in this bustling neighborhood that Dr. Martin Luther King, Jr. was born and raised. The Sweet Auburn Historic District isn't quite as sweet now as it was during its heyday, but many of the houses and businesses have been restored to their original state, including the Atlanta Life Insurance Company. The main attraction is the MLK National Historic Site, and taking a walking tour (guided or un-guided) is the best way to explore this historic district.

The Martin Luther King Jr. National Historic Site

450 Auburn Ave, 404-526-8900; www.thekingcenter.com
The Rev. Dr. Martin Luther King Jr.'s childhood birthplace and home still stands in the district. Ebenezer Baptist Church, the church he co-pastored with his father and the eventual site of his 60,000-attendee funeral in 1969, is just a short walk away. Other points of interest include King's gravesite and memorial park, as well as the Martin Luther King, Jr. Center for Nonviolent Social Change.

The facilities are open from 9 am to 5 pm daily and, although tours are free of charge, tickets are required for Birth Home tours. Tickets can be obtained at the Visitor Center and are issued on a first-come, first-served basis. You should acquire your tickets upon arrival at the Historic Site, as tours fill rapidly and are limited to 15 people. Tours of the Birth Home begin every hour on the hour from September through May,

increasing to every half hour during the summer months. Unfortunately, advance reservations are not accepted. For more info, call 404-331-5190, press zero, and ask for tour information.

Sweet Auburn Curb Market

404- 659-1665; 8 am-6:30 pm Mon-Fri; 8 am-7 pm Sat
This urban farmers' market, which began in 1918, offers everything from Caribbean jerk spices to Southern chitlins. Local cooks love the authentic southern foods they can find here. In addition to chow, the market features entertainers and vendors selling a variety of non-food wares. Vendors come and go, so don't show-up with a rigid shopping list.

How to Get There—Driving

The Sweet Auburn District and the King Center are just east of downtown Atlanta. Take I-75/85 N/S to the Freedom Parkway exit and turn right on Boulevard. Car and bus parking is available in the lot on your right (second driveway).

How to Get There—Mass Transit

The closest MARTA train station to The King Center is King Memorial Station (E2). Exit the station and turn right. Go east on Decatur Street for 2 blocks and turn left on Jackson Street. Turn right on Auburn Avenue (approximately 6 blocks). From the Five Points station, board MARTA bus 3 (Auburn). The district is just a few stops away.

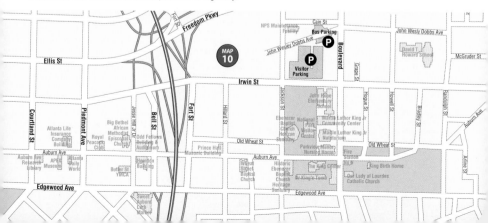

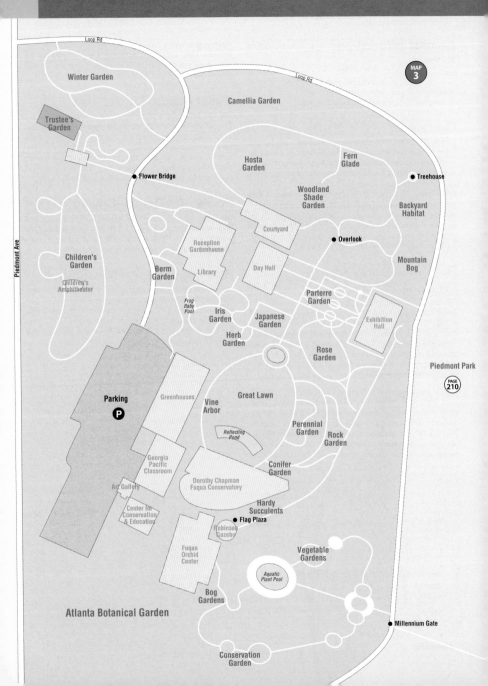

MAP 3

Loop Rd

Loop Rd

Winter Garden

Camellia Garden

Trustee's Garden

Hosta Garden

Fern Glade

● Treehouse

● Flower Bridge

Woodland Shade Garden

Backyard Habitat

Courtyard

Piedmont Ave

Children's Garden

Berm Garden

Reception Gardenhouse

● Overlook

Mountain Bog

Children's Amphitheater

Library

Day Hall

Frog Baby Pool

Iris Garden

Japanese Garden

Parterre Garden

Exhibition Hall

Herb Garden

Rose Garden

Piedmont Park

PAGE 210

Parking

Ⓟ

Greenhouses

Vine Arbor

Great Lawn

Reflecting Pond

Perennial Garden

Rock Garden

Georgia Pacific Classroom

Conifer Garden

Art Gallery

Dorothy Chapman Fuqua Conservatory

Center for Conservation & Education

Hardy Succulents

● Flag Plaza

Robinson Gazebo

Fuqua Orchid Center

Vegetable Gardens

Atlanta Botanical Garden

Bog Gardens

Aquatic Plant Pool

Millennium Gate ●

Conservation Garden

Parks & Places • **Atlanta Botanical Garden**

General Information

NFT Map:	3
Address:	1345 Piedmont Ave NE
	Atlanta, GA 30309
Phone:	404-876-5859
Website:	www.atlantabotanicalgarden.org
Hours:	Apr–Sep, Tues–Sunday, 9 am-7 pm
	Oct–Mar, Tues–Sunday, 9 am-5 pm
	Closed Mondays
Admission:	Adults $12, Seniors $9, Students $7,
	Children under 3 free

Overview

The Atlanta Botanical Garden is located at the northwest corner of Piedmont Park. Gardening nuts should take advantage of the resources offered by the ABG: in addition to classes and demonstrations, garden employees offer a hotline service to answer questions regarding plants and gardening methods, and provide referrals to local area garden clubs. The on-site Sheffield Botanical Library collection includes more than 2,000 books and 80 periodicals for use by visitors.

If you're not into gardening but want to impress your visiting snooty mother-in-law or over-educated cousin, the ABG's thirty acres might be just the place to take them. The gardens feature several formal gardens, a mature hardwood forest, and a conservatory named after the wife of a rich guy—the Dorothy Chapman Fuqua Conservatory houses rare and endangered plants from tropical rainforests and desert regions, as well as displays of citrus trees and carnivorous plants.

Other reasons for visiting the ABG: 1. You need to take a hike (Storza Woods offers a 1.25-mile trail); 2. You need to meditate (The Japanese Garden is rather peaceful); 3. The Cowboy Junkies are performing (The ABG hosts summer concert series); 4. You just like looking at plants.

Food

Give up the thought of food-topped checkered picnic blankets splayed on the grass—outside food is not permitted in the gardens. You can purchase fancy-schmancy (i.e. overpriced) sandwiches, salads, and snacks from the Sun in My Belly café. The café keeps the same hours as the garden, except in winter when it opens at 10 am. Sun in My Belly (www.suninmybelly.com) also provides catering for groups who attend the Concerts in the Garden series. Check out their website for menus and order forms.

Events

Many events held in the garden are one-time or annual occasions and usually coincide with Halloween, Christmas, and other popular holidays. The super-popular Concerts in the Garden series is an annual event that hosts an eclectic line-up of performers; past headliners include Rickie Lee Jones, Roseanne Cash, and the Cowboy Junkies. On the last Wednesday evening of every month, you can enjoy the surrounds with Cocktails in the Garden. From storybook time to drop-in kids' classes, there's always something going on in the garden for children. Check the website for a calendar of events.

How to Get There—Driving

From I-85/I-75, exit at 14th Street and drive east until the street dead-ends at Piedmont Avenue. Turn left and the garden's entrance will be on the right at the first traffic light between 14th Street and Monroe Drive. The Garden is adjacent to Piedmont Park on Piedmont Avenue.

Parking

Limited parking is available during the week. On Saturday and Sunday, off-site parking is provided at Colony Square for $2, with a free shuttle to and from the garden. A proposed new parking deck could solve the parking problem (or perhaps just anger locals).

The Spin: While the arboretum and Piedmont Park were once regarded as neighborhood parks, they are increasingly considered destinations for Atlantans living in all parts of the city. As a result, more people are driving to the park than ever before, creating a need for increased public parking facilities. The ABG has proposed building a unique "green" parking facility into a steep slope on the edge of Piedmont Park's North Woods.

The Reality: The garden needs to make more money, and a six-story parking deck could provide that cash cow. Generally, local residents are not pleased with the idea of a "green" parking deck. AJC editor Cynthia Tucker ranted: "What's next? Will People for the Ethical Treatment of Animals hold pig roasts to raise money?" Until the dispute is resolved, be prepared to park and walk or shuttle.

How to Get There—Mass Transit

Take the MARTA train to the Arts Center Station and transfer to the 36 North bus. On Sundays, take the 27 Monroe/Lindbergh bus.

General Information

NFT Map:	9
Address:	285 Andrew Young
	International Blvd NE
	Atlanta, GA 30313
Event Services:	404-223-4300
Executive Offices:	404-223-4000
Website:	www.gwcc.com

Overview

Combined with the Georgia Dome and Centennial Olympic Park, the World Congress Center was meant to provide Atlantans with a state-of-the-art convention, sports, and entertainment complex. However, since the center opened in 1976, it has hosted mainly private conventions with no relevance to Atlantans.

At over 950,000 square feet, the Georgia World Congress Center is the second largest exhibition facility in the United States. The center primarily hosts conventions, trade shows, and corporate events; greatest hits include the Atlanta Home Builders Banquet, a meeting of the American Urological Association, and the International Woodworking Fair—all members-only affairs.

Unless you're attached to one of the corporate shindigs taking place here, you'll be limited to attending events like the Atlanta Boat Show and the Atlanta Journal Constitution International Auto Show.

Food

If you're going to be stuck in this concrete jungle, you'll need to know the best means of feeding and hydrating yourself. Since the center is located in a fairly remote location, there are really no nearby food alternatives. Budget-conscious exhibitors and attendees should take a packed lunch, as in-house food comes with typically high convention price tags. If lunch can be charged to your business account, MGR Food Services provides an array of healthy sandwiches and salads, with an abundance of caffeine-charged snack carts dotted around the venue. If you're exhibiting with a large group, you can order meals by the dozen in advance on the convention website.

How to Get There—Driving

From the airport and the south, take I-75/85 N to Andrew Young International Boulevard (Exit 248C). Turn left onto Andrew Young International Boulevard then left onto Centennial Olympic Park Drive. Turn right onto Marietta Street and the Green Lot will be located on your left, just past the Omni Hotel.

From the north, take I-75/85 S to Williams Street (Exit 249C). Williams Street bears to the right. Drive five blocks on Williams and make a right onto Andrew Young International Boulevard. Drive one block and make a left onto Centennial Olympic Park Drive and follow the directions above.

From the west and east, take I-20 to Spring Street (Exit 56B). If you're coming from the west, turn left (right if you're coming from the east) onto Spring Street and then left on Marietta Street.

Parking

Getting to the GWCC is easy and, thanks to more than 4,500 onsite parking spaces, so is storing your vehicle for the day. There are five surface lots and two parking decks—all located within the convention, sports, and entertainment complex. Parking never costs more than $8 per day. All lots are gated and attendants are on duty during all show/event hours.

How to Get There—Mass Transit

The GWCC is MARTA-accessible at two stations. For access to events in Buildings A and B, use the Dome/GWCC/Philips Arena/CNN Center Station (W-1). For access to events in Building C, use the W-1 station above or use the Vine City Station (W-2).

If you are coming from Hartsfield-Jackson Atlanta International Airport, MARTA has a rail station located at the north end of the airport, near baggage claim.

General Information

Address:	1978 Island Ford Pkwy
	Atlanta, GA 30350
Phone:	678-538-1200
Website:	www.nps.gov/chat

Overview

When your friends tell you it's time to shoot the Hooch, don't reach for your pistol. Grab your bathing suit and some sunscreen—they're taking you to ride the rapids of Georgia's Chattahoochee River. The Hooch is one of the few watery escapes for landlocked Atlantans, and shooting the Hooch is a must.

Outdoorsy Southerners enjoy daytrips to Chattahoochee National Recreation Area—48 miles of protected land between Atlanta and Lake Lanier. The fishing is phenomenal (the river runs cold all year, making it a great place to catch trout, catfish, and bass), canoeists and rafters enjoy class one and two rapids, and the riverbanks are covered in trails for day-hikers, joggers, and bikers.

But the Hooch is also a river in danger. The sprawl of Atlanta has turned the southern portion of the river into one of the most polluted stretches of river in the country. The river is ranked as one of the twenty most endangered rivers in the nation due to agricultural run-off, industrial discharges, and urban development.

Chattahoochee Nature Center

9135 Willeo Rd, Roswell, 770-992-2055;
www.chattnaturecenter.com
The Chattahoochee Nature Center offers visitors two miles of well-kept trails, a boardwalk that winds its way along the riverbank, a greenhouse (open to the public by appointment only), a picnic rental area, and various special events and programs geared to instill an environmental consciousness in urban-raised children. The center runs Camp Kingfisher, a hands-on environmental education summer program for kids aged 5 to 12 from the Atlanta area.

Visiting the center is free for members, $3 for adults, and $2 for children and seniors. The center is open Monday-Saturday, 9 am–5 pm and Sunday, noon-5 pm. It's closed New Year's Day, Thanksgiving, and Christmas.

Cochran Shoals

1978 Island Ford Pkwy, 770-399-8070
Just a short drive north of Atlanta's metropolitan center, Cochran Shoals is the largest and most popular recreation

South

area along the Hooch. The "Fitness Loop" is a three-mile trail of fairly flat and easy terrain, which is open to walkers (and dogs), joggers, and bikers (although the trail gets pretty crowded and a better spot for bikers is the Sope Creek Trail). Take a detour off of the main loop to do some climbing, bird spotting, or visit the ruins of the old paper mill.

If your motivation for day-tripping out of the city is to escape hordes of people, try the east side of Cochran Shoals, where you'll run into anglers and odd ruins of stacked stone. Cochran Shoals recreation area is for day-use only and closes at sundown. There is a $2 parking fee.

Palisades

The Palisades sit along the east and west banks of the Hooch below Powers Ferry Landing. Rock climbers usually head to the east side. Day hikers head to the west side's wide gravel path or to the loop that travels across the river and over the bluffs. Canoeists and rafters enjoy the class two rapids that run through the Devils Shoals Race Course.

Rentals and Instruction (National Recreation Area)

Alliance for a Better Education, 770-645-5996. Canoe, kayak, raft, and tube rentals.
Atlanta Fly Fishing Guides, 404-664-4823. Fly-casting, fly-fishing, wading, and boat rentals.
Chattahoochee Nature Center, 770-992-2055. Guided canoe floats.
High Country, 404-814-0999. Canoe, kayak, raft rentals, and instruction.
River Through Atlanta, 770-650-8630. Fly-fishing guide service, instruction, and fly-tying classes.
White Water Learning Center of Georgia, 404-231-0042. Canoe and kayak instruction and rentals, guided river trips.
Williamson Brothers Catering, 770-425-1739. Full-service catering.

How to Get There—Driving

For East Palisades hiking, take the Northside Drive exit off I-285. Head south for 1.25 miles and turn right onto Indian Trail. The entrance to the park is at the end of Indian Trail.

For Cochran Shoals hiking and Powers Island paddling, take Interstate North Parkway (Exit 22 off I-285), and head west for about 0.75 miles. The parking area will be on your right. The entrance to the Fitness Trail is across the river.

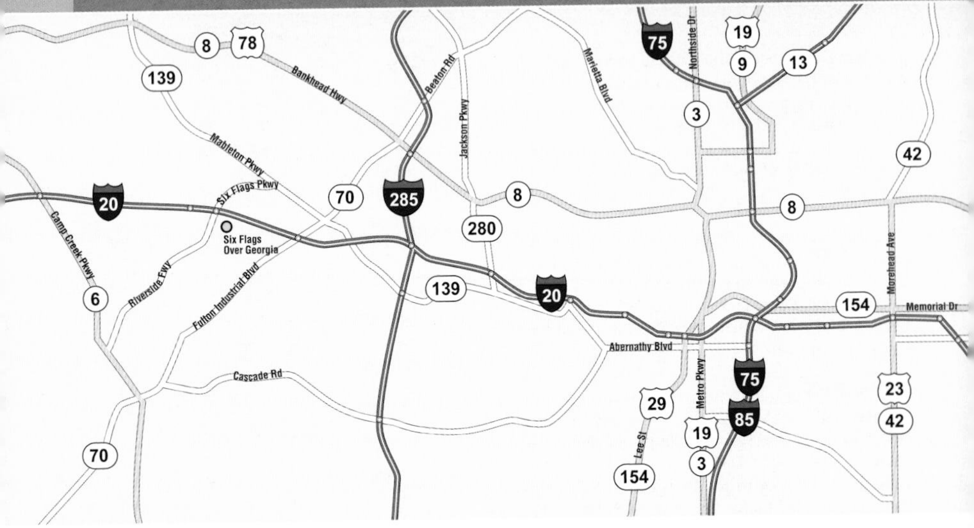

General Information

Address: 275 Riverside Pkwy
Austell, GA 30168
Phone: 770-948-9290
Website: www.sixflags.com/georgia

Overview

While the rollercoasters are the main attraction at Six Flags, you will spend more time in long lines with sweaty people sporting mullets than you will on the rides, and you might have to refinance your home to afford the steep cost of entry. Unless you're a rollercoaster junkie with expendable cash, you should definitely wait until the off-season to visit and do whatever you can to cut costs (at the very least, pack a lunch). Don't show up hungry on a Saturday in June.

After surviving the lines, count on some top-notch thrills on eight different coasters and a variety of other dropping, spinning, and splashing machines. Our fave is the Superman Ultimate Flight coaster, where you're strapped in horizontally to fly through the sky.

There's also plenty to do for the height- and age-restricted park-goers as well—the Wile E. Coyote Canyon Blaster, Splashwater Falls, and Bugs Bunny World provide family fun (and more lines) for visitors of all ages.

The Season

The park opens in the spring and remains open through October. Off-season is pretty much any time that kids are in school and weekdays. The month of October is called "Fright Fest" at Six Flags, during which many of the rides are overhauled with a spooky Halloween theme, and staff take on the roles of singing and dancing ghouls. Halloween night is the last hurrah until Six Flags reopens again in the spring.

Hours of Operation

Park hours vary, depending on the season and the particular day you visit. The park opens at 10 am and closes anywhere from 6 pm to 10 pm. Call or visit the website for date-specific information.

Entrance Fees

If you bought a one-day general admission ticket to the park (*at* the park) for the 2004 season, you would have paid $42.99 (plus tax). You should never do this! You never have to pay the full price unless it's a Saturday (the park's busiest day). Discounted pre-purchased tickets and/or coupons are available at Publix grocery stores, local AAA centers, Georgia Welcome centers, the Atlanta Visitors and Convention Bureau, or through the Six Flags website. If you're a frequent rider, the best thing to do is purchase a Season Pass, which

costs less than the price of two one-day admissions and allows unlimited entry throughout the season. They even have special private pass-holder days.

Fast Lane & "Q-Bot"

If money's still burning a hole in your pocket after admission, spend $10 (rental fee) plus an additional $10 per person (minimum 2, maximum 6) on a "Q-Bot" device. This will allow you to approach the Fast Lane at one of the more popular attractions and electronically declare that you want on (but don't want to physically wait in line). The Q-Bot will then calculate the waiting time required and you can go about other business until the Q-Bot signals that at long last your wait is over—be sure to laugh heartily as you whiz by the sweaty NASCAR fans waiting in line. You can reserve a Q-Bot before your visit by calling 770-948-3389 at least 24 hours prior to your visit ($5 additional charge).

Kennels

You and your friends are the only animals allowed in the park. If, like Paris, you can't go anywhere without your pooch, dogs can be looked after in the kennels located at the main entrance. Water is provided, but not food. Pets can't be kept overnight, so don't have such a good time that you forget to pick them up. Kennel guests must have current vaccinations and registration tags. Best bet: Leave Tinkerbell at home, for goodness sake!

Lockers

Need a place to drop your backpack for the day? Locker wristbands can be purchased at almost any gift shop in the park. No unwanted family members can be stored. Try the kennel.

How to Get There—Driving

Six Flags Over Georgia is located on I-20, approximately 20 minutes west of Atlanta. Exits going in both directions (47 & 46A) are clearly marked for Six Flags

Parking

The daily parking rate is $10, with the lot opening usually no more than 30-60 minutes before the park. For an extra $2, you can experience Gold Parking (a.k.a. More-Expensive-But-Not-Much-Closer-to-the-Gates) in the Georgia Cyclone Lot. Show up on a motorcycle and you've got it made. If you've splurged on the Season Pass for the park then you surely need the Season Pass parking permit—this is available at the bargain price of $25 for unlimited visits ($50 for Gold Parking). These permits can be purchased at the parking booths, which accept cash only—can you believe it?

How to Get There—Mass Transit

A *seasonal* rail-to-bus service departing from the Hamilton E. Holmes (Hightower) Station on the East/West Line is offered by MARTA during the warmer months. Call MARTA directly on 404-848-4711 to see if it's running.

Parks & Places · **Stone Mountain Park**

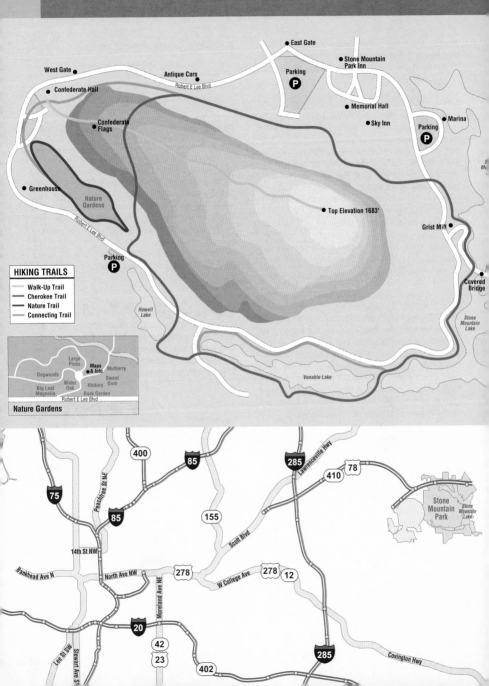

East Gate

Parking

Stone Mountain Park Inn

West Gate

Antique Cars

Robert E Lee Blvd

Confederate Hall

Memorial Hall

Confederate Flags

Sky Inn

Parking

Marina

Greenhouse

Robert E Lee Blvd

Nature Gardens

Top Elevation 1683'

Grist Mill

HIKING TRAILS

Walk-Up Trail
Cherokee Trail
Nature Trail
Connecting Trail

Parking

Covered Bridge

Howell Lake

Stone Mountain Lake

Large Pines

Maps & Info

Mulberry

Dogwoods

Water Oak

Hickory

Sweet Gum

Big Leaf Magnolia

Rock Garden

Robert E Lee Blvd

Venable Lake

Nature Gardens

400

85

285

Lawrenceville Hwy

410

78

75

Peachtree St NE

85

155

Scott Blvd

Stone Mountain Park

Stone Mountain Lake

14th St NW

Bankhead Ave N

North Ave NW

Moreland Ave NE

278

W College Ave

278

12

Lee St SW

Stewart Ave S

20

42

23

402

285

Covington Hwy

General Information

Address: Highway 78 E
              Stone Mountain, GA 30087
Website: www.stonemountainpark.com
Phone: 770-498-5690 (metro Atlanta area)
              800-317-2006 (outside metro Atlanta)

Overview

Stone Mountain is the largest chunk of unearthed granite in the world. If that isn't enough to get your blood rushing, check this out: it has three Confederate heroes carved on the side, including the president of the Confederacy, Jefferson Davis. Hey, we may have gotten whooped in the Civil War, but the confederacy is alive and well at Stone Mountain Park. Yeeeehaw!

From the nature-lover's viewpoint, the park has more than Dixie-pride to offer. Most notable are the incredible views of Atlanta and the Appalachians from the top of the mountain, which can be reached by walking or via the Skylift cable car. The Stone Mountain Scenic Railroad offers a five-mile journey throughout the park as well. For children there are waterslides (the Mountain Screamer and the Southern Pipeline) and the Great Barn, which is filled with rope nets, mazes, and super slides. Golf courses, plantations, farmyards, and museums round out the possible to-do list.

The Lasershow Spectacular is the world's largest laser light show. Using the side of the mountain as a screen, a laser animation projection displays tales and various comical characters synchronized to surround-sound music. In the final scene, the horses and Confederate heroes depicted on the mountain come to life and march off to the sweet serenade of Elvis singing "Dixie." It's enough to bring tears to the eyes of every Southerner. The show occurs nightly during the summer months.

History

In 1790, Americans began settling the area near the giant mass of granite, which they named Rock Mountain. Despite its significant geological interest, the mountain is better known for the enormous 3-acre bas-relief Confederate Memorial on its north face; it's the largest bas-relief in the world. The three carved figures are Stonewall Jackson, Robert E. Lee, and Jefferson Davis.

This explicitly confederate memorial is largely the result of Stone Mountain's historic ties with the Ku Klux Klan. During the early 1900s, Klansmen met regularly at the base of the monolith and they raised a large portion of the initial money to begin the carving. Along with the Daughters of the Confederacy, the KKK helped determine the explicitly Confederate nature of the memorial carving in 1923. Gutzon Borglum, the sculptor responsible for Mount Rushmore, began the project but the carving was not completed until 1970 by a different artist. The social landscape today contrasts sharply and ironically with its history, as the population of the city of Stone Mountain is now almost 70% African-American.

Entrance Fees

Entry to the park costs $7 per vehicle or $20 per bus. An Annual Parking Pass is $30. This permit allows access to many of the park's amenities including the public picnic areas, nature trails, children's playground, walk-up trail, and the Lasershow Spectacular. If you want to experience other attractions in the park, the one-day All Attractions Pass costs $19 for adults and $16 for children (aged 3-11). If you visit often, you should buy an annual membership, which includes all entry fees and parking; the cost for two people is $99. Check the website for other family packages.

Camping

The Stone Mountain Family Campground includes 441 wooded campsites: 44 with full hook-ups; 254 partial hook-ups with water and electricity (for tents, pop-ups, and motor homes); and 43 primitive tent sites.

The following amenities are available for campers: supply/grocery store, bathrooms with full shower facilities, laundry, playground, volleyball court, and swimming pool. Camp site rentals range from $23 to $45 per night.

How to Get There—Driving

Stone Mountain Park is located 16 miles east of downtown Atlanta. From downtown, take I-20 E to I-285 N. From I-285 N, take Exit 39B/US Hwy 78 E (Snellville/ Athens) exit. Drive 7.7 miles and take Exit 8/Stone Mountain Park. Follow the exit ramp to the East Gate entrance of Stone Mountain Park.

How to Get There—Mass Transit

The Avondale MARTA station (E7) on the East Line is the closest to the Park. The #120 bus also stops at the park.

Overview

As a rule, the farther you travel outside of Atlanta, the more stereotypically Southern it becomes. In other words, the number of Confederate flag-sightings is directly proportional to the distance from Atlanta's city limits. Even so, the North Georgia Mountains have plenty to offer, besides Southern pride, if you're looking for a quick weekend get-away. Many Atlantans own mountain pied-a-terres for escaping the urban bustle. The following are just some of the many options for out-of-town trips.

Alpine Helen

Convention & Visitors Bureau, P.O. Box 730, 800-858-8027
Located in the heart of Georgia's Blue Ridge Mountains, this former motherland of the Cherokee tribe was converted into a 19th-century Bavarian alpine village in 1968. Located about 1.5 hours north of Atlanta, this wilderness Disneyland took on its appearance when an artist who was deeply influenced by German culture and architecture was hired by local businessmen to help improve the deteriorating village community. Today, the streets are made of cobblestones, the buildings look like ski lodges, the Glockenspiel chimes on the hour, and tourism is thriving. No Bavarian tribute is complete without Oktoberfest; the celebrations in Alpine Helen are huge and usually begin in September and end in November.

While the city may be a tacky tourist trap, floating down the Chattahoochee on an inner tube is an annual ritual for many Atlantans. There are several tubing companies in Helen and trips down the river take between one to 2.5 hours. For the bargain price of $5, the trip is worth every penny. Check out the folks at www.coolrivertubing.com.

The town also offers fishing, mountain biking, and horseback riding adventures. Peak leaf season begins at the end of October and extends into the first few weeks of November. And if you want to extend the fantasy of living in a different century, check out the annual hot air balloon races.

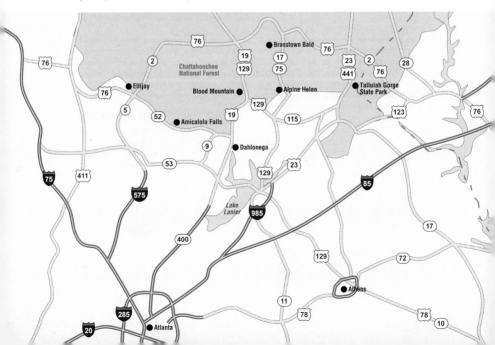

Amicalola Falls

418 Amicalola Falls Lodge Rd, Dawsonville,
706-265-8888

Famous for the 729-foot waterfall (highest drop east of the Mississippi), Amicalola Falls has appropriately kept its poetic Cherokee name, which translates as "tumbling waters." For the ambitious day hiker, the park offers twelve miles of loop trails that pass through 1,000 acres of fairly rugged terrain. The eight-mile Southern Terminus Access Trail approaches Springer Mountain, the beginning of the 2,150-mile Appalachian Trail. For less strenuous enjoyment of the outdoors, other attractions include a stocked stream teeming with trout, three playgrounds for children, and 78 picnic tables. A great reward after a hefty hike is "Hike Inn," a hiker's lodge located five miles into the park, and accessible only by foot along the Len Foote Hike Inn trail; there you can feel the camaraderie that comes with having earned your repose and knowing that everyone around you did too.

Brasstown Bald

Visitor Information Center: 706-896-2556

Standing at an imposing 4,784-feet above sea-level, Brasstown Bald is the state's highest mountain. On clear days, four states are visible from the summit. A steep half-mile walk will take you to the mountain top (as will a shuttle). Four hiking trails, ranging from moderate to strenuous, weave their way around and up the mountain. Located at the top of the mountain, the Visitors Information Center shows videos and exhibitions about the history of the surrounding area. The center and the snack food concession stands are open from Memorial Day through October, but the mountain and surrounding areas are in the height of their glory during the spring and summer months.

Blood Mountain

The highest point on the Appalachian Trail acquired its menacing name from an old Native-American legend. The myth tells of a bloody battle between two warring tribes—the Cherokees and the Creek Nations. So many warriors were killed that blood supposedly ran down the sides of the mountain. Vogel State Park, considered one of the most beautiful parks in the region, is the most popular destination near Blood Mountain.

To hike to Blood Mountain, park your car at the Byron Reece Trail, right off Highway 19. The parking area is about half a mile north of the Walasi-Yi Center. Follow the Reece Access Trail until it connects with the Appalachian Trail. Turn right onto the Appalachian Trail and follow the white blazes to the top of Blood Mountain.

Dahlonega

Twenty years before the famous California gold rush, the small town of Dahlonega (which means "gold" in Cherokee) experienced the country's first enthrallment with the yellow metal when gold was fortuitously stumbled upon during a deer hunt in 1828. In the mid-1800s, more than $6 million dollars of gold was coined in Dahlonega. Today, the Dahlonega Gold Museum exhibits a history of mining in Georgia and gives visitor's the opportunity to pan for gold in the town's exhausted soil.

Dahlonega is the gateway to the North Georgia Mountains and the Chattahoochee National Forest. Overnight horseback riding trips through the Chattahoochee National Forest (706-482-8302) and boating trips along the Chestatee or the Etowah rivers (706-864-7177) all set out from Dahlonega. A wildlife preserve (706-864-9411) and a private game preserve for hunting quail and pheasant are also popular attractions.

Ellijay

Located in the foothills of the Appalachian mountains, a little over an hour drive north from downtown Atlanta, Ellijay serves as a beautiful backdrop for hiking, horseback riding, mountain biking, swimming, boating, and fishing. Carter's Lake, a 3,500-acre lake has a smooth and sandy beach, a marina, and six public boat launch sites along its banks. At Fort Mountain, visitors can view prehistoric rock formations, and Chieftan's Trail offers a guided tour of Native American sites (706-635-7400).

But it's really the apples that make a trip to Ellijay especially worthwhile. This small town is the "apple capital" of Georgia and, if you visit between August and December, roadside produce stands will offer you twelve varieties of the cheapest and sweetest apples you've ever tasted. Visit Apple Orchard Valley, home of eleven apple orchards, located on Highway 52. The annual harvest festival usually takes place at the end of October.

Lake Lanier

Lake Lanier Islands, 6950 Holiday Rd, Buford, 770-932-7255

Lake Lanier is an invaluable resource for all Georgians, even if they don't know it. The lake was created in the mid-20th-century to support industrial growth and to provide drinking water to three million Georgians in the northern parts of the state. Both the Chattahoochee and the Chestatee rivers feed into the lake, which covers 38,000 acres of what was once farmland.

Since its opening in 1958, the lake has become an important recreational facility as well. Located only 35 miles north of Atlanta, Lake Lanier attracts many urban dwellers seeking peace and tranquility. The lake offers 540 miles of shoreline, camping (allowed only in designated areas and as cheap as $12 per night), boating, golf, and hunting. The lake is filled with an array of bass, catfish, yellow perch, walleye, and bream. Some golf hot-spots include Emerald Point, Renaissance Pine Isle, and Chateau Elan. Because of its popularity, using Lake Lanier's facilities is not always free. The park charges "day-use fees" for some of the parking, swimming, picnic areas, and boat launchings, so make sure you take cash with you.

If the lake doesn't do it for you, try Lake Lanier Islands. The water park features four slides, Georgia's largest wave pool, a mile-long beach, volleyball courts, and live entertainment. You can also rent a range of boats, from sailboats to luxury liners complete with hot tubs. Cost of entry to the water park is $26.99 for adults and $16.99 for children and seniors; kids under 2 enter free.

Tallulah Gorge State Park

P. O. Box 248, Tallulah Falls, 706-754-7970

The granite walls of the 1,000-foot-deep crevice into the earth's crust have lent Tallulah Gorge the moniker "Niagara of the South." The gorge has been a death trap for many hikers over the years (in one especially fatal year, six hikers died attempting to hike the trail to the gorge's floor). The gorge received a nod from Hollywood in the 1972 movie *Deliverance*, when Jon Voigt climbed out of the two-mile wide abyss. The State Park, co-managed by the state government and Georgia Power, also serves as a sanctuary for endangered plants and animals, including the Peregrine falcon. Because of the danger of the terrain for hikers, as well as concern over the safety of the gorge's wildlife population, permits must be obtained from the visitor's center before entering the park. But the permit is worth obtaining—once you're in, you have twenty miles of hiking trails, a beach surrounding a 63-acre manmade lake, tennis courts, and campgrounds at your disposal.

Colleges & Universities · **Spelman College**

General Information

NFT Map: 12
Mailing Address: 350 Spelman Ln SW
Atlanta, GA 30314
Phone: 404-681-3643
Website: www.spelman.edu

Overview

Founded in 1881, Spelman College is a private liberal arts college dedicated to the education of African-American women. With a student body comprised of more than 2,100 students hailing from all over the world, the 32-acre campus is located just five minutes from downtown Atlanta. Spelman has four partner institutions (Clark Atlanta University, the Interdenominational Theological Center, Morehouse College, and Morehouse School of Medicine), forming the most impressive grouping of historically black institutions of higher learning in the world. Spelman students can cross-register at any of its undergraduate partners. Because of its outstanding academic resources and commitment to the education of women, the college is consistently ranked among the top 75 best liberal arts colleges by the *U.S. News & World Report*.

Spelman was also the inspiration for the television show *A Different World* that featured a fictional black co-ed college, Hillman College.

Tuition

For the 2004-2005 academic year, the undergraduate tuition and fees totaled $14,940. Room and board for the year were an additional $8,040 (personal expenses, books, and lab fees not included).

Sports

Though Spelman College isn't known for its top-notch athletic department, there is no lack of spirit among these Jaguars. Recently, the school began taking steps towards improving its sports programs. As a provisional member of the NCAA Division III, Spelman competes with other NCAA member institutions in cross-country, soccer, volleyball, basketball, tennis, and golf. Other athletic activities include club track and field and cheerleading. For more information, visit www.spelman.edu/students/athletics.

Culture on Campus

The Spelman College Museum of Fine Art (350 Spelman Ln SW, 404-270-5607) is not only an important academic resource for students, alumni, and faculty, but also for the people of Atlanta. It is the only museum in the nation that showcases works by and about African-American women and its uniqueness complements the philosophies of the college. One of its most impressive permanent exhibits consists of 20th-century painting and sculpture by African-American artists—works by Jacob Lawrence, Faith Ringgold, Valerie Maynard, Selma Burke, Herman "Kofi" Bailey, Elizabeth Catlett, Claudia Widdiss, and Lloyd McNeil. The museum is open Tuesday through Friday from 10 am-4 pm, Saturday from 12 pm-4 pm and is free to the public, though a suggested donation of $3 is encouraged. Visit www.museum.spelman.edu/museum for current exhibition information.

Department Contact Information

Visit www.spelman.edu/parents/directory for a more complete telephone directory.

Office of Admissions 404-270-5190
Registrar 404-270-5230
Health Services. 404-270-5254
Housing and Residence Life. 404-270-5344
Student Activities 404-270-5139
Bookstore 404-270-5151
Spelman College Museum of Fine Art 404-270-5607

Visit www.spelman.edu/academics/programs for a department telephone directory and links to their web pages.

Camilla St

Ashby Grv St

Parsons St

Ogden St

Euhfree St

Fair
Street
Annex

Fair Street
Student Housing

Webster St

Davidson House
Center for
Excellence

Milton St

Raymond St

James P Brawley Dr

ROTC
Headquarters

Robert W Woodruff
Library

Fair St

Joyce St

Ashby St

Franklin L
Forbes Arena

Samuel H
Archer Hall

Brazeal Hall/
Ralph B Ellison
College Infirmary

Triplex

Physical
Plant

Nabrit-Mapp-
McBay Hall

Samuel
T Graves
Hall

MAP
12

William H
Danforth Chapel

Thomas
Kilgore Jr
Campus
Center

Kilgore
Dormitory

1

2

Sale
Hall
Annex

3

4   5   6

Chivers/
Lane
Dining
Hall

Bookstore

Frank St

Residence Hall

Charles D
Hubert Hall

WEB DuBois Hall

William Jefferson
White Hall

Brown St

Benjamin E
Mays Hall

Print
Shop

Lee Ln

1. Joseph T Robert Hall/Post Office
2. Security Office
3. Sale Hall/Howard Thurmond Humanities Center
4. John Hope Hall
5. Technology Tower
6. Charles Merrill Hall
7. Emma and Joe Adams Institute for Community Service

Claude B Dansby Hall

Tennis Courts

John H
Wheeler Hall

Benjamin G Brawley Hall

Greensferry Ave

Joseph E Lowery
(Ashby) Street
Guard Booth

Westview Dr

Spelman
College

PAGE
237

Maintenance
Building

BT Harvey
Stadium/
Edwin Moses
Track

Welborn St

Martin Luther King Jr
International Chapel

Hugh M
Gloster Hall

Westview Dr

Morehouse
Parking Deck

Sells Ave

Gloster Hall
Annex

7

Westview
Guard Booth

Trio Programs

Leadership Center
at Morehouse

West
End
Annex

West End Ave

Colleges & Universities • **Morehouse**

General Information

NFT Map: 12
Mailing Address: 830 Westview Dr SW
Atlanta, GA 30314
Phone: 404-681-2800
Website: www.morehouse.edu

Overview

Located just three miles from downtown Atlanta, Morehouse College, or "The House" as some call it, is a private, four-year liberal arts college for African-American men. Enrolling about 3,000 students on its 61-acre campus, Morehouse awards more degrees to black men than any institution in the nation, and has been called the Harvard of black colleges. Need we say more?

The college hasn't always been "The House." Founded in 1867, it was formerly known as the Augusta Institute, the Atlanta Baptist Seminary, and the Atlanta Baptist College. The most recent name, dating from 1913, honors Henry L. Morehouse, the secretary of the Northern Baptist Home Missions Society.

Now, if you're worried that an all-male school might put a damper on your social life, don't be—Spelman women are a stone's throw away. But for you wallflowers, each Morehouse freshman is paired with a Spelman sister, and co-ed classes are common (not to mention shared parties, sporting events, and the brother-sister Greek scene).

Tuition

For the 2004-05 academic year the total cost for first-time students was $24,488 (including room and board). For returning students, it was slightly less at $23,844. Neither of these prices takes into consideration personal expenses and/or additional fees.

Sports

The Maroon Tigers are affiliated with the Southern Intercollegiate Athletic Conference (SIAC) and Division II of the NCAA. Morehouse athletics teams also compete in first-class facilities: The Samuel H. Archer Student Center houses the James E. Haines Swimming Pool and intramural basketball courts, while the Harvey Stadium is home to the Maroon Tigers football team and the Flying Tigers track and field teams. The Tennis Center is the stomping ground for the tennis team that has won 25 of the last 26 SIAC championships, and the Frank Forbes Arena is where the Maroon Tiger basketball team competes.

Tickets for football games are $12 for adults, $8 for students with ID, free for children under 3. Tickets may be purchased at the gate on game day or in advance from the Business Office, which is located in Gloster Hall, Room 210. Call 404-681-2800 ext. 3252 for more information.

Culture on Campus

Music is a huge outlet on the Morehouse campus. The Concert Band, Glee Club, Jazz Band, and Marching Band are all nationally recognized musical groups. For the most part, these groups perform at either the King Chapel or the Sale Hall Chapel on campus. The Atlanta Symphony Orchestra often accompanies the choral concerts. In addition to music, there are about 70 clubs, organizations, and special interest groups. The eight major fraternities and sororities are located on campus and are very active. Many of them have outstanding step teams that often hold performances and competitions in Atlanta. If you hear about one, don't miss it!

Department Contact Information

Admissions Office 800-851-1254
Registrar's Office 404-681-2800
Student Health Center 404-215-2637
Bookstore 404-507-8685

For all departments, call 404-681-2800 and then the ext.
Division of Business & Economics . . . . . . ext. 2618
Division of Humanities & Social Sciences . ext. 2739
Division of Science & Mathematics . . . . . ext. 2609
Special Academic Program . . . . ext. 3512

Trinity Pl

E Maple St

N McDonough St

Office of
Facilities/
Central
Receiving

E Howard Ave

E College Ave

Avery Glen
Apartments

Main Loop

Milton Candler Dr

Hopkins Hall

W Howard Ave

Inman
Hall

Anna
Young
Alumnae
House

Rebekah
Scott Hall

Agnes
School Hall

Letitia Pate
Evans Hall

S McDonough St

Residential
Village

West
Parking

Public
Safety

Walters Hall

S Candler St

Avery St

Adams St

Presser
Hall

Buttrick Hall

McCain
Library

Alston
Campus
Center

Winship
Hall

MAP
33

Ansley St

Campbell Hall

President's
House

Dana Fine
Arts Building

Science Building

Winnonna Dr

W Dougherty St

E Dougherty St

Dance Center

Byers Tennis Courts

Woodruff
Physical
Activites
Building

Bruton St

342 South
McDonough

Gellerstedt
Track and Field

Bradley
Observatory and
Delafield
Planetarium

W Hancock St

E Hancock St

College Pl

Bucher Dr

General Information

NFT Map: 33
Address: 141 E College Ave
Decatur, GA 30030
Phone: 404-471-6000
Website: www.agnesscott.edu

Overview

A women's Presbyterian college founded in 1889, Agnes Scott College consistently ranks among the top ten liberal arts colleges of the South and as one of the country's most esteemed women's colleges. With just over 1,000 students, the school is rather small but, for those tired of running into the same female faces, the college participates in a cross-registration program with eighteen area colleges. With this fine education and a lack of male distraction, Agnes Scott women do some impressive things: Georgia's first female Rhodes Scholar was an alumna of Agnes Scott, as was the nation's first woman to be ordained a minister of the Presbyterian Church.

The picturesque campus—located six miles from the heart of metropolitan Atlanta in Decatur—has also served as a setting for many movie locations (perhaps most famously featured in *Scream II* in 1999).

Tuition

In the 2004-2005 academic year tuition costs were $22,050, while room and board was $8,200. Perhaps that's why *U.S. News & World Report* featured Agnes Scott on its 2005 list of "Great Schools at a Great Price." Of course, these prices exclude student fees, books, and other personal expenses.

Sports

The varsity sports teams compete at the Division III level, and they're proud of it! Students at Agnes Scott take great satisfaction in becoming future doctors, lawyers, and writers, not future pro athletes, but they still enjoy the thrill of competition. Varsity sports teams include basketball, soccer, cross-country, softball, swimming, tennis, and volleyball.

Culture on Campus

Agnes Scott contributes to the city's art scene through their Dalton Gallery and Winter Theatre. The Dalton Gallery (141 East College Ave, 404-471-5361) is housed in the Dana Fine Arts building on campus. It features contemporary art and at least one student show for graduating art majors each year. For more information on exhibits, visit http://daltongallery.agnesscott.edu.

The Winter Theatre, a 310-seat auditorium also located in the Dana Fine Arts Building, is the home turf of the college's theater troupe "Blackfriars"— the longest performing theater group in Atlanta. Each semester the student troupe presents one major production of a well-known work, one play for children, and an experimental student-authored production. Tickets to all performances cost $5 and you definitely get much more than you pay for. Call 404-471-6248 for tickets.

Department Contact Information

Log onto www.agnesscott.edu/studentlife/p_telecommunications.asp for a more complete university directory.

Admissions Office 404-471-6285
All-Sports Camps. 404-471-6362
Campus Bookstore 404-471-6350
Department of Public Safety 404-471-6355
Health Center. 404-471-6346
McCain Library 404-471-6094
Office of Human Resources 404-471-6384
Office of Multicultural Affairs 404-471-6082
The Dalton Gallery. 404-471-5361

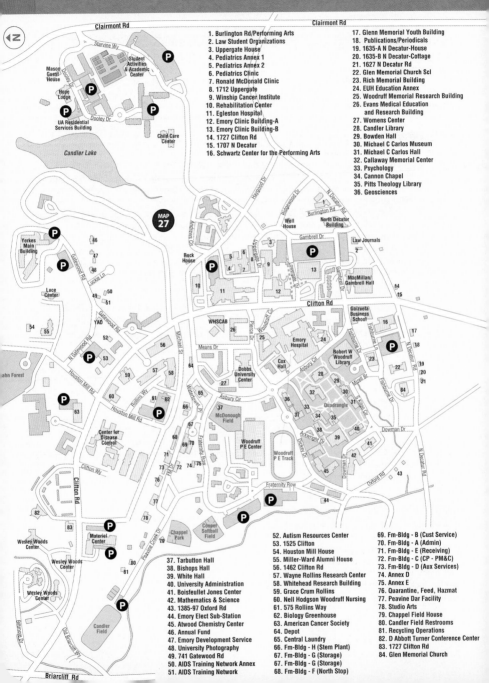

1. Burlington Rd/Performing Arts
2. Law Student Organizations
3. Uppergate House
4. Pediatrics Annex 1
5. Pediatrics Annex 2
6. Pediatrics Clinic
7. Ronald McDonald Clinic
8. 1712 Uppergate
9. Winship Cancer Institute
10. Rehabilitation Center
11. Egleston Hospital
12. Emory Clinic Building-A
13. Emory Clinic Building-B
14. 1727 Clifton Rd
15. 1707 N Decatur
16. Schwartz Center for the Performing Arts

17. Glenn Memorial Youth Building
18. Publications/Periodicals
19. 1635-A N Decatur-House
20. 1635-B N Decatur-Cottage
21. 1627 N Decatur Rd
22. Glen Memorial Church Scl
23. Rich Memorial Building
24. EUH Education Annex
25. Woodruff Memorial Research Building
26. Evans Medical Education
    and Research Building
27. Womens Center
28. Candler Library
29. Bowden Hall
30. Michael C Carlos Museum
31. Michael C Carlos Hall
32. Callaway Memorial Center
33. Psychology
34. Cannon Chapel
35. Pitts Theology Library
36. Geosciences

37. Tarbutton Hall
38. Bishops Hall
39. White Hall
40. University Administration
41. Boisfeuillet Jones Center
42. Mathematics & Science
43. 1385-97 Oxford Rd
44. Emory Elect Sub-Station
45. Atwood Chemistry Center
46. Annual Fund
47. Emory Development Service
48. University Photography
49. 741 Gatewood Rd
50. AIDS Training Network Annex
51. AIDS Training Network

52. Autism Resources Center
53. 1525 Clifton
54. Houston Mill House
55. Miller-Ward Alumni House
56. 1462 Clifton Rd
57. Wayne Rollins Research Center
58. Whitehead Research Building
59. Grace Crum Rollins
60. Nell Hodgson Woodruff Nursing
61. 575 Rollins Way
62. Biology Greenhouse
63. American Cancer Society
64. Depot
65. Central Laundry
66. Fm-Bldg - H (Stem Plant)
67. Fm-Bldg - G (Storage)
67. Fm-Bldg - G (Storage)
68. Fm-Bldg - F (North Stop)

69. Fm-Bldg - B (Cust Service)
70. Fm-Bldg - A (Admin)
71. Fm-Bldg - E (Receiving)
72. Fm-Bldg - C (CP - PM&C)
73. Fm-Bldg - D (Aux Services)
74. Annex D
75. Annex E
76. Quarantine, Feed, Hazmat
77. Peavine Dar Facility
78. Studio Arts
79. Chappel Field House
80. Candler Field Restrooms
81. Recycling Operations
82. D Abbott Turner Conference Center
83. 1727 Clifton Rd
84. Glen Memorial Church

General Information

NFT Map:	27
Mailing Address:	1380 Oxford Rd
	Atlanta, GA 30322
Phone:	404-727-6123
Website:	www.emory.edu

Overview

Founded by the Methodist Church in 1836, Emory University is home to 11,300 undergraduate and graduate students of many cultures and denominations. The school's main campus is located in the tree-lined suburban neighborhood of Druid Hills, 15 minutes from downtown Atlanta, and is by far the greenest campus in the city.

Emory College, the oldest college within the university, is the undergraduate school of arts and sciences, offering students over 50 possible majors. However, Emory is probably best known for its outstanding medical facilities and its School of Medicine, with six departments ranked among the top ten nationally. Though the university has many nationally-ranked programs and is typically found on "top 25" lists of national universities, Emory is often the fallback for Ivy-eyed Southern students. In addition to the College and medical school, the university has a two-year undergraduate program in its Oxford College (38 miles east of Atlanta), a graduate school of arts and sciences, and professional schools of medicine, theology, law, nursing, public health, and business.

Tuition

For the 2004-2005 academic year, the tuition was $28,940, with room and board running an additional $9,650. These prices exclude student fees, books, and other personal expenses. Graduate tuition and expenses vary by college.

Sports

Emory's sports teams are called the Eagles, but you won't find an obnoxious, life-sized mascot flapping around campus. Emory does not excel or even really participate in intercollegiate athletics. In fact, if you were to walk around the campus today, you might see a student wearing a T-shirt proudly stating that the Emory football team is "still undefeated." Emory doesn't have a football team!

Instead, Emory focuses most of its athletic energy on intramural sports, which are quite popular at the university. The George W. Woodruff Physical Education Center (WoodPEC) houses state-of-the-art fitness equipment, racquetball and tennis courts, an outdoor track and field facility, and a swimming pool. The pool is home to the men's and women's swimming teams, the athletic pride and joy of the school, as they consistently rank in the top ten in NCAA Division III competition.

Culture on Campus

The Donna and Marvin Schwartz Center for Performing Arts (1700 N Decatur Rd, 404-727-5050) is the music, dance, and theater center of the campus. The 90,000-square-foot facility includes a concert hall, a dance studio, and a theater lab. Visit http://schwartzcenter.emory.edu for a calendar of events and box office information.

The collections of the Michael C. Carlos Museum (571 S Kilgo Cir, 404-727-4282) span the globe and the centuries. Housed in a distinguished building designed by renowned architect Michael Graves, the Carlos maintains the largest collection of ancient art in the Southeast with objects from ancient Egypt, Greece, Rome, the Near East, and the ancient Americas. The museum is also home to collections of 19th- and 20th-century sub-Saharan African art and European and American works on paper from the Renaissance to the present. Check out www.carlos.emory.edu for more information.

Department Contact Information

Visit www.emory.edu/central/contact.html for a university directory and links to division and department email addresses.

Emory College Admissions 404-727-6036
Candler School of Theology
   (General Information). 404-727-6322
Goizueta Business School
   (General Information). 404-727-8099
Graduate School of Arts & Sciences . . 404-727-6028
Rollins School of Public Health 404-727-5481
School of Law. 404-727-6816
School of Medicine 404-727-5640
Woodruff School of Nursing. 404-727-6910

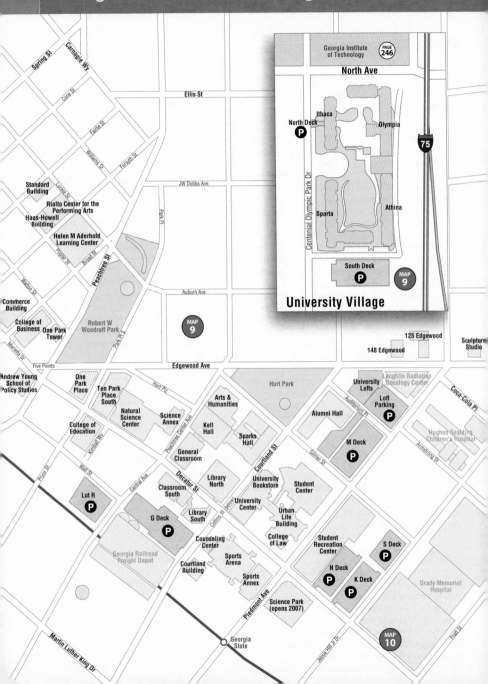

Spring St

Carnegie Wy

Cone St

Fairlie St

Williams St

Forsyth St

Ellis St

Lucke St

Standard Building

Rialto Center for the Performing Arts

Haas-Howell Building

Poplar St

Broad St

Helen M Aderhold Learning Center

Peachtree St

Park Pl

JW Dobbs Ave

Park Pl S

Auburn Ave

Georgia Institute of Technology

PAGE 246

North Ave

Ithaca

North Deck **P**

Olympia

75

Centenial Olympic Park Dr

Sparta

Athina

South Deck **P**

MAP 9

University Village

Walton St

Commerce Building

College of Business

One Park Tower

Marietta St

Robert W Woodruff Park

MAP 9

Five Points

Edgewood Ave

125 Edgewood

148 Edgewood

Sculpture Studio

Andrew Young School of Policy Studies

One Park Place

Ten Park Place South

Hurt Plc

Hurt Park

University Lofts

Loughlin Radiation Oncology Center

Coca-Cola Pl

Natural Science Center

Arts & Humanities

Auditorium Pl

Loft Parking **P**

College of Education

Kimball Wy

Science Annex

Peachtree Center Ave

Kell Hall

Sparks Hall

Alumni Hall

Gilmer St

M Deck **P**

Hughes Spalding Children's Hospital

Armstrong St

Pryor St

Wall St

General Classroom

Courtland St

Lot R **P**

Central Ave

Decatur St

Classroom South

Library North

Collins St (below)

University Bookstore

University Center

Student Center

G Deck **P**

Library South

Urban Life Building

Georgia Railroad Freight Depot

Counseling Center

College of Law

Student Recreation Center

S Deck **P**

Courtland Building

Sports Arena

N Deck **P**

K Deck **P**

Sports Annex

Piedmont Ave

Grady Memorial Hospital

Pratt St

Science Park (opens 2007)

Jessie Hill Jr Dr

MAP 10

Martin Luther King Jr Dr

Georgia State

General Information

NFT Map: 9, 10
Mailing Address: 33 Gilmer St SE
                     Atlanta, GA 30303
Phone: 404-651-2000
Website: www.gsu.edu

Overview

Georgia State is an urban research university in the fields of business, education, and urban affairs, so it helps that its home is downtown Atlanta. The second largest of Georgia's 86 accredited institutions of higher education, GSU enrolls over 28,000 students—more than ten percent of all enrolled students in the state. In other cities, a downtown location would offer students access to valuable resources and diverse experiences, but at GSU, the students and university bring the resources and experience to the city. Unfortunately, when school's out of session, downtown is largely lifeless.

Composed of six colleges (Arts & Sciences, Business Administration, Education, Health Sciences, Law and Public Policy), unique and arguably useless fields of study are also available to students such as entrepreneurship, gerontology (the study of aging), and hydrogeology (the study of the occurrence and effects of ground water), among others.

Tuition

For the 2004-2005 academic year, the undergraduate tuition for Georgia state residents was $4,154, while non-residents paid $14,260. Housing for the academic year was $5,130. Graduate tuition varies by college and, as always, all academic fees exclude student fees, books, and personal expenses.

Sports

Georgia State has a 17-sport athletics program, securing the school as a Division I player. However, because the school fails to have a "sacred" football team, or any football team for that matter, you probably won't hear much about the Panthers around town. Still, when it comes to other sports, the Panthers are alright. In particular, the basketball teams have received abundant press for winning 20 or more games seven times throughout the past 5 years and earning a combined six post-seasons bids. Through automatic conference bids, 13 of the teams have reached the highest goals by competing in NCAA postseason in men's basketball, women's basketball, men's soccer, volleyball, men's cross country, women's cross country, softball, men's golf, women's golf, men's tennis, and women's indoor and outdoor track.

Culture on Campus

Georgia State University's Rialto Center for the Performing Arts (80 Forsyth St, 404-651-4727) is an 833-seat performing arts venue located in the heart of the Fairlie-Poplar district in downtown Atlanta. The venue is home to the Rialto Series, which presents the best of national and international jazz, world music, dance, and cabaret. The center also hosts many School of Music performances and the Atlanta Film Festival. Visit www.rialtocenter.org for a calendar of events.

The campus is home to WRAS-Atlanta, the 100,000-watt voice of Georgia State University. WRAS is the most powerful, completely student-run college radio station in the US and plenty of locals would argue that Album 88 offers the best in Atlanta radio. Tune to 88.5 FM to listen in.

The campus also boasts its own movie theater within the University Center called Cinefest (66 Courtland St, 2nd fl, 404-651-CINE for showtimes) that often features top-notch independent and foreign films. Visit www.student.gsu.edu/~aragsdale1/ for film listings and movie times.

Department Contact Information

Visit http://campusdirectory.gsu.edu/eGuide/servlet/eGuide for a more complete university directory.

Undergraduate Admissions
  Office 404-651-2365
College of Arts & Sciences 404-651-2294
College of Education 404-651-2525
College of Health
  & Human Sciences. 404-651-3032
College of Law 404-651-2048
Robinson College of Business. 404-651-1913
Andrew Young School
  of Policy Studies 404-651-3990

Georgia Institute of Technology

1. Georgia Tech Hotel and Conference Center
2. Paul Heffernan House
3. Lutheran Center
4. Christian Campus Fellowship
5. Wesley Foundation/Methodist Center
6. Baptist Student Union
7. Catholic Center
8. Westminster Christian Fellowshiip
9. Edge Athletic Center
10. Rice Center for Sports Performance
11. Bobby Dobb Stadium
12. Navy ROTC Armory
13. Earth and Atmospheric Science (Old CE)
14. Daniel Laboratory
15. Army Office
16. Army Armory
17. Holland Building
18. WH Emerson Building
19. Lyman Hall
20. A French Building
21. Moore Student Success Center
22. Carnegie Building
23. Junior's Grill

24. Grants and Contracts
25. Athletic Association Conference Room
26. Smith Building
27. Savant Building
28. Guggenheim Building
29. Engineering Science and Mechanics (ESM) Building
30. Knight Building
31. Coon Building
32. Mechanical Engineering Research Building
33. Space Science and Technology Building (SST)
34. Office of Information Technology
35. GTRI Research
36. Crosland Tower
37. Cherry Emerson Building
38. Building Construction and Center for GIS (Arch Annex)
39. Pettit Microelectronics Research Center (MIRC)
40. Mason Civil Engineering Building

41. Lamar Allen Sustainable Education Building
42. Instructional Center
43. Groseclose Building
44. School of Industrial and Systems Engineering
45. UA Whitaker Building
46. Ajax Building
47. Beringause Building
48. Vernon D and Helen D Crawford Pool
49. CEISMC, Electronic Commerce Resource Cen

General Information

NFT Map: 5
Mailing Address: Georgia Institute of Technology
Atlanta, GA 30332
Phone: 404-894-2000
Website: www.gatech.edu

Overview

Consistently ranked among *U.S. News & World Report*'s top ten public universities in the United States, the Georgia Institute of Technology was founded in 1885 as a trade school. Today more than 16,000 undergraduate and graduate students receive an education in a variety of nationally recognized, top-ranked programs. Undergraduate and graduate degrees are offered at the Colleges of Architecture, Engineering, Sciences, Computing, Management, and the Ivan Allen College of Liberal Arts.

Honestly, though, what college with "technology" in the name produces outstanding liberal arts scholars? These students love slide rules and calculus. Random perks of attending Tech: 1. You get to live in the apartments where the Olympic athletes stayed in 1996. 2. You can play kickball on the world's largest expanse of artificial turf (at least that's what proud students and alumni claim). The one big disadvantage, however, is that the 400-acre campus is located in a somewhat seedy part of the city.

Tuition

For the 2004-2005 academic year, the undergraduate tuition and fees for Georgia residents was $2,139, while non-residents paid $8,779. Housing for the academic year ranged from $3,648-$5,308, depending on apartment size, style, and number of occupants. Meal plans vary in price and are in addition to housing prices. Graduate tuition, fees, and housing vary by college.

Sports

The school's sports teams have a variety of nicknames, including the *Ramblin' Wreck* and the *Engineers*, but they are most commonly called the *Yellow Jackets* in honor of their obnoxious bug mascot, Buzz. Tech offers a variety of intercollegiate sports for men and women, but the options are pretty standard. Gymnasts need not apply, and soccer players must be content with intramurals. It's also worth mentioning that Georgia Tech has a longstanding rivalry with another well-known Georgia school, the University of Georgia. Keep an eye out for those yellow baseball caps that proudly read, "To Hell With Georgia!" Visit www.ramblinwreck.collegesports.com for complete sporting event listings and ticket information.

Culture on Campus

The Ferst Center for the Arts (349 Ferst Dr NW, 404-894-9600) showcases concerts, recitals, lectures, dance, film, and theater. The facility houses an intimate 1,155-seat auditorium that is available to students at Georgia Tech and the greater Atlanta arts community. Programming for a season of music, theatre, dance, and opera performances lasts from September to May and the selection of musical genre ranges from jazz, classical, and blues to bluegrass, folk, and pop.

In addition, the center is home to several Atlanta performing arts companies that present all or most of their season at the Ferst: the Atlanta Lyric Theatre, Ballethnic Dance Company, and the Atlanta Gay Men's Chorus. The Georgia Tech Music Department also performs several concerts at the Ferst Center throughout the year. DramaTech, the campus theater group that has its own performance space, performs one show at the Ferst Center each spring as well. Visit www.ferstcenter.gatech.edu for more information or to purchase tickets.

Department Contact Information

Visit www.gatech.edu/offices-departments for a university directory and links to division and department web pages.

Office of Undergraduate Admissions . 404-894-4154
Office of Graduate Admissions 404-894-1610
College of Architecture 404-894-3880
College of Computing 404-894-3152
College of Engineering 404-894-3350
College of Management 404-894-2600
College of Sciences 404-894-3300
Ivan Allen College of Liberal Arts 404-894-1727

General Information

Atlanta Bicycle Campaign: www.atlantabike.org
Atlanta Peachtree
  Roadrollers Skate Club: www.aprr.org
Critical Mass Rides: www.critical-mass.org
General Skating
  Information: www.skateatlanta.com
MARTA: www.itsmarta.com
Southern Off-Road
  Bicycle Association: www.sorba.org
PATH Foundation: www.pathfoundation.org

Overview

Atlanta is consistently ranked as one of the most dangerous cities for pedestrians, which doesn't bode well for those on bikes or skates. Georgians like their cars and love their SUVs. Commutes are long, roads are crowded and hilly, and many streets have no room for alternative transportation such as bikes. Atlanta has recently made efforts to increase facilities for recreational bikers and skaters, so all is not lost.

Biking

Commuting by bike is a hairy affair, but there are plenty of opportunities to safely take to your two-wheeler after work and on weekends.

The PATH Foundation is a non-profit organization dedicated to developing a system of greenway trails throughout metro Atlanta—the results are every biker's dream. The Silver Comet trail connects Atlanta to Alabama, and 48 of the 60 miles are already complete. The Atlanta/DeKalb trail system includes an 18-mile stretch from Georgia Tech to Stone Mountain Park, as well as the Arabia Mountain trail in DeKalb County. Piedmont Park also remains one of the top destinations for urban bikers looking for a quick spin.

If you must take to the streets, residential neighborhoods like Reynoldstown, Grant Park, Little Five Points, Candler Park, Emory, Decatur, and Midtown are your best bets.

Also check out Critical Mass, a monthly event where cyclists join forces to reclaim the traffic-laden streets on the last Friday evening of each month.

Extreme bikers should head to the Georgia International Horse Park (770-860-4190); created for the 1996 Summer Games, it's the only Olympic mountain bike trail in the country.

Bikes Onboard Mass Transit

In an attempt to encourage city dwellers to use bikes for transportation, not just recreation, MARTA imposes no restrictions on bicycle access on trains. They simply ask bikers to use their judgment and to be considerate of other passengers. Bikes are only allowed on the front racks of buses—each bus rack accommodates two bikes.

Skating

Skaters are permitted to share the expansive PATH trails with the biker crowd, and that's just the beginning of Atlanta's numerous skating options. Piedmont Park is a nationally renowned skating venue. With hilly trails, flat terrain, and a roller-dance circle that's packed on weekends, Piedmont accommodates all skating abilities.

While Piedmont Park encourages skaters to show off their moves, not all parks allow skating (Centennial Olympic Park being one of them), so make sure you check park regulations before heading out with your blades.

You'll periodically see renegade groups of skaters from the Atlanta Peachtree Roadrollers Skate Club whizzing around the Highlands. Feel free to join in. The "Athens to Atlanta"—an 87-mile race from Athens, Georgia, to Piedmont Park—is the most famous skate race in America. The event takes place annually in October. For more information, visit www.a2a.net.

Bike/Skate Shops

	Address	Phone	Map
Intown Bicycles	1035 Monroe Dr	404-872-1736	6
Atlanta Pro Bicycle	632 N Highland Ave	404-874-1214	7
Let's Roll	10 Wall St	770-387-4241	9
Outback	1125 Euclid Ave	404-688-4878	11
Atlanta Cycling	4335 Cobb Pkwy	770-952-7731	16
REI Atlanta	1800 Northwest Expy NE	404-633-6508	23
Bicycle South	2098 N Decatur Rd	404-636-4444	29
Dunwoody Schwinn	4480 Chamblee Dunwoody Rd	770-455-3171	37
Atlanta Cycling	1544 Piedmont Rd	404-873-2451	N/A
Roswell Bicycles	670 Houze Wy	770-642-4057	N/A
Skate Escape	1086 Piedmont Ave	404-892-1292	N/A
The Silver Comet Depot	4342 Floyd Rd	770-819-3279	N/A

Boating/Sailing

If you're a big boater or sailor, why did you move to Atlanta? And why are you still here? It's landlocked. Still, a number of boating opportunities do exist in and around Atlanta. The man-made lakes are big enough for boating action, but you'll have to just imagine the ocean breeze. With the limitations on boating and sailing activity, canoeing, kayaking, rowing, and rafting provide alternatives for those with a hankering to experience the water. Your other option: move to Florida.

Rowing

While canoeists paddle on the Chestatee, crew enthusiasts are generally found pulling their oars through the Chattahoochee River. The easiest way to participate in rowing is through the not-for-profit Atlanta Rowing Club, which hosts races and offers lessons for beginners. Call 770-993-1879 for more information, or visit their website at www.atlantarowingclub.org.

Lake Allatoona

651 Marina Rd, Cartersville
There are 27 public recreation areas with boat launching ramps along the 270-mile shore of Lake Allatoona. Pricey motorboat rentals (about $150 per day) are also available by the hour, half-day, full day, or as sunset and moonlight cruises. Make reservations by calling 770-974-2628.

Allatoona Marinas

Allatoona Landing:	770-974-6089
Glade Marina:	770-975-7000
Harbor Town Marina:	770-974-6442
Holiday Marina Harbor:	770-974-2575
Little River Marina:	770-345-2900
Park Marina:	770-974-6063
Victoria Harbour:	770-926-7718
Wilderness Camp:	770-386-2170

Lake Lanier Islands

6950 Holiday Rd, Buford, 770-932-7255;
www.lakelanierislands.com
The resort and water park at Lake Lanier Islands, located just 45 minutes northeast of downtown Atlanta, remain the city's most popular daytrip destinations. If you're not interested in water sports, the 540 miles of shoreline is crowded with plenty of dry activities including golf, horseback riding, and luxury spas. Call 770-932-7255 for motorboat rentals (very pricey at a little more than $100 for two hours), or 770-271-1888 for sailboat rentals. Make sure you call before jumping in the car—several attractions are closed during off-peak seasons. Hours: May-September, Sunday-Friday: 10 am-6 pm; Saturday: 10 am-7 pm.

Sailing Clubs at Lake Lanier

Barefoot Sailing Club:	770-849-9803
Catalina 22, Fleet 58:	770-517-6200
Lake Lanier Sailing Club:	770-967-6441
Southern Sailing Club:	770-967-2224
Windjammer Barefoot Cruises:	630-966-9060

The Chestatee River

Highway 60, Dahlonega, 706-864-7117;
www.canoegeorgia.com
Once the regular stomping grounds of the Cherokees (before settlers in search of gold forced the tribe west), the Chestatee River has become a popular canoeing and kayaking destination that boasts first-rate fishing, secluded beaches, swimming holes, and mild rapids. The strong downstream current lets you relax while the water does the work. The downstream trip is six miles long and takes about two hours. Guided trips depart between 9 am and 3 pm on weekends, and 10 am and 3 pm on weekdays. Canoe rentals cost $42 for two people, and single-person kayaks can be rented for $27 (both prices include a shuttle from the outfitter to the river). For more information, call Appalachian Outfitters on 800-426-7117.

The Chattooga River

1251 Academy Rd, Long Creek, 864-647-9587
Although the address is South Carolina, the Chattooga actually starts in North Carolina and forms the border between Georgia and South Carolina. Used as a location in the Southern classic *Deliverance*, the Chattooga rapids will make you squeal like a pig—in a good way. There are several companies that offer whitewater rafting trips down the Southeast's first "Wild & Scenic" river. For the most thrilling ride, go in spring or early summer.

Atlanta Boat Show

285 Andrew Young International Blvd, NE Atlanta,
770-951-2500; www.atlantaboatshow.com
This three-day Atlanta Boat Show is held annually at the Georgia World Congress Center and caters to novices as well as boating aficionados. Learn about boating opportunities in Atlanta, participate in fishing and casting demos, sign-up for daily sailing seminars, enter the boating photo contest, and take in the largest display of boats in the southeast. Tickets for the boat show cost $8 for adults and $3 for children.

Sports • **Tennis**

General Information

**Atlanta Department of Parks,
  Recreation and Cultural Affairs**
Phone: 404-817-6766
Website:
www.atlantaga.gov/Government/Parks.aspx

Fulton County Department of Parks & Recreation
Phone: 404-730-6348
Website:
www.co.fulton.ga.us/departments/parks_rec.html

Overview

All of the city's public outdoor tennis courts are available on a first-come, first-served basis at no charge. The courts are run by either the City of Atlanta's Recreation Department or the Fulton County Department of Parks and Recreation—you can complain to them if there's a big crack across the court, if the lights have gone out, or if there aren't any court lights at all. Depending on the season and the school, area colleges and universities sometimes open their courts for public use (but you didn't hear that from us).

Outdoor Courts—Open to the Public

Main Parks

	Address	Phone	# Courts	Map
Washington	1125 Lena St NW	404-658-6229	8	8
Chastain	135 W Wieuca Rd NW	404-255-3210	9	18
Piedmont	400 Park Dr	404-853-3461	12	22
Bitsy Grant	2125 Northside Dr NW	404-609-7193	23	24

Northeast Courts

	Address	Phone	# Courts	Map
Bedford Pine Park	400 Merritts Ave NE	N/A	4	10
Selina S Butler Park	98 Wm Holmes Borders Dr NE	N/A	2	10
Lenox Wildwood Park	1760 Lenox Rd NE	N/A	2	26
Candler Park	1500 McLendon Ave NE	N/A	4	31
Goldsboro Park	Goldsboro Rd & Euclid Ave NE	N/A	2	31
Lake Claire Park	Lakeshore Dr (near McClendon)	N/A	1	31
McClatchey Park	Avery Dr & Westminster Dr NE	N/A	3	N/A

Northwest Courts

	Address	Phone	# Courts	Map
Underwood Hills Park	Ridgeway Ave & Harper Wy NW	N/A	2	1
Shady Valley Park	2720 Shady Valley Dr NW	N/A	3	22
Peachtree Hills	308 Peachtree Hills Ave NW	N/A	3	25
Anderson Park	98 Anderson Ave NW	N/A	3	N/A
Center Hill Park	2304 Donald L Hollowell Pkwy	N/A	1	N/A
English Park	1350 Bolton Rd NW	N/A	1	N/A
Frankie Allen Park	100 Bagley St & Pharr Rd NW	N/A	4	N/A
Grove Park	709 Hortense Pl NW	N/A	2	N/A
Knight Park	1194 Church St NW	N/A	1	N/A
Maddox Park	1115 Donald L Hollowell Pkwy	N/A	1	N/A
Mozley Park	1565 Mozley Pl SW	N/A	2	N/A

Southeast Courts

	Address	Phone	# Courts	Map
Grant Park	840 Cherokee Ave SE	N/A	4	13
Rosa L Burney Park	477 Windsor St SE	N/A	2	13
Phoenix II Park	Georgia Ave & Martin St SE	N/A	2	14
Rawson-Washington	Connally St & Kelly St NE	N/A	2	14
Coan Park	1350 Woodbine Ave SE	N/A	4	31
Bessie Branham Park	2051 Delano Dr & Norwood Ave	N/A	2	32
East Lake Park	241 Daniel Ave SE	N/A	2	32
Brownwood Park	Emerson Ave SE & Brownwood Ave SE	N/A	3	34
Pittman Park	950 Garibaldi St SE	N/A	3	45
Chosewood Park	401 Nolan St SE	N/A	1	46
Arthur Langford Park	211 Thornton St SE	N/A	4	N/A
Cleveland Avenue Park	41 Cleveland Ave SE	N/A	1	N/A
Empire Park	245 Oak Dr SE	N/A	2	N/A
Harper Park	Wilson Rd & Gilbert Rd SE	N/A	2	N/A
South Atlanta Park	Gammon St & Bisbee Ave SE	N/A	3	N/A

South Bend Park	1955 Compton Dr SE	N/A	2	N/A
Southside Park	Jonesboro Rd SE	N/A	6	N/A
Thomasville Park	1835 Henry Thomas Dr SE	N/A	1	N/A

Southwest Courts

	Address	Phone	# Courts	Map
Cleopas R Johnson	Fair St & Northside Dr NW	N/A	2	12
Perkerson Park	770 Deckner Ave SW	N/A	6	44
Adair II Park	Murphy Ave & Gillett St	N/A	2	N/A
Adams Park	2300 Wilson Dr SW	N/A	4	N/A
Ben Hill Park	2405 Fairburn Rd SW	N/A	2	N/A
Collier Park	3691 Collier Dr SW	N/A	2	N/A
Deerwood Park	Alexandria Dr & Tampa Trail SW	N/A	2	N/A
Harwell Heights Park	3114 Collier Dr SW	N/A	3	N/A
Melvin Drive Park	3895 Melvin Dr SW	N/A	2	N/A
Oakland City Park	1305 Oakland Dr SW	N/A	2	N/A
West End Park	1111 Oak St SW	N/A	2	N/A
West Manor Park	3204 W Manor Cir SW	N/A	2	N/A
Wilson Mill Park	300 Wilson Mill Rd SW	N/A	2	N/A

Golf

As the home of Bobby Jones (considered the greatest golfer of all time—especially if you live here) and the Masters Tournament, Atlanta has a pretty big golf chip on its shoulder. Pun intended. Pretty much everyone plays golf and, with decent weather year-round and a wide range of courses, there is time and space for all the would-be Bobbys. Well, almost. Feminist Martha Burk recently protested against the Augusta National Golf Course (home of the Masters) for not allowing female members. You can't expect much from a golf course that didn't allow its first black member until 1990. For us peons who don't happen to sport double-x chromosomes or have multi-million dollar bank accounts, Charlie Yates is probably the best course for your buck. Go at twilight and save $6!

Public Golf Courses

	Address	Phone	Par	Fees w/day-w/e
Alfred Tup Holmes	2300 Wilson Dr SW	404-753-6158	72	$22-$25
Arbor Springs	300 Arbor Springs Pkwy	770-683-4727	72	$30-$35
Bobby Jones	384 Woodward Wy NW	404-355-1009	71	$34-$38
Browns Mill	480 Cleveland Ave SE	404-366-3573	72	$35-$41.50
Candler Park 9	585 Candler Dr	404-371-1260	31	$10 all week
Charlie Yates	10 Lakeside Village Dr	404-373-4655	56	$32-$38
Chattahoochee	301 Tommy Aaron Dr	770-532-0066	72	$35-$52.50
Cherokee Run	1595 Centennial Olympic Pkwy	770-785-7904	72	$48-$69
Chestatee	777 Dogwood Wy	706-216-7336	71	$63-$79
Chicopee Woods	2515 Atlantic Hwy	770-534-7322	72	$47-$59
Cross Creek	1221 Cross Creek Pkwy NW	404-352-5612	54	$15-$20
Emerald Pointe	7000 Holiday Rd	770-945-8787	72	$70-$72
John A White	1053 Cascade Cir SW	404-756-1868	35	$12-$18
Lakeside	3600 Old Fairburn Rd	404-344-3629	72	$30-$40
North Fulton	216 W Wieuca Rd NE	404-255-0723	71	$36-$41
Olde Atlanta	5750 Ole Atlanta Hwy	770-497-0097	71	$55-$75
Reunion	5615 Grand Reunion Dr	770-967-8300	72	$39-$59
Stone Mountain	1145 Stonewall Jackson Dr	770-465-3278	72	$47-$60
Sugar Creek	2706 Bouldercrest Rd	404-241-7671	72	$21-$28
White Columns	300 White Columns Dr	770-343-9025	72	$80-$90
Wolf Creek	3000 Union Rd	404-344-1334	72	$49-$65

General Information

Atlanta Outdoor Club:
www.atlantaoutdoorclub.com
Dog Hikers of Georgia: 770-992-2363
Georgia Appalachian
Trail Club: www.georgia-atclub.org
Organized Group Hikes: www.funhikes.com
Women's Outdoor
Network: 770-937-6770;
www.wonatlanta.com

Amicalola State Park

418 Amicalola Falls Lodge Rd, Dawsonville,
706-265-8888; www.gastateparks.org/info/amicalola
Amicalola (Cherokee for "tumbling waters") is most famous for its 729-foot waterfall. The park also boasts twelve miles of wooded hiking trails, including a difficult eight-mile trail leading up to Springer Mountain (the southern tip of the Appalachian Trail) and great wildlife. Hours: 7 am-10 pm, daily. For more information, read the "North Georgia Mountains" page in Parks and Places.

From Atlanta, follow GA 400 to GA 53 towards Dawsonville. Turn right on Elliott Family Parkway (Highway 183), and continue on Highway 183 until it ends at GA 52. Turn right on GA 52, and you'll see the entrance to the park on the left. If you've driven more than a mile past Burt's Pumpkin Farm, you've probably gone too far.

Appalachian Trail Hiking in Georgia

404-634-6495, www.georgia-atclub.org
Moderate to difficult. A rather steep 75-mile section of the 2,150-mile Appalachian Trail cuts right across the Peach State, climbing from 2,500 to 4,400 feet in elevation.

The best way to get to the trailhead is to travel from Atlanta to Gainesville by car or train, then head to the Approach Trail at Amicalola Falls State Park—just one of the many entrances to the Appalachian Trail. Shuttle volunteers called "friends of thru hikers" also offer free rides from several locations in Atlanta to various trail access points. Check out www.georgia-atclub.org/directions.html for more details.

Bartram National Recreation Trail

706-782-3320
Moderate. This underappreciated trail traces the steps of William Bartram, 19th-century naturalist and explorer, who roamed the southern wilderness. Georgia's portion of trail covers 38 miles of terrain and offers a solitary hiking or backpacking experience with river fishing spots along the way. Located in the Chattahoochee National Forest, the northern end of the trail begins near the border of Georgia and North Carolina.

From Atlanta, follow 365 N until it becomes US 441 N. Take 441 N from Clayton to Dillard. A mile north of Dillard, turn right onto GA 246 towards Highlands, North Carolina. Continue on GA 246 and GA 106 for seven miles and turn right on Bald Mountain Road. Continue for 2.1 miles then take Forest Service Road 7 (Hale Ridge Road) for 1.1 miles.

Cloudland Canyon State Park

122 Cloudland Canyon State Rd, Rising Fawn,
706-657-4050; www.gastateparks.org/info/cloudland
The 2,343-acre park straddles a deep gorge, carved into the mountain by Sitton Gulch Creek. Trails range from two to seven miles, and day-hikers should check out the 4.5-mile West Rim and Waterfalls Trail. The hikes are decent, filled with scenic vistas and rugged terrain, and the camping is divine, with backcountry campsites available for $4 per person. Entry to the park is $2 per car, except on Wednesdays when it's free. Hours: 7 am-10 pm daily.

From Atlanta, take I-75 N for about 108 miles. Take Exit 2 to I-24 W, and then take Exit 167 to I-59 S. Get off at Exit 11 toward Trenton and take GA 136 E for about eight miles. The entrance to the park is clearly marked.

Kennesaw Mountain National Battlefield Park

Kennesaw, 770-427-4686
Easy to moderate. The trail (a little over two miles round trip) traces its way in and around Civil War battlefields. This isn't exactly backcountry kind of stuff though—you'll be hiking up a paved road to the mountaintop, and the trail gets pretty crowded on weekends. Even though there's a great view of downtown Atlanta and Cobb County from the apex, real hikers should head elsewhere. And if you're looking for a history lesson, you're better off staying home and reading books.

From Atlanta, follow I-75 to exit 269 (Barrett Parkway). At the light, turn west onto Barrett Parkway. Travel down Barrett Parkway for about three miles, turn left at the light onto Old Highway 41. Turn right at the next light (Stilesboro Road). The visitor center will be on your left. And if you're not the greatest navigator, just look for the brown and white road signs that guide you step by step to Kennesaw.

Stone Mountain Park

Highway 78 East, Stone Mountain, 30087, 770-498-5690; www.stonemountainpark.com
Easy to moderate. Meander through 3,200 acres of forestland, mountains, and lakes on three separate hiking trails of varying difficulty and try to ignore the 3,200 other people doing the same thing. The Walk-Up Trail (most difficult) takes you to the top of the mountain, the Cherokee Trail (medium difficulty) circles the base of the mountain, and the Nature Trail and Gardens (easiest) is a flatter amble for the less-able hiker. Located sixteen miles east of Atlanta, Stone Mountain is the country's largest block of exposed granite. The north mountainside bears a high-relief carving of American Confederacy heroes and also serves as a giant screen for the Lasershow Spectacular in the warmer months. Translation: lots and lots and lots of tourists. Park hours: 6 am-midnight, daily.

Driving from Atlanta, take I-75, exit 269 Barrett Parkway. Go southwest past Highway 41 (North Cobb Parkway) to Old Highway 41. Turn left and go to Stilesboro Road. Turn right and then left into the visitors center.

Sweetwater Creek State Park

1760 Mount Vernon Rd, Lithia Springs, 770-732-5871; www.gastateparks.org/info/sweetwater
Easy to moderate. Fifteen miles west of downtown Atlanta lies four loop trails that cover more than 9 miles of relatively easy hiking. The trails circle Civil War ruins (they're everywhere), secluded ponds, and waterfalls, offering an ideal setting for even a half-day retreat from city tension. Trails range from flat one-mile jaunts to three-mile uphill climbs. Incredible scenic views make the trek well worth the effort. Hours: 7 am-10 pm daily. Trails close at dark.

Driving from Atlanta, take I-20 west from Atlanta to exit 44 at Thornton Road, turn left and drive 1/4 mile. Turn right on Blairs Bridge Road. Drive two miles and turn left on Mount Vernon Road.

Sports • **Swimming**

Swimming

With Hotlanta's average summer temperature reaching 88.7 degrees, chances are you'll be seeking a pool for refuge. There are many city-run outdoor pools scattered throughout Atlanta, but those aren't really your best bet. Virtually every apartment complex in the city has a swimming pool—if you don't have one, make friends with someone who does.

There are five indoor natatoriums in the city for year-round swimming. In addition to standard lap swimming, these centers offer swimming lessons and aqua-aerobics. You can call any of these pools directly for more information or visit the city's website at www.atlantaga.gov, click on Departments, and then on Bureau of Parks.

*Indicates pools open during summer months only. Yearly rates are for Atlanta residents. Yearly rates for non-residents are $165.

Pools	Address	Phone	Fee (day, year)	Map
Maddox Pool*	1142 Donald L Hollowell Pkwy NW	404-892-0119	$2, $90	4
Piedmont Park Pool*	400 Park Dr NE	404-892-0117	$2, $90	6
Washington Park Natatorium	102 Ollie St NW	404-658-1436	$2, $90	8
Martin Luther King Jr. Natatorium	70 Boulevard Dr SE	404-658-7330	$2, $90	10
John F. Kennedy Natatorium	225 James P Brawley Dr SW	404-215-2855	$2, $90	12
Phoenix Pool*	477 Windsor St NW	404-522-0030	$2, $90	13
Rosa L Burney Park	477 Windsor St SE	404-522-0030	$2, $90	13
Chastain Park Pool*	235 W Wieuca Rd NW	404-841-9196	$3	18
Garden Hills Pool*	355 Pinetree Dr NW	404-848-7220	$2, $90	25
Candler Pool*	1500 McLendon Ave NE	404-373-4849	$2, $90	31
Pittman Pool*	950 Garibaldi St SE	404-522-0021	$2, $90	45
Arthur Langford Pool*	1616 Joyland Pl SE	404-622-3043	$2, $90	49
Adams Pool*	1581 Lagoon Ln SW	404-753-6091	$2, $90	N/A
Adamsville Park Natatorium	3201 Martin Luther King Jr Dr SW	404-505-3181	$2, $90	N/A
Anderson Pool*	100 Anderson Ave NW	404-799-0317	$2, $90	N/A
Dynamo Swim Center	3119 Shallowford Rd NE	770-457-7946	$5	N/A
Grant Park Pool*	25 Park Ave SE	404-622-3041	$2, $90	N/A
John A White Pool*	1101 Cascade Cir SW	404-755-5546	$2, $90	N/A
Powell Pool*	1690 Martin Luther King Jr Dr SW	404-753-7156	$2, $90	N/A
Southbend Pool*	2000 Lakewood Ave SE	404-622-3048	$2, $90	N/A
Southeast Natatorium	365 Cleveland Ave SE	404-624-0774	$2, $90	N/A
Thomasville Pool*	1745 Thomasville Dr SE	404-622-3045	$2, $90	N/A
Tucson Pool*	4610 Tucson Trail SW	404-349-4942	$2, $90	N/A

Bowling

When it comes to bowling, Atlanta holds its own in the realm of "dirty bowling halls." All are sketchy, but the shadiest is Express Lanes—if you're looking for a uniquely urban experience, complete with retro décor and an interesting crowd, bowl at Express.

If you'd rather bowl with hicks, Budweiser drinkers, and scads of Abercrombie teens, head to either AMF Snellville or Brunswick Gwinnett Lanes. Gwinnett Lanes caters

mostly to the high school crowd with "cosmic bowling" on summer nights and a huge arcade of games (they also have forty lanes of pure bowling bliss). Lanes fill up quickly on a first-come, first-served basis, so be prepared to wait.

If you don't want to wait to bowl, try the Northeast Plaza Fun Bowl—the dark lanes are underground, giving the bowling experience a unique bomb shelter aesthetic that most people tend to avoid.

Name	Address	Phone	Adult Fees (including shoe rental)	Map
Express Lanes	1936 Piedmont Cir NE	404-874-5703	$5 until 6 pm, $6 evenings	3
Northeast Plaza Fun Bowl	3285 Buford Hwy NE	404-636-7548	$5 weekdays, $6 after 5 pm & w/e	23
Suburban Fun Bowl	2619 N Decatur Rd	404-373-2514	$4.50 until 6 pm, $5.50 evenings & w/e	30
AMF Chamblee Lanes	2175 Savoy Dr	770-451-8605	$7 until 5pm, $8 after 5 pm & w/e	37
Bleachers Chamblee	2175 Savoy Dr	770-451-8605	$7 until 5 pm, $8 evenings & w/e	37
AMF Bowling	4990 Jimmy Carter Blvd	770-923-5080	$6 until 5 pm, $8 evenings & w/e	N/A
AMF Snellville Lanes	2350 Reagan Pkwy	770- 972-5300	$4 until 5 pm, $8 after 5 pm & w/e	N/A
AMF Union City Lanes	5100 Goodson Connector	770-969-0100	$7 until 5 pm, $8 after 5 pm & w/e	N/A
AMF Woodstock Lanes	108 Woodpark Blvd	770-926-2200	$7.50 until 5 pm, $8 evenings & w/e	N/A
Brunswick Gwinnett Lanes	3835 Lawrenceville Hwy	770-925-2000	$7 until 6 pm, $8 evenings	N/A
Cherokee Lanes	1149 Marietta Hwy	770-345-2866	$4 until 6 pm, $6 evenings & w/e	N/A
Forest Park Lanes	4929 Jonesboro Rd	404-366-2810	$5 until 6 pm, $5.50 evenings, $6 w/e	N/A
Glenwood Lanes	4161 Glenwood Rd	404-284-1010	$3.75 until 6 pm, $5.25 evenings & w/e	N/A
Magnolia Lanes	1400 Bowling Lane	770-229-2695	$5.25 until 5 pm, $6.25 evenings & w/e	N/A

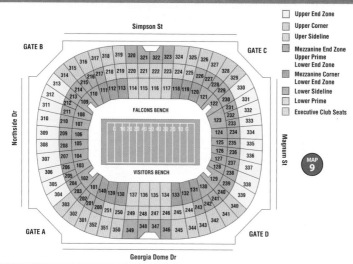

Simpson St

GATE B

GATE C

Northside Dr

Magnum St

FALCONS BENCH

VISITORS BENCH

GATE A

GATE D

Georgia Dome Dr

- Upper End Zone
- Upper Corner
- Uper Sideline
- Mezzanine End Zone
  Upper Prime
  Lower End Zone
- Mezzanine Corner
  Lower End Zone
- Lower Sideline
- Lower Prime
- Executive Club Seats

MAP 9

General Information

NFT Map:	9
Address:	One Georgia Dome Dr
	Atlanta, GA 30313
Phone:	404-223-4636
Website:	www.gadome.com
Falcons Website:	www.atlantafalcons.com
Falcons Phone:	770-965-3115
Ticketmaster:	404-223-8000

Overview

There's a theme to Atlanta professional sports: amazing facilities, not-so-amazing teams. That feeling rings especially true when it comes to the Georgia Dome and the Falcons.

"The Dome" is a gargantuan convention, sports, and entertainment venue. It is 27-stories tall and holds 71,250 seats, making it the largest cable-supported domed stadium in the world. It was built in 1992 in response to the threat that the Falcons would leave the city if they weren't provided with a new and improved nest. It might have been better if they had flown the coop; the team has made only one Super Bowl appearance (in 1998) during its 38 year existence—and they lost. But for some reason (i.e. Michael Vick), Atlantans are still rabid Falcons fans.

How to Get There—Driving

Traveling south on I-75, take Exit 252/Northside Drive. Turn right on Northside Drive and the dome will be on your left. Traveling south on I-85, take Exit 249C/Williams Street. Turn right on Alexander, left on Centennial Olympic Park Drive, right onto Martin Luther King Jr. Drive, and right on Northside Drive. The Dome will be on your right.

Traveling north on the I-75/85 Connector, take Exit 246/Downtown/Central Avenue. Take Central Avenue to Martin Luther King Jr. Drive and turn left. Make a right on Northside Drive and the Dome will be on your right.

Traveling west on I-20, take Exit 58A/Spring-Windsor Street. Turn right on Spring Street, left on Martin Luther King Jr. Drive, and right on Northside Drive. The dome will be on your right.

Parking

Parking is sometimes a problem during events. There are over 4,000 spaces located right next to the dome that cost $8 per day. They fill up quickly, so get in early.

How to Get There—Mass Transit

Highly recommended. MARTA trains run frequently to the dome before and after all events. Take a MARTA train to the Phillips Arena/Dome/GWCC Station. A walkway will take you from the platform to the arena—just follow the crowds.

How to Get Tickets

Tickets for Falcons home games are almost always available, unless the team is doing exceptionally well (unlikely). Ticket prices range from $50 to $5,680 (for a seat in the VIP suite). The Falcons ticket office is located in the Georgia Dome. If you don't want to go in person, give Ticketmaster a call on 404-223-8000 or visit www.ticketmaster.com.

General Information

NFT Map:	9
Address:	1 Philips Dr
	Atlanta, GA 30303
General Information:	404-878-3000
Website:	www.philipsarena.com
Hawks Phone:	404-827-DUNK (3865)
Hawks Website:	www.nba.com/hawks
Thrashers Phone:	404-584-PUCK
Thrashers Website:	www.atlantathrashers.com
Ticketmaster:	404-249-6400

Overview

You'd be forgiven for thinking that the ultra-modern and shiny (it's made of glass and steel) Philips Arena is a sports complex that was built for champions. The only winners at this venue are inevitably Atlanta's opponents. The last time the NBA's Atlanta Hawks won a championship was in 1958—when they were based in St. Louis. Philips is also home to the Thrashers of the NHL. Founded in 1999 and named for the state bird, this young hockey team has had some relatively decent seasons so far. Philips also hosts major music concerts and lots of ice skating. Club seats and luxury boxes are situated along only one side of the playing surface, affording great views for all. Concertgoers, however, must endure some rather horrible acoustics.

How to Get There—Driving

From the north, take I-75/I-85 S and exit at Williams Street (249C). Turn right on Baker Street and left onto Centennial Olympic Park Drive. From the south, take I-75/I-85 N and exit at Andrew Young International Boulevard (248C). Turn left onto Centennial Olympic Park Drive.

From the east, take I-20 W and exit at Windsor/Spring Street (56B). Turn right onto Spring Street, left onto Marietta Street, and left onto Centennial Olympic Park Drive.

Parking

Parking is available in several lots around the arena including the CNN Decks, Centennial Garage on Centennial Olympic Park Drive, and the Philips Arena lot on Park Avenue West (formally Foundry Street). Prices at these lots vary depending on the event, but usually range from $12-$20.

How to Get There—Mass Transit

MARTA is the easiest and most efficient means of transportation to the center. The Philips Arena/CNN Center (W-1) is one stop west of the Five Points Station

How to Get Tickets

Tickets for all events can be purchased through Ticketmaster. You can also visit the arena box office Monday-Friday, 9:30 am-5 pm. The office is closed weekends except on event days, when it opens at 12 pm.

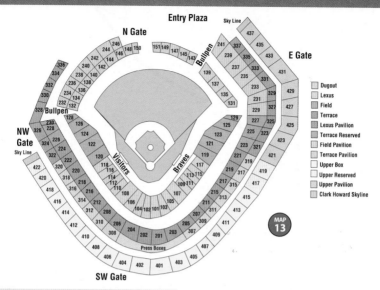

Entry Plaza

N Gate — Sky Line — E Gate — NW Gate — Sky Line — SW Gate — Bullpen — Visitors — Braves — Press Boxes

MAP 13

- Dugout
- Lexus
- Field
- Terrace
- Lexus Pavilion
- Terrace Reserved
- Field Pavilion
- Terrace Pavilion
- Upper Box
- Upper Reserved
- Upper Pavilion
- Clark Howard Skyline

General Information

NFT Map: 13
Address: 755 Hank Aaron Dr
Atlanta, Georgia 30315
Phone: 404-522-7630
Tickets by Phone: 404-249-6400
Websites: www.atlantabraves.com
www.ballparks.com/baseball/national/turner.htm

Overview

Plans were made in 1996 to turn the 50,000-seat Olympic Stadium into the new home of the Braves following the Summer Games. To the dismay of many Atlantans, the old Atlanta-Fulton County Stadium, where the Cinderella team went from worst to first in 1991, was leveled and turned into a parking lot. The first Braves game at Turner Field took place on April 4, 1997, with the Braves ominous loss to the Chicago Cubs, 5-4. Despite impressive teams and strong seasons, the Braves have only won one pennant and not a single World Series since moving into their flashy new digs. Atlantans can only hope that the Braves will overcome their post-season jinx—they're our city's greatest athletic hope.

How to Get There—Driving

From 1-75/85 N/S, take the Fulton Street exit (Exit 246) and turn east onto Fulton Street (toward the Olympic Torch). Make a right onto Hank Aaron Drive and Turner Field will be on the right.

From 1-20 E, exit at Turner Field/Capital Street (Exit 58A). Turn left onto Fulton Street, then make a right onto Hank Aaron Drive. Turner Field is on the right. From 1-20 W, exit at Windsor Street (Exit 56B) and turn right onto Windsor Street. Make a left onto Fulton Street, then turn right onto Hank Aaron Drive. Turner Field is on the right.

Parking

Parking is plentiful, but not cheap—$10 per car and $30 per bus, RV, or limo. Your best bet is the Orange Lot, located at the corner of Fulton Street and Hank Aaron Drive. Start looking for parking signs when you get off the freeway.

How to Get There—Mass Transit

Take the North/South MARTA line to Five Points Station and exit on the Forsyth Street side. The Braves shuttle begins pick-ups from the station one hour before game time and performs drop-offs for one hour after the game.

How to Get Tickets

It's not hard to secure Braves tickets these days. Prices range from $1 (you have to buy the tickets at the box office three hours before the game, and you'll be sitting in the clouds) to $48 for dugout seats. Order tickets by phone or online at www.nettickets.com or www.ticketmaster.com.

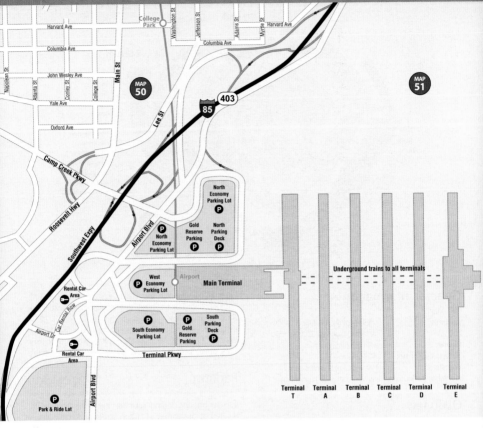

General Information

NFT Map:	50 & 51
Address:	6000 N Terminal Pkwy
	Atlanta, GA 30320
Phone:	404-530-6600
Websites:	www.atlanta-airport.com
Airport Police:	404-530-6630
Ground Transportation:	404-530-6674
Lost & Found:	404-530-2100 x100

Overview

Atlanta proudly claims the "busiest airport in the world" title. With over 78 million travelers passing through the gates, the Hartsfield-Jackson Atlanta International Airport has claimed this title since 1998. Share this trivia with your Yankee friends who doubt that Atlanta is anything close to cosmopolitan, although we do have to admit that Atlanta's "hub" status might account for more travelers in transit than actual visitors.

The airport is easy to get to, but don't count on Southern hospitality once you're there—an Atlanta police officer recently threw a woman to the ground while arresting her for a parking violation. The officers at the airport are not always the friendliest characters, so be sure to obey all traffic rules, and don't linger curbside waiting for passengers. In addition to the usual airport hassles of traffic congestion, check-in lines, and long security lines, the gigantic size of ATL requires riding an "Automated People Mover" (a.k.a. subway train) to get to your gate.

The airport began operation in 1925, when Mayor Walter A. Sims signed a five-year lease on an abandoned auto racetrack and developed it into an airfield. In the 1940s, Delta Airlines moved its headquarters from Monroe, Louisiana to Atlanta, and still calls the airport home. When former mayor William B. Hartsfield passed away in 1971, the airport was renamed in his honor. Most recently, the name was changed to Hartsfield-Jackson in honor of another former Atlanta mayor, the late Maynard H. Jackson.

Transit • **Hartsfield-Jackson Airport**

How to Get There—Driving

From the north and downtown, take I-85 S to Exit 18A. From the south, take I-75 N to I-285 W and get off at Exit 3. From the east and west, take I-285 to I-85, then take Exit 18A. All exits are clearly marked for the airport.

Parking

If you're driving to the airport, there are more than 30,000 short- and long-term parking spaces available. Even so, parking fills up (after all, it *is* the world's busiest airport). Call 877-ATL-PARK for current parking information.

Hourly lots are $1 per hour for the first two hours and $2 per hour thereafter; at $48 per day, don't plan on parking there overnight. Daily parking lots are adjacent to the main terminal and charge $1 per hour and $12 per day. The North and South economy lots are next to the daily parking decks and the West economy lot is at the west end of the main terminal beyond the Ground Transportation Center. (The West lot is usually the best bet because it's rarely full.) All economy lots charge $1 per hour and $8 per day.

Airport Park-Ride lots are $9 per day. They're further away, but the airport provides free shuttle service to the main terminal. To return to the Park-Ride lots, take the shuttle from the Ground Transportation Center. Waiting for the bus can be a hassle, especially if it is cold, rainy, or really busy. Use these lots only as a last resort. There are also several park-ride lots on Camp Creek Parkway that are not affiliated with the airport.

How to Get There—Mass Transit

MARTA is the most efficient way to get to ATL from the Atlanta metro area. MARTA's Airport Station is the final stop on the South Line—a 16-minute trip from Five Points Station. All southbound trains go to the airport and there's plenty of luggage space available at the end of each railcar for your bags. If you're carrying a lot of gear, head for the elevators at each station.

How to Get There—Shuttle

Shared-ride shuttle services are available and include transportation to hotels, metro areas, non-metro areas, businesses, or residential locations. When leaving the airport, visit the Ground Transportation Center's island "F". For reservations, try Airport Metro Shuttle (404-766-6666), Atlanta Link (404-524-3400), or Airport Perimeter Connection (404-761-0260). Check the airport website for other services.

Car Rentals

Avis	404-530-2725
Budget	404-530-3000
Enterprise	404-763-5220
Hertz	404-530-2925
National/Alamo	404-530-2800
Thrifty	770-996-2350
(Off Airport)	
Airport Rent-A-Car of Atlanta	800-905-4997
Dollar	866-434-2226
EZ Rent a Car	404-761-4999
Payless Car Rental	404-766-5034

Hotels

AmeriSuites • 3415 Norman Berry Dr • 404-768-8484
Clarion Suites • 4820 Massachusetts Blvd • 770-996-0000
Courtyard by Marriott • 2050 Sullivan Rd • 770-997-2220
Crown Plaza • 1325 Virginia Ave • 404-768-6660
Days Inn • 4505 Best Rd • 404-767-1224
Embassy Suites • 4700 Southport Rd • 404-767-1988
Hilton • 1031 Virginia Ave • 404-767-9000
Holiday Inn • 1380 Virginia Ave • 404-762-8411
Ramada Inn • 1551 Phoenix Blvd • 770-996-4321
Sleep Inn • 1911 Sullivan Rd • 770-996-6100
The Westin • 4736 Best Rd • 404-762-7676
Wellesley Inn • 1377 Virginia Ave • 404-762-5111

Terminal North

Code	Airline	Phone	Concourse
AC	Air Canada	888-247-2262	D
JM	Air Jamaica	800-523-5585	E
FL	AirTran	800-247-8726	C
AA	American	800-433-7300	T
HP	AmericanWest	800-327-7810	D
BA	BritishAirways	800-247-9297	E
CO	Continental	800-231-0856	D
3C	Corporate	800-555-6565	D
F9	Frontier	800-432-1359	D
D9	Independence Air	800-359-3594	D
KE	Korean Air	800-438-5000	E
LH	Lufthansa	800-645-3880	E
YX	Midwest	800-452-2022	D
NW	Northwest	800-225-2525	D
UA	United	800-241-6522	T
US	US Airways	800-428-4322	D

Terminal South

Code	Airline	Phone	Concourse
AM	Aeromexico	800-237-6639	E
AF	Air France	800-237-2747	E
EV	ASA	800-325-1999	C
DL	Delta Air Lines	800-325-1999	A, B, D & T
DL	Delta Air Lines	800-221-1212 (INT'L)	E
OH	Comair	800-325-1999	C
SA	South African	800-722-9675	E
H1	Hooters Air	888-359-4668	B

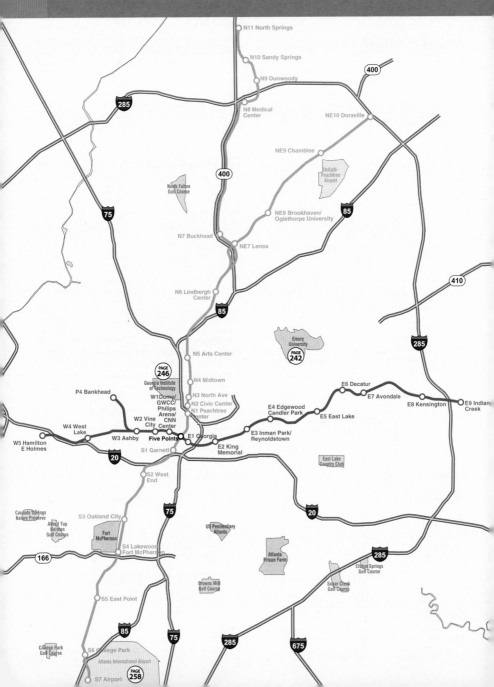

General Information

Mailing Address: 2424 Piedmont Rd NE
                            Atlanta, GA 30324
MBTA Website: www.itsmarta.com
Main Phone: 404-848-5000
Customer Info: 404-848-4711
Customer Service: 404-848-4800
Lost & Found: 404-848-3208
                            (Five Points Station)

Overview

The Metropolitan Atlanta Rapid Transit Authority (MARTA) comprises a network of bus routes that are linked to the metro rail system, allowing passengers to transfer to the higher-capacity trains free of charge (ask your bus driver for a transfer).

If you're expecting MARTA to measure up to New York's subway or Chicago's El, prepare to be disappointed. The claim is that "It'sMARTA," but most Atlantans haven't caught on. This may be because the rail system is limited in service (the network boasts a whopping 38 stations), and riding the bus doesn't make much sense when you can just drive your car.

MARTA is most useful for transportation to the airport or to events at the Georgia Dome and Philips Arena. But even then, you usually have to drive your car to an outlying MARTA station. The good news: parking at most stations is free.

Rail

The Rapid Rail system operates two main lines. The north-south line runs from the North Springs Station (N11) and the Doraville Station (NE10), both outside the I-285 perimeter highway, to Hartsfield-Jackson Atlanta International Airport (S7) in the south. The northeast line branches from the north line after Lindbergh Center (N6) and roughly follows the path of I-85 through Atlanta. The north line parallels the GA 400 toll way.

The east-west line connects the Hamilton E. Holmes Station (W5), near the western interchange of I-285 and I-20, with the Indian Creek Station (E9) at the eastern end of the line.

The rail system operates from approximately 5 am until 1 am Monday through Friday and from 5 am until 12:30 am on weekends and holidays. Trains run approximately every ten minutes on weekdays and every five minutes from Lindbergh Center Station to the Airport. On Saturdays, Sundays, and holidays, trains operate at approximately 15-minute intervals. For major special events, MARTA trains operate as frequently as every five minutes.

Buses

MARTA operates more than 700 buses on 154 routes. The system has the third-largest fleet of buses operating on compressed natural gas, a clean-burning fuel chosen to support the city's effort to improve air quality. Three-quarters of the buses include wheelchair lifts. Buses operate from 5 am until 1:30 am Monday through Friday and from 5:30 am until 12:30 am on weekends and holidays. Check the website for specific routes and schedules.

Fares & Tickets

A single fare token costs $1.75, a roll of ten tokens is $17.50, and a roll of twenty tokens is $30. For regular commuters, weekly or monthly unlimited TransCards cost $13 and $52.50 respectively. For primary and secondary students attending school in Fulton and DeKalb counties, a Student TransCard can be used on buses and trains from 6 am until 7 pm on weekdays—weekly cards cost $10. College students can check with their school to see if they participate in the discounted University Pass program. Half-Fare Cards are available for seniors and the disabled. Out-of-town visitors should check out the Visitor's Pass, which can be purchased in advance for a predetermined number of days.

Bicycles

Atlanta cyclists often use MARTA as part of their journey. Bicycles are permitted on trains at all times. On MARTA buses, bikes have to be stored on the racks on the front (i.e. not inside). Each bus can only handle two bikes at a time—first come, first served.

Parking

Free daily parking is available at twenty-four MARTA rail stations. The following stations offer long-term secure parking for $3-$6 (cash only) per day: Lindbergh Center, Dunwoody, Sandy Springs, North Springs, Lenox, Brookhaven, Doraville, Kensington, and College Park. Sure beats the cost of parking at the airport.

Overview

The MARTA system was originally intended to serve five Atlanta counties, but it only serves Fulton and DeKalb. Cobb, Gwinnett, and Clayton haven't gotten "SMARTA with MARTA" for a variety of reasons—suburban residents fear that the train is a shuttle of mayhem that will pipe crime into their blissful lives and tax-wary conservatives don't want to pay the extra 1% sales tax to support the darned thing. But the deciding factor might be that suburbanites fear that their SUVs might become obsolete with alternative transportation. These counties have created their own bus systems instead. We're not really sure how this appeases their concerns, but it seems to make them happy.

Gwinnett County Transit

770-822-5010; www.gctransit.com
Gwinnett County Transit (GCT) is the public bus system that serves Gwinnett County, one of metro Atlanta's most populated regions. Express buses began running in 2001 and local buses began service in 2002. The express buses to downtown Atlanta are geared to accommodate commuters and run Monday through Friday on six routes. The local buses run Monday through Saturday; no buses run on Sunday (you should be driving your SUV to church).

A one-way fare costs $3 on express buses and $1.75 on local buses. If you transfer from a local bus to an express bus, you pay the $1.25 difference. For daily riders, the best deal is the Express Monthly Pass ($100), which allows unlimited access to both express and local buses. The Local Monthly Pass costs $55. You can transfer for free to any MARTA bus or train line from any GCT bus—just ask the driver for a transfer slip. The converse is also true—when you pay your MARTA fare, ask for a transfer slip and present it to the GCT bus driver. Visit the GCT website or call them for details about discounts for seniors and students, Paratransit for the disabled, and specific route and scheduling information.

Cobb Community Transit

770-427-4444; www.cobbdot.org/cct.htm
Cobb Community Transit (CCT) operates 13 local and two express bus routes in Cobb County. Most lines operate Monday through Friday, but there are some routes that run on Saturday. None of the buses run on Sunday because Chick-fil-A is closed and, honestly, why bother traveling if you can't get to Chick-fil-A?

The one-way fare on a local bus is $1.25. The express route costs $3 one-way and $4 round-trip. If you transfer from a local bus to an express bus, you have to pay the fare difference. You can transfer from any CCT bus to a MARTA train or bus free of charge; be sure to request a transfer slip from the driver. Again, monthly passes are the way to go for frequent bus riders. A monthly Local Pass is $45 and a monthly Express Round-Trip Pass is $70. Visit the CCT website or call them for details about senior/youth/disabled discounts, Paratransit service for the disabled, and specific route and schedule information.

Clayton County C-TRAN

770-472-8800;
http://web.co.clayton.ga.us/ctran/index.htm;
What fun you can have riding in and around Clayton County! The fare system is relatively simple: $1.50 for a one-way adult fare and a $52.50 for an unlimited monthly pass. The usual discounts are available for seniors, children, and disabled individuals. You can transfer between all C-TRAN buses and MARTA bus or rail free of charge. Just ask your driver for a free transfer slip.

Times vary on individual routes. In general, buses operate Monday through Friday from 5 am to 12 am, Saturday from 6 am to 12 am, and Sunday from 7 am to 10 pm (normal life *does* continue on Sundays in Clayton). Visit the website or call for specific details regarding route and scheduling information.

General Information

Address: Parking Violations Bureau
                        City Court of Atlanta
                        150 Garnett St
                        Atlanta, GA 30303

Department of Transportation (GDOT):
Phone: 404-656-5267
Website: www.dot.state.ga.us

Parking Tickets

In many ways, Atlanta is a city of the future. In other ways, Georgians are still living in the past. You'll catch a glimpse of Atlanta's more archaic side when you need to pay a parking ticket or find out where the hell your car went when it was towed. In most cities, this information is made easily accessible on the web. Not so in Atlanta.

Paying parking tickets not only creates a huge dent in your wallet, but it's an enormous hassle: you can pay in person at the Traffic Violations Bureau or you can send a money order, cashier's check, or company check (but not a personal check) to Parking Violations Bureau, City Court of Atlanta, 150 Garnett St, Atlanta, GA 30303. The other option is to call 404-658-6940 and be disconnected eight times before getting through to someone to pay by credit card.

In short, the city of Atlanta doesn't make it easy for residents to pay parking tickets, which could explain why the city is losing millions of dollars every year on unpaid tickets. The parking division of Atlanta's Traffic Court was recently disbanded and, rather than go through the ridiculous state-imposed rigmarole it takes to pay traffic tickets, most drivers choose to simply ignore their parking tickets altogether.

Meters

You can generally find a parking spot without a meter, as there are plenty of neighborhoods and side streets that are meter-free (if you're willing to walk a couple of blocks). Most meters are not 24-hour, so if you go out in the evening in the Highlands (for example), you don't need to worry about dropping change. Parking downtown is another story altogether. Almost all metered parking spaces downtown are enforced 24 hours a day, seven days a week, thanks to the greedy genius of city council and lost revenue from unpaid parking tickets. Carry plenty of change with you.

You should also be equipped with change when heading to Decatur or the Highlands during the daytime. When dealing with meters, make sure you read the posted signs and the instructions on the meter carefully.

Pay-to-Park

There are numerous legitimate parking decks and other pay-to-park operations throughout Atlanta. There are also many pay-to-park hustlers who pretend to work for a parking company, but instead they take your money and run. The best are the homeless folks outside Apache Café who carry around cones, block off free spaces, and then charge customers to park in spaces with which they have no affiliation.

Decks usually charge by the hour and lots range from a couple of bucks to $15 if there is a special event nearby. Make sure that the person you pay is a legitimate employee, and always pay the cash box (not the shady guy) if there's one on the lot. Otherwise you could run the risk of getting booted or towed.

Residential Permit Parking

To obtain a residential parking permit, call Atlanta's Office of Transportation at 404-330-6501 for an application. A residential parking permit costs $12 for two years and is only recognized in the neighborhood for which it is registered.

Tow Pound

Finding out where your car has been impounded after it has been towed depends on where it was parked:

Atlanta: 404-853-4330
Roswell: 770-551-7600
Forsyth: 770-751-0581
Alpharetta County: 770-751-0581

General Information

DMV Website:	www.dmvs.ga.gov
Driver's License Information:	678-413-8400
Motor Vehicle Tag and Title:	404-362-6500
Accident Reporting:	678-413-8647

Overview

Grid is a four-letter word that the masterminds of Atlanta roadways avoid, and logic, although it has five letters, has earned an equally lewd reputation. If Atlanta is the New York of the South, the similarity ends at the roadways. Atlanta has a distinct absence of neat grids, and there is no alternative logic to replace the sequential beauty of streets and avenues in NYC.

To make things worse, Atlanta also has lots of traffic and little public transportation. The traffic results from the large suburban population traveling into the city for work. The irony is that when asked why they moved to the suburbs, people will respond, "To avoid the traffic."

The Highways

Yes, we have highways. Actually they are some of the nicest in the country, but they are also some of the busiest. Three of the nation's biggest bottlenecks are the I-85, I-75, I-20, and I-285. Both I-85 and I-75 run north-south while I-20 runs east-west, and I-285 goes round and round.

I-85 connects Atlanta with Greenville (South Carolina) and Charlotte (North Carolina) to the north and with Montgomery (Alabama) to the south. I-85 S is also the route to the "Redneck Riviera," also known as Panama City, a popular destination for spring break on the Florida panhandle.

I-75 N runs from Atlanta to Chattanooga and Knoxville (Tennessee) and all the way to the Canadian border. Heading south, you will hit Florida east of the Panhandle and along the way visit Macon and Valdosta (Georgia).

Note: I-85 and I-75 merge for seven miles as you enter downtown Atlanta from the north or south, but then re-split. When merged, this stretch of highway is called the Downtown Connector.

I-20 heading west extends from Atlanta to Birmingham (Alabama), Dallas (Texas) and beyond.

Heading east, it passes through the wonderful cities of Augusta (Georgia) and Florence (South Carolina).

I-285 is the highway from which legends are made. There are numerous stories of people getting stuck on the road and making endless circles around Atlanta, most notably a Braves rookie who missed practice. The 62.77-mile road connects all of the major interstates, and is almost always a traffic nightmare during rush hour; avoid it at all costs. I-285 is also the demarcation of "the Perimeter"— anything inside the circle is "Inside the Perimeter" and anything outside the circle is "Outside the Perimeter."

The baby of the Atlanta highway family is Georgia Highway 400, the state's only toll road. GA 400 travels north, servicing Roswell and Alpharetta and ends near Dahlonega. If you travel on 400 frequently, consider purchasing a "cruise card" for paying tolls. Check out www.georgiatolls.com.

Tip for shoppers: if you take I-85 N from downtown to GA 400 and get off at Exit 2/Lenox Road, you will arrive at Atlanta's mega-malls, Lenox Mall and Phipps Plaza. The toll plaza is just north of the Lenox Road exit, so you won't even have to pay a toll to go shopping.

Two other highways worth mentioning are I-675 and I-575. I-675 connects the southeast side of I-285 with I-75 approximately ten miles south of the city. I-575 branches off from I-75 cutting through Cherokee County and heading into the North Georgia Mountains.

Atlanta Highway Lingo

Northeast Expressway:	I-85 N
Southwest Expressway:	I-85 S
Northwest Expressway:	I-75 N
Southeast Expressway:	I-75 S
Perimeter:	I-285

"Spaghetti Junction": The interchange that connects I-85N with I-285 and surrounding side streets—rush hour headache.
The inner loop: The lanes of I-285 closest to the city.
The outer loop: Surprise! The lanes of I-285 farthest from the city.

The Surface Streets

While it may appear that every street in Atlanta is named Peachtree, there are actually only 60—or thereabout.

This multiple-Peachtree hazard is minor compared to the name-changing trick that many of the city's streets play. For example Juniper Street becomes Courtland, Briarcliff turns into Moreland, and Monroe morphs into Boulevard. Why? It's really very simple. Years ago, a change in street name mirrored the racial segregation of the city.

Don't bother paying attention to terms such as "street," "avenue," or "boulevard" as they do not indicate a darned thing—streets can run north-south or east-west, and the same is true of avenues and boulevards.

The longer you remain in Atlanta, the more you will understand the "God is My Co-Pilot" bumper stickers, as He is really the only one who can help you.

Here are some pointers:

Peachtree Street runs north-south starting in Downtown, passes through Midtown where it becomes Peachtree Road, and heads into Buckhead, where it forks. To the right, it continues past Lenox Mall and becomes Peachtree Industrial. To the left, it becomes Roswell Road and travels through Sandy Springs, Roswell, and Alpharetta.

Piedmont Avenue runs parallel to Peachtree and can also take you from Midtown into Buckhead.

Ponce de Leon travels east-west and is a good bet to get you to Decatur and Stone Mountain. Ponce is located off Peachtree Street, close to the Fox Theater. North Highland runs off of Ponce and will take you to the Highlands to the north. Moreland also runs off Ponce and will take you to Little Five and East Atlanta to the south. Ponce is a beautiful stretch with several large Southern mansions and plenty of lush greenery.

In Midtown, a grid magically appears, albeit short-lived. East-west streets bear numbers between 4th and 27th Streets. 10th and 14th Streets are major thoroughfares.

Our best advice is to use your NFT maps and don't be shy about asking for directions.

Atlanta DMVs

DMV Headquarters
2206 East View Pkwy
P.O. Box 80447
Conyers, GA 30013

Covington
8134 Geiger St
Covington, GA 30014

Lithonia
8040 Rockbridge Rd
Lithonia, GA 30058

South DeKalb
2801 Candler Rd, Ste 82
Decatur, GA 30034

Forest Park
5036 Hwy 85
Forest Park, GA 30297

Marietta
1605 County Services Pkwy
Marietta, GA 30008

Sandy Springs
8610 Roswell Rd, Ste 710
Sandy Springs, GA 30350

North Cobb
2800 Canton Rd
Piedmont Village Shopping Center
Marietta, GA 30066

General Information

Amtrak Reservations: 1-800-USA-Rail (872-7245)
Amtrak Website: www.amtrak.com
Brookwood Station: 1688 Peachtree St NW
                    Atlanta, GA 30309
Phone: 404-881-3060
Hours: Mon-Sun: 7:30 am-10 pm

Overview

Atlanta's Amtrak station is located along the Crescent Route, which heads south to New Orleans and north to New York City. Unless you are absolutely petrified of flying, or have a train fetish, traveling to and from Atlanta by Amtrak is a most uneconomical and ill-advised endeavor. Atlanta is not a reasonable train distance from anywhere worth going. Furthermore, Brookwood Station is nowhere near downtown, nor is it connected to the MARTA rail system. The only way to reach downtown from the station is by taxi or MARTA bus. With the world's busiest airport, it is really easy to find cheap flights into and out of the city—do this.

Fares

Riding on Amtrak can get pricey, so their discounts and deals are worth looking into. Use Amtrak's "Fare Finder" to find discounts of up to 90 percent off regular prices. Discounts are available only on certain routes and only if you purchase tickets online. Check the website regularly, as the different discounts and deals change often.

Amtrak also offers student and senior discounts and special promotional fares year-round. For more information, visit www.amtrak.com.

Service

Delays have become status quo for those familiar with Amtrak trains. Consider yourself lucky if you arrive at your destination less than an hour and a half later than expected. But at least the trains are clean, the seats are roomy and equipped with electrical sockets to make your trip more productive, and the food is edible, if overpriced. Complaining about how much Amtrak sucks is a way to bond with your fellow passengers.

Going to New York City

One way tickets to the Big Apple cost between $101 and $197. The trip takes about eighteen hours. The train runs only once a day.

Going to Washington DC

One way tickets to our nation's capital cost between $82 and $128. The trip takes a little under fourteen hours and departs once a day.

Going to New Orleans

One way tickets to a Fat Tuesday celebration will cost you between $48 and $60. The trip takes about twelve hours and runs once a day.

Going to Springer Mountain

The one-hour train ride to the southern point of the Appalachian Trail costs $15 one-way.

General Information

Address: 232 Forsyth St
              Atlanta, GA 30303
Phone: 800-229-9424
Website: www.greyhound.com

Overview

Greyhound Lines, the country's leading intercity bus transportation service, plays an important role not only in Atlanta's public transportation system, but also in its history. In 1961, it was a Greyhound bus that carried the famous Freedom Riders of the Civil Rights Movement from Washington DC to the South. Blacks and Whites traveled together aboard Greyhound to Atlanta in an attempt to desegregate intercity buses, encountering extreme violence from the Klan along their route through the South.

Today, Greyhound buses may be notoriously smelly, but at least they no longer serve as backdrops to unfortunate scenes of violent racism. The relatively cheap fares (at least compared to Amtrak) draw frugal and adventurous travelers alike, and everyone is seated on a first-come, first-served basis. Be prepared for a little bit of chaos and some sketchy characters at the station, as the Atlanta Greyhound terminal is the company's eighth-busiest terminal in the country.

Ticket Information

Reservations are not needed. Passengers are encouraged to arrive an hour before departure time to purchase tickets. Tickets purchased online allow passengers to travel only between two points (i.e. leave from one city and arrive in another). But Greyhound offers more flexible options for more spontaneous travelers—unrestricted tickets are available for purchase at Greyhound ticket offices. You can buy a ticket on a whim, travel to a new city, hole up for a couple of days, and get back on board the dog to discover someplace new. Tickets can be purchased with cash, travelers checks, major credit cards, or local bank checks.

Greyhound also runs seven daily departures from Atlanta Hartsfield-Jackson International Airport to downtown Atlanta and points northeast of the city (less luxurious, but cheaper than taking a cab). Board the bus on the lower level of the airport's North Terminal.

Fares

Greyhound participates in Student Advantage, which gives students a fifteen percent discount on bus fares and a fifty percent discount on packages sent through Greyhound PackageXpress. Greyhound also offers discounts for seniors. Through the "Friendly Fares" program, passengers can travel 300 miles from their starting destination for $29 one-way and $58 round-trip (you just need to purchase your ticket seven days in advance). Beware: these tickets, unlike all other Greyhound tickets, are not refundable! For more information on "Friendly Fares" and other discounts, check out the Greyhound website.

Baggage Procedures

With the purchase of one adult ticket, you can check up to two pieces of luggage for free (and yes, you can check a bike—it counts as one piece of luggage). Each piece of luggage must weigh less than fifty pounds, and you will be charged $15 to $25 for any bags that exceed the weight limit. Carry-on bags must be small enough to fit under the seat or in the overhead compartment. No pets allowed.

Pharmacies

	Address	Phone	Map
CVS	520 Boulevard SE	404-624-0022	15
CVS	1943 Peachtree Rd	404-351-4932	2
CVS	2350 Cheshire Bridge Blvd	404-486-7289	26
CVS	1554 N Decatur Rd NE	404-373-4534	28
CVS	2830 N Druid Hill Rd	404-679-4666	27
CVS	5764 Peachtree Industrial Blvd	770-457-4401	43
Walgreens	595 Piedmont Ave NE	404-685-9665	10
Walgreens	585 DeKalb Industrial Wy	404-292-8878	30
Walgreens	5373 Peachtree Industrial Blvd	678-547-1672	42

Supermarkets

	Address	Phone	Map
Kroger	725 Ponce de Leon Ave NE	404-875-3009	7
CVS	2738 N Decatur Rd	404-508-8058	30
Kroger	2685 Metropolitan Pkwy SW	404-209-6638	51
Walgreens	595 Piedmont Ave NE	404-685-9665	10
Walgreens	585 DeKalb Industrial Wy	404-292-8878	30

Veterinarians

	Address	Phone	Map
Pets Are People, Too	4280 N Peachtree Rd	770-452-1001	42
Georgia Veterinary Specialists	455 Abernathy Rd	404-459-0903	35

Copying

	Address	Phone	Map
Kinko's	3637 Peachtree Rd NE	404-233-1329	22
Kinko's	100 Peachtree St NE	404-221-0000	9
Kinko's	2088A N Decatur Rd	404-321-3990	29

Gas Stations

	Address	Phone	Map
BP/Amoco	448 Boulevard SE	404-627-7977	15
Chevron	2195 Monroe Dr NE	404-558-2981	3
Exxon	486 Ponce de Leon Ave NE	404-745-9745	6
Exxon	507 Ralph David Abernathy Blvd SW	404-752-7270	12
Exxon	247 Moreland Ave SE	404-659-6758	15
Exxon	1400 W Paces Ferry Rd NW	404-237-5040	16
Exxon	635 Lindbergh Dr NE	404-237-9221	25
Exxon	1675 Memorial Dr	404-371-3333	31
Exxon	1981 Flat Shoals Rd SE	404-244-9256	34
Exxon	77 Perimeter Ctr E	770-393-1150	36
Exxon	180 University Ave SW	404-622-4013	45
Quiktrip	2804 Paces Ferry Rd NW	770-432-9908	16
Quiktrip	3292 Buford Hwy NE	404-633-6193	23
Quiktrip	761 Sidney Marcus Blvd NE	404-240-0089	26
Quiktrip	1836 Briarcliff Rd	404-320-6828	26
Quiktrip	1910 Lawrenceville Hwy	404-633-2849	99
Quiktrip	2375 North Druid Hills Rd	404-315-1501	23
Shell	1521 Peachtree St NE	404-876-1377	2

Investigators

Allen Investigative Services	770-977-0404	

Locksmiths

A&A Safe, Lock & Door Co	404-361-8360
A-Abbot Safe & Lock Service	770-993-8751
Absolute Friendly Discount Lock	404-495-9899
Bakee Lockout & Tow	404-454-0110
Decatur Lock and Key	404-658-9800
Integrity Locksmith	404-237-1198
Libterty Locksmith	404-815-8910
V&G Lock & Key	678-768-8311

Plumbing

All Star Plumbing	404-351-1922
Citywide Plumbing and Drain	404-209-0011
Mr Rooter Plumbing	770-638-4038
Now Plumbing	678-407-2821
Payless Sewer & Drain	770-237-8171
Rooter One!	404-608-1919
Roto-Rooter Plumbers	404-892-7000
Superior Plumbing	404-231-5412

Post Offices

Atlanta	3900 Crown Rd	404-684-2308

Television

2	(ABC)	WSB	www.wsbtv.com
5	(FOX)	WAGA	www.wagatv.com
8	(PBS)	WGTV	www.gpb.org
11	(NBC)	WXIA	www.11alive.com
17	(TBS)	WTBS	www.superstation.com
30	(PBS)	WPBA	www.pba.org
36	(WB)	WATL	http://wb36.trb.com
46	(CBS)	WGCL	www.wgcltv.com
69	(UPN)	WUPA	www.paramountstations.com

FM Stations

88.5	WRAS	Diversified Rock—GSU
89.3	WRFG	Indie Public Radio
90.1	WABE	NPR News/Classical
90.7	WUWG	Public Radio-SUWG
91.1	WREK	Diversified—Georgia Tech
91.5	WWEV	Christian
91.9	WCLK	Jazz/Soul—Clark Atlanta University
92.1	WJGA	Contemporary/Oldies
92.9	WZGC	Adult-Alternative
93.3	WVFJ	Contemporary Christian
94.1	WSTR	Top 40
94.9	WLTM	Soft Rock
95.5	WBTS	Top 40
96.1	WKLS	Rock
97.1	WFOX	Urban/R&B
97.5	WPZE	Gospel
98.5	WSB	Adult Contemporary
99.7	WNNX	Modern Rock
100.1	WNSY	Oldies
100.5	WWWQ	Top 40
101.5	WKHX	Country
102.3	WLKQ	La Raza–Spanish
102.5	WAMJ-FM	Classic Soul
102.9	WMJE	Oldies
103.3	WVEE	R&B
104.1	WALR	R&B/Oldies
104.7	WFSH	Contemporary Christian
105.3	WMAX-FM	Spanish Top 40
105.7	WLCL	Oldies
106.1	WNGC	Country
106.7	WYAY	Classic Country
107.1	WTSH	Country
107.5	WJZZ	Contemporary Jazz
107.9	WHTA	Rap

AM Stations

550	WDUN	News/Talk
590	WDWD	Pre-teen/Disney
610	WPLO	Spanish
640	WGST	News/Talk
680	WCNN	Sports
750	WSB	News/Talk
790	WQXI	Sports
860	WAEC	Christian
920	WGKA	Christian
970	WNIV	Christian/Talk
1010	WGUN	Religious
1040	WPBS	Gospel
1080	WFTD	Mexican Music
1100	WWWE	Spanish
1160	WMLB	Classic Oldies
1190	WGKA	Religious
1230	WFOM	News/Talk (simulcasts with WALR 1340)
1260	WTJH	Gospel
1290	WCHK	News/Talk
1310	WPBC	Mexican Music
1340	WALR	News/Talk
1380	WAOK	News/Talk
1400	WNIV	Christian Talk
1410	WKKP	Contemporary/Oldies
1420	WATB	Spanish
1430	WGFS	Oldies
1440	WGMI	Southern Gospel
1460	WXEM	Spanish
1480	WYZE	Gospel
1500	WDPC	Gospel
1520	WDCY	Gospel
1550	WAZX	Hispanic
1570	WSSA	Christian
1600	WAOS	Spanish
1690	WSWK	Classic Country

Print Media

ATL: Magazine	949 W Marietta St	404-815-1177	Free monthly entertainment guide.
Atlanta Business Chronicle	1801 Peachtree St, Ste 1	404-249-1000	Business weekly.
Atlanta Daily World	145 Auburn Ave NE	404-659-1110	Daily news.
The Atlanta Inquirer	947 Martin Luther King Jr NW	404-523-6086	Weekly news.
Atlanta Journal-Constitution	72 Marietta St NW	404-526-5151	City's main daily.
Atlanta Magazine	260 Peachtree St, Ste 300	404-527-5500	Monthly lifestyle.
Atlanta Voice	633 Pryor St SW	404-524-6426	African-American weekly.
Atlanta Woman Magazine	3379 Peachtree Rd NE, Ste 300	404-760-1204	Monthly women's mag.
Creative Loafing	750 Willoughby Wy	404-688-5623	Free alternative weekly.
The Daily Tribune News	251 S Tennessee St, Cartersville	770-382-4545	Daily news.
Deep Magazine	2418 DeSoto Ave, Savannah	888-677-DEEP	"New South" women's mag.
The Emory Wheel	1380 Oxford Rd	404-727-6175	Emory biweekly.
Fulton County Daily Report	190 Pryor St SW	404-521-1227	Daily legal paper.
The GSU Signal	33 Gilmer St, Rm 200	404-651-2242	GSU daily.
Jezebel	14 Piedmont Ctr NE	404-233-1147	Monthly lifestyle.
Paper City Magazine	1776 Peachtree St NW	404-591-3145	Monthly style trends.
Piedmont Review	1425 Dutch Valley Pl NE	404-249-7474	Free A&E monthly.
Southern Voice	1075 Zonolite Rd, Ste 1-D	404-876-1819	Free weekly gay/lesbian.
Stomp and Stammer	PO Box 55233	404-635-0937	Free monthly music.
The Sunday Paper	763 Trabert Ave, Ste D	404-351-5797	Free alternative weekly.
Technique	353 Ferst Dr, Rm 137	404-894-2831	GA Tech weekly.

Useful Phone Numbers

Emergencies:	911
General Information:	411
Police Department:	404-853-3431
Fire Department:	404-853-7000
Traffic Concerns:	404-330-6501
Atlanta City Hall:	404-330-6100
Cobb County Board of Elections:	770-528-2581
Fulton County Board of Elections:	518-736-5526
DeKalb County Board of Elections:	404-298-4020

Websites

http://atlanta.citysearch.com · Reviews of restaurants, landmarks, and businesses in town.

www.atlanta.craigslist.org · Job listings, personals, part-time gigs, sublets, etc.

www.atlantadailyworld.com · The daily newspaper online.

www.atlanta.about.com · Information about… Atlanta.

www.atlantaga.gov · Atlanta Government's home on the web.

www.accessatlanta.com · Movies, restaurants, listings, news, sports stats, etc.

www.toprestaurants.com/atlanta.htm · Pretty self-explanatory.

www.notfortourists.com · The ultimate web index for Atlanta can be found on the NFT website.

We're Number One!!!

- Georgia is the nation's largest producer of peaches, peanuts, and pecans.
- Golf's most elite tournament, the Masters, is played annually in April at Augusta National.
- Spelman College, founded in 1881, was the first college for black women in the country.
- Atlanta was the first southern city to host the Olympic Games (1996).

Essential Atlanta Books

Gone With the Wind, by Margaret Mitchell
A Man in Full, by Tom Wolfe
Wise Blood, by Flannery O'Connor
The Wind Done Gone, by Alice Randall
The Autobiography of Martin Luther King Jr., by Martin Luther King, Jr.
Peachtree Road, by Anne Rivers Siddons
The Hearts of Men, by Travis Hunter
Atlanta Blues, by Robert Lamb
That Faith, That Trust, That Love, by Jamellah Ellis
The Last Night of Ballyhoo, by Alfred Uhry
Down on Ponce, by Fred Willard
The Color Purple, by Alice Walker
The Heart is a Lonely Hunter, by Carson McCullers

Essential Atlanta Movies

Gone With the Wind (1939)
Juke Girl (1942)
Deliverance (1972)
The House on Skull Mountain (1974)
Let's Do It Again (1975)
Smokey and the Bandit (1977)
Sharky's Machine (1981)
Cyborg (1989)
Driving Miss Daisy (1989)
Fried Green Tomatoes (1991)
Scream II (1997)
Remember the Titans (2000)
Mission: Impossible II (2000)
The Calling (2002)
Catch Me If You Can (2002)
The Fighting Temptations (2003)

General Information • **Practical Information**

Essential Atlanta Songs

"85"—Youngbloodz
"Atlanta Blues"—Various, written by Dave Elman
"Atlanta Bound"—Gene Autrey
"Atlanta Gal"—Charles Fulcher & His Orchestra
"Atlanta Moan"—Barbecue Bob
"Atlanta Song"—David Allan Coe
"Atlanta"—Pretty Things
"Atlanta"—Stone Temple Pilots
"Atlanta—That's Where I Stay"—MC Shy D
"Chattahoochee"—Alan Jackson
"Devil Went Down to Georgia"—Charlie Daniels Band
"Dying Crapshooter's Blues"—Blind Willie McTell
"Georgia on My Mind"—Various, written by Hoagy Carmichael
"Grant Park"—Marvelous 3
"Hot 'Lanta"—Allman Brothers Band
"I'm on My Way to Atlanta"—Freddy King
"Love Shack"—B-52's
"Marching Through Georgia"—Various, words by Henry Clay Work
"Midnight Train to Georgia"— Gladys Knight & The Pips, written by Jim Weatherly
"Oh Atlanta"—Bad Company
"Oh Atlanta"—Little Feat
"Welcome to Atlanta"—Jermaine Dupri featuring Ludacris
"Why Georgia"—John Mayer

Atlanta Timeline

A timeline of significant events in Atlanta's history (by no means complete)

1834: Cherokee territories in North Georgia surrender to white settlers. 16,000 Cherokees are moved out West on the Trail of Tears.
1837: Town of Marthasville, renamed Atlanta, becomes a city.
1861: Georgia secedes from the United States.
1864: Battle of Atlanta.
1868: Atlanta named as the capital of Georgia.
1881: Spelman College, the first college for black women in the United States, is founded in Atlanta.
1892: Asa Candler founds the Coca-Cola Company in Atlanta.
1913: Georgia State University founded.
1915: Emory University moves to Atlanta.
1924: Booker T. Washington High School, the city's first black high school, opens.
1928: Atlanta Daily World founded.
1929: Martin Luther King, Jr. born in Atlanta.
1936: Margaret Mitchell publishes *Gone with the Wind*.
1941: Delta Airlines moves its headquarters to Atlanta.
1947: Negro Voter League established.
1964: Nobel Peace Prize awarded to Martin Luther King, Jr.
1965: The Braves move from Milwaukee to Atlanta.
1968: Martin Luther King, Jr.'s funeral held in Atlanta.
1974: Hank Aaron breaks Babe Ruth's record with 715 home runs.
1976: Ted Turner purchases the Atlanta Braves.
1976: Jimmy Carter, Georgia native, elected President of the United States.
1988: Democratic National Convention held in Atlanta.
1995: The Braves win World Series for the first time in 38 years.
1996: Atlanta hosts Centennial Summer Olympic Games.

General Information • **Calendar of Events**

January

Peach Bowl	Georgia Dome	College football galore. New Year's Eve parade warms you up.
Martin Luther King, Jr. Week	The King Center	Various services, musical tributes, seminars, award dinners, and speeches. 2nd weekend in January.
Cathedral Antiques Show	Cathedral of St Philip, 2744 Peachtree Rd	Antique extravaganza. Last week in January.
Atlanta Boat Show	Georgia World Congress Center	Boats & more boats.
ATLart	Various galleries/museums	Coordinated art event between more than 30 galleries and museums (www.atlart.com).

February

Southeastern Flower Show	Georgia World Congress Center	4-acre gardening gala. February or March.
The Best of Atlanta Party	Cobb Galleria Center	Celebrating the best food & drink Atlanta has to offer. One night in mid-February.

March

St. Patrick's Day Parade	Downtown	Irish pride. Lots of beer. Saturday closest to March 17th.
Conyers Cherry Blossom Fest	Georgia International Horse Park	Cherry blossoms. Late March.
Cracker Barrel 500	Atlanta Motor Speedway	NASCAR, man. A Sunday not to miss.

April

Easter Sunrise Services	Stone Mountain Park	VERY early services at the top and base of Stone Mountain. Easter Sunday.
Atlanta Dogwood Festival	Piedmont Park	Dogwoods in blossom with fair-like activities and hot air balloons. 3 days in mid-April.
Atlanta Steeplechase	Rome, GA	Atlanta's premiere social spring event with horses and hats.
Spring Campaign	Stone Mountain Park	Full-scale civil war encampment reenacted. Late April.
Georgia Renaissance Festival	Fairburn–Exit 61 on I-85	Craft Fair meets Medieval Times. A 7-weekend stretch starting in late April.
Sweet Auburn Spring Fest	Sweet Auburn District	Multi-cultural celebration. Weekend in late April.
AJC Auto Show	Georgia World Congress Center	Vroom. Vroom. (Sometimes happens in March.)
Masters Golf Tournament	Augusta, GA	All for the green jacket. Early April.

May

Gardens for Connoisseurs Tour	Various gardens	Benefits the Atlanta Botanical Gardens, tours of private gardens. Mother's Day weekend.
Lasershow Spectacular	Stone Mountain	Laser beams and rednecks. Every night through Labor Day.
Decatur Arts Festival	South lawn of Old Courthouse	Great fun for kids including arts & crafts, mimes, and clowns. Memorial Day weekend.
Atlanta Jazz Festival	Various locations	Major week-long jazz fest. Memorial Day-ish.
Atlanta Film & Video Festival	The IMAGE Film/Video Center	Indie media fest. Late May to early June.
March of Dimes Annual "Dining Out" Event	Various restaurants & after-party	Top culinary fundraising event. Night in mid-May.
Atlanta Celtic Festival	Georgia International Horse Park	Celebration of Celtic culture. Weekend in May.
On the Bricks	Centennial Olympic Park	Cheap ($5) concert series. Friday nights through August.

June

Music Midtown	Midtown/various locations	Major musical guests, artist's market, food booths. Early June.
Virginia-Highland Summerfest	Virginia Ave & N Highland Ave	Arts and crafts blowout. Weekend in mid-June.
Screen on the Green	Piedmont Park	Free movies in the park. Thursdays in June.
AthFest	Athens, GA	Music and arts festival in cool college town.
Georgia Shakespeare Festival	Oglethorpe University	Shakespeare meets lawn luncheon. Mid-June-November.
Coca-Cola Summer Film Fest	Fox Theater	Movies in a classic theatre. Happens through August.
Atlanta Pride Festival	Piedmont Park, Midtown	Atlanta's GLBT celebration. Weekend in June.
Stone Mountain Village Annual Arts & Crafts Festival	Stone Mountain Village	Family craft/food fun. Father's Day weekend.

July

Asian Cultural Experience	Atlanta Botanical Garden	Asian cultural celebration. Early July weekend.
Independence Day	Various locations	Peachtree 10-K Road Race, parades, music, and fireworks, of course. July 4th.
National Black Arts Festival	Various locations	A celebration of the sights, sounds, and expressions of the African American culture. 10 days in late July and early August.

August

Montreaux Atlanta Music Fest	Various parks including Piedmont & Centennial Olympic	Jazz, blues, gospel, reggae, and zydeco. Weekly, leading up to and including Labor Day.
Bark in the Park	Piedmont Park	Atlanta Symphony Orchestra provides an evening of outdoor music for you and your pooch. One night in August.
Atlantis Music Festival	Music venues around the city	Music conference featuring unsigned bands from across the southeast.
Atlanta Restaurant Week	Various restaurants	A week of dining discounts in downtown Atlanta.

September

Yellow Daisy Festival	Stone Mountain Park	Crafts, music, dance, flowers, food & storytellers. Weekend after Labor Day.
Taste of Atlanta	Lenox Square	Name says it all. Weekend in September.
Wine South	Gwinnett Center	Major wine tasting. Weekend in late September.
JapanFest	Stone Mountain Park	Celebration of Japanese culture.
Sandy Springs Festival	Sandy Springs	Community celebration weekend.
Walk for Wildlife	Freedom Parkway Trail in Downtown	Raise funds and awareness for wildlife conservation. Late September.

October

American Association of University Women's Annual Book Fair	Lenox Square Mall	Books, books, and more books. 4 days in early October.
Annual Scottish Festival & Highland Games	Stone Mountain Park	Dancers, pipe, and drums, Scottish harping & fiddling, sword dancing. Mid-October.
ArtScape	Woodruff Park	Local and regional art and food. Mid-October.
Sunday in the Park at Oakland	Oakland Cemetery	Storytellers, historians, guided tours, hat & costume contest, music. One Sunday in October.
AIDS Walk Atlanta	Piedmont Park	AIDS fundraiser. Mid-October.

November

Veterans Day Parade	16th St & Peachtree St	The usual fanfare. Veterans' Day.
Atlanta Marathon & Half-Marathon	Turner Field & Peachtree Rd	Thanksgiving Day road race.
An Olde Fashioned Christmas	Stone Mountain Park	Crafters, carolers, storytellers, live nativity, train rides, and Santa Claus. Mid-November - December 30th.
Holiday High Lights	Plaza b/w Underground and World of Coca-Cola kids	Holiday tree lighting with trains and polar bears for Sunday after Thanksgiving.
Christmas at Callanwolde	Callanwolde Fine Arts Center	Holiday crafts, children's breakfasts with Santa, caroling and hymn singing. Two weeks in late November or early December.

December

County Christmas	Atlanta Botanical Garden	Holiday crafts, carolers, bell ringers, children's theater, pony rides. 1st Sunday in December.
Children's Healthcare of Atlanta Christmas Parade & Festival of Trees	Georgia World Congress Center	Lavish parade, 9-day Festival of Trees, vignettes, roller-coaster, balloon ride. 1st Saturday in Dec.
Peach Bowl Game	Georgia Dome	Football. Sometime between Christmas & New Year.
New Year's Eve	Underground Atlanta	Big Peach dropped from 138-foot light tower.

Overview

Websites: www.dogfriendly.com; www.dog-play.com

Atlanta is a great place to be a dog: trees, fire hydrants, and plenty of open spaces make it easy for pet owners to enjoy the outdoors with their best friends. Just remember to take seriously all rules and regulations imposed upon pet owners: failing to clean up after your dog, or allowing your dog to run off-leash (unless it's a designated area), can cost you up to $1,000 in fines, a prison term of up to one year, community service for up to six months, or a combination of all of the above. Sounds like harsh punishment for a little dog-doo, but a little here and a little there adds up.

Piedmont Park Off-Leash Dog Park

404-875-7275

Piedmont Park is the place to see and be seen with your canine companion. While the 185-acre park allows leashed dog walking on almost all of its paths, the main doggie attraction is the 1.5-acre fenced-in, off-leash area located north of the Park Drive Bridge. Here, dogs can roam free, swim, and socialize with their doggie-playmates. So dog-friendly is Piedmont Park that once a year (usually in August) the Atlanta Symphony Orchestra holds a "Bark in the Park" concert, where dog owners and their beloved pets take in the symphony together.

Mason Mill Dog Park

404-371-4925

This half-acre dog park is DeKalb County's only public dog park. Dogs of all sizes are free to run unleashed from sunrise to sundown. Dog owners, as usual, are responsible for scooping doggie doo.

Stone Mountain Park

770-498-5600

Dogs are prohibited from entering most of the park and its trails. But if you keep those puppies leashed, they can accompany you on the Cherokee Trail, the Nature trail, or in the Gardens.

Cochran Shoals Dog Beach

770-399-8070

Cochran Shoals Dog Beach has become another hot spot for dog owners. Dogs are technically supposed to be kept on leashes but, as long as they're kept near the water's edge and away from the trail, most owners just let them run wild in the waves. The best way to get to the beach is to take I-75 N to the Windy Hill Road exit. Drive along Interstate North Parkway for about two miles and keep an eye out for Powers Ferry Parking Lot, which will be on your left.

Americans spend an estimated six million dollars a year on clothing, accessories, and toys for their new-born babies. And that's only the first phase in eighteen years of subsidizing your adorable, loveable little money hole. So, among other things, we've come up with a list of places where *you* might even enjoy spending some of that hard-earned cash on your kids.

The Best of the Best

★ **Funnest Park**: Piedmont Park (400 Park Dr NE, 404-875-PARK). The city's urban hub is the funnest park for everyone—not just kids—but the playscape by sculptor Isamu Noguchi, the kite-flying scene, the swimming pools, and baseball fields make it a true children's wonderland. Word on the street is that it's also a great place for kids to learn how to bike and roller skate.

★ **Bestest Bookstore**: Hobbit Hall (120 Bulloch Ave, 770-587-0907). A waterfall, goldfish pond, and floating water lilies welcome you into the world of Hobbit, where each floor of the six-story building is devoted to a different genre of children's literature. Free story times take place throughout the week, and the bookstore also hosts birthday parties and school field trips.

★ **Yummiest Kid-Friendly Restaurant**: OK Café (1284 W Paces Ferry Rd NW, 404-233-2888). The burgers, salads, and comfort foods are larger than kid's size, and the little tykes may get distracted from their meals with the jukeboxes, shiny '50s-style diner booths, and the money-tree sculpture in front. But the bottom line is that kids love the restaurant, the restaurant loves kids, and you really can't argue with that.

★ **Best Rainy Day Alternative**: Fernbank Museum of Natural History (767 Clifton Rd NE, 404-929-6300). Kids will look forward to rainy days if they include trips to the IMAX, admiring 123-feet long dinosaurs, and playing with the interactive nature exhibitions. In fact, they might even ask you to move to rain-soaked Seattle, but then they'd miss out on Fernbank's marine biology and ecology summer camp. So there.

★ **Neatest Birthday Party Venue**: Center for Puppetry Arts (1404 Spring St NW, 404-881-5159).

If you rent out the puppet theater for a party, the reigning birthday girl or boy of the day gets a red wagon for collecting presents, a private party room, and a throne. If you bring your own food, you can throw a picnic outside. But your kid has got to be popular—there's a ten kid minimum for parties (and you have to be a member of the Center, which costs $35 per year).

★ **Coolest Outdoor Holiday Activity**: Centennial Olympic Park Holiday Ice Rink (265 Luckie St NW, 404-222-7275). It's not hard to be the best outdoor ice rink around when you're the *only* outdoor ice rink in town. But having a monopoly on the industry isn't all this rink has got going for it: the lights on the rink and the observational seating make you feel like a returning Olympic champion, and the Christmas decorations really get you into that cozy holiday spirit.

★ **Niftiest Indoor Holiday Avctivity**: The Pink Pig (3393 Peachtree Rd NE, 404-231-2800). Originally located inside the downtown Atlanta Rich's, Priscilla the Pink Pig began making her rounds in 1953. The ride, a large pig that hung from a track and circled the toy department at Christmas, brought squeals of joys to countless Atlanta children (and was a rather effective marketing gimmick). In fact, Priscilla was so frickin' popular, Rich's had to add a second pig named Percival. The store retired the ride in 1996, but now it's back at the Lenox Macy's every Christmas. For $3 your children (and you) can ride the new Pink Pig and get a nifty sticker proclaiming: "I rode the Pink Pig."

Shopping Essentials

Here's a sampling of the top shops for tots in Atlanta:

- **Pickle Patch Books** • 41 W Park Sq, Marietta • 770-419-7524 • Coziest of the cozy children's bookshop.
- **The Inner Child** • 308 W Ponce de Leon Ave, Decatur • 404-377-7775 • Unique independently owned children's toys and friendly staff.
- **Richards Variety Store** • 2347 Peachtree Rd NE • 404-237-1412 • No matter what you're looking for, however obscure, you can probably find it here. Games, books, kitchen equipment, socks, costumes, and just plain junk. It's a sight to see.

- **Pottery Barn Kids** • Lenox Square Mall, 3393 Peachtree Rd NE • 404-442-9122 • Kids' furniture and popular baby shower registry site.
- **Precious Soles** • 2140 Peachtree Rd NW• 404-355-3314 • Specialty kids' shoe store.
- **Angel's Consignment** • 5380 Roswell Rd • 404-459-7001 • Children's clothing consignment store.
- **Playgrounds To Go** • 5891 New Peachtree Rd • 770-455-7390 • Swing sets and outdoor play equipment for sale.
- **Babies R Us** • 1155 Mt. Vernon Hwy • 770-913-0222 • The baby superstore.
- **Aiko Baby** • 427 Candler St • 404-223-3223 • Unique kids' clothing and gifts.
- **Bear & Gabby** • 1212 Cumberland Mall • 770-434-3444 • Upscale children's clothing.
- **Children's Shop** • 2385 Peachtree Rd • 404-365-8496 • Reasonably priced kids' clothes for boys and girls.
- **Tadpoles** • Town Center Plaza, 425 Earnest Barrett Pkwy, Kennesaw • 770-499-7010 • Family-owned resale store that specializes in children's and maternity clothes, toys, baby furniture, and accessories.
- **Hansel & Gretel's Children's Boutique** • 3205 Woodward Crossing Blvd, Ste 100, Buford • 770-614-6860 • High-end kids' clothes.
- **All-Stitch** • 445 Plasamour Dr NE • 404-872-0577 • Children's dance wear.
- **Jacadi** • Lenox Square Mall, 3393 Peachtree Rd NE• 404-848-3460 • Designer Parisian clothes for kids 12 and under.
- **Bellini Children's Furniture** • 5285 Roswell Rd • 404-851-1588 • Classy baby furniture and bedding.
- **Million Dollar Baby** • 100 Piedmont Cir • 770-248-0388 • Baby furniture galore.
- **Hobbit Hall** • 120 Bulloch Ave • 770-587-0907 • Children's bookstore housed in a make-believe cottage with a goldfish pond and wooden deck. Each floor devoted to different genre of children's literature.
- **The Toy Store** • 1544 Piedmont Rd • 404-875-1137 • Large array of toys for kids, from cheap plastic bouncy balls to designer dolls.
- **The Right Start** • 3330 Piedmont Rd • 404-233-8610 • School supplies.
- **Toys R Us** • 2997 Cobb Pkwy S • 770-951-8052 • 1 Buckhead Loop Dr NE • 404-467-8697 • The toy superstore.
- **Bounce Atlanta** • Roswell • 770-641-7034 • Moonwalk and waterslide rental service for parties, also sells Carvel cakes and party supplies.
- **Mimi Maternity** • Lenox Square Mall • 404-365-0426 • Maternity wear.
- **Changing Times Diaper Service** • 5616 New Peachtree Rd • 770-455-8362 • Diaper delivery service.

Fun in the Sun

Outdoor adventures that can't be beat!

- **Tanglewood Farm** (171 Tanglewood Dr, Canton, 770-667-6464) 100 small farm animals to pet and play with, including pot-bellied pigs, donkeys, and miniature horses. They also host birthday parties and offer riding courses for children under the age of 15.
- **American Adventures** (250 Cobb Pkwy N, 770-424-9283) Amusement park geared toward children 12 and under. Rides, mini-golf, arcade, foam factory, and go-karts galore.
- **Zoo Atlanta** (800 Cherokee Ave, 404-624-5600) The wildlife park is rated one of the top zoos in the country. Attractions include the Ford African Rain Forest as well as Lun Lun and Yang Yang, the Chinese pandas. The zoo also runs a children's day camp in the summer months.
- **Piedmont Park** (400 Park Dr NE, 404-875-PARK) The 285-acre park is full of playgrounds, open fields, a public pool, sports fields, and Playscape, a system of slides and ladders created by sculptor Isamu Noguchi. Great place to fly a kite. And it's all free!
- **Six Flags White Water** (250 Cobb Pkwy N, 770-424-9283) On a hot day, this place is an unbeatable water wonderland for family fun.
- **Holiday Ice Skating Rink** (265 Luckie St, 404-222-7275) Atlanta's only outdoor ice skating rink, located in Centennial Olympic Park.
- **Swan Center Outreach** (75 Swan Center Dr, 770-893-3525) Horseback riding center that offers trail rides, riding lessons, and after-school activities about animal care and nature studies. They also host birthday parties.
- **All Children's Playground** (Lake Peachtree, Peachtree City, 770-631-2542) $100,000 went into building this massive steel, rubber, fencing, and ropes course. Handicapped-accessible.
- **Fanplex (**768 Hank Aaron Dr, 404-522-7374) Mini-golf course.

Indoor Alternatives

Indoor activities are good distractions on rainy days when cabin fever takes hold, but even better for those sweltering summer days, when playing outside becomes nothing more than a sweaty and uncomfortable mess for the little tykes.

- **Center for Puppetry Arts** (1404 Spring St, 404-873-3391) Puppet theater and museum that puts on puppet-adaptations of traditional stories. A souvenir puppet is included with your ticket purchase.
- **Imagine It! Children's Museum** (275 Centennial Olympic Park Dr NW, 404-659-KIDS) Targeting kids 10 and under, the museum is completely interactive with hands-on exhibitions involving finger painting, sand sculptures, dancing, and splashing.
- **Michael's: The Arts & Crafts Store** (locations around Atlanta, 770-565-0872; www.michaels.com) You buy the supplies and choose a craft, and you'll get an instructor and a room for free. Great for group activities or birthday parties.
- **Build-a-Bear** (2929 Turner Hill Rd, Ste 1220, Lithonia, 770-482-9239) Toy store/workshop where kids, ages 5 and up, make their own stuffed animals from provided materials.
- **Red Door Playhouse** (587 Atlanta St, Roswell, 770-649-9994) Offers drama, theater, and music classes for kids.
- **Children's Art Museum** (6400 Sugarloaf Pkwy, Ste 300, 770-623-6002) Key words: hands-on. The museum has ceramic studios, black-box theater, and puppet theater. Just make sure your kids aren't already bored of the place because they've been there so many times on school field trips. Professional performances take place in the black-box theater on Saturday mornings.
- **Art Station** (5284 Manor Dr, 770-469-1105) A non-profit arts center that offers kids' classes in art and theater. Classes conducted in professional theater and studio spaces.
- **Imagine That!** (5054 Nandina Ln, 770-392-1627) Science museum geared at children ages 3-14. Art and sciences are taught by professionals, and they'll even come to your house for a science-themed birthday party.
- **Fernbank Museum of Natural History** (767 Clifton Rd, 404-929-6300) What self-respecting kid doesn't like dinosaurs? And who doesn't get a kick out of IMAX movies? 'Nuff said.

Kid-Friendly Restaurants

So, you don't feel like cooking, you want to go out, but it's just too late to find a babysitter? Well, these restaurants smile upon children and serve up decent food in jovial atmospheres that should keep the kids happy and satisfy your own desire to be dined and entertained.

- **Sweet Java Brown** (1994 Hosea L. Williams Dr, 404-377-9223) Coffee and ice cream shop with singing and storytelling hour for kids.
- **Cici's Pizza** (6690 Roswell Rd, Ste 410, 404-257-9944) Family-friendly pizza buffet, featuring sixteen different kinds of pizza, as well as dessert pizzas. The place gets busy on the weekends, but a small game room keeps kids from getting restless. Birthday parties encouraged.
- **OK Café** (1284 W Paces Ferry Rd NW, 404-233-2888) Modern diner serving up standard diner fare. Kids like sliding around in the red vinyl booths and gawking at the waitresses in 1950's Flo-style attire.
- **ESPN Zone** (3030 Peachtree Rd, 404-682-3776) Arcade and restaurant in one. Kids might become more interested in the games than in the food, but at least they won't complain when there's a wait for a table.
- **Hard Rock Café** (215 Peachtree St NE, 404-688-7625) Average food tastes better when you're staring at a signed Elvis EP. No matter how tacky you might find it, the fact of the matter is that kids really dig this place.
- **Jake's Ice Cream & Muncheteria** (676 Highland Ave, 404-523-1830) A family-friendly restaurant that also caters and hosts birthday parties.

Websites

www.atlanta-kids.com
www.gocitykids.com
www.factmonster.com
www.atlanta-midtown.com/kids
atlanta.babyzone.com
atlanta.parenthood.com

General Information · LGBT

Overview

For Southern gays and lesbians, Atlanta is a small oasis of open-mindedness in an arid desert of intolerance. The city ranks third in the country for its number of gay residents, most of whom have settled in Midtown, the scene of an electrifying gay and lesbian nightlife. With the exception of Decatur (the old stomping ground of the Indigo Girls), not too many gay-friendly areas can be found outside of Midtown. Shirley Franklin, Atlanta's first female African-American mayor, launched a tourism campaign in 2002 to encourage more gay and lesbian travelers to visit the city. Outside of Atlanta, the GLBT community suffers persecution from the state government and its non-Atlanta constituents. The state amended the constitution to prohibit same-sex marriage on the same day it helped re-elect Dubya. However, within Atlanta the vibrancy of the GLBT scene makes you almost forget you're in the South.

Health Centers and Support Organizations

- **Atlanta Gay & Lesbian Center**, First MCC of Atlanta, 1379 Tullie Rd, 404-325-4143—Founded in 1975, the center hosts support group discussions about GLBT issues and personal experiences every Wednesday evening. Reservations required, as groups are limited to twelve people.
- **Atlanta Executive Network (AEN)**, 1379 Tullie Rd NE, Ste 101, 404-321-0079; www.aen.org—GLBT business and professional network that advocates for equal rights of gays and lesbians in the business world.
- **Atlanta Gay & Lesbian Chamber of Commerce (AGLCC)**, 2103 N Decatur Rd, 404-377-4258; www.atlantagaychamber.org—The only legally recognized gay and lesbian chamber of commerce in the country. The group promotes the growth of businesses that support the GLBT community in Atlanta.
- **Atlanta Lesbian Cancer Initiative**, 1530 DeKalb Ave NE, Ste A, 404-688-2524; www.alci.org—Provides education and services for lesbians and their families dealing with cancer.
- **AIDS Survival Project**, 139 Ralph McGill Blvd, Ste 201, 404-874-7926; www.aidssurvivalproject.org—Provides free support, education, advocacy, and testing for people living with HIV and AIDS.
- **AID Atlanta**, 1438 W Peachtree St NW, Ste 100, 404-870-7773; www.aidatlanta.org—Offers services for individuals living with HIV/AIDS.
- **Fourth Tuesday**, 1530 DeKalb Ave NE, Ste A, 770-662-4353; www.fourthtuesday.org—Provides services for lesbians, bi females, and transgendered females in Atlanta including social gatherings, scholarships, educational programs, and networking opportunities.
- **Georgia Equality**, 1379 Tullie Rd, 404-327-9898; www.georgiaequality.org—A statewide political advocacy group representing the GLBT community.
- **Project Open Hand**, 176 Ottley Dr NE, 404-419-3309; www.projectopenhand.org—They cook. They Deliver. They Care. They supply fresh-cooked meals to people living with HIV/AIDS, as well as elderly and disabled members of the community.

Bookstores

- **A Cappella**, 1133 Euclid Ave NE, 404-681-5128; www.acappellabooks.com
  Specializes in hard-to-find literature, including gay and lesbian titles.
- **Brushstrokes**, 1510 Piedmont Ave, 404-876-6567; www.brushstrokesatlanta.com
  Atlanta's gay and lesbian gift shop includes GLBT books and magazines.
- **Charis Books & More**, 1189 Euclid Ave, 404-524-0304; www.charis.booksense.com—The only independent feminist bookstore in Atlanta.
- **Outwrite Bookstore and Coffee House**, 991 Piedmont Ave, 404-607-0082, www.outwritebooks.com—Atlanta's only specifically gay and lesbian bookstore doubles as a community meeting place.

Websites

- **For Atlanta's Gay Visitors**—www.gay-atlanta.com
  All-purpose website for gays visiting Atlanta.
- **Gay Atlanta**—www.gayatlanta.com
  Great gay website with links to other great gay websites with gym listings, arts listings, and more.

Out in Atlanta—www.outinatlanta.com
GLBT chat room, news, and information on culture and community in Atlanta.
• **Pridenet**— www.pridenet.com
Self-proclaimed G-rated GLBT website that you can navigate by subject.

Publications
• **Southern Voice**—www.southernvoice.com
The free weekly paper is Atlanta's "authoritative gay news source."
• **David Atlanta Magazine**—http://davidatlanta.com
Weekly social rag full of photos of hunky, bare-chested gay guys.

Annual Events
• **Atlanta Pride Celebration**—Weekend of entertainment, parades, and unification of LGBT community held annually in June. www.atlantapride.org.
• **Atlanta AIDS Walk**—Annual October 5K walkathon that raises money for AIDS research, beginning and ending in Piedmont Park. 404-876-9255; www.aidatlanta.org.
• **Out on Film**—LGBT film festival usually held in November each year. 404-352-4225; www.outonfilm.com.

Venues—Gay
Blake's On the Park · 227 10th St · 404-892-5786 · www.blakesontheparkatlanta.com
Blue · 960 Spring St NW · 404-877-1221
Bulldogs · 893 Peachtree St NE · 404-872-302 · members.aol.com/bulldognco
Burkhart's Pub · 1492 Piedmont Ave · 404-872-4403 · www.burkharts.com
Eagle · 2821 Main St · 404-873-2453 · www.atlantaeagle.com
Felix's on the Square · 1510 Piedmont Ave NE · 404-249-7899
Heretic · 2069 Cheshire Bridge Rd NE · 404-325-4241 · www.hereticatlanta.com
Mary's · 1287 Glenwood Ave SE · 404-624-4411
The Metro · 1080 Peachtree St NE · 404-874-9869
New Order · 1544 Piedmont Rd NE · 404-874-8247
The Oscars Atlanta · 1510 Piedmont Ave NE · 404-874-7748
The Phoenix · 567 Ponce De Leon Ave NE · 404-892-7871
Scandals · 1510-G Piedmont Rd NE · 404-875-5957
Swinging Richards · 1715 Northside Dr NW · 404-355-6787
Wetbar · 960 Spring St · 404-745-9494
Woofs on Piedmont · 2425 Piedmont Rd NE · 404-869-9422 · www.woofsatlanta.com

Venues—Lesbian
Girls in the Night · 831 Juniper St NE · 404-881-9280
My Sister's Room · 222 E Howard Ave · 404-370-1990 · www.mysistersroom.com

Venues—Mixed
Armory · 836 Juniper St NE · 404-881-9280
Charlie Brown's Cabaret· 50 Upper Alabama St (Underground Atlanta) · 678-904-4512
Hoedowns · 931 Monroe Dr NE · 404-876-0001 · www.hoedownsatlanta.com
Miss Q's · 560 Amsterdam Ave · 404-875-6255
Red Chair Restaurant & Video Lounge · 550 C Amsterdam Ave NE · 404-870-0532 · www.redchairatlanta.com
Rico's View · 736 Ponce de Leon Ave NE · 404-873-3220

In the event of biological warfare, Atlanta could be the safest place to reside—the headquarters of the Centers for Disease Control and Prevention are located here. Then again, it could be the worst place too, due to all the germs, bacteria, viruses, and infected animals in our backyard. The good news: the germs and animals don't actually live in the city, they're located in the pleasant town of Lawrenceville.

In the event of a Robin Cook *Outbreak* scenario, Atlanta has plenty of top-notch hospitals: **Grady** is one of the largest public hospitals in the southeast; **Emory** is ranked in the top-10 in heart health and heart surgery by *U.S. News & World Report*; and **Piedmont Hospital** is celebrating is centenary in 2005.

Hospital	Address	Phone	Map
Atlanta Medical Center	303 Parkway Dr NE	404-265-4000	10
Children's Healthcare of Atlanta at Egelston	1405 Clifton Rd NE	404-325-6000	27
Children's Healthcare of Atlanta at Scottish Rite	1001 Johnson Ferry Rd NE	404-501-1000	41
Emory Crawford Long	550 Peachtree St NW	404-686-4411	9
Emory University Hospital	1364 Clifton Rd NE	404-712-2000	29
Emory-Dunwoody Medical Center	4575 N Shallowford Rd	770-454-2000	37
Grady Memorial	80 Jesse Hill Jr Dr SE	404-616-4307	10
Hughes Spalding Children's	35 Jesse Hill Jr Dr	404-616-6402	10
Northside	1000 Johnson Ferry Rd NE	404-851-8785	41
Piedmont	1968 Peachtree Rd NW	404-605-5000	2
St Joseph's of Atlanta	5665 Peachtree Dunwoody Rd NE	404-851-7001	41
South Fulton Medical Center	1170 Cleveland Ave	404-305-3500	51

Ian Schrager hasn't lent his design prowess to Atlanta, so we don't really have "cool" hotels. The closest thing to cool is the **Georgian Terrace**, a.k.a. The Grand Dame. Built in 1911, the hotel's claim to fame is that it hosted the reception for the premiere of *Gone With The Wind* in 1939.

Atlanta does have plenty of nice hotels including the Four Seasons, two Ritz-Carltons, and a Westin. Southern hospitality can be found at bed and breakfasts such as the **Gaslight**—B&Bs in Atlanta are our version of the chic boutiques found in other cities. Call Bed & Breakfast Atlanta at 404-875-0525 or 800-967-3224 to find the perfect fit.

Map 1 • Underwood Hills / Blandtown

			Rate per night	Stars
Holiday Inn	1810 Howell Mill Rd	404-351-3831	110	
Intown Suites	1375 Northside Dr NW	404-350-8102	25	

Map 2 • Collier Hills / Brookwood Hills

Fairfield Inn & Suites	1470 Spring St NW	404-872-5821	79	★★★
Residence Inn	1365 Peachtree St	404-745-1000	144	
Super 8	1641 Peachtree St NE	404-873-5731	54	

Map 3 • Ansley Park / Piedmont Heights

Hello B&B	1865 Windemere Dr	404-892-8111	89	
Intown Suites	1944 Piedmont Cir NE	404-875-0023		

Map 5 • Georgia Tech / Arts Center

Four Seasons	75 14th St NE	404-881-9898	375	★★★★★
Hampton Inn	1152 Spring St NW	404-872-3234	99	★★★
Hotel Indigo	683 Peachtree St NE	404-874-9200	116	
Marriott Suites	35 14th St	404-876-8888	149	★★★
Regency Suites Hotel	975 W Peachtree St	404-876-5003	104	
Residence Inn	1041 W Peachtree St	404-872-8885	104	
The Georgian Terrace Hotel	659 Peachtree St NE	404-897-1991	134	★★★★
Villager Lodge	144 14th St NW	404-267-0925	57	

Map 6 • Midtown

Ansley Inn	253 15th St NE	404-872-9000	120	★★★1/2
Shellmont Inn	821 Piedmont Ave NE	404-872-9290	165	
Virginia Highland Bed & Breakfast	630 Orme Cir NE	404-892-2735	125	
Wyndham	125 10th St NE	404-873-4800	149	

Map 7 • Virginia Highland

Clermont Hotel	789 Ponce de Leon Ave NE	404-874-8611	57	
Ponce de Leon Place	929 Ponce de Leon Pl	404-873-6267	95	
The Gaslight Inn	1001 St Charles Ave NE	404-875-1001	165	

Map 9 • Downtown / Centennial Place / Techwood

AmeriSuites	330 Peachtree St NE	404-577-1980	75	★★★
Super 8	111 Cone St	404-524-5200	84	
Hampton Inn & Suites	161 Spring St NW	404-589-1111	120	
Holiday Inn	101 International Blvd	404-524-5555	119	★★★
Howard Johnson Plaza Hotel & Suites	54 Peachtree St	404-223-5555	84	

General Information · **Hotels**

Map 9 · Downtown / Centennial Place / Techwood—*continued*

			Rate per night	Stars
Hyatt Regency	265 Peachtree St NE	404-577-1234	200	★★★★
Quality	89 Luckie St	404-524-7991	144	★★★
The Ritz-Carlton	181 Peachtree St NE	404-659-0400	314	★★★★
Westin Peachtree Plaza	210 Peachtree St SW	404-659-1400	250	★★★
Wyndham	160 Spring St NW	404-688-8600	149	★★★★

Map 10 · Downtown / Sweet Auburn

Courtyard	175 Piedmont Ave NE	404-659-2727	149	★★
Fairfield Inn	175 Piedmont Rd NE	404-659-7777	106	★★★
Hilton	255 Courtland St NE	404-659-2000	137	★★★★
Marriott Marquis	265 Peachtree Center Ave	404-521-0000	210	★★★★
Savannah Suites	140 Pine St	404-591-2400	60	
Sheraton	165 Courtland St	404-659-6500	299	★★★★

Map 11 · Inman Park / Cabbagetown / Little Five Points

1890 King-Keith House (B&B)	889 Edgewood Ave NE	404-688-7330	140	
Heartfield Manor (B&B)	182 Elizabeth St NE	404-523-8633	100	
Sugar Magnolia (B&B)	804 Edgewood Ave NE	404-222-0226	115	

Map 13 · Mechanicsville / Summerhill

Holiday Inn Select	450 Capitol Ave SE	404-591-2000	109	★★★1/2
Residence Inn	134 Peachtree St NW	404-522-0950		

Map 14 · Grant Park

Hill Street Resort B&B	729 Hill St SE	404-627-6788	119	

Map 15 · Ormewood Park North / Woodland Hills

Atlanta Motel	277 Moreland Ave SE	404-659-2455	45	

Map 16 · Paces / Northside

Homewood Suites	3200 Cobb Pkwy SW	770-988-9449	124	

Map 19 · West Brookhaven

Sierra Suites	3967 Peachtree Rd NE	404-237-9100	99	★★★

Map 21 · Central Buckhead

Courtyard	3332 Peachtree Rd NE	404-869-0818	159	
Crowne Plaza	3377 Peachtree Rd NE	404-264-1111	159	★★★1/2
Doubletree Hotel	3342 Peachtree Rd NE	404-231-1234	169	★★★★
Fairfield Inn & Suites	3092 Piedmont Rd NE	404-846-0900	109	★★★★
Hampton Inn	3398 Piedmont Rd NE	404-233-5656	96	
Homewood Suites	3566 Piedmont Rd NE	404-365-0001	129	★★★
InterContinental	3315 Peachtree Rd NE	404-946-9000	312	★★★★
The Westin Buckhead	3391 Peachtree Rd NE	404-365-0065	309	★★★
Wingate Inn	3600 Piedmont Rd NE	404-869-1100	139	★★★★

Map 22 · Lenox

Embassy Suites	3285 Peachtree Rd NE	404-261-7733	161	★★★
Hampton Inn	1975 N Druid Hills Rd	404-320-6600	89	★★★

General Information • **Hotels**

Holiday Inn	2061 N Druid Hills Rd	404-321-4174	99	★★★
Homestead Studio Suites	1339 Executive Park Dr NE	404-325-1223	75	★★★
JW Marriott Hotel	3300 Lenox Rd	404-262-3344	259	★★★★
Microtel Inns & Suites	1840 Corporate Blvd	404-325-4446	49	
Sheraton	3405 Lenox Rd NE	404-261-92159		★★★
The Ritz-Carlton	3434 Peachtree Rd NE	404-237-2700	319	★★★★★

Map 23 • Briarcliff / Clairmont

Days Inn	2910 Clairmont Rd NE	404-633-8411		
Clairmont Lodge	10108 Cannon Farm Hill Rd NE	404-267-1300	89	
Extended StayAmerica	3115 Clairmont Rd NE	404-679-4333	66	
Wingate Inn	2920 Clairmont Rd NE	404-248-1590		★★★

Map 25 • Garden Hills / Peachtree Heights / Peachtree Hills

Beverly Hills Inn	65 Sheridan Dr NE	404-233-8520	99	★★★
Holiday Inn Express	505 Pharr Rd	404-262-7880	105	★★★
Ramada Limited	2115 Piedmont Rd NE	404-876-4444	84	
Staybridge Suites	540 Pharr Rd	404-842-0800	108	

Map 26 • Morningside / Lenox Hills

Baymont Inns & Suites	2535 Chantilly Dr NE	404-321-0999	70	★★
Cheshire Motor Inn	1865 Cheshire Bridge Rd NE	404-872-9628	55	
MainStay Suites	800 Sidney Marcus Blvd	404-949-4820	159	★★
Sleep Inn	800 Sidney Marcus Blvd	404-949-4000	134	★★

Map 27 • Toco Hills / Emory University

Emory Conference Center Hotel	1615 Clifton Rd	404-712-6000	160	★★★★
Emory Inn	1641 Clifton Rd	404-712-6000	110	★★★

Map 29 • North Decatur / Druid Hills East

Garden House B&B	135 Garden Ln	404-377-3057	85

Map 30 • Decatur

Holiday Inn Select	130 Clairmont Ave	404-371-0204	99	★★★
Super 8	917 Church St	404-378-3765	63	
Sycamore House B&B	624 Sycamore St	404-378-0685	118	

Map 32 • Kirkwood

Laurel Hill Bed & Breakfast	1992 McLendon Ave	404-377-3217	106

Map 35 • Sandy Springs (North)

Residence Inn	6096 Barfield Rd	404-252-5066	154
Staybridge Suites	760 Mt Vernon Hwy NW	404-250-0110	100

Map 36 • West Dunwoody

AmeriSuites	1005 Crestline Pkwy	770-730-9300	99	
Bentley's Bed & Breakfast	6860 Peachtree Dunwoody Rd	770-396-1742		
Comfort Suites	6110 Peachtree Dunwoody Rd	770-828-0330	89	★★★
Courtyard	6250 Peachtree Dunwoody Rd	770-393-1000	159	
Crowne Plaza	4355 Ashford Dunwoody Rd	770-395-7700	129	★★★
Doubletree Guest Suites	6120 Peachtree Dunwoody Rd	770-668-0808		★★★

General Information • **Hotels**

Map 36 • West Dunwoody—*continued*

			Rate per night	Stars
Embassy Suites	1030 Crown Pointe Pkwy	770-394-5454	161	★★★
La Quinta Inn & Suites	6260 Peachtree Dunwoody Rd	770-350-6177	94	★★★
Microtel Inns & Suites	6280 Peachtree Dunwoody Rd	678-781-4000	60	★★
W Atlanta	111 Perimeter Ctr W	770-396-6800	190	

Map 38 • Vinings

Crowne Plaza	6345 Powers Ferry Rd NW	770-955-1700	109	★★★★
Hawthorn Suites	1500 Parkwood Cir	770-952-9595	99	
Sierra Suites	2010 Powers Ferry Rd	770-933-8010	79	★★★

Map 40 • Sandy Springs (South)

Comfort Inn	5739 Roswell Rd NE	404-252-6400	79	★★★1/2
Hampton Inn	769 Hammond Dr	404-303-0014	99	
Holiday Inn Express	765 Hammond Dr	404-250-4479		★★★
Intown Suites	355 Hammond Dr NE	404-531-0067	32	

Map 41 • North Atlanta West

Fairfield Inn & Suites	1145 Hammond Dr	770-350-0000	119	★★★
Homestead Studio Suites	1050 Hammond Dr	770-522-0025	60	★★
Marriott	246 Perimeter Center Pkwy NE	770-394-6500	159	★★★★★
The Westin	7 Concourse Pkwy	770-395-3900	234	★★★

Map 42 • North Atlanta East / Silver Lake

Holiday Inn Select	4386 Chamblee-Dunwoody Rd	770-457-6363	99	
Residence Inn	1901 Savoy Dr	770-455-4446	129	
Savannah Suites	5280 Peachtree Industrial Blvd	678-805-3400	52	
Suburban Extended Stay Hotel	2050 Peachtree Industrial Ct	770-234-9005	54	

Map 43 • Chamblee / Doraville

Comfort Inn	2001 Clearview Ave	770-455-1811	69	★★★

Map 50 • College Park

Crowne Plaza	1325 Virginia Ave	404-768-6660	117	★★★
Drury Inn & Suites	1270 Virginia Ave	404-761-4900	72	
Econo Lodge	1360 Virginia Ave	404-761-5201		★★
Holiday Inn	1380 Virginia Ave	404-762-8411	104	
Ramada Plaza Hotel	1419 Virginia Ave	404-768-7800	74	★★★
Wellesley Inn & Suites	1377 Virginia Ave	404-762-5111	134	★★★

Map 51 • Hapeville

Days Inn	2788 Forrest Hills Dr SW	404-768-7755		
Fairfield Inn & Suites	1255 Walker Ave	404-767-5374	104	
Hampton Inn & Suites	3450 Bobby Brown Pkwy	404-767-9300	104	
Hilton	1031 Virginia Ave	404-767-9000	149	★★★★
Intown Suites	845 N Central Ave	404-766-9960	22	
Red Roof Inn	1200 Virginia Ave	404-209-1800	71	
Renaissance Concourse Hotel	1 Hartsfield Centre Pkwy	404-209-9999	159	★★★★

A sore spot for many Atlanta residents (not to mention the tourism industry) is the lack of original, worthwhile landmarks within Atlanta's city limits. Ask an Atlanta old-timer and they will blame it on the fact that Atlanta was burned down almost completely during the Civil War. We think that 140 years is enough time to create something worthy of a tourist attraction, if not of artistic merit. It's not that Atlanta hasn't had its share of remarkable architecture and interesting entertainment venues, it's just that we have a penchant for tearing them down and putting up really ugly buildings (or highways) in their place.

Ironically, the area's most well known landmarks aren't even in Atlanta. The Big Chicken in Marietta is interesting if you are into huge, tacky mechanical advertisements for lousy fried chicken. And the Confederate hero granite rock carvings of Stone Mountain are, well, for rednecks. **Centennial Olympic Park** is fine if you like to run through water fountains or watch the homeless take baths, but it's really only worth a visit when an event is taking place, like the summer concert series or the Holiday in Lights display.

Atlanta takes a tip from Las Vegas—create fake landmarks if you don't have any of your own. A fake Arc de Triomphe called Millennium Gate is coming soon to a Midtown landscape near you. Also on the horizon is the Georgia Aquarium, a boat-shaped monstrosity that seems a bit redundant, since the

impressive Tennessee Aquarium in Chattanooga is only 2 hours away. **Atlantic Station** is like The Sims come to life—a live-work-play city within the city. Atlanta also has a new, painfully ugly yellow bridge at 17th Street in Midtown to help transport the trendsetters to their Sims-like environment. **The Varsity** is a landmark for people that wax nostalgic for artery-clogging fast food.

The Landmarks We Love

The gorgeous **Fox Theatre** is a national historic landmark, and one of the city's best live entertainment venues. The ornate **Georgian Terrace Hotel**, which hosted the premiere party for *Gone with the Wind*, is a city jewel. The **Sun Dial Restaurant, Bar, and View** offers the best views of the city high atop the **Westin Peachtree Plaza** in Downtown Atlanta. **Piedmont Park** provides a green oasis in the heart of the bustling city, and is Atlanta's best answer to Central Park in New York City. **Oakland Cemetery** provides the final resting place for many local notables, including author Margaret Mitchell. Visiting the proud-to-be-seedy **Clermont Lounge** has become an unofficial rite of passage. For a powerful civil rights history experience, the **King Center** remains one of the country's most important resources. And the original **Krispy Kreme** location in Atlanta, on Ponce De Leon Avenue, with its glowing "Hot Now" sign has fed generations of cops and potheads.

Map 2 • Collier Hills / Brookwood Hills

Atlantic Station	1349 W Peachtree St NE • 404-876-2616	Vast new live-work-play development in West Midtown.
Brookwood Station AMTRAK	1688 W Peachtree St NE • 800-872-7245	Atlanta's AMTRAK station is an architectural treasure.
Center for Puppetry Arts	1404 Spring St NW • 404-873-3391	Puppets for the people!
Sherwood Forest	Beverly Rd & Peachtree St	Get lost in the winding streets of this gorgeous neighborhood.

Map 3 • Ansley Park / Piedmont Heights

Atlanta Botanical Garden	1345 Piedmont Ave NE • 404-876-5859	Great for green thumbs.
Fat Matt's Rib Shack	1811 Piedmont Ave NE • 404-607-1622	BBQ/blues dive as shown on the Food Network.

Map 4 • West Midtown / Home Park

Atlanta Humane Society	981 Howell Mill Rd NW	Find a furry friend here.
King Plow Arts Center	887 W Marietta St NW	Fine/performing arts complex housed in historic industrial building.

Map 5 · Georgia Tech / Arts Center

Fox Theatre	660 Peachtree St NE · 404-881-2100	Beautiful temple-turned-theatre. Check out the sky ceiling.
Georgian Terrace Hotel	659 Peachtree St NE · 800-651-2316	Historic hotel with *Gone with the Wind* ties.
High Museum	1280 Peachtree St NE · 404-733-4400	Atlanta's best-known art museum.
Margaret Mitchell House	990 Peachtree St · 404-249-7015	Called "the dump" by the *Gone with the Wind* author.
The Varsity	61 North Ave NW· 404-881-1706	The world's largest drive-in restaurant.

Map 6 · Midtown

The Abbey	163 Ponce de Leon Ave NE · 404-876-8532	Dinner served by "monks" in a former church.
Corner of 13th Street & Peachtree Street	Peachtree St & 13th St	Where Margaret Mitchell was killed by a speeding taxi.
Krispy Kreme Doughnuts	295 Ponce de Leon Ave · 404-876-7307	Flagship Ponce store, where the hot & glazed await the drunk & dazed.
Mary Mac's Tea Room	224 Ponce de Leon Ave NW · 404-876-1800	Southern meat-and-three legend is classiest thing on Ponce.
Piedmont Park	400 Park Dr NE · 404-876-4024	Atlanta's answer to Central Park.
Ponce de Leon	Ponce de Leon Ave & Monroe Dr	Notoriously seedy strip of Atlanta.

Map 7 · Virginia Highland

Clermont Lounge	789 Ponce de Leon Ave NE · 404-874-4783	The anti-strip club. Don't miss Blondie's beer-crushing act.
Freedom Park	North Ave & Freedom Pkwy	Pedestrian- and bike-friendly destination inside the city.
Manuel's Tavern	602 N Highland Ave NE · 404-525-3477	Favorite hangout for local journalists, politicians, and cops.

Map 8 · Vine City

Herndon Home	587 University Pl NW · 404-581-9813	Home of Atlanta's first African American millionaire, Alonzo Herndon.

Map 9 · Downtown / Centennial Place / Techwood

Centennial Olympic Park	265 Park Ave NW · 404-222-7275	Kids love running through the fountains.
CNN Center	1 CNN Ctr, 190 Marietta St NW · 404-827-2300	24-hour news headquarters. Take the behind-the-scenes tour.
Five Points	30 Alabama St SW · 404-848-4711	Main MARTA hub and where major Downtown streets unite.
Georgia Dome	1 Georgia Dome Dr · 404-223-4636	Where the Falcons play to a fickle crowd.
Georgia World Congress Center	285 Andrew Y International Blvd NE · 404-223-4300	Where conferences happen.
Imagine It! The Children's Museum of Atlanta	275 Centennial Olympic Park Dr NW · 404-659-5437	"Don't touch" doesn't apply here.
MARTA Peachtree Center Station Escalator	216 Peachtree St NE · 404-848-4711	Longest escalator in the Southeastern United States!
The Tabernacle	152 Luckie St NW · 404-659-9022	Former church converted into raucous live music venue.
Underground Atlanta	50 Upper Alabama St · 404-523-2311	The ultimate tourist trap.
Woodruff Park	Auburn Ave & Peachtree St	Homeless on parade.

Map 10 · Downtown / Sweet Auburn

The Apex	135 Auburn Ave · 404-523-2739	African-American Panoramic Experience.
Ebenezer Baptist Church	407 Auburn Ave NE · 404-688-7263	Where Martin Luther King Jr. first preached.

Grady Memorial Hospital	80 Jesse Hill Jr Dr SE • 404-616-4307	Superb trauma center. If you're shot, go here.
King Center	449 Auburn Ave NE • 404-526-8923	Preserves Martin Luther King Jr.'s legacy through educational exhibits.
Sweet Auburn District	Auburn Ave b/w Courtland Ave & Jackson St	Historically African-American business district.
Sweet Auburn Curb Market	209 Edgewood Ave • 404-659-1665	Overrated indoor farmer's market.
Shakespeare Tavern	499 Peachtree St NE • 404-874-5299	Superb live Shakespearean theatre in authentic pub setting.

Map 11 • Inman Park / Cabbagetown / Little Five Points

Carter Presidential Center and Library	441 Freedom Pkwy • 404-420-5145	Tribute to a great humanitarian and so-so president.
Charis Books	1189 Euclid Ave NE • 404-524-0304	Lesbian/feminist bookstore veteran.
Inman Park Neighborhood	Euclid Ave & Elizabeth St	Historic Victorian homes, and a quirky annual neighborhood parade.
Little Five Points	Moreland Ave NE & Euclid Ave NE	Quirky, bohemian neighborhood with great shops.
The Vortex Bar & Grill	438 Moreland Ave NE • 404-688-1828	Giant skull entrance doesn't scare tattooed clientele.

Map 12 • West End

Atlanta University Center	440 Westview Dr • 404-523-5148	Historic African-American higher learning complex.
Paschal's	180 Northside Dr SW • 404-525-2023	Civil rights-era meeting place that was spared demolition.

Map 13 • Mechanicsville / Summerhill

Shrine of the Immaculate Conception	48 Martin Luther King Jr Dr SW 404-521-1866	Atlanta's oldest Catholic church. One of the few things Sherman didn't burn down.
Turner Field	755 Hank Aaron Dr SE • 404-577-9100	Will the Braves ever win another World Series?
World of Coca Cola	55 Martin Luther King Jr Dr • 770-578-4325	Soft drink ad disguised as museum.

Map 14 • Grant Park

Cyclorama	800 Cherokee Ave SE • 404-624-1071	Oddest Atlanta tourist attraction uses rare storytelling device.
Oakland Cemetery	248 Oakland Ave SE• 404-688-2107	Final resting place for notable Atlantans. Gorgeous architecture.
Zoo Atlanta	800 Cherokee Ave SE • 404-624-5600	Starring Lun Lun and Yang Yang, those adorable Commie pandas!

Map 17 • Northwest Atlanta / Mt Paren

Chastain Park Amphitheatre	4469 Stella Dr • 404-233-2227	Outdoor music venue favored by cell-phone chatting yuppies.
Tuxedo Park	Vicinity of 3661 Tuxedo Rd NW	Ritzy homes in a ritzy neighborhood.

Map 21 • Central Buckhead

Atlanta History Center	130 W Paces Ferry Rd NW • 404-814-4000	Start here to learn Atlanta's history.
Buckhead Pool Hall	30 Irby Ave NW • 404-841-8989	Buckhead's oldest bar that's been in Levi's jeans TV commercials.
Swan House	130 W Paces Ferry Rd NW • 404-814-4000	Recently restored gorgeous mansion from the 1920s.

Map 24 · Peachtree Battle / Woodfield

Bobby Jones Golf Course	384 Woodward Wy NW · 404-355-1009	Tee off at the course named for one of golf's greatest.
Governor's Mansion	391 W Paces Ferry Rd NW · 404-656-1776	Greek Revival masterpiece in the heart of Buckhead.

Map 25 · Garden Hills / Peachtree Heights / Peachtree Hills

Atlanta Fish Market	265 Pharr Rd NE · 404-262-3165	You can't miss the giant copper fish!
Beverly Hills Inn	65 Sheridan Dr · 404-233-8520	Stylish bed and breakfast in Buckhead.
Buckhead Nightclub District	Peachtree Rd, Pharr Rd, & Paces Ferry Rd	Lots of bling-bling; too much bang-bang.
Miami Circle Antique Marketplace	700 Miami Cir NE	Antiques shopping on steroids.

Map 27 · Toco Hills / Emory University

Center for Disease Control and Prevention	1600 Clifton Rd NE · 404-639-2080	A little ebola, a little plague, a lot of security.

Map 28 · Druid Hills West

Callanwolde Fine Arts Center	980 Briarcliff Rd NE · 404-872-5338	Gorgeous multi-use fine arts facility.
Fernbank Museum of Natural History	767 Clifton Rd NE · 404-929-6300	Fossils, IMAX, and martinis.
The Mansion	822 Lullwater Rd NE	Home featured in *Driving Miss Daisy*.
Michael C Carlos Museum	571 S Kilgo Cir NE · 404-727-4282	Mummies and lots of other cool stuff.

Map 29 · North Decatur / Druid Hills East

Watershed	406 W Ponce de Leon Ave · 404-378-4900	Indigo Girls' Emily Saliers restaurant venture. Awesome fried chicken.

Map 30 · Decatur

Eddie's Attic	515 N McDonough St · 404-377-4976	Live acoustic music venue where John Mayer played.

Map 31 · Edgewood / Candler Park

Ann's Snack Bar	1615 Memorial Dr SE · 404-687-9207	Atlanta's version of "The Soup Nazi."

Map 32 · Kirkwood

Bessie Branham Park	2051 Delano Dr NE	Modern recreation center in the 'hood.

Map 42 · North Atlanta East / Silver Lake

Chamblee Antique Row	3519 Broad St · 770-455-4751	Antique Capital of the South!

Map 44 · Adair Park

Couer D'Allene Studio Lofts	1213 Allene Ave SW · 404-753-2914	Capitol View's first loft development.
House of Prayer	1136 Metropolitan Pkwy SW · 404-753-2914	Known as "House of Reverend Whip-Ass" to locals.

Map 46 · Peoplestown

Harold's Barbecue	171 McDonough Blvd SE · 404-627-9268	Serving pulled pork by the prison for over 50 years.
US Federal Penitentiary	601 McDonough Blvd SE · 404-635-5100	Time out for terminal misfits.

The Atlanta system is disorganized and frustrating—you may have to visit three different branches before you find what you're looking for. The main branch downtown offers the best, but still not great, one-stop browsing (with the added hassle of finding parking). It helps if you think of the nearest bookstore as an additional local library.

Atlanta's special libraries include: The **Auburn Avenue Research Library** on **African-American Culture and History**; the **King Library and Archives**, the world's largest repository of primary source materials on both Dr. Martin Luther King, Jr. and the American Civil Rights Movement; and the **Jimmy Carter Library**.

Library	Address	Phone	Map
Auburn Avenue Research Library	101 Auburn Ave NE	404-730-4001	10
Briarcliff Library	2775 Briarcliff Rd	404-679-4400	23
Brookhaven Library	1242 N Druid Hills Rd	404-848-7140	19
Buckhead Branch	269 Buckhead Ave NE	404-814-3500	25
Central (Main) Library	1 Margaret Mitchell Sq	404-730-1700	9
Chamblee Library	4115 Clairmont Rd	770-936-1380	20
College Park Branch	3647 Main St	404-762-4060	50
Decatur Library	215 Sycamore St	404-370-3070	30
Doraville Library	3748 Central Ave	770-936-3852	43
Dunwoody Library	5339 Chamblee-Dunwoody Rd	770-512-4640	36
East Atlanta Branch	457 Flat Shoals Ave SE	404-730-5438	34
Georgia-Hill Branch	250 Georgia Ave SE	404-730-5427	14
Hapeville Branch	525 King Arnold St	404-762-4065	51
Jimmy Carter Library	441 Freedom Pkwy NE	404-865-7100	11
King Library & Archives	449 Auburn Ave NE	404-526-8900	10
Kirkwood Branch	11 Kirkwood Rd NE	404-377-6471	32
Mechanicsville Branch	400 Formwalt St SW	404-730-4779	13
Northside Branch	3295 Northside Pkwy NW	404-814-3508	16
Peachtree Branch	1315 Peachtree St NE	404-885-7830	2
Ponce de Leon Branch	980 Ponce de Leon Ave NE	404-885-7820	7
Sandy Springs Regional	395 Mt Vernon Hwy	404-303-6130	39
Stewart-Lakewood Branch	2893 Lakewood Ave	404-762-4054	49
West End Branch	525 Peeples St SW	404-752-8740	12

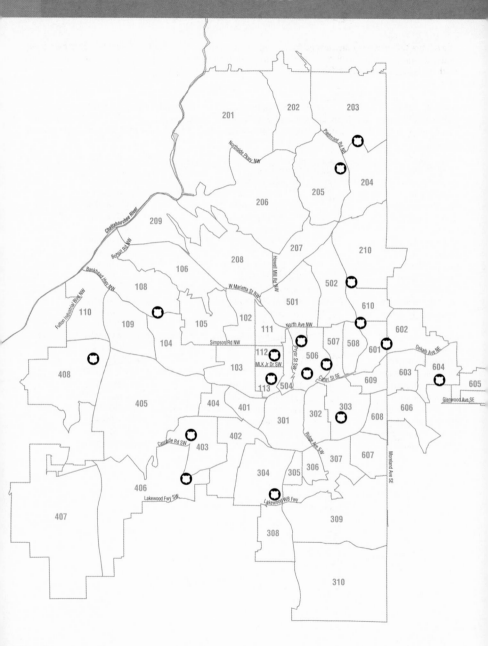

Important Phone Numbers

Life Threatening Emergencies: 911
Non-Emergency Police Service: 404-853-3434
Wanted Persons: 404-853-4220
Rape Victims Hotline: 404-853-4260
Crime Victims Hotline: 404-853-4255
Family Violence Hotline: 404-853-4215
Missing Persons Unit (Adults): 404-853-4235 x5090
Crimes Against Children: 404-817-7895
Sex Crimes Report Line: 404-658-6666
GLBT Liaison: 404-817-6710
Central Records: 404-853-7461
Public Affairs: 404-817-6873
Impounded Vehicles: 404-853-4330
Atlanta PD Website: www.atlantapd.org

Statistics

	2003	2002	2001
Murders	149	152	143
Rapes	281	276	367
Robberies	3,701	4,168	4,341
Aggravated Assaults	4,360	5,373	5,956
Burglaries	8,065	8,554	8,731
Larcenies	22,931	23,706	25,721
Auto Theft	7,235	7,222	6,935

Station	Address	Phone	Map
APD Zone 1 Fair Street Mini Precinct	676 Fair St SW	404-658-6274	12
APD Zone 1 Magnolia Street Mini Precinct	612 Magnolia St NW	404-658-6486	8
APD Zone 2 Lenox Mall Mini Precinct	3393 Peachtree Rd NE	404-467-8061	21
APD Zone 2 Station	3120 Maple Dr NE	404-848-7231	21
APD Zone 3 Metropolitan Parkway	2027 Metropolitan Pkwy SW	404-230-9604	49
APD Zone 3 Station	880 Cherokee Ave SW	404-624-0674	46
APD Zone 4 Campbellton Road Mini Precinct	2000 Campbellton Rd SW	404-755-1499	48
APD Zone 5 Auburn Avenue Mini Precinct	247 Auburn Ave NE	404-658-6452	10
APD Zone 5 Midtown Mini Precinct	1320 Monroe Dr NE	404-853-3300	6
APD Zone 5 Station	398 Centennial Olympic Park Dr NW	404-658-7054	9
APD Zone 5 Underground Mini Precinct	94 Pryor St SW	404-658-6364	9
APD Zone 6 Station	2025 Hosea L Williams Dr NE	404-371-5002	32
APD Zone 6 Little Five Points Mini Precinct	428 Seminole Ave NE	404-658-6782	11
APD Police Operations Bureau	675 Ponce de Leon Ave	404-817-6791	7
Decatur Police Department - Oakhurst Office	707 E Lake Dr	404-370-4161	32
Doraville Police Department	3760 Park Ave	770-455-1000	43
Chamblee Police Department	3518 Broad St	770-986-5005	42
East Point Law Enforcement Center	2727 East Point St	404-761-2177	50
Hapeville Police Department	700 Doug Davis Dr	404-669-2149	51

30068

30067

30092

30338

30328

30360

30071

30339

30380

30342

30319

30341

30340

30009

30339

30327

30326

30345

30084

30305

30324

30329

30318

30306

30033

30021

30322

30079

30008

30309

30313

30002

30314

30307

30030

30303

30317

30032

30334

30312

30035

30310

30316

30311

30330

30315

30034

30331

30344

30337

30354

30288

30294

Post Office	Address	Phone	Zip	Map
Broadview Station	780 Morosgo Dr NE	404-233-9401	30324	26
Brookhaven Branch	3851 Peachtree Rd NE	404-262-9794	30326	19
Buckhead Station	3495 Buckhead Loop NE	404-816-9486	30326	21
Central City Carrier Station	400 Pryor St SW	404-222-0765	30303	13
Central City Retail	183 Forsyth St SW	404-521-2053	30303	13
Chamblee	3545 Broad St	770-216-1968	30341	42
Civic Center Station	570 Piedmont Rd	404-874-8718	30308	10
Decatur	520 W Ponce de Leon Ave	404-373-8827	30030	29
Doraville	4700 Longmire Ext	770-216-8475	30340	43
Druid Hills	1799 Briarcliff Rd NE	404-875-7590	30333	26
Dunwoody	1551 Dunwoody Village Pkwy	770-352-9070	30338	36
Dunwoody Post Offices	4444 N Shallowford Rd	770-458-7387	30338	37
East Atlanta Station	1273 Metropolitan Ave SE	404-521-2064	30316	34
East Point	2905 East Point St	404-767-3973	30344	50
Eastwood Station (Finance)	1926 Hosea L Williams Dr NE	404-373-2164	30317	31
Executive Park Station	4 Executive Park Dr NE	404-634-5811	30329	23
Federal Center Station	41 Marietta St	404-524-2963	30301	9
Gate City Station	486 Decatur St SE	404-521-2855	30312	10
Glenridge	5400 Glenridge Dr NE	404-256-1977	30342	40
Hapeville	650 S Central Ave	404-768-2389	30354	51
Howell Mill Postal Store	1984 Howell Mill Rd NW	404-350-9193	30327	1
Little Five Points Station	457 Moreland Ave NE	404-521-1982	30307	11
Martech Carrier Station	967 Brady Ave NW	404-885-1037	30318	4
Martech Finance Station	794 Marietta St NW	404-523-7374	30318	4
Midtown	1072 W Peachtree St NW	404-873-4869	30309	5
Morris Brown Station	50 Sunset Ave NW	404-302-9470	30314	8
North Atlanta Station	1920 Dresden Dr NE	404-636-8764	30319	20
North Highland Station	1190 N Highland Ave NE	404-873-0878	30306	7
Northside Carrier Facility	3840 Roswell Rd NE	404-239-0894	30305	21
Peachtree Center	240 Peachtree St SW	404-523-5057	30303	13
Perimeter Center	4707 Ashford Dunwoody Rd	770-913-0790	30338	36
Pharr Road	575 Pharr Rd NE	404-869-4413	30355	25
Sandy Springs Postal Store	227 Sandy Springs Pl NE	404-255-9643	30328	35
US Post Office	1 CNN Ctr, 190 Marietta St NW	404-524-3394	30303	9
US Post Office	133 Peachtree St NE	404-765-7300	30303	9
West End	848 Oglethrope Ave SW	404-755-4412	30310	12

Times listed are last pick-up time, pm.

Map 1

Drop Box	1 Northside 75 NW	6:00
Drop Box	1575 Northside Dr NW	6:30
Drop Box	1661 Defoor Ave NW	6:30
Drop Box	1715 Howell Mill Rd NW	7:30
FedEx	1715 Howell Mill Rd NW	7:30
Drop Box	1900 Emery St NW	5:30
Drop Box	1984 Howell Mill Rd NW	7:00
Drop Box	485 Bishop St NW	6:00
Drop Box	763 Trabert Ave NW	6:30

Map 2

Drop Box	1315 Peachtree St NE	6:00
Drop Box	1350 Spring St NW	7:00
Drop Box	1355 Peachtree St NE	7:00
Drop Box	1360 Peachtree St NE	7:30
FedEx	1375 Peachtree St NE	7:00,
Kinkos		3:00
Drop Box	1409 Peachtree St NE	7:30
Drop Box	1447 Peachtree St NE	7:00
Drop Box	1545 Peachtree Rd NE	7:00
Drop Box	1708 Peachtree St NW	6:00
Drop Box	1718 Peachtree St NW	6:45
Drop Box	1740 Peachtree St NW	7:00

Map 3

Drop Box	1874 Piedmont Rd NE	7:00
Drop Box	469 Plasters Ave NE	7:00
Drop Box	593 Dutch Valley Rd NE	6:30

Map 4

Drop Box	505 10th St NW	6:30
Drop Box	530 Means St NW	6:00
Drop Box	700 14th St NW	6:00
Drop Box	794 Marietta St NW	6:00

Map 5

Drop Box	600 Peachtree St NE	7:30
Drop Box	615 Peachtree St NE	6:30
Drop Box	710 Peachtree St NE	6:00
Drop Box	715 Peachtree St NE	6:30
Drop Box	730 Peachtree St NE	6:30
Drop Box	754 Peachtree St	7:00
Parcel Plus	85 5th St NW	7:00
Drop Box	10 Peachtree Pl NW	7:00
Drop Box	1100 Spring St NW	7:00
Drop Box	1170 Peachtree St	6:45
Drop Box	1201 W Peachtree St	7:30
Drop Box	1275 Peachtree St NE	6:30
Drop Box	75 14th St NW	7:00
Drop Box	999 Peachtree St NE	7:00
Drop Box	247 4th St NW	7:30
Drop Box	197 14th St NW	6:30
Drop Box	250 14th St NW	6:30
Drop Box	400 10th St NW	6:30
Drop Box	410 14th St NW	6:30
Drop Box	347 Ferst Dr	7:30

Map 6

Drop Box	597 Cooledge Ave NE	7:00
Drop Box	621 North Ave	6:30

Map 8

Drop Box	643 Martin Luther King Jr Dr NW	6:00

Map 9

FedEx	100 Peachtree St NE	7:00,
Kinkos		3:00
FedEx	100 Peachtree St NE	8:30
Drop Box	101 Marietta St NW	7:00
Drop Box	127 Peachtree St NE	7:30

Map 10 (continued)

Drop Box	133 Luckie St NW	7:00
Drop Box	133 Peachtree St NE	7:00
Drop Box	191 Peachtree St NE	6:00
Drop Box	2 Peachtree St NW	7:00
FedEx	229 Peachtree St NE	8:30
Drop Box	25 Park Pl NE	7:00
Drop Box	250 Spring St NW	7:30
Drop Box	250 Williams St NW	7:30
Drop Box	42 Marietta St NW	7:00
Drop Box	50 Hurt Plz SE	7:00
Drop Box	55 Park Pl NE	7:00
Drop Box	58 Edgewood Ave NE	7:00
Drop Box	75 Spring St SW	5:00
FedEx	285 International	4:00
Kinkos	Blvd NW	

Map 10

FedEx	255 Courtland St NE	7:00,
Kinkos		12:00
FedEx	265 Peachtree	7:00,
Kinkos	Center Ave NE	3:00
Drop Box	285 Peachtree Center Ave NE	6:45
Drop Box	303 Peachtree Center Ave NE	7:00
Drop Box	51 Peachtree Center Ave NE	7:00
Drop Box	69 Butler St SE	7:00
Drop Box	70 Ellis St NE	7:30
Drop Box	75 Piedmont Ave NE	7:00
Drop Box	250 Piedmont Ave NE	7:00
Drop Box	570 Piedmont Ave NE	7:30
Pak Mail	595 Piedmont Ave NE	5:30,
		12:30

Map 11

Drop Box	1 Copenhill Ave NE	6:00
Drop Box	280 Elizabeth St NE	6:00
Drop Box	99 Krog St NE	6:00

Map 12

Drop Box	720 Westview Dr SW	6:30
Drop Box	504 Fair St Sw	6:30
Drop Box	350 Spelman Ln SW	6:30

Map 13

Drop Box	183 Forsyth St SW	7:00
Drop Box	230 Peachtree St NW	7:30
Drop Box	270 Peachtree St SW	7:15
FedEx	401 Windsor St SW	8:30, 5:00

Map 15

Drop Box	566 Boulevard SE	6:30

Map 16

Drop Box	2060 Mt Paran Rd NW	6:30
Drop Box	3290 Northside Pkwy NW	7:00
FedEx	3401 Northside Pkwy NW	6:30,
Kinkos		2:30
Drop Box	3715 Northside Pkwy NW	7:00

Map 17

Drop Box	4401 Northside Pkwy NW	7:00
Drop Box	173 W Wieuca Rd	6:45

Map 18

Drop Box	4651 Roswell Rd NE	7:00

Map 19

Drop Box	3851 Peachtree Rd NE	6:45

Map 21

Drop Box	3098 Piedmont Rd NE	7:00
Drop Box	3312 Piedmont Rd NE	7:30
Drop Box	3405 Piedmont Rd NE	6:45
Drop Box	3423 Piedmont Rd NE	6:45
Drop Box	3475 Piedmont Rd NE	7:30
Drop Box	3490 Piedmont Rd NE	7:15
Drop Box	3495 Piedmont Ctr NE	6:45
Drop Box	3500 Piedmont Rd NE	7:30
Drop Box	3520 Piedmont Rd NE	7:30
Drop Box	3525 Piedmont Rd NE	6:45
Drop Box	3535 Piedmont Rd NE	6:45
Drop Box	3565 Piedmont Ctr	6:45
Drop Box	3333 Peachtree Rd NE	6:45
FedEx	3340 Peachtree Rd NE	8:00, 4:30
Drop Box	3343 Peachtree Rd NE	6:45
Drop Box	3348 Peachtree Rd NE	7:30
Drop Box	3350 Peachtree Rd NE	7:30
Drop Box	3379 Peachtree Rd NE	6:30
Drop Box	3384 Peachtree Rd NE	7:00
Drop Box	3391 Peachtree Rd NE	6:15
Drop Box	3399 Peachtree Rd NE	7:00
Drop Box	3400 Peachtree Rd NE	7:15
Drop Box	3414 Peachtree Rd NE	7:00
Drop Box	3833 Roswell Rd NE	6:30

Map 22

Drop Box	3210 Peachtree Rd NE	7:30
Drop Box	1055 Lenox Park Blvd	5:45
Drop Box	66 Lenox Pointe NE	7:30
Drop Box	1 Buckhead Loop NE	7:00
Drop Box	3355 Lenox Rd NE	5:45
Drop Box	3424 Peachtree Rd NE	6:45
Drop Box	3455 Peachtree Rd NE	6:00
Drop Box	3475 Lenox Rd NE	6:45
Drop Box	3500 Lenox Rd NE	7:00
Drop Box	2801 Buford Hwy NE	6:30

Map 23

Drop Box	1645 Tullie Cir NE	7:30
Drop Box	17 Executive Park Dr NE	5:00
Drop Box	1945 Cliff Valley Wy NE	6:30
Mail Boxes Etc	2480 Briarcliff Rd NE	6:00
Drop Box	2957 Clairmont Rd NE	7:15
Drop Box	2970 Clairmont Rd NE	7:00
Drop Box	2987 Clairmont Rd NE	7:00
Drop Box	3105 Clairmont Rd NE	6:00
Drop Box	4 Executive Park Dr NE	6:00

Map 24

Drop Box	75 Bennett St NW	6:00

Map 25

Drop Box	2901 Piedmont Rd NE	7:15
Drop Box	2996 Grandview Ave NE	6:45
Drop Box	3060 Peachtree Rd NW	7:00
Drop Box	550 Pharr Rd NE	7:15
Drop Box	575 Pharr Rd NE	7:00
Drop Box	2581 Piedmont Rd NE	7:00
Drop Box	700 Miami Cir NE	7:00

Map 26

Drop Box	1123 Zonolite Rd NE	7:00
Drop Box	1799 Briarcliff Rd NE	7:00
FedEx	2441 Cheshire Bridge Rd NE	8:30, 5:00
Drop Box	780 Morosgo Dr NE	7:00
Drop Box	1841 Clifton Rd NE	7:30

Map 27

Drop Box	1600 Clifton Rd NE	7:00

Map 28

Drop Box 1256 Briarcliff Rd NE 6:30

Map 29

Drop Box 201 Swanton Wy 6:00
Drop Box 315 W Ponce de Leon Ave 6:00
Drop Box 520 Ponce de Leon Ave 5:30
Drop Box 1300 Clifton Rd NE 7:00
Drop Box 1327 Clifton Rd NE 7:00
Drop Box 1639 Pierce Dr 6:30

Map 30

Drop Box 1 W Court Sq 4:00
Drop Box 101 W Ponce de Leon Ave 6:00
Drop Box 125 Clairmont Ave 6:30
Drop Box 150 Ponce de Leon Ave 6:30
Drop Box 160 Clairmont Ave 6:30
Drop Box 250 E Ponce de Leon Ave 6:30
Drop Box 755 Commerce Dr 6:30

Map 31

Drop Box 250 Arizona Ave 6:00
Drop Box 1599 Memorial Dr SE 6:30

Map 32

Intown Business Center 147 College Ave NE 6:00, 2:00

Map 35

Drop Box 1 Glenlake Pkwy 6:45
Drop Box 10 Glenlake Pkwy SE 6:30
Drop Box 50 Glenlake Pkwy NE 5:30
Pak Mail 6025 Sandy Springs Cir NE 5:00, 12:00
Drop Box 6045 Barfield Rd NE 6:30
Drop Box 6065 Roswell Rd NE 7:00
Drop Box 6195 Barfield Rd NE 6:30
Drop Box 6255 Barfield Rd NE 6:30
Drop Box 800 Mt Vernon Hwy NE 5:30

Map 36

Drop Box 1000 Abernathy Rd NE 7:00
Drop Box 1100 Abernathy Rd NE 6:00
Drop Box 6160 Peachtree Dunwoody Rd NE 6:30
Drop Box 6600 Peachtree Dunwoody Rd NE 7:00
Drop Box 7000 Central Pkwy NE 7:00
Drop Box 7000 Peachtree Dunwoody Rd NE 6:30
Drop Box 100 Ashford Ctr N 6:30
Drop Box 1040 Crown Pointe Pkwy 6:30
Drop Box 1050 Crown Pointe Pkwy 6:30
Drop Box 1200 Ashwood Pkwy 6:30
Drop Box 1532 Dunwoody Village Pkwy 7:00
Drop Box 1724 Mt Vernon Rd 7:00
Drop Box 200 Ashford Ctr N 7:00
Drop Box 4707 Ashford Dunwoody Rd 6:30
Drop Box 4800 Ashford Dunwoody Rd 6:30
American Mail Plus 5579 Chamblee Dunwoody Rd 5:00
Post Net 5588 Chamblee Dunwoody Rd 6:00, 2:00
Drop Box 900 Ashwood Pkwy 7:00
Drop Box 1 Ravinia Dr 7:15
Drop Box 115 Perimeter Ctr W 7:00
Drop Box 121 Perimeter Ctr W 6:30
FedEx Kinkos 126 Perimeter Ctr W 7:30, 4:00
Drop Box 1455 Lincoln Pkwy E 7:00
Drop Box 3 Ravinia Dr 7:00
Drop Box 302 Perimeter Ctr E 6:30
Drop Box 64 Perimeter Ctr E 6:30
Drop Box 66 Perimeter Ctr E 7:00

Map 37

Drop Box 1867 Independence Sq 6:30

Map 38

Drop Box 2000 Riveredge Pkwy NW 6:00
Drop Box 2100 Riveredge Pkwy NW 6:00
Drop Box 5660 New Northside Dr NW 6:30
Drop Box 1300 Parkwood Cir SE 6:30
Drop Box 1600 Parkwood Cir SE 7:00
Drop Box 2018 Powers Ferry Rd SE 6:30
Drop Box 2100 Powers Ferry Rd SE 7:00
Drop Box 2120 Powers Ferry Rd SE 6:30
Drop Box 2997 Cobb Pkwy 6:30
Drop Box 3101 Towercreek Pkwy SE 6:45
Drop Box 3200 Cobb Galleria Pkwy 6:30
Drop Box 3330 Cumberland Blvd 6:30
Drop Box 3350 Riverwood Pkwy SE 6:30
Drop Box 6151 Powers Ferry Rd NW 6:00
Drop Box 6190 Powers Ferry Rd NW 6:00
Drop Box 6400 Powers Ferry Rd NW 7:00
Drop Box 6520 Powers Ferry Rd NW 7:00

Map 39

Drop Box 5780 Powers Ferry Rd NW 6:00

Map 40

Drop Box 180 Allen Rd NE 6:30
Drop Box 270 Carpenter Dr NE 6:30
Drop Box 5730 Glenridge Dr NE 6:30
Drop Box 5775 Glenridge Dr NE 6:30
Drop Box 5825 Glenridge Dr NE 6:30
Drop Box 5871 Glenridge Dr NE 6:00
Drop Box 5881 Glenridge Dr NE 6:00
Drop Box 5887 Glenridge Dr NE 6:00
FedEx 5975 Roswell Rd 7:30
Drop Box 6000 Lake Forrest Dr NW 6:15
Drop Box 80 Cliftwood Dr NE 6:30
Drop Box 4840 Roswell Rd NE 7:00
Mail USA 4920 Roswell Rd NE 4:00, 2:00
Drop Box 5064 Roswell Rd NE 6:30
Drop Box 5180 Roswell Rd NE 6:15
Drop Box 5188 Roswell Rd NE 7:00
Drop Box 5400 Glenridge Dr NE 6:30
Drop Box 5447 Roswell Rd NE 6:30
Drop Box 5600 Glenridge Dr NE 6:30
Drop Box 5600 Roswell Rd NE 6:30
Drop Box 5605 Glenridge Dr NE 5:30

Map 41

Drop Box 4151 Ashford Dunwoody Rd NE 6:45
Drop Box 1 Concourse Pkwy NE 6:30
Pak Mail 1100 Hammond Dr NE 4:30, 12:30
Drop Box 1140 Hammond Dr NE 7:00
Drop Box 1150 Hammond Dr NE 7:00
Drop Box 1155 Hammond Dr NE 6:30
Drop Box 2 Concourse Pkwy NE 6:00
Drop Box 4 Concourse Pkwy NE 6:00
Drop Box 5 Concourse Pkwy NE 6:30
Drop Box 5901 Peachtree Dunwoody Rd NE 7:00
Drop Box 5909 Peachtree Dunwoody Rd NE 7:00
Drop Box 6 Concourse Pkwy NE 6:30
Drop Box 990 Hammond Dr NE 6:00
Drop Box 1100 Johnson Ferry Rd NE 6:30
Drop Box 1150 Lake Hearn Dr NE 6:30
Drop Box 5505 Peachtree Dunwoody Rd NE 6:30
Drop Box 5565 Glenridge Connector NE 7:00
Drop Box 5671 Peachtree Connector NE 6:45
Drop Box 5775 Peachtree Dunwoody Rd NE 6:00
Drop Box 5780 Peachtree Dunwoody Rd NE 6:00
Drop Box 975 Johnson Ferry Rd NE 6:00
Drop Box 211 Perimeter Center Pkwy NE 7:00
Drop Box 223 Perimeter Center Pkwy NE 6:30

Map 42

Drop Box 1835 Savoy Dr 5:45
Drop Box 2080 Peachtree Industrial Ct 6:30
Drop Box 3525 Broad St 7:00
Drop Box 4201 N Peachtree Rd 6:45
Drop Box 4360 Chamblee Dunwoody Rd 6:30
Drop Box 5383 New Peachtree Rd 6:00

Map 43

Drop Box 2000 Clearview Ave 6:00
Drop Box 2830 Clearview Pl 6:00
Drop Box 5600 Buford Hwy NE 7:00, 4:00
Drop Box 3510 Shallowford Rd NE 7:15
Drop Box 5000 Kristie Wy 7:00
Drop Box 3990 Flowers Rd 6:30

Map 47

Drop Box 601 McDonough Blvd SE 7:00

Map 48

Drop Box 2905 East Point St 6:30

Map 50

Drop Box 1513 Cleveland Ave 6:45

Map 51

Drop Box 1136 Cleveland Ave NE 6:30
Drop Box 1 Clay Pl 7:30
Renaissance Business Center 1 Hartsfield Center Pkwy 6:00
Drop Box 100 Hartsfield Center Pkwy 6:30
Drop Box 1001 Virginia Ave 7:30
Drop Box 1025 Virginia Ave 7:30
Drop Box 650 S Central Ave 6:45
Drop Box 760 Doug Davis Dr 7:30

Arts & Entertainment • **Art Galleries**

In 1962, 106 Atlantans boarded a plane to Paris to participate in an art tour. As the plane taxied down the runway, it was unable to reach takeoff speed and crashed killing everyone on-board, save two flight attendants. In one day, Atlanta lost its most passionate patrons of the arts. In their memory, $13 million was raised to build the Atlanta Memorial Arts Center, known today as the **Woodruff Arts Center**. The center is located next door to the High Museum of Art. In between the two buildings is a casting of Rodin's *L'Ombre*, donated by the French government in memory of the 106 Atlantans who lost their lives in the plane crash.

The thriving arts scene in Atlanta is an on-going tribute to the legacy of these patrons. The gallery scene is ever-changing as in most cites, but the Highlands and Buckhead have always been a hotbed for artists, while Castleberry Hill is the new kid on the block.

Highlands

Located near several restaurants, **Aliya Gallery** showcases Canadian works and stays open later to

accommodate hungry crowds. Down the street, the **Modern Primitive** provides a taste of folk, self-taught, and local art.

Buckhead

There are numerous galleries in Buckhead—the old-timer in the gallery scene. The prestigious 7,000 square-foot **Fay Gold Gallery** could be called the grandmother. Ms. Gold changed the art scene in Atlanta when she started selling works by Yankee artists at high-dollar prices during the '80s. **Jackson Fine Art** offers 20th-century and contemporary photography including works by Ansel Adams and Eudora Welty. For a one-stop shopping experience, cruise East Paces Ferry, as there are several galleries here including **Galerie Timothy Tew**.

Castleberry Hill

The baby art district, the Hill, offers lots of new and avant-garde galleries. **Marcia Wood Gallery** moved here from Buckhead and showcases contemporary art.

Galleries

Galleries	Address	Phone	Map
ACA Gallery	1280 Peachtree St NE	404-733-5050	5
Aliya Gallery	1402 N Highland Ave	404-892-2835	7
Atlanta Artists Center Grandview Gallery	2979 Grandview Ave	404-237-2324	25
Atlanta Photography Group and Gallery	Tula Art Ctr, 75 Bennett St NW	404-605-0605	24
Barbara Archer Gallery	280 Elizabeth St	404-523-1845	11
Bennett Street Gallery	22 Bennett St	404-352-8775	24
City Gallery East	675 Ponce de Leon Ave	404-817-7956	7
Darius Gallery	3255 Peachtree Rd NE	404-264-1133	22
Eyedrum	290 Martin Luther King Jr Dr SE, Ste 8	404-522-0655	14
Fay Gold Gallery	764 Miami Cir NE	404-233-3843	25
Frances Aronson Fine Art	631 Miami Cir NE	404-949-9975	25
Galerie Timothy Tew	309 E Paces Ferry Rd	404-869-0511	21
GASP! Gallery	Tula Art Ctr, 75 Bennett St NW	404-355-5540	24
High Museum	1280 Peachtree St NE	404-733-4562	5
Lagerquist Gallery	3235 Paces Ferry Pl NW	404-261-8273	21
Lambert Gallery	805 Lambert Dr NE	404-897-1109	26
The Lowe Gallery	75 Bennett St	404-352-8114	24
The Madison Gallery	351 Peachtree Hills Ave	404-816-4033	25
Marcia Wood Gallery	263 Walker St	404-827-0030	13
Matre Gallery	Tula Art Ctr, 75 Bennett St NW	404-350-8399	24
the Modern Primitive gallery	1393 N Highland Ave	404-892-0556	7
Momus Gallery	Tula Art Ctr, 75 Bennett St NW	404-355-4180	24
Museum of Contemporary Art of Georgia	1447 Peachtree St	404-881-1109	2
Naomi Silva Gallery	Tula Art Ctr, 75 Bennett St NW	404-350-8890	24
Sandler Hudson Gallery	1009 Marietta St	404-350-8929	4
Skot Foreman Fine Art	315 Peters St SW	404-222-0440	13
Swan Coach House Gallery	3130 Slaton Dr NW	404-266-2636	21
Trinity Gallery	315 E Paces Ferry Rd	404-237-0370	21
Ty Stokes Gallery	261 Walker St SW	404-222-9863	13
Woodruff Arts Center	1280 Peachtree St NE	404-733-4200	5
Yo Yo Boutique and Gallery	188 Carroll St	404-389-0912	15
Youngblood Gallery	629 Glenwood Ave	404-627-0393	15

The South loves chains—chain restaurants, chain supermarkets, and Wal-Mart. When it comes to bookstores, the love continues; most of the books you buy will be from **Borders** or **Barnes & Noble**. If you've seen one chain, you've seen them all. But with a little effort, you can maintain your independent book-buying spirit.

General Independent

For general independent bookstores, **Tall Tales Book Shop** is great. There are lots of friendly, older ladies who work there, so it's is like buying a book from your grandmother (if your grandmother is nice). Useless side note: **Kudzu Book Fair** is named after the annoying green weed that grows everywhere in Georgia.

Cheap Books

For cheap books, the local chain (there's that word again), **Chapter 11**, offers discounts on a variety of books, from summer reading to cookbooks. All books are discounted by at least 11%, and with 13 locations statewide, there is sure to be one near you. In addition to offering discounted and used books, **Book Nook** has a great comic book selection.

Old Books

For antiquarian selections, visit either **C. Dickens** or **Antonio Raimo**, who is said to resemble Charles Dickens. In addition to books, Raimo's shop offers fun browsing with maps, globes, and thousands of antique prints.

Comic Books

Oxford Comics is really the place to go for your favorite cartoon literature.

Gay/Lesbian Lit

Charis, along with **Outwrite**, **Brushstrokes**, and **A Cappella** offer gay and lesbian literature. A Cappella in Little Five specializes in hard-to-find gay and lesbian lit, while Outwrite in Midtown is also a coffee shop and a great resource for information about gay and lesbian services in Atlanta.

Specialty

If you want the knowledge without the effort, **Bookears** carries about 10,000 audiobook titles. (If you are tempted to make a joke about illiteracy and the South, don't.) Fiery feminists head to **Charis Books** for an excellent selection of feminist titles. **Afrobooks** offers a selection of African-American titles. And, if after all this running around, you need some spiritual rejuvenation, make a final stop at the **Phoenix & Dragon**, which specializes in personal growth, healing, and transformation—or just head to Wal-Mart for some bubble-bath.

Map 1 • Underwood Hills / Blandtown

Books & Cases & Prints/ Defoor Centre Book Marketplace	1710 Defoor Ave NW	404-231-9107; 404-591-3901	Used and antiquarian.

Map 2 • Collier Hills / Brookwood Hills

Borders	1745 Peachtree St NE	404-810-9004	Chain.

Map 3 • Ansley Park / Piedmont Heights

Bookears	1579 Monroe Dr NE	404-815-7475	Audio books.
Brushstrokes	1510 Piedmont Ave NE	404-876-6567	Gay & lesbian.
Chapter 11	1544 Piedmont Ave NE	404-872-7986	Local bargain books chain.

Map 5 • Georgia Tech / Arts Center

American Management Association Bookstore	1170 Peachtree St NE	404-892-7599	Business, IT, and career.
Engineer's Bookstore	748 Marietta St NW	404-221-1669	Technical bookstore.
Majors Bookstore	748 Marietta St NW	404-873-3229	Engineering and medical books.
Park Place Bookstore	22 Park Place South SE	404-525-5100	Textbooks.

Map 6 • Midtown

Outwrite Bookstore and Coffeehouse	991 Piedmont Ave NE	404-607-0082	Gay & lesbian.

Arts & Entertainment • **Bookstores**

Map 7 • Virginia Highland

Atlanta Book Exchange	1000 N Highland Ave NE	404-872-2665	Discounted general.
Beaver Book Sale	696 Cleburne Ter NE	404-876-1068	Discounted general.
Borders	650 Ponce de Leon Ave	404-607-7903	Chain.

Map 9 • Downtown / Centennial Place / Techwood

B Dalton Bookseller	231 Peachtree St NE	404-577-2555	Chain.
Waldenbooks	1 CNN Ctr, 190 Marietta St NW	404-659-1949	Chain.

Map 10 • Downtown / Sweet Auburn

Georgia Bookstore	124 Edgewood Ave NE	404-659-0959	Textbooks.
Georgia State University Bookstore	66 Courtland St NE	404-651-2155	Textbooks.

Map 11 • Inman Park / Cabbagetown / Little Five Points

A Cappella Books	1133 Euclid Ave NE	404-681-5128	General used.
Charis Books & More	1189 Euclid Ave NE	404-524-0304	Feminist books.
Dancing Frog Books @ Jake's Ice Cream	676 Highland Ave	404-522-0760	Used.

Map 12 • West End

Afrobooks	871 Ralph David Abernathy St	404-755-0095	Discounted African American books.

Map 16 • Paces / Northside

Chapter 11	3509 Northside Pkwy	404-841-6338	Local bargain books chain.

Map 19 • West Brookhaven

Bookears	3944 Peachtree Rd NE	404-816-2665	Audio books.

Map 20 • East Brookhaven

Atlanta Vintage Books	3660 Clairmont Rd	770-457-2919	Used and rare.

Map 21 • Central Buckhead

C Dickens	56 E Andrews Dr NW	404-231-3825	Rare & collectible books and maps.
Waldenbooks	3393 Peachtree Rd NE	404-261-2781	Chain.

Map 22 • Lenox

Borders	3637 Peachtree Rd NE	404-237-0707	Chain.
Doubleday Bookshop	3500 Peachtree Rd NE	404-816-1755	Chain.

Map 25 • Garden Hills / Peachtree Heights / Peachtree Hills

Antonio Raimo Galleries	700 Miami Cir NE	404-841-9880	Used and rare.
Barnes & Noble	2900 Peachtree Rd NE	404-261-7747	Chain.
Chapter 11	2345 Peachtree Rd NE	404-237-7199	Local bargain books chain.
Oxford Comics	2855 Piedmont Rd NE	404-233-8682	Comics.

Map 27 • Toco Hills / Emory University

Book Nook	3073 N Druid Hills Rd	404-633-1328	Mainly used.
Discount Books	2795 N Druid Hills Rd NE	404-634-0591	Discount bookstore.
Tall Tales Book Shop	2105 Lavista Rd NE	404-636-2498	General new.

Map 28 · Druid Hills West

| Druid Hills Bookstore | 1401 Oxford Rd NE | 404-727-2665 | Emory University bookstore. |

Map 30 · Decatur

| Books Again | 225 N McDonough St | 404-377-1444 | General used, rare, and out-of-print. |

Map 35 · Sandy Springs (North)

| Chapter 11 | 6237 Roswell Rd | 404-256-5518 | Local bargain books chain. |

Map 36 · West Dunwoody

B Dalton Bookseller	4400 Ashford-Dunwoody Rd	770-394-4185	Chain.
Barnes & Noble	120 Perimeter Ctr W	770-396-1200	Chain.
Borders	4745 Ashford-Dunwoody Rd	770-396-0004	Chain.

Map 38 · Vinings

| Borders | 3101 Cobb Pkwy | 770-612-0940 | Chain. |

Map 40 · Sandy Springs (South)

Bookears	5980 Roswell Rd NE	770-671-8273	Audio books.
Hoot Owl Attic	185 Allen Rd NE	404-303-1030	Metaphysical books.
Phoenix & Dragon	5531 Roswell Rd NE	404-255-5207	Human spirit and metaphysical.

Map 42 · North Atlanta East / Silverlake

| Kudzu Book Fair | 5488 Peachtree Industrial Blvd | 770-458-9277 | General new. |

Map 43 · Chamblee / Doraville

| Books Japan | 6251 Peachtree Industrial Blvd | 678-209-0555 | Japanese books. |

Map 48 · East Point

| Barnes & Noble | 3685 Market Place Blvd | 404-349-0359 | Chain. |

Arts & Entertainment • **Movie Theaters**

It may not be a uniquely Southern phenomena, but on the weekends the popular, mainstream theaters are crowded with movie-surfers—people who purchase one ticket and then spend the evening going from movie to movie. Movie-surfers talk on cell-phones and sit on the aisles, just in case they need to make a quick exit for the next movie. Unless you're one of the people surfing, you'll find the experience to be quite annoying. If you must go to a movie on the weekend, try one of the "independent" theaters.

Movie-Surfer Joints

Atlanta has a wide variety of 10+ screens theaters that charge $8 per ticket and show all the blockbuster movies. Not too much varies between **Regal Hollywood Stadium 24**, **AMC Parkway Pointe 15**, and **Magic Johnson Atlanta**. Note that **AMC Phipps Plaza 14** does not have stadium seating, so try elsewhere if you're not tall. Given that Phipps is a high-dollar shopping center, you would think they could spring for some decent seating.

"Independent"

Independent is in quotes because although **United Artists Tara** is not technically an independent theater, it does show indie films and keeps away the movie-surfers.

LeFont theaters and the **Landmark Midtown Cinema** also show indie films—better atmosphere, better movies.

Specialty

The **Starlight Drive-In** is a must-do-once experience and a good deal at $6 for 2 movies. For a different date experience or for a date you don't want to talk to, the **AMC Buckhead Backlot** offers dinner during your movie. You can also check out the **Fernbank Museum's IMAX** for really big nature flicks. During the summer, there are two special treats: **Screen on The Green** offers movies in Piedmont Park and the historic **Fox Theatre** shows movies twice a week.

If you are a big movie buff, check out IMAGE, an organization working to promote the production, exhibition, and awareness of film and video. They offer classes, organize film competitions, and produce the Atlanta Film Festival at various locations. Visit their website at www.imagefv.org.

Movie Theaters

	Address	Phone	Map
AMC Buckhead Backlot 6	3340 Peachtree Rd NE	404-467-0862	21
AMC Phipps Plaza 14	3500 Peachtree Rd NE	404-816-4262	22
Buford Highway Twin Theaters	5805 Buford Hwy	770-458-5234	43
Cinefest Film Theatre	66 Courtland St NE	404-651-2463	10
Fernbank Museum's IMAX Theatre	767 Clifton Rd NE	404-929-6400	28
Fox Theatre	660 Peachtree St NE	404-881-2100	5
Landmark Midtown Art Cinema	931 Monroe Dr NE	404-872-5796	6
Lefont Garden Hills Cinema	2835 Peachtree Rd NE	404-266-2202	25
Lefont Plaza Theatre	1049 Ponce de Leon Ave NE	404-873-1939	7
Lefont Sandy Springs	5920 Roswell Rd NE	404-255-0100	40
Regal Perimeter Pointe 10	1155 Mt Vernon Hwy	770-481-0194	36
Screen on the Green (outdoors)	Piedmont Park, The Meadow, 10th St & Monroe Dr	404-878-2600	6
United Artists Tara Cinemas-Atlanta	2345 Cheshire Bridge Rd NE	404-634-5661	26

Art and Pretty Things

Atlanta's grand dame of museums is the **High Museum of Art**. There are actually two locations: the Meier-designed main facility in Midtown and the **High Museum of Art Folk Art & Photography Galleries** downtown in the Georgia-Pacific Center. Collections include African art, American art, decorative arts, European art, folk art, modern and contemporary art, and photography. Through a partnership with the Smithsonian, the **Museum of Design** brings some interesting exhibits to Atlanta. If you're interested in ancient civilizations, visit Emory's **Michael C. Carlos Museum**; it maintains the largest collection of ancient art in the southeast, including objects from ancient Egypt, Greece, Rome, the Near East, and the ancient Americas.

Atlanta History

Since Atlanta was burnt to the ground during the Civil War, people around here have a hard time forgetting. The **Atlanta Cyclorama** depicts the 1864 Battle of Atlanta in a panoramic painting complete with 3-D features and audio. If you have seen *Gone With the Wind*, this painting captures the scene where the entire city was on fire. You can be sure to find details of the bloody battle, as well as other details of Atlanta's past, at the **Atlanta History Center. The King Center** provides an in-depth look at the Civil Rights Movement and the **Jimmy Carter Center** addresses national and international issues of human rights and participates in conflict mediation around the world.

Atlanta's Own

The **World of Coca-Cola** is worth a visit (once), although the entry fee is a little steep for an interactive Coke advertisement. Invented in 1886 by Atlanta pharmacist John Pemberton, the tasty beverage is one of Atlanta's proudest achievements. (A kid was suspended from school for wearing a Pepsi shirt in South Georgia!)

Science

With the SciTrek Museum closing down, check out the **Fernbank Museum of Natural History and Science Center** for a taste of science.

Museums

	Address	Phone	Map
Atlanta Botanical Garden	1345 Piedmont Ave NE	404-876-5859	3
Atlanta Cyclorama & Civil War Museum	800 Cherokee Ave SE	404-624-1071	14
Atlanta History Center	130 W Paces Ferry Rd NW	404-814-4000	25
Braves Museum and Hall of Fame	Turner Field, 755 Hank Aaron Dr	404-614-2311	13
Center for Puppetry Arts	1404 Spring St NW	404-873-3089	2
Fernbank Museum of Natural History	767 Clifton Rd NE	404-929-6300	28
Fernbank Science Center	156 Heaton Park Dr NE	678-874-7102	29
The Herndon Home	587 University Pl NW	404-581-9813	8
High Museum of Art	1280 Peachtree St NE	404-733-4400	5
High Museum of Art Folk Art & Photography Galleries	133 Peachtree St NE	404-577-6940	9
Imagine It! The Children's Museum of Atlanta	275 Centennial Olympic Park Dr NW	404-659-5437	9
Jimmy Carter Library & Museum	441 Freedom Pkwy	404-865-7100	11
The Margaret Mitchell House & Museum	990 Peachtree St	404-249-7015	5
Monetary Museum	1000 Peachtree St NE	404-498-8777	5
Museum of Design	285 Peachtree Center Ave	404-688-2467	10
NAMES Project Foundation and AIDS Memorial Quilt	101 Krog St	404-688-5500	11
The William Breman Jewish Heritage Museum	1440 Spring St NW	678-222-3700	2
World of Coca-Cola Atlanta	55 Martin Luther King Jr Dr	770-578-4325 ext. 1465	9

Atlanta's nightclub owners fought the law, and the law won. Atlanta's strip clubs used to be considered some of the best in the nation, but with the government shut-down of the infamous Gold Club, the city's adult entertainment scene has lost a bit of its glitz, though expensive, scantily clad girls are still in plentiful supply.

With a rash of Buckhead nightclub shootings and deaths, the Atlanta City Council had the bright idea that closing the bars earlier would help reduce the violence. This decision ran some clubs out of business, and ended the 24-hour private nightclubs in the city, including Backstreet, arguably the most famous gay dance club in the Southeast. The city is now putting a lot of money and effort into touting their brand new "nightlife district" at the much-maligned Underground Atlanta. Through a legal loophole, the clubs there can skirt the earlier 2:30 am bar closing time and keep pouring alcohol until 4 am, and patrons can carry open containers of alcohol from club to club. However, due to Georgia's antiquated blue laws, on Saturday and Sunday they have to shut down the party at the same time as everyone else. (That's right, Saturday night, when most people are looking to party.) Bottom line: Underground Atlanta's track record of success is about the same as our Atlanta Hawks (downright atrocious).

Where Booty-Shaking is The Bomb

Hip hop music lovers can be found at **Vision, Club 112,** and **The Velvet Room,** all within easy walking distance of each other on Peachtree Street in Midtown. **The Mark** is one of the downtown area's better dance destinations. The legendary **MJQ Concourse** on Ponce De Leon Avenue has been dishing out the beats for years to a loyal crowd. **Blu** and **Wetbar** are where the gay dance scene is now that Backstreet is closed. For two-stepping gay men, saddle up to **Cowtippers** at the Midtown Promenade. **Compound** and **Eleven50** in Midtown feature the beautiful people of Atlanta dancing with top-notch DJ action. In Buckhead, veteran club **Tongue & Groove** still packs them in by keeping up with the latest dance club trends. **Havana Club** is good for some salsa dancing. **Mako, Uranus,** and **Bell Bottoms** offer decent dance club action in the heart of Buckhead.

Single and Swilling

Crescent Street in Midtown is a single and hipster haven. Try the **Leopard Lounge, Cosmopolitan,** and the **Lava Lounge** for an active singles scene. The Virginia-Highlands bar scene caters to a more relaxed, thirty-something crowd. Neighborhood pubs rule, so grab a pint and make some new friends. **Highland Tap** has earned its rightful reputation as a warm and friendly meat market. If you're looking for love in Buckhead, head to Phipps Plaza, where you can search for your future mate at **Twist** and **The Tavern at Phipps. Dailey's Downstairs** in the heart of Downtown is an after-work singles magnet.

Atlanta Drinking Institutions

NFT loves the "no idiots" rule in effect at the **Vortex**. Too bad it can't be applied to all aspects of life. The giant skeleton entrance at the original Little Five Points location is pretty cool too. **Atkins Park** in the Virginia-Highlands has been pouring since 1922, making it the oldest tavern in Atlanta. **Manuel's Tavern** has been the site of many a spirited debate, drawing a high-profile crowd of local politicians, cops, and journalists. **The Sun Dial Restaurant, Bar, and View** is one of Atlanta's classiest venues to sip a cocktail. **Limerick Junction** in the Virginia Highlands is Atlanta's oldest Irish pub. For a bar that matches its surrounding neighborhood perfectly, check out the **Euclid Avenue Yacht Club** (simply "The Yacht" to regulars) in Little Five Points.

Strip Clubs

The Cheetah is one of Atlanta's classier establishments, boasting the upscale restaurant, Alluvia. If you've ever wondered where old strippers go to die, **The Clermont Lounge** in the basement of the seedy Clermont Motor Hotel in the Poncey-Highlands will answer that question in gruesome detail. The Cheshire Bridge Road area is chock full of "gentlemen's clubs," including **Doll House, Tattletale, Flashers,** and the **24K Club** along with a plentiful supply of "health spas." Other well-known Atlanta strip clubs include **Fantasy Fare, Goldrush Show Bar,** and **The Pink Pony.** For gay men, **Swinging Richards** is an all nude, all gay extravaganza.

Dive Bars

Lenny's in Downtown Atlanta is a local landmark for grungy carousing. In Buckhead's electric clubbing district, the **Buckhead Amusement Center** offers a special charm. For a real blues experience, don't miss **Northside Tavern**. On the gay side of life, the **Phoenix** is *not* where the pretty boys go. The **Star Community Bar** in Little Five Points is a funky retro dive complete with an Elvis shrine. **The Earl** in East Atlanta offers a damn fine burger to go along with beer swilling and some hard rocking live music; their Sunday "Dunch" is the stuff of legend as well.

Live Music

There are a lot of great live music venues in Atlanta. **The Tabernacle** in Downtown Atlanta is a former church. **Smith's Olde Bar** in Midtown features Americana music acts. **Eddie's Attic** in Decatur helped John Mayer get his break and showcases acoustic talents, both local and national. For the finest in live jazz, check out **Churchill Grounds** next to the Fox Theatre. For the real deal in blues music, head to the gritty **Northside Tavern** or **Blind Willie's** in the Virginia-Highlands for a toe-tapping good time. Don't forget about **The Fox Theatre** as a music venue. With the right band or musician, it is a memorable concert experience. **Andrews Upstairs** is where a thirty-something Buckhead singles crowd goes for live music.

Take the Party Outdoors

Atlantans love to drink outdoors as much as they like to dine outdoors. The most picturesque place to sip a beer or cocktail may be **Park Tavern**, on the corner of Piedmont Park. Cheapskates should wait until it rains, when a beer goes for a buck. **Prince of Wales**, on the other side of the park, is good for people watching as well. **Fuego** in the Crescent Street club area offers a spacious patio and is a good place to put some tapas in your tummy to counteract all of the booze you'll be consuming for the rest of the night. Sapphic lovers chat amidst the cozy garden at **My Sister's Room** in Decatur. **CJ's Landing** in Buckhead boasts a 100-year-old oak tree on its deck—perfect for hugging if the world starts spinning after an afternoon of tequila shots. The deck at the **Treehouse Restaurant & Pub** offers a bird's eye view of surrounding Buckhead (and the pub's hip, yet professional, clientele).

Map 1 • Underwood Hills / Blandtown

Swinging Richards	1715 Northside Dr NW	404-355-6787	Wild, all-nude gay men's extravaganza!

Map 2 • Collier Hills / Brookwood Hills

Black Bear Tavern	1931 Peachtree Rd NE	404-355-9089	Great neighborhood bar outside of main Buckhead club district.
The Loft	1374 W Peachtree St	404-885-9198	Snazzy renovation of former Vinyl concert venue.

Map 3 • Ansley Park / Piedmont Heights

Burkhart's Pub	1492 Piedmont Ave NE	404-872-4403	Fun and friendly gay neighborhood bar.
Deux Plex	1789 Cheshire Bridge Rd	404-733-5900	Trendy nightclub with world-class DJ's.
New Order	1544 Piedmont Ave NE	404-874-8247	Where graying gays go for meaningful conversations and cocktails.
Scandals	1510 Piedmont Ave NE	404-875-5957	Friendly neighborhood gay bar that attracts older crowd.
Smith's Olde Bar	1578 Piedmont Ave NE	404-875-1522	Americana and roots rock live music showcase.
Tripp's	1931 Piedmont Cir NE	404-724-0067	Trashy fun with friendly staff.

Map 4 • West Midtown / Home Park

Compound	1008 Brady Ave	404-872-4621	Posh West Midtown nightspot.
The Library	800 Marietta St NW	404-874-5400	Grungy college crowd hangout.
Northside Tavern	1058 Howell Mill Rd NW	404-874-8745	Authentic dive bar with blues music.

Map 5 • Georgia Tech / Arts Center

Apache Café	64 3rd St NW	404-876-5436	Cool spoken word, jazz, and hip-hop lounge.
Atlanta Brewing Company	1219 Williams St	404-275-6701	Great tours and tasting every Friday.
Blu	960 Spring St NW	404-877-1221	No alcohol, but plenty of sweaty, shirtless gay men.
Bulldog's	893 Peachtree St NE	404-872-3025	Friendly gay bar popular with African Americans.
Charlie G's	1041 W Peachtree St NW	404-724-9060	Easily overlooked neighborhood bar. Good lunch destination.
The Cheetah	887 Spring St NW	404-892-3037	Where the strippers are since the Feds busted the Gold Club.
Churchill Grounds	660 Peachtree St	404-876-3030	Snazzy, sophisticated jazz club next to the Fox Theatre.
Cosmopolitan Lounge	45 13th St NE	404-873-6189	Where trendy thirty-somethings go to hook up.
Fantasy Fare	700 Marietta St NW	404-681-5600	Theme rooms and hot girls galore.
Dragonfly	67 12th St NE	404-875-7473	Vision stepchild, but still good people-watching.
Halo	817 W Peachtree St NW	404-962-7333	Trendy unmarked lounge in Biltmore Hotel basement.
Lava	57 13th St NE	404-873-6189	Three-floor club with excellent house DJ.
Leopard Lounge	84 12th St NE	404-874-2704	Lounge for more down-to-earth clubbers.
The Velvet Room	1021 Peachtree St	404-249-6400	Strict dress code but plenty of skin.
Wetbar	960 Spring St NW	404-745-9494	Where dancers take a break from the action at adjacent Blu.
Whiskey Peach	44 12th St NW	404-745-9551	Glam meets underground vibe.

Map 6 • Midtown

Armory	836 Juniper St NE	404-881-9280	Stiff drinks and stiff muscles at this gay and lesbian hangout.
Atlanta Eagle	306 Ponce de Leon Ave	404-873-2453	A little Levi/leather, big bears, and gay cruising galore.
Blake's	227 10th St NE	404-892-5786	Neighborhood gay bar with fun drag shows.
Club 112	1055 Peachtree St NE	404-261-0155	Bling-bling, ballers, and booty-shaking.
Eleven50	1150B Peachtree St NE	404-874-0428	Cool crowd central in Midtown.
The Highlander	931 Monroe Dr NE	404-872-0060	Shots, beers, and burgers next to a movie theatre.
Hoedown's	931 Monroe Dr NE	404-876-0001	Where the gay boys and girls go to two-step.
Jocks and Jills Midtown	112 10th St NE	404-873-5405	Local sports bar chain. Offers free shuttles to games.
Loca Luna	836 Juniper St NE	404-875-4494	Terrific tapas and hot, fun Brazilian vibes.
The Metro	1080 Peachtree St NE	404-874-9869	Seedy gay bar always running into trouble with the law.
Miss Q's	560 Amsterdam Ave NE	404-875-6255	More relaxed attitude than neighboring Red Chair Lounge.
Park Tavern	500 10th St NE	404-249-0001	Great view of the city; dollar brews when it rains.
Phoenix	567 Ponce de Leon Ave	404-892-7871	Rough riders paradise.
Prince of Wales	1144 Piedmont Ave NE	404-876-0227	Pub with great patio overlooking Piedmont Park.

Red Chair Lounge	550-C Amsterdam Ave	404-870-0532	Non-smoking video lounge draws primarily gay crowd.
Red Light Café	553 Amsterdam Ave NE	404-874-8728	Top notch bluegrass and folk music in barebones environment.
Vision	1068 Peachtree St NE	404-874-4460	Hip hop hotspot where Ludacris and P. Diddy party.

Map 7 • Virginia Highland

10 High	816 N Highland Ave NE	404-873-3607	Basement club located beneath Dark Horse Tavern.
Atkins Park	794 N Highland Ave NE	404-876-7249	Atlanta's oldest tavern still a popular nightlife spot.
Blind Willie's	828 N Highland Ave NE	404-873-2583	Blues dive with live music nightly.
Dark Horse Tavern	816 N Highland Ave NE	404-873-3607	Single, straight hook-up spot.
Dugan's	777 Ponce de Leon Ave NE	404-885-1217	Great place to cheer on the home team.
Hand in Hand	752 N Highland Ave NE	404-872-1001	British-style pub with great patio.
Highland Tap	1026 N Highland Ave NE	404-875-3673	Martinis, steaks, and mingling.
Limerick Junction	822 N Highland Ave NE	404-874-7147	Atlanta's oldest Irish pub.
The Local	758 Ponce de Leon Ave NE	404-873-5002	PBR's and pub grub on Ponce.
Manuel's Tavern	602 N Highland Ave NE	404-525-3447	Landmark bar popular with politicians and journalists.
Masquerade	695 North Ave NE	404-577-8178	3-for-1 subculture magnet plays punk to goth.
Midtown Saloon & Grill	736 Ponce de Leon Ave NE	404-874-1655	Neighborhood bar with diverse set of regulars.
MJQ Concourse	736 Ponce de Leon Ave NE	404-870-0575	Underground club veteran with loyal following.
Model T's	699 Ponce de Leon Ave NE	404-872-2209	Thirty-something gay men hangout.
Moe's and Joe's	1033 N Highland Ave NE	404-873-6090	Grungy neighborhood beer-only bar.
Neighbor's Pub	752 N Highland Ave NE	404-872-5440	Bar with happening patio all year long.
Rico's View	736 Ponce de Leon Ave NE	404-873-3220	Ever-changing crowd keeps things lively.
Righteous Room	1051 Ponce de Leon Ave NE	404-874-0939	Neighborhood hangout in strip-mall location.

Map 8 • Vine City

617 Club	310 Joseph E Lowery Blvd NW	404-659-2555	For hard-core players only.

Map 9 • Downtown / Centennial Place / Techwood

Club 720	904 Martin Luther King Jr Dr	404-524-5331	720 refers to the weight of the club's bouncer.
Dailey's Downstairs	17 Andrew Young International Blvd	404-681-3303	Atlanta icon with retro cuisine and cigar/ martini bar.
Sidebar	79 Poplar St	404-588-1850	Downtown drinking destination with good Cuban sandwiches.
The Mark	79 Poplar St	678-904-0050	Where to get your groove on downtown.
Sun Dial	210 Peachtree St NW	404-659-1400	Tallest hotel in the Western Hemisphere. Revolving top floor bar/restaurant.
Traxxx	339 Marietta St NW	404-681-4252	Exotic girls and a high energy crowd.

Map 10 · Downtown / Sweet Auburn

Charlie and Barney's Bar & Grill	231 Peachtree Center Ave NE	404-688-0928	Chug some brews, and down some chili.
O'Terrill's	510 Piedmont Ave	404-815-0079	Home of the Guinness ice cream topped brownie.
Royal Peacock	186 Auburn Ave NE	404-524-1488	Hey mon', it's reggae music all night long!
Shakespere Tavern	499 Peachtree St NE	404-874-5299	Superb live Shakespearean theatre in authentic pub setting.

Map 11 · Inman Park / Cabbagetown / Little Five Points

97 Estoria	727 Wylie St SE	404-522-0966	Cabbagetown watering hole.
Brewhouse Café	401 Moreland Ave NE	404-525-7799	Soccer fan central.
Euclid Avenue Yacht Club	1136 Euclid Ave NE	404-688-2582	Where all of the characters of L5P meet for a drink.
Little 5 Points Corner Tavern	1174 Euclid Ave NE	404-521-0667	Replacement for the defunct 9 Lives Saloon.
Star Community Bar	437 Moreland Ave	404-681-9018	Elvis shrine with a bit of grime.
The Vortex	438 Moreland Ave NE	404-688-1828	Cool giant skull entrance. Thursday is biker night.

Map 14 · Grant Park

Lenny's	307 Memorial Dr SE	404-577-7721	A true dive bar in all its glory.

Map 15 · Ormewood Park North / Woodland Hills

Carroll Street Café	208 Carroll St SE	404-577-2700	Chillin' Cabbagetown-style.
Crazy Horse Bar & Grill	687 Memorial Dr SE	404-523-5495	Blue-collar dive on the wrong side of the tracks.

Map 18 · Chastain Park

Brandy House and Tavern	4365 Roswell Rd NE	404-252-7784	Providing good live music and libations since the 1970s.

Map 21 · Central Buckhead

Andrew's Upstairs	56 E Andrews Dr NW	404-467-1600	Live music venue for the ultra-hip clubbers.
Beluga Martini Bar	3115 Piedmont Rd	404-869-1090	Martinis pour as fast as the money at this classy nightspot.
Buckhead Amusement Center	30 Irby Ave NW	404-237-9152	Greasy hole-in-the-wall with frat-boy Buckhead crowd.
Buckhead Saloon	3107 Peachtree Rd NE	404-261-7922	Honky-tonk heaven in the middle of dance-club Buckhead.
Che	268 E Paces Ferry Rd NE	404-231-2224	Ritzy rum bar in former Blais spot.
Churchill Arms	3223 Cains Hill Pl NW	404-233-5633	English pub theme draws primarily college co-eds.
Coyote Ugly	287 E Paces Ferry Rd NE	404-659-8459	Like the movie, only lamer.
East Andrews Bar	56 E Andrews Dr NW	404-869-1132	Sophisticated Buckhead nightspot with live music.
Electra	3081 E Shadowlawn Ave NE	404-627-8464	Smoke-free retro lounge.
Fado	3035 Peachtree Rd NE	404-841-0066	Pints of Guinness for lads and lasses.
Five Paces Inn	41 Irby Ave NW	404-365-0777	Buckhead's original dive bar. Rugby fan hangout.
Fluid	3067 Peachtree Rd NE	404-995-0064	Chaos owners strike gold again with this Buckhead club.

Hole in the Wall	3177 Peachtree Rd NE	404-233-9801	Where drunken Buckhead singles go to hook up.
Jellyroll's Dueling Pianos	295 E Paces Ferry Rd NE	404-261-6866	Piano bar with a mixed-age crowd.
Johnny's Hideaway	3771 Roswell Rd NE	404-233-8026	Where the geriatric crowd gets down.
The Living Room	3069 Peachtree Rd NE	404-816-1116	A little grungy, a little sweaty, a lot of fun.
Lulu's Bait Shack	3057 Peachtree Rd NE	404-262-5220	Order their signature 96 oz fishbowl drink, if you dare.
Mako	3065 Peachtree Rd NE	404-846-8096	Mardi Gras-style madness.
McDuff's Irish Pub	56 E Andrews Dr NW	404-816-8008	Not that authentic, but still a decent place for a pint.
Mike 'n Angelo's	312 E Paces Ferry Rd	404-237-0949	Down-to-earth dive in the heart of Buckhead.
Moondogs	3179 Peachtree Rd NE	404-231-4201	College co-ed hangout.
Park Bench	256 E Paces Ferry Rd NE	404-264-1334	Popular tavern with late 20s and 30s clientele.
Rose and Crown	288 E Paces Ferry Rd NE	404-233-8168	Great deck and beer selection.
Sambuca Jazz Café	3102 Piedmont Rd NE	404-237-5299	Jazz sophistication for the Buckhead crowd.
Sanctuary	3209 Paces Ferry Pl	404-262-1377	Upscale Latin music nightclub.
Tongue and Groove	3055 Peachtree Rd NE	404-261-2325	Buckhead veteran still attracts the beautiful people.
Uranus	3049 Peachtree Rd NE	404-816-9931	No, it's not a gay bar.
World Bar	3071 Peachtree Rd NE	404-266-0627	Wicked weekend-only hotspot.

Map 22 · Lenox

Chapparel	2715 Buford Hwy NE	404-634-3737	Mainly Hispanic clientele, gay night offered.
Fuzzy's Place	2015 N Druid Hills Rd NE	404-321-6166	Baby boomers club; local blues diva, Francine Reed, performs regularly.
Pink Pony	1837 Corporate Blvd NE	404-634-6396	One of Atlanta's best strip clubs. National acts perform weekly.
The Tavern at Phipps	3500 Peachtree Rd NE	404-814-9640	The bartenders don't just mix drinks, they put on a show.
Twist	3500 Peachtree Rd NE	404-869-1191	Cocktails, low-carb tapas at this trendsetter hook-up spot.

Map 23 · Briarcliff / Clairmont

Sidelines	2775 Clairmont Rd NE	404-321-0303	Family-friendly sports bar chain.

Map 24 · Peachtree Battle / Woodfield

Libby's, A Cabaret	3401 Northside Pkwy	404-237-1943	One of the only true cabarets in town.

Map 25 · Garden Hills / Peachtree Heights / Peachtree Hills

Bell Bottoms	225 Pharr Rd	404-816-9669	Diverse, unpretentious crowd dances under the disco ball.
CJ's Landing	270 Buckhead Ave NE	404-237-7657	Laid-back atmosphere, 100-year-old oak tree anchors patio.
Frequency	220 Pharr Rd	404-760-1975	Bi-level Buckhead clubbing favorite.
Havana Club	247 Buckhead Ave	404-869-8484	Salsa dancing, cigars, and Buckhead beauties.
Tongue and Groove	3055 Peachtree Rd NE	404-261-2325	Buckhead veteran still attracts the beautiful people.
Jack Rabbit Lounge	3055 Bolling Wy NE	404-261-2325	Swanky nightclub offers cheese plates, tapas, and dancing.
Tattletale Lounge	2075 Piedmont Rd NE	404-873-2294	Boobs and beer without the attitude.

Map 25 • Garden Hills / Peachtree Heights / Peachtree Hills—*continued*

Three Dollar Café	3002 Peachtree Rd	404-266-8667	Beer and sports at this Buckhead institution.
Treehouse Restaurant and Pub	7 Kings Cir NE	404-266-2732	Great outdoor drinking destination.
Woofs on Piedmont	2425 Piedmont Rd NE	404-869-9422	Where gay sports fans unite.

Map 26 • Morningside / Lenox Hills

24K Club	2284 Cheshire Bridge Rd NE	404-320-1923	Friendly and pretty strippers, what a concept.
Doll House	2050 Cheshire Bridge Rd NE	404-634-0666	This strip club is as dim as the girls.
Buddies	2345 Cheshire Bridge Rd NE	404-634-5895	Where the anti-trendy gay guys hang out.
Heretic	2069 Cheshire Bridge Rd NE	404-325-3061	Gay leather bar with the world famous hallway.

Map 27 • Toco Hills / Emory University

Famous Pub and Sports Palace	2947 N Druid Hills Rd	404-633-3555	For those who live and breath sports.
Maggie's	2937 N Druid Hills Rd NE	404-636-5300	Where Emory students go to get drunk.

Map 30 • Decatur

Azul Tequila and Wine Bar	141 Sycamore St	404-377-3311	Raging Burrito restaurant by day, relaxed lounge scene at night.
Brick Store Pub	125 E Court Sq	404-687-0990	Decatur's neighborhood bar destination.
Eddie's Attic	515 N McDonough St		Live acoustic music venue where John Mayer played.
Java Monkey	205 E Ponce de Leon Ave	404-378-5002	Cool coffee and wine bar with relaxed attitude.
My Sister's Room	222 E Howard Ave	404-370-1990	Watering hole for dykes and femmes.
Pin-ups	2788 E Ponce de Leon Ave	404-377-2956	Strip club that treats couples well.
Surburban Lanes Bowling	2619 N Decatur Rd	404-373-2514	Bowling for the masses!

Map 32 • Kirkwood

Mulligan's	630 E Lake Dr	404-377-0108	Oakhurst dive with deep fried everything.
Thinking Man Tavern	537 W Howard Ave	404-370-1717	Warm and cozy wind-down spot.
Universal Joint	906 Oakview Rd	404-373-6260	Former gas station turned neighborhood bar.

Map 34 • East Atlanta

The Earl	488 Flat Shoals Ave	404-522-3950	Burgers, brews, and top notch indie rock acts.
The Flatiron	520 Flat Shoals Ave SE	404-688-8864	Laid-back beer joint for East Atlanta hipsters.
Fountainhead Lounge	485 Flat Shoals Ave	404-522-7841	As stylish as it gets in East Atlanta.
Gravity Pub	1257 Glenwood Ave SE	404-627-5555	Where East Atlanta residents gather for drinks and games.
Mary's	1287 Glenwood Ave SE	404-624-4411	Fun karaoke at this East Atlanta gay bar.

Map 35 • Sandy Springs (North)

Café 290	290 Hilderbrand Dr NE	404-256-3942	Jazz for the older, sophisticated set.

Flashers	6420 Roswell Rd NE	404-843-1167	Lots of naked girls, but go with a wad of cash.
The Punchline	280 Hilderbrand Dr NE	404-252-5233	Local and national comedians perform here.

Map 36 · West Dunwoody

CB South	5500 Chamblee Dunwoody Rd	770-828-0355	Ski lodge tavern with a southern twist.
Derby Food & Spirits	1155 Hammond Dr NE	770-396-8808	Happy hour for the Perimeter crowd.
Dunwoody Tavern	5488 Chamblee Dunwoody Rd	770-394-4164	OTP see-and-be-seen spot for singles after work.

Map 38 · Vinings

Sidelines Bar & Grille	5525 Interstate North Pkwy	770-952-0001	Fun, family-friendly sports bar.

Map 40 · Sandy Springs (South)

American Pie	5480 Roswell Rd NE	404-255-7571	Cheesy, trashy debauchery.
Maxim Cabaret	5275 Roswell Rd NE	404-250-0244	Nude entertainment complex. Formerly The Coronet Club.

Map 42 · North Atlanta East / Silver Lake

Bleachers Sports Bar and Billiards	2175 Savoy Dr	770-452-7655	Neighborhood sports bar hangout.

Map 43 · Chamblee / Doraville

Barnacles	6365 Peachtree Industrial Blvd	770-451-6778	Seafaring-themed debauchery with radio DJ appearances, live music.
Oasis Goodtime Emporium	6363 Peachtree Industrial Blvd	770-454-8065	Wait out the rush hour at this strip club near I-285.
Rooster's Barnyard	5805 Buford Hwy	770-452-8543	International strippers on three stages.

Map 44 · Adair Park

Little King Lounge	1081 Lee St SW	404-758-8990	Not related to that other King family of Atlanta.

Map 49 · Sylvan Hills

Club Nikki	1785 Stewart Ave SW	404-753-5525	Nikki is naughty, and so are you for going here.
FJ's Tavern	2202 Metropolitan Pkwy SW	404-762-1062	Site of a triple murder a few years ago.

Map 50 · College Park

Brake Pad	3403 Main St	404-766-1515	Trains, planes, beer, and burgers.
East Point Corner Tavern	2783 Main St	404-768-0007	Neighborhood bar with loyal following.
Main Street Bar & Grill	2787 Main St	404-305-0685	East Point neighborhood hangout.

Map 51 · Hapeville

B-52's	3420 Norman Berry Dr	404-765-0280	Karaoke rules here.
Central Station	387 N Central Ave	404-209-1157	The wings keep locals coming back.
Crystal Palace	502 Connell Ave SW	404-762-7241	Seedy club in the ghetto.
Goldrush Show Bar	2608 Metropolitan Pkwy SW	404-766-2532	Bachelor Party Headquarters

What a difference a decade makes. The 1996 Olympic Games helped usher in a restaurant revolution in Atlanta, which almost makes up for "Whatizit?"—the worst Olympics mascot ever. Though Atlanta will never shed its old-school mentality completely, there are enough grits- and sweet tea-hating transplants here now to help diversify the local restaurant industry. Dining out is an integral part of Atlanta's social scene, where trendy style can overshadow true substance. Opening a restaurant here is like being a Las Vegas high roller: one can crash and burn in record time or one can become the talk of the town. Rising stars receiving national attention include **Rathbun's** in Inman Park, **MidCity Cuisine** in Midtown and **Restaurant Eugene** in Buckhead. Don't be surprised to see Atlantans filling up those heated patios in the dead of winter: we love our outdoor dining.

Southern for Southerners

There is no shortage of "meat-and-threes" in Atlanta, despite the city sophistication. **Mary Mac's Tea Room** is one of the best examples of old school Southern dining. Here, servers call you "sweetie" and mean it, the tea is always sweet, and mac-n-cheese is a vegetable. With a name like **Bobby and June's Country Kitchen**, you expect Southern goodness and receive it in generous portions. The **Colonnade Restaurant** is an Atlanta institution, a meat-and-three that draws everyone from blue-haired church ladies to drag queens. The two "silver" restaurants, **Silver Grill** and **Silver Skillet**, are down-home cooking destinations as well; the latter is known for their awesome breakfasts.

Southern for Non-Southerners

Take your visiting relatives or friends to **South City Kitchen** for ultra-cool Southern cuisine that's anything but your typical meat-and-three. **Wisteria** serves delectable Southern cuisine in an upscale, yet inviting, ambience that is also good for non-natives. **Horseradish Grill** in Buckhead is sure to impress out-of-towners. **Watershed** in Decatur, including chef Scott Peacock's sublime fried chicken, should convert any hardened Northerner.

Soul Food

The large African American population in Atlanta means that we have some of the finest soul food joints to be found in the country. **Son's Place** in Inman Park is known for their fried chicken and biscuits. **Thelma's Kitchen** in Downtown Atlanta draws nearby college students, cops, and politicians, so you know it must be good. And while the original **Paschal's**, a historical civil rights era landmark, has closed for business, the other location is still serving up its brand of upscale soul food. **Beautiful Restaurant** is aptly named not for its caféteria-style ambience, but for its real-deal ribs, cornbread, and heavenly banana pudding. **Busy Bee Café** is another sure-fire soul food spot, frequented by nearby Atlanta University Center students.

Sushi A-Plenty

Atlanta continues to go crazy over sushi. It seems to be everywhere, from restaurants that aren't actual sushi places, to sushi bars in nightclubs, to grocery stores, and, of course, the Asian food Mecca of Buford Highway. What's next, sushi at the QT? For a bona fide sushi experience, **Soto** in Buckhead offers some of the most dynamic and artistic creations in the city. Make sure you have a couple of hours to spare, as the chef works at his own painstaking pace. The ultra-hip **MF Sushibar** is where black-clad beautiful people nibble sushi and sip hazelnut-flavored sake. More beautiful sushi lovers can be found at **Twist**, where the sashimi tuna pizza is a hit. Sign up for the "Taka Tuna Club" at **Café Taka Sushi** and you will be notified by email whenever a special fish delivery comes in to the restaurant.

Barbecue

Barbecue joints are popping up all over the city, and that's a good thing for 'cue-loving city dwellers that used to have to traipse out to the country for decent pulled pork and ribs. Barbecue in the South is a serious culinary phenomenon and is fiercely subjective. A place you love will be absolutely hated by your co-workers, and vice versa. NFT's picks include **Pig-N-Chik** for fast take-out barbecue, and **Rolling Bones BBQ** in the Edgewood district for drive-thru barbecue. For blues and 'cue head to the world famous **Fat Matt's Rib Shack**, or **5th Street Ribs n Blues** in the new Technology Square development. For some finger-lickin' good ethnic BBQ, don't miss the Korean-style barbecue at **Hae Woon Dae** on Buford Highway. But for the real deal, both **Daddy D'z** and **Harold's Barbecue** offer authentic barbecue in the heart of the 'hood. Recommended dress code: bulletproof vests.

Cheap Eats

The aptly named **Eats** on Ponce De Leon has fed poor college students and fringe members of society for years. Their jerk chicken kicks ass. A dozen hot and glazed **Krispy Kreme** doughnuts is Atlanta's best junk food breakfast, and guarantees a sugar rush all morning long. A monster slice at **Cameli's Gourmet Pizza Joint** is a meal in itself. Grab one of the best Cuban sandwiches in Atlanta at **Kool Korners Grocery** for less than a five-spot. A ghetto burger at **Ann's Snack Bar** could feed a small village, but it's so good you won't want to share. Other cheap meals can be had at just about any ethnic restaurant on Buford Highway, barbecue joints, and most meat-and-three's around town.

Anything But Cheap Eats

For Russian cuisine fit for a Czar, head to **Nikolai's Roof**. **Seegers** is the place to go when you have a few hundred dollars to spare and a craving for the cuisine of a brilliant, temperamental chef. **Restaurant Eugene** is sure to dazzle the well-heeled set, with its serene refinement and tastefully presented dishes. You can't go wrong with old-school steakhouses like **Bones** or **Chops** when trying to make an impression. Downtown Atlanta icons like the **Sun Dial Restaurant, Bar, and View**, and **City Grill** also are perfect for the mature and moneyed crowd.

Vegetarian

The new and upscale **Lush** is trying to raise the bar by offering creative vegan cuisine for patrons not in college and wearing Birkenstocks. **Café Sunflower**, with locations in Sandy Springs and Buckhead, continues to draw a loyal vegetarian crowd. **Broadway Café** is a good place to go kosher and vegetarian. **Flying Biscuit Café**, with locations in Candler Park and Midtown, doesn't offer solely vegetarian cuisine, but their meatless offerings are yummy comfort food; try the black bean love cakes or the angel/devil veggie burgers. Leave it to the South to come up with a barbecue joint that includes tofu: **Patio Daddy-O BBQ** in East Point also offers vegetarian-friendly side dishes. For pregnant vegetarians who get those middle-of-the-night tofu cravings, there is **Eighty Eight Tofu House** on Buford Highway in Doraville, which is open 24 hours a day. For more Asian vegetarian cuisine, including a crispy Chinese pizza, don't miss **Harmony Vegetarian** on Buford Highway in Chamblee.

Late Night Noshing

Atlanta caters to a late night crowd, so there are plenty of night owl spots to cure hunger and hangovers. **The Majestic Diner** on Ponce is Atlanta's legendary diner that can be considered a people-watching paradise or hell, depending upon your perspective. **Landmark Diner**, open 24/7 in Buckhead is a great place to catch business people starting off their workday, along with clubbers sobering up after all-night parties. **Da Vinci's Innovative Italian Joint** caters to the Midtown clubbing crowd by staying open until 2:30 am most nights. **R. Thomas Deluxe Grill** in Buckhead offers quirky and healthy vegetarian options and is open 24 hours a day. **Café Intermezzo** is the perfect place for late night coffee, cocktails, and sinful desserts. One cannot overlook the ubiquitous **Waffle House** that has helped many Atlantans nurse a hangover with an order of scattered, smothered, and covered hashbrowns and strong black coffee. **Apres Diem** offers a cool vibe with a comfy lounge area and is open until 2 am on weekends—perfect for a stop after a midnight movie next door at the Landmark Midtown Art Cinema. **Teaspace** in Little Five Points stays open past midnight most nights for those late night cravings of noodles and bubble tea.

Patio Dining

Atlantans will sit outside to dine any time of the year, with even the ugliest, most forlorn patios considered primo seating. **Park Tavern** offers merely average food and service, but the breathtaking view of Piedmont Park and the Midtown skyline make up for it. For fun and lively patio scenes, try **Front Page News**, **Vickery's**, **Joe's on Juniper**, and **Zocalo**, which are all in Midtown. If gay guy eye candy is your thing, then the huge patio at **Einstein's** was made just for you. Oh, and they have a fine view of the Midtown skyline as well. For romantic dining with a great view, **Canoe**, overlooking the Chattahoochee River, is hard to beat. Just about all of the pizza joints in Atlanta have excellent patios as well, including **Osteria 832** in Virginia Highland.

Favorite Dish

Rocky the Free-Range Chicken at **Woodfire Grill**.

Best Restaurant in the Least Likely Location

Oscar's in College Park.

Key: $: Under $10 / $$: $10-$20 / $$$: $20-$30 / $$$$: $30+ .

Map 1 • Underwood Hills / Blandtown

Fellini's Pizza	1991 Howell Mill Rd	404-352-0799	$	Pizza on the patio: a simple Atlanta pleasure.
Malaya	857 Collier Rd NW	404-609-9991	$$	Malaysian cuisine that turns up the heat.
Melting Pot	857 Collier Rd NW	404-351-1811	$$$	Fondue for the masses.
Misto	1950 Howell Mill Rd NW	404-425-0030	$	Italian value by Burrito Art owner.
Salsa	2020 Howell Mill Rd NW	404-352-3101	$	Decent Cuban but overrun with children.

Map 2 • Collier Hills / Brookwood Hills

Café Intermezzo	1845 Peachtree Rd	404-355-0411	$	Desserts, cordials, and espressos for the black-clad hip crowd.
Huey's	1816 Peachtree Rd	404-873-2037	$$	Go for the beignets and the chicory coffee; skip the rest.
Mamma Fu's	1935 Peachtree Rd	404-367-5443	$	Noodles are to Mamma's as burritos are to Moe's.
MidCity Cuisine	1545 Peachtree St	404-888-8700	$$	Sean Doty's modern day brasserie offers fun and fine food.
Nan	1350 Spring St NW	404-870-9933	$$$	Upscale, creative Thai from respected Tamarind owners.
R Thomas Deluxe Grill	1812 Peachtree Rd NW	404-872-2942	$	Healthy eats 24/7.
Satay Ria	1861 Peachtree Rd NE	404-609-9990	$	Malaysian that's middle-of-the-road.
Shipfeifer on Peachtree	1814 Peachtree St NE	404-875-1106	$$	Try the curly fries with feta dip.
Ted's Montana Grill	1874 Peachtree Rd	404-355-3897	$$	Ted Turner's bison chain good for casual business lunches.
Wolfgang Puck Express	1745 Peachtree St NE	404-815-1500	$	Upscale fast food that's hit or miss.

Map 3 • Ansley Park / Piedmont Heights

Agnes and Muriel's	1514 Monroe Dr	404-885-1000	$$	Kitschy Southern-themed restaurant with subpar food.
Atmosphere	1620 Piedmont Ave NE	678-702-1620	$$	Modern French in high-energy setting.
Bangkok Thai	1492 Piedmont Ave NE	404-874-2514	$$	Good, cheap Thai popular with the gay crowd.
Cowtippers	1600 Piedmont Ave NE	404-874-3751	$$	Quirky Midtown spin on the usual steakhouse.
Fat Matt's Rib Shack	1811 Piedmont Ave NE	404-607-1622	$	BBQ and blues, grunge included.
Green Sprout	1529 Piedmont Ave NE	404-874-7373	$	Creative vegetarian Chinese cuisine.
King & I	1510 Piedmont Ave NE	404-892-7743	$$	Always dependable and friendly Thai spot perfect for takeout.
Moe's Southwest Grill	1544 Piedmont Ave NE	404-879-9663	$	Perpetually perky Fresh-Mex chain.
Nakato	1776 Cheshire Bridge Rd NE	404-873-6582	$$$	Locals prefer their sushi over the tired hibachi act.
ONE.Midtown Kitchen	559 Dutch Valley Rd	404-892-4111	$$	Ultra-hip restaurant offering bottomless glasses of wine.
Ru San's	1529 Piedmont Ave NE	404-875-7042	$$	Below average sushi, above average prices, and lousy service to boot.
Taco Cabana	1895 Piedmont Ave NE	404-874-6152	$	24-hour Mexican fast food.
Tierra	1425 Piedmont Ave NE	404-874-5951	$$	Superb Latin American cuisine in easily missed location.
Woodfire Grill	1782 Cheshire Bridge Rd	404-347-9055	$$$	Sensational seasonal cuisine. Exceptional service.

Map 4 • West Midtown / Home Park

Bacchanalia	1198 Howell Mill Rd NW	404-365-0410	$$$$	West Midtown Gourmet Wonderland.
Figo Pasta	1210 Howell Mill Rd NW	404-351-3700	$$	Cheap Italian in now trendy West Midtown location.
The Food Studio	887 W Marietta St NW	404-815-6677	$$$	Excellent Contemporary American cuisine next to Actor's Express.
Octane	1009 Marietta St NW	404-815-9886	$	Swill coffee in the loft you wish you owned.
Pangaea	1082 Huff Rd	404-350-8787	$	Sandwiches from around the world.
The Real Chow Baby	1016 Howell Mill Rd	404-815-4900	$	Create your own noodle adventure.
Taqueria Del Sol	1200 Howell Mill Rd NW	404-352-5811	$	Fresh Mexican cantina fare with sometimes rude service.
Thelma's Kitchen	768 Marietta St	404-688-5855	$	Soul food Caféteria popular with AUC students, cops, and politicians.

Map 5 • Georgia Tech / Arts Center

5th Street Ribs n Blues	86 5th St NW	404-249-8808	$	BBQ joint with live blues in Technology Square.
Baraonda	710 Peachtree St	404-879-9962	$$	Trendy Italian neighborhood bistro.
Bobby & June's Country Kitchen	375 14th St NW	404-876-3872	$	Country cookin' in the heart of Midtown.
Bridgetown Grill	689 Peachtree St	404-873-2996	$$	Inexplicably popular faux Jamaican cuisine chain.

Celebrity Café	903 Peachtree St NE	404-870-0002	$	Breakfast and lunch fare that's nothing special.
Cherry	1051 W Peachtree St NW	404-872-2020	$$	Ultra-cool sushi-focused restaurant. Popular with clubbers.
Eno	800 Peachtree St	404-685-3191	$$$	Wine focused menu with thoughtful service.
Front Page News	1104 Crescent Ave NE	404-897-3500	$$	Great patio, decent Cajun-inspired bar food.
Fuego	1136 Crescent Ave	404-389-0660	$	Tapas and cocktails before clubbing destination.
Gordon Biersch	848 Peachtree St NE	404-870-0805	$$	Chain brewery restaurant offers good beer, food, service.
JR Crickets	631 Spring St	404-881-1950	$	The original "wing is the thing" joint.
Kool Korners Grocery	349 14th St NW	404-892-4424	$	Best Cuban sandwiches in town at tiny, nondescript location.
Little Azio	903 Peachtree St NE	404-876-7711	$	Pizza joint that attracts gay hipsters and families.
Mick's	557 Peachtree St NE	404-875-6425	$	Ho-hum glorified American fast food, tourists galore, spotty service.
Moe's Southwest Grill	85 5th St NW	404-541-9940	$	Perpetually perky Fresh-Mex chain.
Noodle	903 Peachtree St NE	404-685-3010	$	Asian cuisines unite for cheap, tasty meal.
Park 75	75 14th St NE	404-253-3840	$$$$	Upscale decadence at this Four Season hotel restaurant.
Pasta Da Pulcinella	1123 Peachtree Wk	404-876-1114	$$	Hidden Italian gem. The Granny apple-sausage ravioli is magnifico!
The Savoy Bar and Grill	659 Peachtree St NE	404-898-8350	$$$	Contemporary American cuisine in gorgeous restored hotel.
Silk	919 Peachtree St	678-705-8888	$$$	Vast upscale, high-energy Asian cuisine hot spot.
The Silver Skillet	200 14th St NW	404-874-1388	$	Southern served up right.
South City Kitchen	1144 Crescent Ave NE	404-873-7358	$$	Sophisticated Southern cuisine.
St Charles Deli	22 5th St NW	404-249-7733	$	Breakfast, lunch, and dinner for those on the go.
Tamarind	80 14th St NW	404-873-4888	$$$	Best Thai in Atlanta. Parking sucks.
Tin Drum	88 5th St NW	404-881-1368	$	Noodle shop in Technology Square.
Toast	817 W Peachtree St NE	404-815-9243	$$	Well-executed light fare behind the Biltmore.
Touch of India	1037 Peachtree St NE	404-876-7777	$$	Below average Indian fare.
Twisted Taco	66 12th St NE	404-607-8771	$	Designer tacos in popular clubbing area.
The Varsity	61 North Ave NW	404-881-1706	$	Historic drive-in. Order the F.O. and a naked dog.
Veni Vidi Vici	41 14th St NE	404-875-8424	$$$$	Longtime classic, romantic Italian restaurant.
Vickery's	1105 Crescent Ave NE	404-881-1106	$$	Beautiful patio, standard American fare.
Vinocity	36 13th St NE	404-870-8886	$$$	Wine without the snobs.
Vortex	878 Peachtree St	404-875-1667	$	No idiots allowed at this burger joint with real attitude.

Map 6 • Midtown

Apres Diem	931 Monroe Dr NE	404-872-3333	$	Bohemian bistro. Decadent desserts.
Babs	814 Juniper St NE	404-541-0888	$	Kitschy, health-conscious breakfast, lunch and dinner.
Bread Garden	549 Amsterdam Ave NE	404-875-1166	$	Fresh baked goods and yummy sandwiches to-go.
Cha Gio/Wild Curry Thai Kitchen	132 10th St NE	404-885-9387	$$	Combined Vietnamese/Thai restaurant.
Corner Bakery Café	1201 Peachtree St NE	404-817-7111	$	Gourmet breakfast and lunch hotspot.
DaVinci's	674 Myrtle St	404-389-0567	$	Late night upscale pizza joint for post-clubbing cravings.
Eats	600 Ponce de Leon Ave NE	404-888-9149	$	Cheap chow. Great jerk chicken.
Einstein's	1077 Juniper St NE	404-876-7925	$$	Midtown veteran offers plenty of male eye candy, decent food.
Fishmonger	980 Piedmont Ave NE	404-459-9003	$$	Average seafood offerings in former Balance spot.
Flying Biscuit	1001 Piedmont Ave NE	404-874-8887	$	Breakfast all day, vegan-friendly.
Gilbert's Mediterranean Café	219 10th St NE	404-872-8012	$$	Meze and martinis.
Jake's Ice Creams & Sorbets	970 Piedmont Ave NE	404-685-3101	$	Ice cream parlor with flavors like, "Chocolate Slap Yo' Mama."
Joe's on Juniper	1049 Juniper St NE	404-875-6634	$	Wings, Brew, and a View.
Krispy Kreme	295 Ponce de Leon Ave	404-876-7307	$	The flagship store. Open 24 hours. Yummy.
Las Palmeras	368 5th St NE	404-872-0846	$	Hidden gem offering authentic Cuban cuisine for a song.
Mary Mac's Tea Room	224 Ponce Leon Ave NE	404-876-1800	$	Meat-and-three, with sweet tea.
Mellow Mushroom	931 Monroe Dr NE	404-874-2291	$	Popular Atlanta pizzeria chain offers dependable cheap eats.
MF Sushibar	265 Ponce de Leon Ave	404-815-8844	$$$	Magic fingers, indeed.
Mitra	818 Juniper St NE	404-875-5515	$$	South American cuisine in high-energy Midtown bungalow.
Moe's Southwest Grill	1197 Peachtree St NE	404-870-0884	$	Perpetually perky Fresh-Mex chain.
Mu Lan	824 Juniper St NE	404-877-5797	$$	Good, not great upscale Chinese. Delivery available.

Key: $: Under $10 / $$: $10-$20 / $$$: $20-$30 / $$$$: $30+

Map 6 • Midtown—*continued*

Nam	931 Monroe Dr NE	404-541-9997	$$$	Sensuous Vietnamese cuisine.
Nancy's Pizza	265 Ponce de Leon Ave	404-885-9199	$$	Chicago-style pizza in the ATL.
Nickiemoto	990 Piedmont Ave NE	404-253-2010	$$	Average sushi, but don't miss the drag queen show.
Papi's East Cuban Cuisine	216 Ponce de Leon Ave NE	404-607-1525	$	Authentic East Cuban cheap eats.
Park Tavern	500 10th St NE	404-249-0001	$	$1 beers when it rains at this Piedmont Park tavern.
Salt	794 Juniper St NE	404-541-1988	$$	Where the trendy crowd goes that can't afford Spice.
Shout	1197 Peachtree St	404-846-2000	$$	Trendy tapas and sushi noshing. Killer Midtown views.
Silver Grill	900 Monroe Dr NE	404-876-8145	$	Meat-and-three favorite. Country fried steak rules.
Spice	793 Juniper St NE	404-875-4242	$$$	See-and-be-seen spot with maturing kitchen.
Thai Chili	1197 Peachtree St NE	404-875-2275	$$$	Thai classics at Colony Square.
Thai Palate	265 Ponce de Leon Ave NE	404-685-9988	$$	Good Thai with efficient delivery.
Willy's Mexicana Grill	1071 Piedmont Ave NE	404-249-9054	$	Parkside patio saves Midtown locale of bland burrito chain.
Zesto Drive-In	544 Ponce de Leon Ave NE	404-607-1118	$	Real fast food, retro style.
Zocalo	187 10th St NE	404-249-7576	$$	Authentic Mexican with best tequila selection in Southeast US.

Map 7 • Virginia Highland

Alon's	1394 N Highland Ave	404-872-6000	$	Popular gourmet bakery and sandwich shop.
American Roadhouse	842 N Highland Ave	404-872-2822	$	Diner food in fun atmosphere. Kids love it.
Babette's Café	573 N Highland Ave	404-523-9121	$$$	Classic French cuisine. Sunday brunches are sublime.
Belly General Store	722 N Highland Ave	404-872-1003	$	Fresh made bagels, yummy cupcakes, tasty sandwiches.
Cameli's Gourmet Pizza Joint	699 Ponce de Leon Ave	404-249-9020	$	The monster slice, baby!
Caramba Café	1409 N Highland Ave	404-874-1343	$$	Ay, caramba! Good Tex-Mex, killer margaritas.
Chin Chin	699 Ponce de Leon Ave	404-881-1511	$$	Reliable Chinese restaurant that delivers.
Dish	870 N Highland Ave	404-897-3463	$$	Hip spot for small plates.
Everybody's	1040 N Highland Ave	404-873-4545	$	Best salads in town, and the pizzas rock too.
Fellini's Pizza	909 Ponce de Leon Ave NE	404-873-3088	$	Pizza on the patio: a simple Atlanta pleasure.
Fontaine's Oyster Bar	1026 1/2 N Highland Ave NE	404-872-0869	$$	OK oysters, fun and hopping bar scene.
Harry & Son's	820 N Highland Ave NE	404-873-2009	$$	Where Highland hipsters go for sushi and Thai.
Harvest	853 N Highland Ave	404-876-8244	$$$	Upscale American cuisine in warm, romantic atmosphere.
Horizon	1397 N Highland Ave NE	404-876-0676	$$$	Seafood focused menu and nice, covered patio.
Java Jive	790 Ponce de Leon Ave	404-876-6161	$	Eclectic Midtown breakfast spot on seedy strip of Ponce De Leon.
La Fonda Latina	923 Ponce de Leon Ave	404-607-0665	$	Cheap, no frills carnita chain. Good for kids.
La Tavola Trattoria	992 Virginia Ave	404-873-5430	$$$	Tiny, romantic Italian spot that packs them in.
Majestic	1031 Ponce de Leon Ave NE	404-875-0276	$	Priceless people-watching at this seedy diner.
Mali	961 Amsterdam Ave	404-874-1411	$$	Outstanding Thai in the Highlands.
Moe's Southwest Grill	863 Ponce de Leon Ave	404-607-7892	$	Perpetually perky Fresh-Mex chain.
Murphy's	997 Virginia Ave NE	404-872-0904	$$	Best brunch in the city. Nice wine program.
Noche	1000 Virginia Ave	404-815-9155	$$	Steamy Southwestern sophistication.
Olive Bistro	650 Ponce de Leon Ave NE	404-874-5336	$	Dependable, cheap Mediterranean favorites.
Osteria 832	832 N Highland Ave NE	404-897-1414	$	Cheap, family-friendly Italian. Lovely patio.
Pad Thai	1021 Virginia Ave NE	404-892-2070	$	A touch of Buford Hwy in the Highlands.
Paolo's Gelato Italiano	1025 Virginia Ave NE	404-607-0055	$	Willy Wonka goes to Italy.
Pura Vida	656 N Highland Ave	404-870-9797	$	Puerto Rican tapas on Ponce.
Qdoba	650 Ponce de Leon Ave NE	404-892-0644	$	Flavorful and friendly burrito joint.
Sala	1186 N Highland Ave NE	404-872-7203	$$	Upscale Mexican cuisine with designer margaritas.
Soul Vegetarian Restaurant	652 N Highland Ave	404-875-4641	$	Soul food without the meat.
Surin of Thailand	810 N Highland Ave	404-892-7789	$	Good Thai at reasonable prices.

Map 8 • Vine City

Busy Bee Café	810 Martin Luther King Jr SW	404-525-9212	$	Simple soul food attracts cops and college students.
Eggroll Corner Chinese Restaurant	825 Martin Luther King Jr Dr NW	404-526-9099	$	Egg rolls and stir-fry in the hood.
KFC	23 Joseph Lowery Blvd SW	404-752-9903	$	The Original Fried Chicken chain.

Map 9 • Downtown / Centennial Place / Techwood

Ali Baba	61 Broad St	404-681-3997	$	Falafels, hummus, and gyros.
Atlanta Bread Company	231 Peachtree St NE	404-688-6393	$	The A.B.C. special is one kickass sandwich.
Atlanta Grill	181 Peachtree St NE	404-659-0400	$$$$	Where the legendary "Cheater's Booth" is located.
Azio	229 Peachtree St NE	404-222-0808	$$	Modern take on traditional Italian in Peachtree Center.
Benihana	229 Peachtree St NE	404-522-9627	$$$	Japanese steakhouse chain with average hibachi fare.
Corner Bakery Café	270 Peachtree St NW	404-215-9000	$	Gourmet breakfast and lunch hotspot.
City Grill	50 Hurt Plz	404-524-2489	$$$$	Former bank becomes award-winning restaurant.
Ginseng Café	52 Broad St	404-688-4437	$	Chinese lunch joint.
Hard Rock Café	215 Peachtree NE	404-688-7625	$$	If relatives drag you here, find a new family.
Landmark Diner	60 Luckie St NW	404-659-1756	$	24-hour diner food downtown.
Lombardi's	94 Pryor St NE	404-522-6568	$$$	Italian in the Underground.
Luxe	89 Park Pl	404-389-0800	$$$	Inventive, upscale fare in former Mumbo Jumbo space.
McCormick & Schmick's	190 Marietta St NW	404-521-1236	$$$	High-end chain fine for business luncheons.
Mick's	229 Peachtree St NE	404-688-6425	$	Standard American fare. Safe bet for picky eaters.
Moe's Southwest Grill	1 CNN Ctr, 190 Marietta St NW	404-529-9922	$	Perpetually perky Fresh-Mex chain.
Moe's Southwest Grill	70 Peachtree St NE	404-688-4288	$	Perpetually perky Fresh-Mex chain.
Mr Everything Café	870 Martin Luther King Jr Dr SW	404-577-3336	$	Yummy soups for everyone.
Pittypat's Porch	25 International Blvd	404-525-8228	$$$	Southern dining for tourists, souvenir glass included.
Ray's in the City	240 Peachtree St NE	404-524-9224	$$	Huge, corporate-style menu with seafood focus.
Sun Dial Restaurant, Bar, and View	210 Peachtree St NW	404-589-7506	$$$$	Revolving dining room on 73rd floor. Amazing ciy views.
Ted's Montana Grill	133 Luckie St NW	404-521-9726	$$	Ted Turner's bison chain good for casual business lunches.

Map 10 • Downtown / Sweet Auburn

Dailey's	17 Andrew Young International Blvd	404-681-3303	$$$	Atlanta icon with retro cuisine and cigar/martini bar.
Gladys Knight Chicken and Waffles	529 Peachtree St	404-874-9393	$	R&B legend scores another hit.
Hsu's Gourmet Chinese	192 Peachtree Center Ave NE	404-659-2788	$$	Gourmet Chinese attracts tourists, conventioneers.
Morton's, The Steakhouse	303 Peachtree Center Ave NE	404-577-4366	$$$$	Dependable high-end steakhouse chain.
Nikolai's Roof	255 Courtland St NE	404-221-6362	$$$$	Russian for the richest of palates and wallets.
Pacific Rim Bistro	303 Peachtree Center Ave NE	404-893-0018	$$	Pan-Asian bistro caters to business, tourist crowd.
Pleasant Peasant	555 Peachtree St NE	404-874-3223	$$$	Downtown veteran for romantic dining.
Rolling Bones Premium Pit BBQ	377 Edgewood Ave	404-222-2324	$	Barbecue with a drive-thru.
Thumbs Up Diner	573 Edgewood Ave	404-223-0690	$	Breakfast hot spot. Try The Heap.
Trader Vic's	255 Courtland St NE	404-221-6339	$$$	Polynesian for yuppies and conventioneers.

Map 11 • Inman Park / Cabbagetown / Little Five Points

Brewhouse Café	401 Moreland Ave NE	404-525-7799	$	Tavern food for soccer fans.
Fritti	311 N Highland Ave	404-880-9559	$$	Sotto Sotto's sister restaurant is upscale pizza joint.
Front Page News	351 Moreland Ave	404-475-7777	$$	Cajun-themed restaurant is fun and loose.
Il Localino	467 N Highland Ave	404-222-0650	$$	Eccentric and energetic Italian dining experience.
Inman Park Patio	1029 Edgewood Ave	404-659-5757	$$	Great private outdoor patio. Wine specials are popular.
Lush	913 Bernina Ave	404-223-9292	$$	Upscale all-vegan with dramatic presentation.
Miro's Garden	1150 Euclid Ave NE	404-221-1604	$$	Health-conscious trendy dining.
Olive Bistro	1099 Euclid Ave NE	404-582-0029	$	Dependable, cheap Mediterranean favorites.
Rathbun's	112 Krog St	404-524-8280	$$$	Emeril protégé receiving buzz for his own restaurant.
Roman Lily Café	668 Highland Ave	404-653-1155	$	Unique, Southern-flavored menu in retro setting.
Savage Pizza	484 Moreland Ave NE	404-523-0500	$	Pizza for the tattooed and pierced crowd.
Son's Place	100 Hurt St NE	404-581-0530	$	Soul food with mouth-watering fried chicken.
Sotto Sotto	313 N Highland Ave	404-523-6678	$$$$	Rustic Italian in trendy, high-energy setting.
Sweet Lime	1128 Euclid Ave NE	404-589-9696	$	Sushi at proletariat prices.
Teaspace	1133 Euclid Ave NE	404-577-9793	$	Bubble teas, noodles, and Birkenstocks.
Tijuana Garage	353 Moreland Ave NE	404-475-8888	$	Cheerful Mexican cantina.
Two Urban Licks	820 Ralph McGill Blvd NE	404-522-4622	$$	Rockin' rotisserie, smokin' blues, and scenesters galore.

Arts & Entertainment • **Restaurants**

Key: $: Under $10 / $$: $10-$20 / $$$: $20-$30 / $$$$: $30+

Map 11 • Inman Park / Cabbagetown / Little Five Points—*continued*

The Vortex	438 Moreland Ave NE	404-688-1828	$	Brave the skull head entrance—their burgers kick ass.
Wisteria	471 N Highland Ave	404-525-3363	$$$	Savory Southern in upscale but friendly atmosphere.
Zesto	377 Moreland Ave	404-523-1973	$	Real fast food, retro style.

Map 12 • West End

Pascal's Restaurant at Castleberry	180 Northside Dr SW	404-525-2023	$$	Upscale soul food. Original is a civil rights landmark.
Satterwhite's	851 Oak St SW	404-756-0963	$	AUC meat-and-three joint.
Soul Vegetarian Restaurant	879 Ralph David Abernathy Blvd SW	404-752-5194	$	Soul food without the meat.

Map 13 • Mechanicsville / Summerhill

Haveli Indian Cuisine	225 Spring St	404-522-4545	$$	Indian food buffet popular with Downtown business crowd.
Lunatique Café	160 Spring St	678-686-3370	$$	Eccentric Chef Paul Luna's Downtown venture.
Slice	259 Peters St	404-588-1820	$	Pizzas, cocktails, and DJs in hip Downtown spot.

Map 14 • Grant Park

Daddy D'z	264 Memorial Dr SE	404-222-0206	$	Their slogan: "We Ain't Pretty, But We're Good."
Dakota Blue	454 Cherokee Ave SE	404-589-8002	$	Burritos and free wi-fi.
Grand Central Pizza	451 Cherokee Ave SE	404-523-8900	$	Pizza and beer joint.
Ria's Bluebird	421 Memorial Dr	404-521-3737	$	Bohemian café with great view of Oakland Cemetery.
Six Feet Under	415 Memorial Dr SE	404-523-6664	$	Seafood shack sheik. Nice view of Oakland Cemetery.

Map 15 • Ormewood Park North / Woodland Hills

Agave	242 Boulevard SE	404-588-0006	$$	Southwestern cuisine and snazzy tequila bar.
The Automatic	313 Boulevard	404-588-9062	$	Atlanta's coolest drive-thru.
Da'Bomb Take Out Restaurant	371 Boulevard SE	404-681-5300	$	It's da'bomb, what more do you want?!
Thunder Alley Grill & Grocery	632 McDonald St SE	404-584-0474	$	Best chili in Cabbagetown.

Map 16 • Paces / Northside

Blue Ridge Grill	1261 W Paces Ferry Rd	404-233-5030	$$$	Southern for the upper crust.
Goldberg's Bagels and Deli	1272 W Paces Ferry Rd	404-266-0123	$	Closest to NYC bagels you can get in the South.
Houston's	3539 Northside Pkwy	404-262-7130	$$$	Fancy dining for dummies.
Joel	3290 Northside Pkwy	404-233-3500	$$$$	Breathtaking French-inspired avant garde cuisine.
OK Café	1284 W Paces Ferry Rd	404-233-2888	$	Popular café with typical diner fare.
Pano's & Paul's	1232 W Paces Ferry Rd	404-261-3662	$$$$	Veteran upscale dining icon.

Map 17 • Northwest Atlanta / Mt Paran

Horseradish Grill	4320 Powers Ferry Rd	404-255-7277	$$$	Ritzy Southern. Great brunches.

Map 18 • Chastain Park

10 Degrees South	4183 Roswell Rd NE	404-705-8870	$$$	South African sensation not to be missed.
Chopstix	4279 Roswell Rd	404-255-4868	$$	Upscale, dependable Chinese restaurant.
Fellini's Pizza	4429 Roswell Rd NE	404-303-8248	$	Pizza on the patio: a simple Atlanta pleasure.
La Fonda Latina	4427 Roswell Rd NE	404-303-8201	$	Cheap, no frills carnita chain. Good for kids.

Map 19 • West Brookhaven

Au Rendez-Vous	1328 Windsor Pkwy	404-303-1968	$$	Inexpensive French bistro.
Bajaritos	3877 Peachtree Rd	404-239-9727	$	Most creative made-to-order burritos around.
Chin Chin	3887 Peachtree Rd	404-816-2229	$$	Dependable Americanized Chinese. Fast delivery.
Jock's and Jill's Sports Grill	4046 Peachtree Rd NE	404-816-2801	$$	Standard sports bar fare.
Meehan's Ale House	4058 Peachtree Rd NE	404-467-9531	$$	Grab a pint with some bangers and mash. Formerly Mangia 101.
Mellow Mushroom	5058 Peachtree Rd	404-266-1661	$	Popular Atlanta pizzeria chain offers dependable cheap eats.
Pig-N-Chik	3929 Peachtree Rd	404-869-0038	$	Awesome BBQ inside the perimeter.

Map 20 • East Brookhaven

57th Fighter Group	3829 Clairmont Rd	770-457-7227	$$$	Swing music club that attracts younger crowd.
Haven	1411 Dresden Dr	404-969-0700	$$	Neighborhood bistro with long waits.

Map 21 • Central Buckhead

Aiko	128 E Andrews Dr NW	404-869-4800	$$	Sushi and martinis. What else do you need?
Anthony's	3109 Piedmont Rd	404-262-7379	$$	Homestyle Italian dining.
Antica Posta	519 E Paces Ferry Rd	404-262-7112	$$$$	Authentic Tuscan cuisine in romantic Buckhead bungalow.
Atlanta Bread Company	3365 Piedmont Rd	404-814-9990	$	The A.B.C. special is one kickass sandwich.
Au Pied De Cochon	3315 Peachtree Rd NE	404-946-9070	$$$	Pig's feet for the wealthy crowd.
Bone's	3130 Piedmont Rd	404-237-2663	$$$$	Steakhouse perfect for power lunches.
Brasserie Le Coze	3393 Peachtree Rd NE	404-266-1440	$$$	Surprisingly exquisite French in shopping mall locale.
Buckhead Diner	3073 Piedmont Rd	404-262-3336	$$	Not your typical diner crowd.
Café at East Andrews	56 E Andrews Dr NW	404-869-1132	$$	Trendy dining destination in club-hopping Buckhead.
The Capital Grille	255 E Paces Ferry Rd	404-262-1162	$$	Lunchtime favorite with the Buckhead business crowd.
Chipotle	3424 Piedmont Rd NE	404-869-7921	$	Gourmet chain with fast, fresh burritos and salads. The guac rocks.
Chops	70 W Paces Ferry Rd	404-262-2675	$$$$	Steakhouse for carnivores with expense accounts.
Clubhouse	3393 Peachtree Rd NE	404-442-8891	$$$	Mainly Buckhead business crowd with meat-market vibes.
Copeland's	3365 Piedmont Rd NE	404-475-1000	$$	Cajun chain offers okay French Quarter cuisine with spotty service.
Corner Bakery Café	3368 Peachtree Rd NE	404-816-5100	$	Gourmet breakfast and lunch hotspot.
Corner Bakery Café	3393 Peachtree Rd NE	404-266-8227	$	Gourmet breakfast and lunch hotspot.
Dantanna's	3400 Around Lenox Dr	404-760-8873	$$$	Friendly, ritzy sports bar atmosphere with fresh seafood.
Dante's Down the Hatch	3380 Peachtree Rd	404-266-1600	$$$	Jazz, fondue, and live alligators.
Fogo de Chao	3101 Piedmont Rd	404-266-9988	$$$	All-you-can-eat meat at this Brazilian steakhouse.
Hal's on Old Ivy	30 Old Ivy Rd NE	404-261-0025	$$$$	Steak and seafood for the old-school crowd.
Hashiguchi	3400 Around Lenox Dr	404-841-9229	$$	Above-average sushi next to the mall.
Henri's Bakery	61 Irby Ave NW	404-237-0202	$	Serious sandwiches, pastries, and cakes!
Kyma	3085 Piedmont Rd	404-262-0702	$$$	Buy airfare to Greece for the price of dinner here.
Landmark Diner	3652 Roswell Rd NW	404-816-9090	$	Gussied up greasy spoon frequented by Buckhead clubbers.
Maggiano's	3368 Peachtree Rd	404-816-9650	$$$	Family-style Italian in warm, welcoming atmosphere.
McKinnon's Louisiane	3209 Maple Dr NE	404-237-1313	$$$	Down-home Cajun in comfortable atmosphere. Seafood focus.
Milan	3377 Peachtree Rd	678-553-1900	$$$	Italian cuisine and beautiful people with a great patio.
Moe's Southwest Grill	3722 Roswell Rd	404-231-1690	$	Perpetually perky Fresh-Mex chain.
Morton's - The Steakhouse	3379 Peachtree Rd NE	404-816-6535	$$$$	Ritzy steakhouse chain delivers the goods.
Nava	3060 Peachtree Rd	404-240-1984	$$$$	Southwestern sheik and awesome décor.
The Palm	3391 Peachtree Rd NE	404-814-1955	$$$$	Bobby Brown and Whitney Houston are regulars.
Portofino	3199 Paces Ferry Pl NW	404-231-1136	$$$	Italian-inspired, primarily American cuisine with excellent wine list.
Prime	3393 Peachtree Rd	404-812-0555	$$$	Surf-n-turf in the mall.
Roy's	3475 Piedmont Rd	404-231-3232	$$$	Ritzy Hawaiian cuisine in Buckhead office tower.
Seeger's	111 W Paces Ferry Rd	404-846-9779	$$$$	Great dining experience if you can shell out the dough.
Soleil	3081 Maple Dr NE	404-467-1790	$$	Reasonable bistro with nice patio.
Soto	3330 Piedmont Rd	404-233-2005	$$$	Best sushi in town, but expect slow dining experience.
Souper Jenny	56 E Andrews Dr NW	404-239-9023	$$$	Tiny, healthy lunch spot with line out the door.
Surin of Thailand	318 E Paces Ferry Rd NE	404-442-7522	$	Decent, but Americanized Thai food.
Swan Coach House	3130 Slaton Dr NW	404-261-0636	$	Southern tearoom fare at its finest.
White House	3172 Peachtree Rd NE	404-237-7601	$	Popular diner with Southern and Greek favorites.

Map 22 • Lenox

Ali-Oli	3535 Peachtree Rd NE	404-266-0414	$$$	Mediterranean-inspired cuisine in flawless setting.
Bluepointe	3455 Peachtree Rd NE	404-237-9070	$$$$	Ultra-cool Asian fusion.
The Cabin Room	2678 Buford Hwy	404-315-7676	$$$$	Like a really fancy hunting lodge.
The Dining Room at the Ritz Carlton	3434 Peachtree Rd NE	404-237-2700	$$$$	For a true dining experience, this can't be beat.
Emeril's	3500 Lenox Rd	404-564-5600	$$$$	Locally disappointing endeavor from famed chef Emeril.
Havana Sandwich Shop	2905 Buford Hwy NE	404-636-4094	$	Excellent, authentic Cuban sandwiches at this

legendary hole-in-the-wall.

Key: $: Under $10 / $$: $10-$20 / $$$: $20-30 / $$$$: $30+

Map 22 · Lenox—*continued*

Houston's	3321 Lenox Rd	404-237-7534	$$$	Fancy dining for dummies.
Johnny Rockets	3500 Peachtree Rd NE	404-233-9867	$	Retro burger joint chain brings wholesome fun to Buckhead.
New York Prime	3424 Peachtree Rd NE	404-846-0644	$$$$	Steak the Yankee way.
Phuket Thai Restaurant	2839 Buford Hwy NE	404-325-4199	$	One of Atlanta's oldest Thai restaurants. Quick lunch service.
Roaster's	2770 Lenox Rd NE	404-237-1122	$	Chain specializing in rotisserie chicken and ribs. Finger-lickin' good.
Twist	3500 Peachtree Rd NE	404-869-1191	$$	Cocktails, low-carb tapas at this trendsetter hook-up spot.

Map 23 · Briarcliff / Clairmont

El Porto Mexican Restaurant	3396 Buford Hwy NE	404-325-9312	$	Traditional Mexican cuisine.
El Rey de Todos Mexican Restaurant	3249 Buford Hwy NE	404-633-0130	$	Just like being south of the border.
El Torero Mexican Restaurant	2484 Briarcliff Rd NE	404-633-1177	$$	Their white cheese dip is muy bueno!
Fortune Cookie	2480 Briarcliff Rd NE	404-636-8899	$	Decent Chinese in strip mall location. Fast delivery.
Machu Picchu	3375 Buford Hwy NE	404-320-3226	$	Peruvian dining destination in strip mall locale.
Moe's Southwest Grill	2484 Briarcliff Rd	404-248-9399	$	Perpetually perky Fresh-Mex chain.
Panahar	3375 Buford Hwy	404-633-6655	$	The only Bangladeshi restaurant in Atlanta.
Violette	2948 Clairmont Rd NE	404-633-3363	$$	Simple French classics with uneven service.
Waffle House	2886 Clairmont Rd NE	404-634-7812	$	Scattered, smothered, and covered. Hmmm, good.

Map 24 · Peachtree Battle / Woodfield

Benihana	2143 Peachtree Rd NE	404-355-8565	$$$	The chef's show is better than the food.
Café Sunflower	2140 Peachtree Rd	404-352-8859	$$	Vegetarian food for real people.
Figo Pasta	1170 Collier Rd NW	404-351-9667	$	Cheap, quick Italian.
Fratelli di Napoli	2101 Tula St NW	404-351-1533	$$$	Bring an army to be fed at this family-style Italian restaurant.
Houston's	2166 Peachtree Rd NW	404-351-2442	$$$	Fancy dining for dummies.
Justin's	2200 Peachtree Rd	404-603-5353	$$$	P. Diddy's upscale soul food endeavor.

Map 25 · Garden Hills / Peachtree Heights / Peachtree Hills

Anis Café & Bistro	2974 Grandview Ave NE	404-233-9889	$$	Romantic bistro with French and Mediterranean influences.
Aria	490 E Paces Ferry Rd NE	404-233-7673	$$$$	Memorable upscale cuisine, award-winning restaurant.
Atlanta Fish Market	265 Pharr Rd	404-262-3165	$$$	Seafood central in Buckhead.
Bite	10 Kings Cir NE	404-231-4113	$$$	Hearty Bavarian fare for the upscale crowd.
Café Tu Tu Tango	220 Pharr Rd NE	404-841-6222	$$	Tapas in an acid-trip setting.
The Cheesecake Factory	3024 Peachtree Rd NE	404-816-2555	$$$	Who knew expensive crap was so popular?
Coco Loco	2625 Piedmont Rd NE	404-262-0198	$	Trendy hole-in-the-wall Cuban cuisine. Skip the seafood.
Eclipse Di Luna	764 Miami Cir NE	404-846-0449	$$	Tapas galore amidst antique shopping district.
Fellini's Pizza	2809 Peachtree Rd NE	404-266-0082	$	Pizza on the patio: a simple Atlanta pleasure.
Georgia Grille	2290 Peachtree Rd NE	404-352-3517	$$$	Southwestern meets seafood.
Imperial Fez	2285 Peachtree Rd	404-351-0870	$$$$	Belly dancing and B'stella.
Jalisco	2337 Peachtree Rd NE	404-233-9244	$	Basic Mexican fare at one of Buckhead's most family-friendly restaurants.
Jim White's Half Shell Restaurant	2349 Peachtree Rd NE	404-237-9924	$$$	Where cronies go for crustaceans.
Moe's Southwest Grill	2915 Peachtree Rd	404-442-8932	$	Perpetually perky Fresh-Mex chain.
Pasta Vino	2391 Peachtree Rd NE	404-231-4946	$	Neighborhood Italian. No surprises.
Pricci	500 Pharr Rd	404-237-2941	$$$$	Fun yet stylish Italian dining.
Ray's New York Pizza	3021 Peachtree Rd NE	404-364-0960	$	Specialty pizzas and calzones rule at this pre-clubbing spot.
Restaurant Eugene	2277 Peachtree Rd	404-355-0321	$$$	Mature cuisine for a mature crowd.
Taka Sushi Café	375 Pharr Rd NE	404-869-2802	$$$	Excellent sushi in low-key fish-shack environment.
Toulouse	2293 Peachtree Rd NE	404-351-9533	$$	French-inspired cuisine and superb wine program in artsy setting.

Waffle House	3016 Piedmont Rd NE	404-231-0023	$	Scattered, smothered, and covered. Hmmm, good.

Map 26 · Morningside / Lenox Hills

Alfredo's	1989 Cheshire Bridge Rd	404-876-1380	$$	Traditional Italian on Cheshire Bridge.
Broadway Café	2168 Briarcliff Rd NE	404-329-0888	$	Kosher vegetarian cuisine, anyone?
The Colonnade	1879 Cheshire Bridge Rd NE	404-874-5642	$	Southern meat-and-three institution.
Doc Chey's	1424 N Highland Ave NE	404-888-0777	$	Noodles and more for pocket change.
Dusty's Barbecue	1815 Briarcliff Rd NE	404-320-6264	$	North Carolina barbecue draws the Emory University crowd.
Floataway Café	1123 Zonolite Rd	404-892-1414	$$$	Romantic venue with California and Italian influences.
Hong Kong Harbour	2184 Cheshire Bridge Rd NE	404-325-7630	$$	Authentic Chinese. Open til 3 am on weekends.
Jitlada	2329 Cheshire Bridge Rd	404-728-9040	$	Average Thai near Tara movie theatre.
Las Margaritas	1842 Cheshire Bridge Rd NE	404-873-4464	$	Mexican, and yes, margaritas at this festive spot.
Little Bangkok	2225 Cheshire Bridge Rd	404-315-1530	$	Hole-in-the-wall offers cheap, spicy Thai and Chinese.
Mambo	1402 N Highland Ave NE	404-876-2626	$$	Fun and tasty Cuban.
Meskerem	2329 Cheshire Bridge Rd NE	404-417-0991	$	Ethiopian in bare-bones atmosphere.
Nicola's	1602 LaVista Rd NE	404-325-2524	$$	Superb Lebanese hole-in-the-wall.
Nino's	1931 Cheshire Bridge Rd	404-874-6505	$$$	One of Atlanta's oldest Italian restaurants. Big menu, big portions.
Olde Towne Pizza	1394 N Highland Ave	404-876-1111	$	Real homemade pizzas, chocolate milk for the kids.
Red Snapper	2100 Cheshire Bridge Rd	404-634-8947	$$	Old-school seafood.
Rustic Gourmet	1145 Zonolite Rd NE	404-881-1288	$$$	Simple New American cuisine with great wine list.
South of France	2345 Cheshire Bridge Rd NE	404-325-6963	$$	Homestyle French cuisine in romantic setting.
Sundown Café	2165 Cheshire Bridge Rd	404-321-1118	$$	Locally beloved taqueria.
Taverna Plaka	2196 Cheshire Bridge Rd	404-636-2284	$$	It's all Greek here, and you get to be part of the show!
Thai Chili	2169 Briarcliff Rd	404-875-2275	$$	Standard Thai for the non-adventurous.
The Varsity Jr	1085 Lindbergh Dr NE	404-261-8843	$	Mini-Me version of local drive-thru legend.

Map 27 · Toco Hills / Emory University

Edo	2945 N Druid Hills Rd NE	404-728-0228	$$$	Hibachi-style dining and sushi. Not cheap.
Houston Mill House	849 Houston Mill Rd	404-727-8311	$$	Upscale Southern luncheon destination near Emory campus.
Le Giverny	1641 Clifton Rd NE	404-325-7252	$$$	French for the romantics.
Mellow Mushroom	1679 LaVista Rd NE	404-325-0330	$	Popular Atlanta pizza chain with healthy vibe.
Petite Auberge	2935 N Druid Hills Rd NE	404-634-6268	$$$	French and Bavarian bistro popular with the older crowd.
Top Spice	3007 N Druid Hills Rd	404-728-0588	$$	Thai and Malaysian cuisine in serene setting.
Touch of India	3017 N Druid Hills Rd	404-728-8881	$$	Just so-so Indian.

Map 28 · Druid Hills West

Burrito Art	1451 Oxford Rd NE	404-377-7786	$	Emory student hangout with cheap, creative burritos.
Doc Chey's Noodle House	1556 N Decatur Rd NE	404-378-8188	$	Emory students flock to this fun, cheap noodle house.
Everybody's	1593 N Decatur Rd NE	404-377-7766	$	Reliable pizza and giant custom-made salads rule at Emory hangout.

Map 29 · North Decatur / Druid Hills East

Athens Pizza	1341 Clairmont Rd NE	404-636-1100	$	Greek food and pizza popular with Emory students.
Bhojanic	1363 Clairmont Rd	404-633-9233	$$$	Upscale mix of Indian, tapas, and fusion cuisine.
Café Lily	308 W Ponce de Leon Ave	404-371-9119	$$	Inventive Mediterranean cuisine. Very friendly, attentive service.
Mexico City Gourmet	2134 N Decatur Rd	404-643-1128	$	Not-so-gourmet Mexican food complete with mariachis.
The Supper Club	308 W Ponce de Leon Ave	404-370-1207	$$$	Romance is the draw at this intimate dining spot.
Taqueria Del Sol	359 W Ponce de Leon Ave	404-377-7668	$	Cheap Southwestern fare packs them in.

..

| Watershed | 406 W Ponce de Leon Ave | 404-378-4900 | $$$ | Indigo Girl's Emily Saliers restaurant offers amazing fried chicken. |

Key: $: Under $10 / $$: $10-$20 / $$$: $20-$30 / $$$$: $30+

Map 30 • Decatur

Atlanta Bread Company	205 E Ponce de Leon	404-378-6600	$	The A.B.C. special is one kickass sandwich.
Café Alsace	121 E Ponce de Leon Ave	404-373-5622	$$	Very French bistro just off the Decatur Square.
Carpe Diem	105 Sycamore Pl	404-687-9696	$$	Apres Diem's sister restaurant offers more ambitious cuisine.
Crescent Moon	174 W Ponce de Leon Ave	404-377-5623	$$	Quirky tapas and romance.
Eurasia Bistro	129 E Ponce de Leon Ave	404-687-8822	$$$	Seafood-centric Asian cuisine in romantic setting.
Johnny's New York Pizza	340 Church St	404-373-8511	$	Respected pizza chain knows its pies.
Moe's Southwest Grill	1524 Church St	404-373-0675	$	Perpetually perky Fresh-Mex chain.
Noodle	205 E Ponce de Leon Ave	404-378-8622	$	Asian cuisines unite for cheap, tasty meal.
Our Way Café	2831 E College Ave	404-292-9356	$	Simple, delectable café fare.
Raging Burrito	141 Sycamore St	404-377-3311	$	California-inspired burrito joint with great patio space.
Sage on Sycamore	121 Sycamore Sq	404-373-5574	$$	Casual bistro setting on the Decatur Square.
Zocalo	123 E Court Sq	404-270-9450	$$	Authentic Mexican draws in family-friendly crowd.

Map 31 • Edgewood / Candler Park

Ann's Snack Bar	1615 Memorial Dr SE	404-687-9207	$	Order a ghetto burger, and mind your manners.
Cold Cream	1645 McLendon Ave NE	404-378-8500	$	Funky ice cream parlor with gourmet coffee and tea.
Fellini's Pizza	1634 Mclendon Ave NE	404-687-9190	$	Pizza on the patio: a simple Atlanta pleasure.
Flying Biscuit Café	1655 McLendon Ave NE	404-687-8888	$	Breakfast all day, vegan-friendly. Original location.
Gato Bizco Café	1660 McLendon Ave NE	404-371-0889	$	Diner with Latin influences.
Radial	1530 DeKalb Ave NE	404-659-6594	$	Hip breakfast joint. Expect long lines on weekends.

Map 32 • Kirkwood

| Billy Goat's Cantina | 653 E Lake Dr | 404-687-0007 | $ | Fresh Mexican fare with strong margaritas. |
| Sweet Devil Moon | 350 Mead Rd | 404-371-3999 | $$ | Tapas with an edge. |

Map 33 • East Lake

Oz Pizza	309 E College Ave	404-373-0110	$	Best pizza in Decatur.
Subway	2889 Memorial Dr SE	404-377-2663	$	Jared is annoying, but their sandwiches are ok.
Wing Factory	307 E College Ave	404-378-2515	$	Wings, wings, and more wings.

Map 34 • East Atlanta

East Atlanta Thai & Sushi	467 Flat Shoals Ave SE	404-522-5992	$$	Below-average Thai and sushi.
Heaping Bowl and Brew	469 Flat Shoals Ave SE	404-523-8030	$	Create your own bowl of goodness.
Iris	1314 Glenwood Ave	404-221-1300	$$$	Bistro with cult following.
Pastificio Cameli	1263 Glenwood Ave SE	404-622-9926	$	Vegetarians rule at this no-meat café.
Zesto	1181 E Confederate Ave SE	404-622-4254	$	Real fast food, retro style.

Map 35 • Sandy Springs (North)

Atlanta Bread Company	220 Sandy Springs Cir NE	404-843-0040	$	The A.B.C. special is one kickass sandwich.
Minado	6690 Roswell Rd NE	404-459-0040	$$	Supersized sushi buffet. Surprisingly good quality.
Savories Bistro	206 Johnson Ferry Rd NE	404-389-0333	$	Over 125 different kinds of cream pies!

Map 36 • West Dunwoody

Atlanta Bread Company	1155 Mt Vernon Hwy	770-392-1944	$	The A.B.C. special is one kickass sandwich.
The Cheesecake Factory	4400 Ashford Dunwoody Rd	678-320-0201	$$$	Who knew expensive could be so popular?
Corner Bakery Café	4400 Ashford Dunwoody Rd	770-804-8233	$	Gourmet breakfast and lunch hotspot.
Eatzi's	4504 Ashford Dunwoody Rd	678-634-0000	$$	Gourmet-to-go chain.
Farmhouse Tea Shoppe	5455 Chamblee Dunwoody Rd	770-673-0099	$$	Sip tea and nibble crumpets.
Fire of Brazil	118 Perimeter Ctr W	770-551-4367	$$$$	Gauchos and a gazillion cuts of meat.
Houston's	4701 Ashford Dunwoody Rd	770-512-7066	$$$	Fancy dining for dummies.
Moe's Southwest Grill	5562 Chamblee	678-320-0360	$	Perpetually perky Fresh-Mex chain.

Map 37 · East Dunwoody

Chopsticks	4639 N Shallowford Rd	770-458-3373	$$	Familiar and fine Chinese cuisine.
Garcia's Mexican Restaurant	4515 Chamblee Dunwoody Rd	770-458-6122	$	Go South of the Border in the strip mall.
Goldberg's Bagel Company	4520 Chamblee Dunwoody Rd	770-455-1119	$	The only real NYC bagel you'll find down South.
Hot Dogs Etc	4639 N Shallowford Rd	770-452-0456	$	Weiners and other unidentifiable meats.
Milano Pizza & Subs	4498 Chamblee Dunwoody Rd	770-451-3200	$	Italian-style fast food.
Moe's Southwest Grill	4401 N Shallowford Rd	770-645-5535	$	Perpetually perky Fresh-Mex chain.
Santi Thai Restaurant	4639 N Shallowford Rd	770-234-9954	$$	Thai hits the suburban strip mall.

Map 38 · Vinings

Café the Pointe	5660 New Northside Dr NW	770-951-5553	$	Popular with the perimeter office park crowd.
Chevy's	5565 New Northside Dr NW	770-952-3241	$$	Fresh Mex just inside the perimeter.
Get Away Café	1600 Riveredge Pkwy NW	770-690-2200	$	Get away from work and have a bite to eat!
Olives Waterside	6450 Powers Ferry Rd NW	770-226-0201	$$	Where singles mingle along the river.
Ray's on the River	6700 Powers Ferry Rd NW	770-955-1187	$$$	Food is overpriced, but what a view!
Riveredge Café	1500 Riveredge Pkwy NW	770-690-2200	$	Vittles for the office park masses.
Sushi-Huku	6300 Powers Ferry Rd NW	770-956-9559	$$$	Regarded as among the best for sushi.

Map 39 · Northside

Powers Ferry East Café	6151 Powers Ferry Rd NW	770-951-2555	$	Keeps the cubicle slaves fed.

Map 40 · Sandy Springs (South)

Fragile	6010 Sandy Springs Cir NE			
Moe's Southwest Grill	860 Johnson Ferry Rd	404-303-0081	$	Perpetually perky Fresh-Mex chain.
RiceSticks	5920 Roswell Rd NE	404-252-6337	$$	Upscale Vietnamese Cuisine in strip-mall locale.

Map 41 · North Atlanta West

Caffe Christina	4000 Summit Blvd	678-686-4277	$$	High-end takeout for the Villa Christina jet-set.

Map 42 · North Atlanta East / Silver Lake

Athens Pizza House	5550 Peachtree Industrial Blvd	770-452-8282	$	Greek-owned pizza chain features good pizza, awesome Greek salads.
Oriental Pearl	5399 New Peachtree Rd	770-986-9866	$	Dim sum divinity.
Salsa con Sabor	5567 Peachtree Industrial Blvd	770-455-6727	$	Puerto Rican and Peruvian cuisine share the spotlight.

Map 43 · Chamblee / Doraville

88 Tofu House	5490 Buford Hwy NE	770-457-8811	$	Spicy tofu stews, Korean BBQ 24/7 in no-frills space.
Bien Thuy	5095 Buford Hwy NE	770-454-9046	$	Quirky Vietnamese veteran remains an Atlanta favorite.
El Azteca	5800 Buford Hwy NE	770-452-7192	$	Mediocre Mexican chain. Mean margaritas and patio dining are main draw.
El Taco Veloz	5000 Buford Hwy	770-454-9964	$	Bare bones taqueria chain.
First China	5295 Buford Hwy	770-457-6788	$$	Huge menu with both Americanized and authentic Chinese selections.
Hae Woon Dae	5805 Buford Hwy NE	770-458-6999	$$$	Korean BBQ at its finest.
Harmony Vegetarian	4897 Buford Hwy NE	770-457-7288	$	Stick with the real veggies at this ethnic vegetarian restaurant.
Little Szechuan	5091 Buford Hwy	770-451-0192	$$	Among the best Chinese restaurants in Georgia. Be adventurous here.
Pho Hoa	5150 Buford Hwy	770-455-8729	$	Huge bowls of pho for next to nothing.
Phung Mie	5145 Buford Hwy NE	770-455-0435	$$	Family-friendly authentic Chinese restaurant.
Toyo Ta Ya	5082 Buford Hwy	770-986-0828	$	Atlanta sushi veteran. All-you-can-eat sushi buffet.

Arts & Entertainment · **Restaurants**

Map 44 · Adair Park

Yag's Soul Food	1219 Metropolitan Pkwy SW	404-755-7212	$	Soul food in the 'hood.

Map 45 · Pittsburgh

Brook's Family Restaurant	309 University Ave SW	404-752-7171	$	Simply down-home cookin'.
Oceanfront	355 University Ave SW	404-758-3560	$	Seafood shack in the heart of the 'hood.

Map 46 · Peoplestown

El Potosino Restaurant	500 McDonough Blvd SE	404-622-0058	$	Mexican grub in the barrio.
Harold's Barbecue	171 McDonough Blvd SE	404-627-9268	$	Kick-ass barbecue in a bad ass area of Atlanta.

Map 47 · Ormewood Park

Cinco de Mayo	1332 Boulevard SE	404-624-0210	$$	Celebrating Mexican culture every day.
Mrs Winner's Chicken & Biscuits	590 McDonough Blvd SE	404-622-5517	$	The best of both artery-clogging worlds.

Map 48 · East Point

Chester Fried Chicken	2091 Headland Dr	404-768-9729	$	Crispy, greasy delight.
Family Griddle	1722 Campbellton Rd SW	404-756-6800	$	Kind of like Waffle House, but less known.
Ida's Country Kitchen	1821 Delowe Dr SW	404-758-4236	$	Ida knows a thing or two about cooking.
Keur Khadim African Restaurant	2105 Campbellton Rd SW	404-758-4833	$	A whole other kind of soul food.
Philly & Wings	2062 Headland Dr	404-767-4044	$	When only one artery-clogging food just won't do.

Map 49 · Sylvan Hills

Afro Dish	1919 Metropolitan Pkwy SW	404-761-0047	$	Serving up soul food on seedy Metropolitan.
Caribbean Experience Restaurant	1747 Metropolitan Pkwy SW	404-756-0107	$	Hey mon! Oxtails and conch fritters!
Hot Spicy Fast Food	1780 Metropolitan Pkwy SW	404-524-6063	$	The food tastes as original as the restaurant's name

Map 50 · College Park

The Brake Pad	3403 Main St	404-766-1515	$	Former gas station turned hip casual eats destination.
Kosmos	3383 Main St	404-766-3788	$$	Low-key neighborhood bistro.
Liz and Lee's Live	1613 White Way St	404-767-1188	$	Everything is fried and served with a side of blues.
Matilda Bean	1603 White Way St	404-762-5136	$	Burrito joint named after a pet Chihuahua.
Oscar's	3725 Main St	404-766-9688	$$$	Upscale American cuisine in unlikely location.
Patio Daddy-O	2714 East Point St	404-767-6764	$	Vegetarian-friendly barbeque with tasty sides.

Map 51 · Hapeville

623	623 N Central Ave	404-768-5559	$$	As ritzy as it gets in Hapeville.

You know a city has reached retail sophistication when a day spa just for men opens. Atlanta metrosexuals looking for a facial, body waxing, or a jar of face mud can head to **Joq** in Buckhead. Shopping is a full-time hobby for many in Atlanta and the options are endless, from country flea markets, to high-end boutiques, to quirky antique shops, and ethnic supermarkets.

It's all spread out, so take the car because you will be driving great distances and filling the trunk. There are lots of bargains to be found and the sales tax is lower than most other shopping destinations like Los Angeles or New York City. For gifts your mother would not approve of, **Junkman's Daughter** cannot be beat; whips, go-go boots, and ahem, "smoking accessories" can all be found at this Little Five Points icon.

For sports fans, **Distant Replays** in Buckhead offers really cool vintage jerseys, jackets, and other memorabilia. For retro toys and hilarious gag gifts, check out the selection at **Outwrite Bookstore and Coffeehouse**. Since this is a gay bookstore, fabulous items featuring scantily clad hunks are also available. And the only convenience store that we found in Atlanta that sells 40 oz malt liquor, lottery tickets, and fine wine is the **Midtown Food Mart**.

Shopping Districts

Miami Circle Design District (Map 25) is antique shopping headquarters, though don't overlook their custom-designed home furnishing offerings. For antiques and quirky boutiques, the Virginia Highland (Map 7) neighborhood is a good destination. Expect to pay top dollar in Buckhead (Map 22) with their concentration of high-end boutiques. For all things outside of America's border, head to Buford Highway (Map 23), where Latino/a and Asian grocery and variety stores are as plentiful as gas stations—but much more exciting. Even if you are not an adventurous foodie, this area is also great for antique bargains. Little Five Points and the Cheshire Bridge Road area (Map 26) can take care of all of your naughty needs, such as tattoos, body piercings, dominatrix gear, XXX videos, and hand-blown glass pipes.

Malls

A good starting place is Lenox Square Mall in Buckhead (Map 22). It's nothing special, but offers a decent mix of higher-end and mid-priced department stores, along with home furnishing chains like **Crate & Barrel** and **Pottery Barn**. The **Apple Store** is where geeks drool over the latest gadgets. Skip the ho-hum food court

and head to **Brasserie le Coze** for some excellent French cuisine. If you really have money to burn, head across the street to Phipps Plaza (Map 22). Here you will find even higher-end stores, designer boutiques, and a movie theatre. Twist and The Tavern at Phipps are good dining/drinking choices for the single, ultra-cool set in between pricey shopping sprees. Underground Atlanta is the place to go for cheap souvenirs and other junk with the word "Atlanta" emblazoned on it—perfect for all of those out-of-state relatives that you have to buy a gift for. Walk (Map 6) is a brightly colored in-town version of a mini-mall that includes **Shoemaker's Warehouse**, where you can find the hippest shoes at the lowest prices, **Cook's Warehouse** for the latest kitchen gadgetry and cooking classes, and **Gado Gado**, for all of your Indonesian home furnishing needs. Ansley Mall (Map 3) is where the gay consumers of Midtown gather, to sip skinny lattes at Starbucks and then flex their abs at L.A. Fitness. The **Publix** supermarket at Ansley has won local awards as one of Atlanta's best cruising spots for gay men.

Gourmet Food and Wine

The Barrelman specializes in unique, limited barrel vintages and each selection on the shelf is hand-picked by proprietor Kenneth Green. It's just about impossible to pick a bad wine at this store and with their bread, gourmet cheese, and meat selections, you can acquire the ingredients for a nice romantic meal in one stop. **Star Provisions**, the gourmet store attached to the divine upscale restaurant, **Bacchanalia**, is a gourmand's dream come true. Here you can find the finest deli selections, cheeses, breads, and desserts, along with wine, and high-end kitchen appliances.

Wine Gallery+Market is a new wine store located near the old Lindbergh Plaza in Buckhead. They offer an extensive wine selection, along with wine accessories, gourmet food, and a deli. The staff is friendly and laid-back but they know their wine. **Eatzi's** is a national chain, but their prepared gourmet offerings are such a hit with Atlantans that a second location has opened in the Dunwoody area. **World Market**, another national chain, offers unique international food selections, candy, and desserts from around the world, and a very nice, reasonably priced wine selection.

Sherlock's Wine Merchants, with four metro Atlanta locations, offers an excellent selection of wines in all price ranges, and they employ a staff that is well-educated in the store's inventory. **Ansley Wine Merchants** offers a great value-priced selection of wines, and the store supplies witty commentary tags to many of their favorites, which are always amusing

to read. **Ali-Oli** offers a small gourmet store attached to their upscale Mediterranean restaurant, with to-go selections from the restaurant kitchen, along with gourmet sauces and wines. **D'Vine Wine Bar and Shop** (near the Perimeter area) offers a good wine selection, as well as wine tastings and light menu.

Healthy eaters need not despair as Atlanta has several natural food stores, including **Sevananda**, a co-op in Little Five Points, **Return to Eden** in the Cheshire Bridge area, **Unity Natural Foods** in Buckhead, and the national chain **Whole Foods**, which is packed to the gills after work and on weekends.

Clothing

For high end department stores, Lenox Square Mall (Map 22) offers **Macy's**, **Bloomie's**, and **Neiman Marcus**. Phipps Plaza (Map 22) offers **Parisian** and **Saks Fifth Avenue**, and a Nordstrom is on the horizon. But boutique shopping is where it's at, both trend-wise and value-wise in Atlanta. Find retro fashion bargains at one of the many vintage clothing consignment shops in town like **Psycho Sisters** or **Stefan's Vintage Clothing**. A new boutique seems to pop up almost daily, but some good ones to keep on your shopping radar include **Bella Azul** in West Midtown, **Blue Genes** at Around Lenox, **Ego Denim** in Emory Village, **Sage Clothing** in Buckhead, and **Luxe** in Miami Circle.

Find hip kids' clothes at **The Owl and the Pussycat**, which has two Atlanta locations. Sports fans flock to **Distant Replays** in Buckhead for authentic and replica vintage jerseys of national and local sports teams. Shoe fanatics march straight to **Shoemaker's Warehouse** for bargains on the latest shoe fashions, where salespeople avoid tailing you around the store. **Abbadabba's** is the place to go for Doc Martens, Birkenstocks, and any other cool shoes that you can think of. For men's shoes and shoe repairs, the dependable **Bennie's Shoes** has been serving the community for decades. Eclectic and new age jewelry can be found at **Soul Kiss Jewelry** in the heart of Little Five Points.

Pet Supplies

Atlantans love their animals so pet supply stores are bountiful. **Highland Pet Supply** offers a good selection of healthy diets for your pets, in addition to some nifty toys and accessories. They also have a convenient self-serve bathing station. **Pet Supplies Plus** is a no-frills pet supermarket that offers a discount card that comes in handy for multi-pet households. **The Pet Set** offers boarding services in addition to food and supplies. The **Posh Pup** in Decatur can serve all of your designer pet needs. **Pet Fancy** at Lenox Square Mall is a tiny shop where you can spend way too much on your furry friends with their selection of designer toys and pet-lover merchandise. **Canine Showcase & Wild Bird** moved to the Cheshire Bridge area, but still provides natural food diets for a variety of animals and some really cool toys and accessories.

Antiques

Maybe it's a Southern thing, but Atlantans love their antique stores. There seems to be one on almost every corner, and they make a great way to spend a lazy Saturday afternoon. The Miami Circle Design District (Map 25), with over 80 stores, offers a great selection of European antiques. **Paris on Ponce** is a treasure-digger's paradise, with several winding rooms chock full of vintage items. The **Lakewood Antiques Market** is open for business the second weekend of each month and, with over 1,500 dealers, is referred to as "America's biggest treasure hunt." The Virginia Highland neighborhood offers a good selection of 20th-century antiques and folk art, along with woodworking tools at **Highland Hardware**. The Cheshire Bridge area has a mini-row of antique shops, including **Cherub's Attic**. Chamblee's Antique Row (Map 42) has been around since 1979 and offers over 20,000 square feet of antique shopping. If you can't find it here, it probably doesn't exist.

Music

Criminal Records in Little Five Points is Atlanta's best independent music store. For sheer volume, a nice local section, and a great used section, **Tower Records** near Disco Kroger in Buckhead is hard to beat. They've added a coffee bar/ice cream stand and a little makeshift living room area so you can make yourself at home while listening to the latest music. **Corner Compact Disc** in Virginia Highland has a knowledgeable and friendly staff on hand to track down that obscure album for you. **Wax N Facts** and **Fantasyland Records** are cool indie music shops as well. For hard-to-find and treasured jazz, rock, and blues albums, visit **Wuxtry** for its unbelievable collection and super-knowledgeable staff.

Map 1 • Underwood Hills / Blandtown

Sam Flax Art & Design Store	1460 Northside Dr	404-352-7200	Art supply store.

Map 2 • Collier Hills / Brookwood Hills

Andrew: Men Women Home	1545 Peachtree St	404-607-1747	High-end boutique with European designer focus.
Baby Cakes	1833 Peachtree Rd NE	404-367-8772	Children's clothing, bedding, furniture, and gifts.
Joq	1545 Peachtree St NE	404-892-7771	Where metrosexuals get manicures and massages.
Standard	1841 Peachtree Rd	404-355-1410	Upscale sportswear for men.
Swoozies	1745 Peachtree St	404-888-0115	For all of your printing and paper goods. Fun gift selection.

Map 3 • Ansley Park / Piedmont Heights

Ansley Mall	1544 Piedmont Ave NE	N/A	Where gay men go to shop.
Ansley Wine Merchants	1544 Piedmont Ave NE	404-876-6790	Decidedly unstuffy wine shop.
Antique Collections	1586 Piedmont Ave NE	404-876-0075	Treasure hunters paradise.
Atlanta Costume	2089 Monroe Dr	404-874-7511	Huge inventory of costumes. Used by local theatres companies.
Bookears	1579 Monroe Dr	404-815-7475	Thousands of audio titles, perfect for the long Atlanta commute.
The Boy Next Door	1447 Piedmont Ave NE	404-873-2664	Specializes in men's swimwear. Sizeable gay clientele.
Classic Comics	1860 Piedmont Ave NE	404-892-4442	Comic book collectors dream come true.
Domus	1919 Piedmont Rd NE	404-872-1050	European furniture and accessories.

Map 4 • West Midtown / Home Park

Bella Azul	1011-B Marietta St	404-249-9150	Boutique owned by wife of former Falcons player Bob Whitfield.
Sprout	1198 Howell Mill Rd NW	404-352-0864	Where tykes with cool parents shop.
Star Provisions	1198 Howell Mill Rd NW	404-365-0410	As gourmet as you can get for take-out shop.

Map 5 • Georgia Tech / Arts Center

The Barrelman	800 Peachtree St	404-685-3191	Eno's wine shop, all hand-picked selections.
The Bath Experience	900 Peachtree St	404-872-2525	Luxurious bath soaps, beauty products, and candles.
Directions	915 Peachtree St	404-870-2133	Really cool furniture for your ultra hip pad.
Earwax Records	565 Spring St	404-875-5600	Meets all your vinyl needs.
fab'rik	1114 W Peachtree St	404-881-8223	Affordable, friendly clothing and accessories boutique.
French Kiss	900 Peachtree St	404-815-8727	Boutique with focus on more daring, provocative clothing.
Inserection	1023 W Peachtree St	404-815-9622	X-rated and proud.
Lui-B	1116 W Peachtree St	404-810-0031	Men's custom shirt shop for those fashion-conscious metrosexuals.
Mac's Beer & Wine	21 Peachtree Pl NW	404-872-4897	Also have a decent selection of liquor. Discount on cash purchases.
Universal Gear	935 Peachtree St	404-872-5700	Mid-priced casual trendy wear for men.

Map 6 • Midtown

Cook's Warehouse	549-I Amsterdam Ave NE	404-815-4993	Cooking gadgets, gizmos, and classes.
Gado Gado	549 Amsterdam Ave NE	404-885-1818	Indonesian furniture and accessories.
Intown Bicycles	1035 Monroe Dr NE	404-872-1735	Bicycles, repairs, accessories.
Midtown Food Mart	225 10th St NE	404-685-8372	Convenience store with good wine selection. No, really.
Outwrite Bookstore and Coffeehouse	991 Piedmont Ave NE	404-607-0082	Gay/lesbian bookstore, gift shop, hangout.
Shoemaker's Warehouse	500 Amsterdam Ave NE	404-881-9301	Designer shoes galore without the sales pitch hassle.
Skate Escape	1086 Piedmont Ave NE	404-892-1292	Rental skate shop across the street from Piedmont Park.
Worthmore Jewelers	500 Amsterdam Ave NE	404-892-8294	Part of inventory comes straight from designers.

Map 7 • Virginia Highland

Belly General Store	772 N Highland Ave NE	404-872-1003	Eclectic meats, cheeses, candies, and gifts.
Bill Hallman Boutique	792 N Highland Ave NE	404-876-6055	Latest trends from Atlanta sweetheart.
Bill Hallman Shoes	776 N Highland Ave NE	404-607-1171	Shoes to match.

Arts & Entertainment • **Shopping**

Map 7 • Virginia Highland—*continued*

Dakota J's	1030 N Highland Ave	404-870-0690	Gifts galore in the Highlands.
Gazzelle's	842 N Highland Ave NE	404-875-4999	Plus-sized designer wear.
Highland Hardware	1045 N Highland Ave NE	404-872-4466	Handmade tools for specialty woodworking projects.
Home Concepts	729 Ponce de Leon Pl	404-885-1505	Discount furniture. Great futon selection.
Java Vino	579 N Highland Ave	404-577-8673	Coffee and wine. The best of both worlds.
Metropolitan Deluxe	1034 N Highland Ave NE	404-892-9337	Eclectic and trendy gift items.
Movies Worth Seeing	1409 N Highland Ave NE	404-892-1802	Where film snobs go to rent movies.
The Owl and the Pussycat	996 Virginia Ave	404-873-3460	Casual, hip kids' clothing, toys, shoes, accessories.
Paris on Ponce	716 Ponce de Leon Pl	404-249-9965	Sprawling antiques store that can take an afternoon to browse.
Planetarian Ornaments	784 N Highland Ave NE	404-607-7694	Exotic accessories, home furnishings, and clothing.
Ten Thousand Villages	1056 St Charles Ave	404-892-5307	Unique non-profit store showcases third-world artists.

Map 9 • Downtown / Centennial Place / Techwood

Americasmart Atlanta	240 Peachtree St NE	404-220-3000	Giant wholesaler complex.
Estee's Children Shop	65 Peachtree St NE	404-688-7779	For hip-hop babies and kids.
The Executive Shop	56 Walton St	404-577-2898	Dapper hats and sleek boots for men.

Map 10 • Downtown / Sweet Auburn

Bella Cucina Artful Food	493 Peachtree St	404-881-0078	Gourmet food sauce company headquarters.

Map 11 • Inman Park / Cabbagetown / Little Five Points

A Cappella Books	1133 Euclid Ave	404-681-5128	Haven for rare, underground, and gay and lesbian books.
Abbadabba's	421 Moreland Ave	404-588-9577	Satisfy your shoe fetish.
Cherry Bomb	1129-A Euclid Ave	404-522-2662	Men's streetwear headquarters.
The Clothing Warehouse	420 Moreland Ave	404-524-5070	Vintage clothing from the 1940's-1980's.
Criminal Records	466 Moreland Ave NE	404-215-9511	Indie record mecca. Local artists promoted nicely.
Crystal Blue	1168 Euclid Ave	404-522-4605	Cool jewelry and of course, crystals.
Envy	1143 Euclid Ave NE	404-525-3689	High-end hodgepodge of local and international fashions.
Identified Flying Objects	1164 Euclid Ave NE	404-524-4628	For all of your high flying needs.
Junkman's Daughter	464 Moreland Ave NE	404-577-3188	Coolest junk shop ever.
Lucky Devil	1158 Euclid Ave NE	404-681-5825	Goth, fetish, and other clothes mom wouldn't approve of.
Psycho Sisters Consignment Shop	428 Moreland Ave	404-523-0100	Like a really cool yard sale.
Rene Rene	1142 Euclid Ave NE	404-522-7363	Owner designs everything in boutique.
Sevananda	467 Moreland Ave SE	404-681-2831	One of the largest natural food cooperatives in the Southeastern US.
Soul Kiss	1154 Euclid Ave NE	404-525-9668	Designer watches, exotic jewelry, and body art.
Stefan's Vintage Clothing	1160 Euclid Ave NE	404-688-4929	Vintage clothing from the 1900's-1960s.
Stratosphere Skateboards	1168 Euclid Ave NE	404-521-3510	Their boards are out of this world.
Tease	1166 Euclid Ave NE	404-584-0220	Where flirts find trends.
Wax N Facts	432 Moreland Ave NE	404-525-2275	Record store with excellent jazz selection.
Wish	447 Moreland Ave	404-880-0402	Streetwear mecca.

Map 12 • West End

Shrine of the Black Madonna Cultural Center and Bookstore	946 Ralph David Abernathy Blvd	404-752-6125	African-American artifacts, art and more.
The Mall West End	850 Oak St SW	404-755-1001	Where hip-hoppers shop for their bling bling.

Map 15 • Ormewood Park North / Woodland Hills

Urban Gardner	347 Boulevard SE	404-529-9980	Where green thumbs are cool.

Map 16 • Paces / Northside

Gretchen's Children's Shop	1246 W Paces Ferry Rd	404-237-8020	Atlanta children's clothing store for over half-century.

Map 17 • Northwest Atlanta / Mt Paran

Mt Paran Country Store	4480 Northside Dr NW		Because driving through snobby neighborhoods makes the average Joe thirsty.

Map 19 · West Brookhaven

Cook's Warehouse	4062 Peachtree Rd	404-949-9945	Heaven for aspiring Iron Chefs.
Sherlock's Wine Merchants	4062 Peachtree Rd	404-949-9945	Great wine selection, this location has cooking school attached.

Map 20 · East Brookhaven

Burlington Coat Factory	4166 Buford Hwy NE	404-634-5566	Everyone knows what this is.
Fiddle-dee-dee	1441 Dresden Dr	404-969-3233	Gifts from Southern treats to college memorabilia.

Map 21 · Central Buckhead

Almanac	22 E Andrews Dr NW	404-266-1188	Women's clothing, lingerie in the heart of Buckhead.
Apple Store	3393 Peachtree Rd NE	404-926-3085	Who knew geeky gadgets could be so cool?
Atlanta Beach	3145 Peachtree Rd NE	404-239-0612	Designer swimwear clothing boutique.
BD Jeffries	3736 Roswell Rd	404-231-3004	Great selection of men's gifts.
Binders	3330 Piedmont Rd	404-237-6331	Art supplies and frames.
Blue Genes	3400 Around Lenox Dr	404-231-3400	Designer denim boutique.
Buckhead's Upscale Resale	3655 Roswell Rd	404-262-7783	Atlanta's only all-designer resale boutique.
Buckles	3145 Peachtree Rd NE	404-365-0746	Children's shoe store with European brands.
C'est Moi	3198 Paces Ferry Pl NW	404-467-0095	If it's French, you can find it here.
DR Mercantile	324 E Paces Ferry Rd	404-869-9087	Nostalgic and retro items for the refined crowd.
Distant Replays	324 E Paces Ferry Rd	404-262-7741	Retro sports jerseys and memorabilia for die-hard fans.
Eatzi's	3221 Peachtree Rd NE	404-237-2266	Gourmet-to-go chain.
Fitigues	26 E Andrews Dr	404-467-1119	Casual, comfortable clothing boutique for all ages.
Greenwood Ice Cream Co. Outlet Store	4829 Peachtree Rd	770-455-6166	Atlanta restaurant ice creams made available to the public.
Henri's	61 Irby Ave	404-237-0202	Buckhead bakery since 1929.
Interior Dimensions	3185 Maple Dr NE	404-467-0488	Leather furniture that Fido won't be allowed on.
Joe Muggs Newstand	3275 Peachtree Rd NE	404-364-9290	Primarily newstand, also carry some books.
K-la	3400 Around Lenox Dr	404-848-1414	Brazilian fashion boutique.
Merci Woman	3209 Paces Ferry Pl NW	404-869-9980	Clothing for full-figured women, sizes 14w-24w.
Now & Again	56 E Andrews Dr	404-262-1468	Antique and fine furnishings consignment shop.
Oh! Fine Lingerie	3209 Paces Ferry Pl	404-949-9901	Designer and vintage lingerie and jewelry.
The Owl and the Pussycat	3145 Peachtree Rd NE	404-237-1900	Casual, hip kid's clothing, toys, shoes, accessories.
Patagonia	34 E Andrews Dr	404-266-8182	Environmentally-conscious outdoor wear.
Pearl Paints	3756 Roswell Rd NE	404-233-9400	For the artist in us all.
Pearson's Wine of Atlanta	3072 Early St NW	404-231-8752	Wine, liquor, beer, and cigars for the well-heeled set.
Pink Lemonade	3802 E Roswell Rd	404-846-0841	Only Lily Pulitzer signature store in Atlanta.
Pollen	22 E Andrews Dr	404-262-2296	Fresh flowers, gifts, bath and body products.
Razzle Dazzle	49 Irby Ave NW	404-233-6940	Sportswear, vintage jeans, jewelry.
Sage Clothing	37 W Paces Ferry Rd	404-233-8280	Young hipsters love this affordable boutique with L.A. fashions.
Susan Lee	56 E Andrews Dr	404-365-0693	Buckhead veteran of boutiques.
Topaz Gallery	3145 Peachtree Rd NE	404-995-0155	Custom jewelry design, repair, and restringing.
Tower Records	3232 Peachtree Rd	404-264-1217	Chain music store. Carry offbeat books.
Urban Frontier	3210 Paces Ferry Pl NW	404-240-0960	Eclectic home furnishings, and folk art.
Urban Outfitters	3393 Peachtree Rd NE	404-264-8849	Chain store for cool stuff. Good book selection.
White Dove	18 E Andrews Dr NW	404-814-1994	Very feminine clothing boutique.
World Market	4733 Piedmont Rd NE	404-814-0801	Ethnic food, wine, gifts, and furniture chain.

Map 22 · Lenox

Dick's Sporting Goods	3535 Peachtree Rd	404-267-0200	Sports equipment and recreation gear.
Fem Deluxe	2770 Lenox Rd NE	404-995-0299	Where clubbers shop for their clubwear.
Filene's Basement	3535 Peachtree Rd NE	404-869-4466	Annual bridal sale is legendary; good deals all year long.
Metropolitan Deluxe - Phipps Plaza	3500 Peachtree Rd NE	404-812-39494	Eclectic and trendy gift items.
Signature Boutique	2770 Lenox Rd NE	404-261-7373	Urban culture focused boutique.

Map 23 · Briarcliff / Clairmont

Guitar Center	1485 Northeast Expy NE	404-633-2522	Everything for the guitar music lover and more.
The Pet Set	2480 Briarcliff Rd	404-633-8755	High-end pet boutique, and boarding, grooming facility.
REI	1800 Northeast Expy NE	404-633-6508	Outdoor recreation specialists.
Sam's Club	2901 Clairmont Rd NE	404-325-4000	Buy cases of crap for discount prices!

Map 24 • Peachtree Battle / Woodfield

Bittersweet Ltd	45 Bennett St NW	404-351-6594	Direct importer of British antiques.
City Art Works	2140 Peachtree Rd NW	404-605-0786	The place to find gifts created by local artists.
Interiors Market	55 Bennett St NW	404-352-0055	Multi-store complex for antiques and art.
Jules Burt Gallery	75 Bennett St	404-875-3047	Sells "Sassy Ladies" collection, as seen on *Friends*.
Monkee's	2140 Peachtree Rd	404-351-9050	Luxury shoe boutique.
Nottingham Antiques	45 Bennett St NW	404-352-1890	European antique pine furniture.
Pickles and Ice Cream	2140 Peachtree Rd	404-351-6262	Maternity apparel that manages to be hip.
Precious Soles	2140 Peachtree Rd	404-355-0864	High-end children's shoes and accessories.
Sherlock's Wine Merchants	3401 Northside Pkwy	404-233-1514	Great wine selection with educated, enthusiastic staff.
The Stalls	116 Bennett St NW	404-352-4430	A bunch of antique stores in one.

Map 25 • Garden Hills / Peachtree Heights / Peachtree Hills

Animals	375 Pharr Rd	404-816-5588	Children's clothing boutique. Personalization available.
Architectural Accents	2711 Piedmont Rd NE	404-266-8700	High-end antiques.
Bennie's Shoes	2581 Piedmont Rd	404-262-1966	Discount designer men's shoe store. On-site repair.
Beverly Hall Furniture Gallery	2789 Piedmont Rd NE	404-261-7580	Staff are professional interior designers.
Books & Cases & Prints Etc	800 Miami Cir NE	404-231-9107	Antique books and prints.
Fantasyland Records	2839 Peachtree Rd NE	404-237-3193	Used CDs in a wide variety of genres.
Highlighters	690 Miami Cir NE	404-264-1599	Funky, modern lamps and light fixtures.
Just the Thing!	529 Pharr Rd NE	404-869-4100	Jewelry, handbags, accessories, and gifts.
Luxe	764 Miami Cir NE	404-869-2493	Top-notch designer wear at 30-80% off retail.
Oxford Comics and Books	2855 Piedmont Rd NE	404-233-8682	Comic books, figurines, TV and B-movie memorabilia.
Pet Pearls	2819 Peachtree Rd	404-906-3000	For the ritzy Rover and the fashonista Fluffy.
Richard's Variety Store	2347 Peachtree Rd NE	404-237-1412	Retro five-and-dime with lots of cool junk.
Spin Street Music	2327 Peachtree Rd NE	404-261-4999	Indie music store with a nifty jukebox.
Unity Natural Foods	2955 Peachtree Rd NE	404-261-8776	Everything from vegan food to vitamins.

Map 26 • Morningside / Lenox Hills

A Flea Antique II	1853 Cheshire Bridge Rd	404-872-4342	Antiques galore.
Canine Showcase & Wild Bird	2036 Manchester St NE	404-875-0611	All-natural pet food, and high-end pet accessories.
Cherub's Attic	2179 Cheshire Bridge Rd	404-634-4577	Antiques at discount prices.
Fickle Manor	1402-4 N Highland Ave	404-541-0960	Colorful, laid back boutique where Va-Hi moms shop.
Happy Herman's	2299 Cheshire Bridge Rd	404-321-3012	Gourmet grocery store.
Milou's Market	1927 Cheshire Bridge Rd	404-892-8296	Antiques and decorative accessories.
Quality Kosher Emporium	2153 Briarcliff Rd	404-636-1114	If you're Jewish, you better shop here.
Return to Eden	2335 Cheshire Bridge Rd	404-320-3336	Health food nut heaven.

Map 27 • Toco Hills / Emory University

Book Nook	3073 N Druid Hills Rd	404-633-1328	New and used books, CD's, videos; excellent comic book selection.
Pike's Nursery	2101 LaVista Rd NE	404-634-8604	Plants and green thumb stuff.

Map 28 • Druid Hills West

Ego	1581 N Decatur Rd NE	404-370-1667	Local designers featured at this denim and T-shirt boutique.
Shield's Market	1554 N Decatur Rd NE	404-377-0204	Aged-beef specialists.

Map 29 • North Decatur / Druid Hills East

The 17 Steps	235 Ponce de Leon Pl	404-377-7564	Wide selection of unique specialty gifts.
Boogaloos	246 W Ponce de Leon Ave	404-373-3237	Designer brands, leather handbags, and cool T-shirts.
Sole	419 W Ponce de Leon Ave	404-377-9006	Brillant shoe shop.
Wuxtry Records	2096 N Decatur Rd NE	404-329-0020	Best selection of rare vinyl in Atlanta.

Map 30 • Decatur

Domestic Instincts	416 Church St	404-377-9188	Former furniture store now offers more homey gifts.
Kudzu Antiques	2874 E Ponce de Leon Ave	404-373-6498	20,000 square feet of antique shopping.

The Posh Pup	419 Church St	404-378-5881	Luxury pet supply store.
Rue de Leon	131 E Ponce de Leon Ave	404-373-6200	Gifts from the French wine country.
Square Roots	117 E Court Sq	404-371-9900	Regional folk art and gifts.
Squash Blossom	427 Church St	404-373-1864	Down-to-earth clothing for today's busy woman.

Map 31 • Edgewood / Candler Park

Frock of Ages	1653 McLendon Ave	404-370-1006	Hats and all of their accessories.
Kelly's Closet	1649 McLendon Ave NE	404-377-9923	One-of-a-kind dresses.

Map 34 • East Atlanta

Earthshaking Music	543 Stokewood Ave SE	404-577-0707	Instruments of all sizes and kinds.
The Dressing Room	504 Flat Shoals Ave SE	404-584-2200	Retro clothes, purses, shoes.
Traders	485 Flat Shoals Ave SE	404-522-3006	Where hipsters furnish their houses.

Map 35 • Sandy Springs (North)

Bell Carpet Galleries	6223 Roswell Rd NE	404-255-2431	High-end floor covering central.
Chocolate Soup	6681 Roswell Rd NE	404-303-9047	Infants and children's designer wear up to 50% off.
Fragile	6010 Sandy Springs Cir NE	404-257-1323	Glassware everywhere!
the petite place	6309 Roswell Rd NE	404-252-1223	Little women only clothing boutique.
The Scarlet Tassel	6235 Roswell Rd NE	404-843-0387	Unique gifts and home accessories.
Smoke 911	6124 Roswell Rd NE	404-256-1116	For all of your smoking needs.

Map 36 • West Dunwoody

Best Buy	1201 Hammond Dr NE	770-392-0454	Wall to wall electronics.
Chickenlips	5484 Chamblee Dunwoody Rd	770-395-1234	Toys, furniture, and children's designer clothes.
D'Vine Wine Bar and Shop	5486 Chamblee Dunwoody Rd	770-350-9463	Good wine selection, handy vino accessories.
Eatzi's	4504 Ashford Dunwoody Rd NE	678-634-0000	Gourmet-to-go chain.
World Market	4733 Ashford Dunwoody Rd	678-731-0014	Ethnic food, wine, gifts, and furniture chain.

Map 37 • East Dunwoody

Pet Supermarket	4498 Chamblee Dunwoody Rd	770-234-9905	Spoil your furry friends without breaking the bank.

Map 40 • Sandy Springs (South)

Fragile	6010 Sandy Springs Cir NE	404-257-1323	Glassware everywhere!
Sunlighting Lamp and Shade Center	4990 Roswell Rd NE	404-257-0043	This place will light up your life, or at least your room.

Map 42 • North Atlanta East / Silver Lake

Great Estates Antiques and Auctions	5180 Peachtree Industrial Blvd	770-457-8454	Direct importers of European antiques.
International Farmers Market	5193 Peachtree Industrial Blvd	770-455-1777	Indoor market where immigrants shop for authentic ingredients.
Wallbedzzz	3838 Green Industrial Wy	404-892-5523	Hide-a-bed madness.

Map 47 • Ormewood Park

Charlie's Trading Post	648 McDonough Blvd SE	404-627-4242	Buy an ex-con's jeans and work boots.

Map 48 • East Point

Carpet Mill Outlet	2084 Headland Dr	404-763-0776	Wall-to-wall carpets.

Map 50 • College Park

East Point Antiques	1595 White Wy	404-767-5170	Treasure hunters flock to this antiques outpost.

The **Fox Theatre** is the pride of Atlanta. This historic performing arts center (and the city's oldest movie theater) gained landmark status when it hosted the 1939 world premier of *Gone With the Wind*. The movie's cast and crew stayed across the street at the Georgian Terrace. Although the Fox has faced threats of demolition, Atlanta citizens won't let the gilded structure go, and the devoted have stepped in to save the Fox many times. Today, the theater hosts concerts and theater productions, including traveling Broadway shows.

7 Stages has been offering up solid productions for over 25 years and is considered the center for contemporary theater in Atlanta. Perhaps you'll find your Romeo at the **Tavern,** where performers produce traditional Shakespeare plays accompanied by an authentic British pub menu and a broad selection of Irish ales and tasty brews.

Peachtree Battle, a comedy about a dysfunctional Buckhead family, is the longest-running play in Atlanta's history. Be sure to catch it at the **Ansley Park Playhouse** but book early—tickets generally sell out up to six weeks in advance. For avant-garde/improv, swing over to **Dad's Garage** or the **Whole World Theater**. Local publication *Creative Loafing* also hosts monthly town hall discussions at the Garage.

Same-day, half-price tickets to all theater, music, and dance performances can be purchased through **AtlanTIX**. At their booths, located at the corner of Upper Alabama and Pryor Streets and at Lenox Square in the Southeast, bargain-hunters can purchase discounted tickets to performances scheduled for that evening if they're not sold out. AtlanTIX accepts cash, credit cards, traveler's checks, and gift certificates. The ticket booths are open Tuesday though Saturday from 11 am to 6 pm, and on Sunday from noon to 4 pm.

Theaters

Theaters	Address	Phone	Map
14th Street Playhouse	173 14th St	404-733-4750	6
7 Stages Theatre	1105 Euclid Ave	404-523-7647	11
Alliance Theatre	1280 Peachtree St NE	404-733-5000	5
Ansley Park Playhouse	1545 Peachtree St	404-875-1193	2
Center for Puppetry Arts	1404 Spring St	404-873-3391	2
Dad's Garage Theatre	280 Elizabeth St	404-523-3141	11
Fox Theatre	660 Peachtree St NE	404-881-2100	5
Horizon Theater Company	1083 Austin Ave NE	404-584-7450	11
Michael C Carlos Museum	571 S Kilgo Cir NE	404-727-5050	28
Peachtree Playhouse	878 Peachtree St	404-875-1193	5
PushPush Theater	121 New St	404-377-6332	30
Rialto Center	80 Forsyth St NW	404-651-1234	9
Stage Door Players (North Dekalb Cultural Arts Center)	5339 Chamblee Dunwoody Rd	770-396-1726	36
Symphony Hall Atlanta	1280 Peachtree St NE	404-733-5000	5
The New American Shakespeare Tavern	499 Peachtree St NE	404-874-5299	10
Variety Playhouse	1099 Euclid Ave	404-524-7354	19
Whole World Theatre	1214 Spring St	404-817-0880	5

- ☐ Orchestra
- ☐ Box Seats
- ☐ Back Seats

General Information

Address: 2000 Lakewood Ave
Atlanta, GA 30315
Phone: 404-443-5090
Websites: www.hob.com/venues/concerts/
hifibuys
Ticketmaster: 404-249-6400; www.ticketmaster.com

Overview

What screams "It's summer!" louder than an outdoor concert at a massive 20,000-seat amphitheater? With the likes of Tim McGraw, Dave Matthews, and Britney Spears gracing the stage, the HIFI Buys Amphitheatre continues to draw A-list mainstream rockers and their hordes of fans during the summer months.

You can either pay a lot of money to sit in the reserved seating area, or save a few bucks and slum it on the sprawling lawn with the masses. But be aware that you get no more than you pay for— from the lawn you probably won't even be aware that you're at the same venue as your favorite performer, unless you glance up at the giant video screens. Either way, the tailgating scene in the parking lot, where concert goers start the pre-party in the blistering Atlanta sun, is definitely not to be missed.

How to Get There—Driving

Located 3.8 miles south of downtown Atlanta and 3.5 miles from Hartsfield Airport, HIFI Buys Amphitheatre is a short and easy drive from downtown. Take I-75/85 to the Langford Freeway East exit and follow signs to the amphitheater.

Parking

With 7,500 secure, well-lit parking spaces, parking is easy and free!

How to Get There—Mass Transit

Take MARTA to the HIFI Buys Amphitheatre/Ft McPherson station. Shuttle buses are available to and from the front gate of the amphitheater.

How to Get Tickets

Tickets are available through Ticketmaster's website, www.ticketmaster.com, or by calling 404-249-6400.

Boisfeuillet Jones Atlanta Civic Center

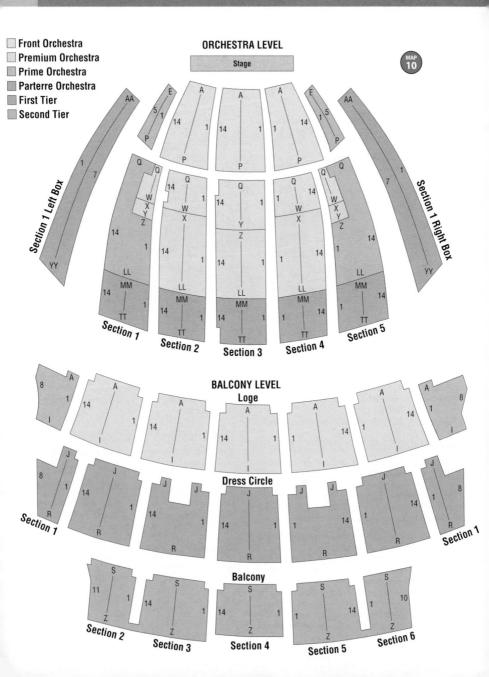

Legend:
- Front Orchestra
- Premium Orchestra
- Prime Orchestra
- Parterre Orchestra
- First Tier
- Second Tier

MAP 10

ORCHESTRA LEVEL

Stage

Section 1 Left Box
Section 1 Right Box

Section 1
Section 2
Section 3
Section 4
Section 5

BALCONY LEVEL

Loge

Dress Circle

Balcony

Section 1
Section 2
Section 3
Section 4
Section 5
Section 6

Boisfeuillet Jones Atlanta Civic Center

General Information

NFT Map:	10
Address:	395 Piedmont Ave NE
	Atlanta, GA 30308
Box Office:	404-658-7159
	(Automated Recording)
Websites:	www.atlantaciviccenter.com
	www.atlantaopera.org
Ticketmaster:	404-249-6400; www.ticketmaster.com

Overview

The Boisfeuillet Jones Atlanta Civic Center (don't worry, Atlantans just call it the Civic Center) is the largest performance stage in the Southeast. With 4,600 seats, the center has the girth to host events ranging from major Broadway shows to A-list musical tours. But for one reason or another, the venue's offerings have remained meager and disjointed. One week, you can catch the Atlanta Opera performing *La Boheme*. The next week, audiences will be singing along with the urban musical *Baby Mama Drama*. Unless you love opera and/or urban entertainment, there's probably no reason for you ever to come here. But if you hum arias, or if you followed the short-lived Urban Broadway series, the Civic Center will be your home away from home.

The Atlanta Opera

In 2003, the Atlanta Opera made the Boisfeuillet Center its official home. Tickets for individual events can be purchased online at www.atlantaopera.org, or by calling 404-881-8885. If you're a real opera fan, multi-show subscriptions are a good way to save yourself some cash. Ticket prices range from $17 to $145, depending on the seats and the evening of the performance (mid-week shows are much cheaper than weekends).

How to Get There—Driving

Take I-20 E/W to I-75/85 N and exit at 249B (Pine Street/Civic Center). Stay in the middle lane. Cross over Peachtree Street and make a right on Courtland Street. Drive two blocks to Ralph McGill Boulevard and make a left. Drive one block and cross over Piedmont Avenue. The Civic Center will be on your left.

From Georgia 400/I-85 S, exit at 249D (North Avenue). Make a left turn on North Avenue and drive four blocks to Courtland Street (one way going south). Make a right on Courtland Street and drive five blocks to Ralph McGill Boulevard. Make a left at the traffic light, go one block and cross over Piedmont Avenue. The Civic Center will be on your left.

Parking

Parking at the Civic Center Lot costs $5 per event. There are also several other parking lots (costs vary depending on location) in the surrounding area.

How to Get There—Mass Transit

From the Five Points station, take bus 16 going north (Noble). This bus stops at the front entrance of the Civic Center.

How to Get Tickets

The Civic Center box office sells tickets on a walk-up, cash-only basis (with the exception of Atlanta Opera tickets purchased the night of the performance, which you can pay for by credit card). The box office hours are Monday-Friday, 10 am-5 pm. Purchasing tickets over the phone or online (using a credit card) can only be done through Ticketmaster.

Chastain Park Amphitheatre

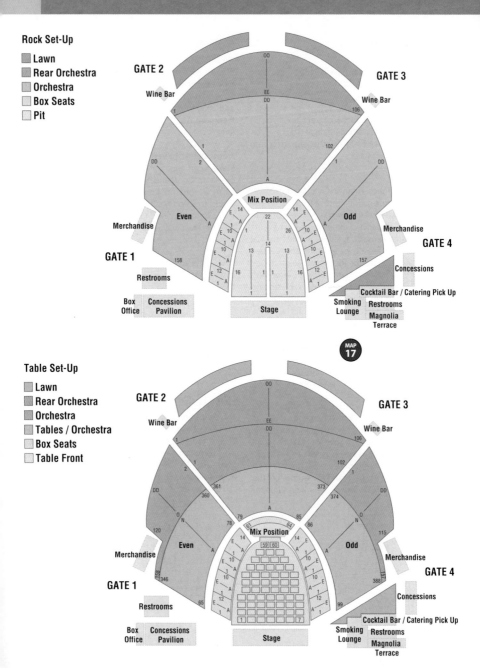

Rock Set-Up
- Lawn
- Rear Orchestra
- Orchestra
- Box Seats
- Pit

GATE 2

GATE 3

Wine Bar

Wine Bar

Merchandise

Merchandise

GATE 1

GATE 4

Concessions

Restrooms

Cocktail Bar / Catering Pick Up

Box Office

Concessions Pavilion

Smoking Lounge

Restrooms

Magnolia Terrace

Stage

Mix Position

Even

Odd

MAP 17

Table Set-Up
- Lawn
- Rear Orchestra
- Orchestra
- Tables / Orchestra
- Box Seats
- Table Front

GATE 2

GATE 3

Wine Bar

Wine Bar

Merchandise

Merchandise

GATE 1

GATE 4

Concessions

Restrooms

Cocktail Bar / Catering Pick Up

Box Office

Concessions Pavilion

Smoking Lounge

Restrooms

Magnolia Terrace

Stage

Mix Position

Even

Odd

General Information

NFT Map: 17
Address: Stella Dr & Pool Rd
              Atlanta, GA 30327
Phone: 404-233-2227
Websites: www.chastainparkamphitheatre.com
              www.classicchastain.org
Ticketmaster: 404-249-6400; www.ticketmaster.com

Overview

Chastain Park Amphitheatre is a small outdoor venue located in Buckhead. The setting provides an idyllic atmosphere for the amphitheater's summer concert series. The musical offerings, for better or for worse, appeal to baby boomer sensibilities, with headlining acts such as Chicago, Kenny Loggins, Jackson Browne, and the occasional ZZ Top or Matthew Sweet. If these names excite you, then a show here is well worth your money. If not, you may want to look into the Atlantic Symphony Orchestra series. Tickets for the 2005 Classic Chastain Season go on sale in March, and purchasing season tickets saves you up to 15% off regular admission prices and guarantees you great seats.

Like the music at most outdoor concert venues, performances at Chastain often take a backseat to picnicking and socializing activities. Your seats can therefore determine your entire concert experience. Seating is divided into three sections: six-person tables, orchestra seats, and general admission lawn seats. The best way to obtain table seats is to purchase season tickets or make friends with wealthy people. The general admission lawns are also fun picnicking spots for the hoi polloi. If you sit in the orchestra, you'll need to bring your own tray for your wines and cheeses and, if you don't want to cart in your own chow (or for shows that don't allow you to bring your own), food and drink are always available for purchase inside the amphitheater.

How to Get There—Driving

From the north, take I-285 S to the Roswell Road exit. Heading south, drive about 2.5 miles and take a right onto W Wieuca Road. At the second stop sign, turn right onto Powers Ferry Road. The amphitheater will be on your right at the intersection of Powers Ferry Road and Stella Drive.

From the south, take I-75 N to the Moores Mill exit (254). Turn left off the exit. Turn right onto West Paces Ferry Road (you'll pass the Governor's Mansion on your left). Just past the Atlanta History Center on your right, turn left at the light onto East Andrews Street. At the next light, turn left onto Roswell Road. Continue north on Roswell Road until just after the Piedmont Road intersection, and then turn left onto Powers Ferry Road. The amphitheater will be on your right after the second stop sign.

Parking

Series Holders can pre-purchase parking permits for one of the four parking lots at Chastain. For everyone else, parking in the red or blue lots costs $9. Parking fills up fast, so we recommend arriving early and carpooling when possible.

How to Get There—Mass Transit

From the Lindbergh MARTA station, take the 38 bus, which stops at Chastain Park.

How to Get Tickets

Series and Mini-Series tickets go on sale on the first Sunday after the official announcement of the Series schedule. To purchase tickets, call the Concert/Southern Tickets at 404-233-2227 between 10 am and 6 pm. When the two-week Series and Mini-Series selling period ends, all remaining tickets can be purchased through Ticketmaster at 404-249-6400, or on their website.

Tickets for the Atlanta Symphony Orchestra season at the amphitheater are available by visiting www.classicchastain.org, or by calling 404-733-5000.

Arts & Entertainment · **Gwinnett Center**

Legend:
- Floor
- Concourse
- Club
- Mezzanine

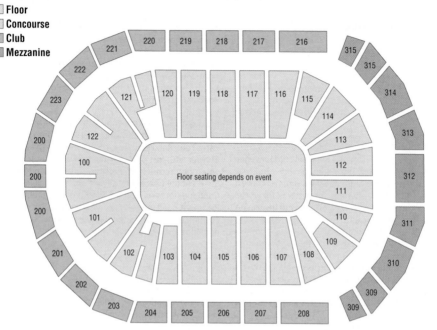

Floor seating depends on event

The Arena at Gwinnett Center

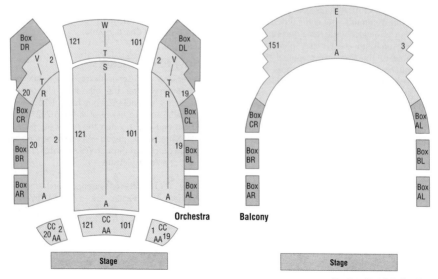

Orchestra

Balcony

Stage

Stage

Performing Arts Center

General Information

Address: 6400 Sugarloaf Pkwy
                  Duluth, GA 30097
Phone: 800-224-6422
Websites: www.gwinnettcenter.com
                  www.gwinnettgladiators.com
Ticketmaster: 800-326-4000; www.ticketmaster.com

Overview

Some Atlantans never leave the city, and this might not be a bad plan given that things outside Atlanta can be, well, different. But, the Arena at Gwinnett Civic Center provides some compelling reasons to visit Gwinnett County—notably Coldplay, Velvet Revolver, Elton John, Big & Rich, The Eagles, and Yanni. (Okay, maybe not Yanni.) The 13,000-seat Arena is *the* place to see major touring acts of all kinds.

The Arena, the Convention Center, and the Performing Arts Center all share the 80-acre Gwinnett Center campus. The Convention Center's main attractions are the luxurious meeting rooms, a grand ballroom for corporate and civic events, and a 50,000-square-foot Exhibit Hall that hosts trade shows, conventions, concerts, and sporting events. The 702-seat Performing Arts Center stages theater productions and musical performances. The Gwinnett Center is also home to the ECHL Gwinnett Gladiators and the Gwinnett Philharmonic.

How to Get There—Driving

From the south, take I-85 N to the Sugarloaf Parkway exit. Turn right off the exit, go back under the interstate and cross over Satellite Boulevard. The center will be on your left.

From the north, take I-85 S to the Sugarloaf Parkway exit. Turn right off the exit and cross over Satellite Boulevard. The center will be on your left.

Parking

The 4,000 parking spaces in the Gwinnett Center lot service all three venues. All parking is free.

How to Get There—Mass Transit

From the Doraville MARTA station, take bus 10, and transfer to bus 50 at the Gwinnett Place Mall. Bus 50 stops at the Gwinnett Center.

How to Get Tickets

Tickets can be purchased at the Gwinnett Center box office Monday-Friday, 10 am–5 pm, and Saturdays and Sundays on event days only starting at noon. Tickets can also be purchased at all Ticketmaster outlets, on the web at www.ticketmaster.com, or by phone by calling 800-326-4000.

Arts & Entertainment • Fox Theatre

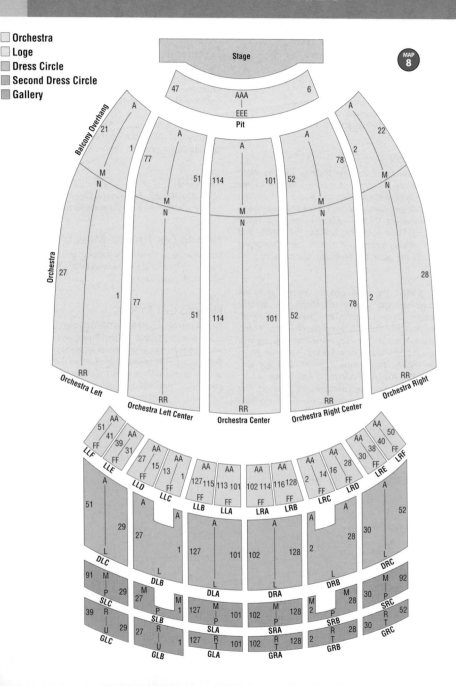

Orchestra
Loge
Dress Circle
Second Dress Circle
Gallery

Stage

MAP 8

General Information

NFT Map: 8
Address: 660 Peachtree St NE
              Atlanta, GA 30308
Phone: 404-881-2100
Website: www.foxtheatre.org
Ticketmaster: 404-817-8700; www.ticketmaster.com

Overview

The Fox Theatre has undergone many crises of identity since its construction in the pre-Depression 1920 s. Originally the Yaarab Temple Shrine Mosque, the Fox became Atlanta's premiere movie venue from the 1940s through the 1960s, and eventually outgrew movies to become the multi-purpose performing arts center it is today. The Fox Theatre hosts local and traveling opera, ballet, and theater companies.

When Clark Gable and Vivien Leigh entered the gilded doors of the Fox Theatre for the 1939 world premier of *Gone With the Wind*, the theater's landmark status was settled. Today, the Fox is a National Historic Landmark and has been fully restored to its original Arabian-style splendor. It's worth getting tickets to a performance at the Fox just to set eyes on the ornate theater itself. The Fox is also the home of "Mighty Mo," the second-largest theater organ in the world. Check out the summer movie series at the Fox to hear Mo in action.

How to Get There—Driving

From the north, take I-75/I-85 S and exit at North Avenue. Take a left at the end of the ramp. Turn left at third traffic light (Peachtree Street) and the theater will be one block down on the left.

From the south, take I-75/I-85 N (I-20 to I-75/I-85 N) and exit at the West Peachtree/Spring Street exit. Drive two blocks to Peachtree Street and turn left—the theater will be two blocks down on the left.

Parking

The Fox Theatre doesn't have its own parking facility. Instead, there are a number of pay parking lots nearby and some street parking. Parking in a lot usually costs between $4 and $10.

How to Get There—Mass Transit

Take MARTA to North Avenue Station (N3 on the North Line) and walk two blocks east to the theater.

How to Get Tickets

Tickets are available online through www.ticketmaster.com or by calling them on 404-817-8700. You can visit the box office in person Monday–Friday, 10 am-6 pm, and Saturday 10 am-3 pm.

The Fox Theatre doesn't sell season tickets. Season tickets can only be purchased through one of the independent companies that perform at the Fox:

Atlanta Ballet	404-892-3303
Broadway in Atlanta Series:	800-278-4447
Delta International Series:	404-881-2000
Theater for the Stars:	404-252-8960

99X New Rock &
90's Alternative
connecting you to...

the *BIGGEST* PARTIES

- Sinners Ball

the *BEST* CONCERTS

- MistleToe Jam 2004
  featuring Velvet Revolver, Muse, & Jimmy Eat World

the *RIGHT* MUSIC

- Nirvana, Green Day, Red Hot Chili Peppers, Jet, and Queens of the Stone Age
- *Demand* your music @ 404-741-0997

Get Connected, become a 99X Freeloader TODAY. Log onto

99X®

Become Official.

Register online at www.notfortourists.com today.

Official NFT Members receive:

- access to the complete **NFT** online database
- the ability to rate **NFT** listings
- access to our entire guidebook series in PDF form
- event listings
- 10% discount on **NFT** books & apparel purchased on our website
- special promotions
- your very own handy dandy Official **NFT** Member Patch
- and oh, so much more!!

Become an Official **NFT** Member and you'll gain entry to exclusive areas on our website including information about discounts, special promotions, and access to TONS of great new online content available to Official **NFT** Members ONLY.

Street Index

Street Index

Street Index

Street Index

Street Index

Street	No.	Grid
Sparta St SW	44	B1
Spelman Ln SW	12	A2
Spence Ave NE	33	B1/C1
Spence Ave SE	33	C1
Spencer Ave		
(1200-1269)	49	C1
(1270-1399)	48	C2
Spencer St NW	8	B1/B2
Spring Ave	48	C1
Spring Rd NW	4	A1
Spring St		
(1-644)	32	B2
(645-3799)	42	B2
Spring St NW		
(1-539)	9	A2/B2/C2
(540-1321)	5	A2/B2/C2
(1322-1599)	2	C2
Spring St SW		
(1-133)	9	C1/C2
(134-303)	13	A1
Spring Garden Dr SW	49	C2
Spring House Cv NE	29	A1
Spring Mill Cv	37	A2
Spring Oaks Ct	39	A1
Spring Valley Ln NE	7	A2
Spring Valley Rd NW	1	A2
Spring Walk Ct	42	A2
Springdale Cir SW	49	B1/B2/C1
Springdale Dr NE	25	B1/B2
Springdale Pl SW	49	B1
Springdale Rd	51	B1
Springdale Rd NE	28	A2/B1/C1
Springdale Rd SW		
(2100-2647)	49	B2/C1
(2648-2999)	51	A1
Springdale St	30	B2
Springer St NW	1	B1
Springfield Ct	37	B1
Springfield Dr		
(4700-4938)	37	B1
(4933-4999)	36	B2
Springhaven Ave	51	B1
Springlake Dr NW		
(1990-2099)	1	A2
(2100-2117)	24	C1
Springlake Pl NW	1	A1
Springmill Cv	37	A2
N Springs Ct	37	B1
N Springs Dr		
(1470-1559)	36	C2
(1560-1799)	37	C1
Springside Ct NE	19	B1
Springside Pointe	36	B2
Springvale Cir	36	C2
Spruce St NE	11	C1
Spruell Ave NE	40	C1
Spruell Springs Rd NE	40	C1
Squire Pl NE	25	C2
St Annes Ln NW	24	A1
St Augustine Pl NE	7	C2
St Charles Ave NE		
(500-611)	6	C2
(700-1099)	7	C1/C2
St Charles Way NE	6	C2
St Clair Ct	41	A2
St Claire Ln NE	22	C1
St Francis Ave	48	B2/C2
St James Xing	41	C1
St Johns Ave SW	49	B2
St Johns Cir SW	49	B2
St Jose St SW	12	A1
St Joseph Ave	48	C2
St Louis Pl NE	7	C2
St Lukes Pl NE	10	A1
St Michael Ave	48	B2
St Paul Ave SE	14	B1
Stadium Dr	42	B2
Staff Row SW	48	A2
Stafford Pl	43	C1
Stallings Ave SE	34	B2
Standard Dr NE		
(1000-1211)	22	A2
(1204-1299)	19	C2
Standish Ave NW	2	B1
Stanton Cir	48	B1
Stanton Ct	48	B1
Stanton Rd	48	
Stanton Rd SW	48	A2
Stanwood Ave SE	31	C2
Star Dr	19	C2
Starcross Ct	37	A2
Stark Ln	42	B2
Starlight Cir NE	19	A1
Starlight Ct	19	A1
Starlight Ct NE	18	A2
Starlight Dr NE	18	B2
(500-999)	19	A1
Starlight Ln NE	19	A1
State St NW		
(508-551)	9	A1
(600-1299)	5	A1/B1/C1
State Route 13	3	A2
	2	B2
State Route 400	40	A2
State Route 400 NE	40	A2/C2
	35	B2
Statewood Rd NE	18	C2
Steele Dr NW	2	B1/C1
Stella Dr NW		
(4401-4506)	17	A2
(4501-4699)	39	C2
Stephen Long Dr NE	25	C1
Stephens Dr NE	27	B1
Stephens St SW		
(317-502)	13	C1
(503-599)	12	C2
Stephens Mill Run NE	18	C2
Stephens Walk Dr	37	A2
Sterling St	32	B2
Sterling St NE	31	A1
Steve Dr SW	51	A2
Stewart Ave SW	12	B2
Stewart Ct	43	C2
Stewart Dr NE	40	B1
Stewart Rd	43	B2/C2
Stillwood Dr	51	B1
Stillwood Dr NE	7	B2
Stillwood Chase	28	B1
Stockbridge Dr SE	34	B1
Stokeswood Ave SE	34	A1/B1
Stoland Dr NE	20	C2
Stone Brook Pl NE	19	B2
Stone Mill Trl	35	B1
Stone Mill Trl NE	35	A1/B1
Stone Quarry Rd SE	34	C1
Stonegate Way NW	16	A2
Stonewall St SW	12	A2
Stoneybrook Dr SE	34	B1
Stonington Dr NE	35	A1
Stovall Blvd NE		
(600-735)	18	C2
(736-1199)	19	C1
Stovall Pl NE	19	C1
Stovall St SE	15	A2/B2
Stovall Ter NE	19	C1
Strait St	43	C1
Strasburg Ct	37	B2
Stratfield Cir NE	41	C2
Stratfield Dr NE		
(3200-3344)	20	A1
(3329-3599)	41	C2
Stratford Pl NE	19	B1
Stratford Rd NE	21	B2
N Stratford Rd NE		
(3552-3751)	21	A2
(3752-4299)	19	B1/C1
Stratford Hall Pl NE	18	B1
Stratham Dr	37	A1
Strathmore Dr NE	26	A1
Strong St NW	5	C1
Sudbury Rd NE	35	A2
Sugar Creek Pl SE	34	C2
Summer Dr NE	36	C1
Summer Rose Ct	42	B2
Summer Rose Dr	42	A2/B2
Summer Terrace Ln NE		
	40	C1
Summerford Ct	36	B2
Summerford Dr	36	A2/B2
Summerset Ln	37	B2
Summerset Ln NE	36	A1
Summit St NE	40	C1
Summit North Dr NE	22	C1
Summit Pointe Dr	27	B1
Summit Pointe Way NE		
(100-2209)	27	B1
(1600-2499)	26	B2
Sunbury Pl NW	1	A2
Sunderland Cir NE	41	B2/C2
Sunderland Ct NE	41	B2/C2
Sunderland Way NE	41	C2
Sunland Dr NE		
(1200-1306)	19	C2
(1307-1399)	20	C1
Sunny Brook Ln NE	35	B1
Sunny Brook Pl NE	35	B1
Sunset Ave	51	C2
Sunset Ave NW		
(1-526)	8	A2/B2/C2
(527-599)	4	C2
Sunshine Way	49	B1
Sunstede Dr	30	A1
Superior Ave	29	A2/B2
N Superior Ave	29	A2
Surrey Ln	20	B2
Sussex Rd NE	26	C1
E Sussex Rd NE	26	C1
W Sussex Rd NE	26	C1
Sutters Point NE	40	A2
Sutton St SE	32	C1
Suzanne Dr	30	A1
Swann Cir	2	B2
Swanton Way		
(100-176)	30	C1
(177-498)	29	C2
Swanton Hill Ct	29	C2
Swathmore Dr NW	17	A1
Sweetwood Ct NE	27	B1
Swims Valley Dr NW	38	C2
Sycamore Dr	30	A2/B2/C2
Sycamore Pl	30	C1
Sycamore Sq	30	C1
Sycamore St	30	C1/C2
Sycamore Ridge Dr	30	B2
Sycamore Station	30	B2
Sydney St SE	14	B1/B2
Sylvan Cir NE	19	C2
Sylvan Cir SW	49	B1
Sylvan Pl SW	49	A1
Sylvan Rd		
(2100-2621)	49	B1/C1
(2622-3199)	51	A1/B1
Sylvan Rd SW		
(1000-1555)	44	A1/B1/C1
(1556-2100)	49	A1/B1
Sylvan Ter	49	C1
Sylvan Way SW	49	B1
Sylvan Ridge Dr SW	49	A1
Sylvania Dr	27	B2
Sylvester Cir SE	34	B2
Taft Ave NE	6	B2
Taft Pl SW	49	A2
Taft St SW	49	A2
Talbot Colony NE	36	A1
Tall Oaks Dr NE	40	B2
Tall Pines Ct NW	18	A1
Tall Pines Dr NW	18	A1
Tall Tree Dr NE	22	B2
Talley Dr		
(2226-2299)	42	B2
(2300-2519)	43	B1
(2520-2699)	33	A2
Tallulah Dr NE	19	B2
Tallulah St NW	1	B2
Tamarisk Dr NE	40	B2
Tamassee Ct	37	B2
Tamer Ln NW	39	A2
Tamworth Dr NE	36	C1
Tanbark Ct NE	41	C2
Tanglewood Cir NE	23	A2
Tanglewood Ct	39	C1
Tanglewood Trl NW	39	C1
Tanner St SE	10	C1/C2
Tanyard Creek Ct	29	C2
Tara Trl NW	39	C2
Tate St NW	8	A1
Tatnall St SW		
(400-471)	13	A1
(584-609)	8	C2
Taunton Way NE	41	C1
E Taylor Ave	50	B2
W Taylor Ave	50	B1/B2
Taylor St NW	1	B1
Tazor St NW	8	A1
Teal Rd	42	B1
Tech Pky NW	4	C2

Street Index